Elements of

SUPERVISION

....

William R. Spriegel, Ph.D.

Professor of Management
and Dean of the College of Business Administration,
the University of Texas;
Management Consultant

Edward Schulz, Ph.B.

Manager, Personnel, RCA Laboratories,
Radio Corporation of America, Princeton, New Jersey

William B. Spriegel, M.D.

Instructor in Neurology and Psychiatry,
the Medical School, Northwestern University,
and Assistant Attending Physician,
Chicago Wesley Memorial Hospital

Elements of

SUPERVISION

Second Edition

NEW YORK · JOHN WILEY & SONS, INC.

London · Sydney

Library of Congress Catalog Card Number: 57–5934

Printed in the United States of America

Preface to the Second Edition

Our original edition of *Elements of Supervision* was written to meet the specific needs of the war effort. Although the current interest in executive development lacks the urgency of a war crisis, it continues to hold a leading place in management thinking. The present revision of *Elements of Supervision* was undertaken to include some of the more important developments during the past fifteen years. We have retained most of the original material, bringing it up to date. We have also added some seven chapters and an appendix on Statistical Quality Control.

These seven chapters have been added to provide additional material in areas where the modern supervisor finds himself hard pressed. The two chapters, "Interviewing—A Skill Needed in Supervising" and "The Supervisor and Mental Health," are added to strengthen the consideration given to the supervisor's responsibility in *human relations*. "The Supervisor and Motion and Time Study" and "The Supervisor and Stores and Material Control" are two new chapters included to provide additional material on the operational responsibilities of the supervisor. In industry, most of the time of the supervisor is spent on directing the efforts of people (human relations) toward efficient work (which requires motion and time study) on "materials and assemblies." Naturally these efforts strive to accomplish the material production within the framework of *competitive costs*. It was with this phase of the supervisor's responsibility in mind that the chapter on cost control was added.

While Mr. Edward Schulz did not participate in the revision, his original contribution in the first edition is recognized. The revised chapters retain much of Mr. Schulz's philosophy as expressed in our early joint efforts.

It would be impossible to recognize by name the many operating men, authors, research agencies, professional associations, and magazines that have provided ideas and suggestions that have been presented in this book. Most of us are the product of our environments. We, as authors, are deeply indebted to our professional associates in industry and universities whose experiences have influenced this revision.

WM. R. SPRIEGEL
WM. B. SPRIEGEL

Austin, Texas
Evanston, Illinois
October 1, 1956

Preface to the First Edition

For many years in management circles the functions of an executive have been discussed under three headings, namely, organization, deputization, and supervision. With each crisis in management, renewed emphasis is placed upon each of these three functions, especially supervision. This was true during World War I, 1914–1918, during the expansion of the nineteen twenties, and more recently during the present international crisis. During any period of rapid industrial expansion or rapid shifting from one type of activity to another, almost invariably two bottlenecks or shortages develop, a shortage in skilled mechanics and an insufficient supply of trained supervisors. It is only natural that both of these shortages should develop since men become skilled in either of these fields only by careful planning and long-run training. During slack periods business curtails its training programs either from necessity or because of the short-run viewpoint which prevails in most enterprises.

Although publication was hastened by the demand for an increase in the effectiveness and number of supervisors for our defense program, this book, whose material has been developed over a period of more than twenty years of industrial experience and consultation, is designed not only for use in the current emergency but also for the long-run program, which it is hoped industry will not abandon with the first signs of a contraction in the present production demands. In writing a book for general use it is, of course, necessary to omit the names of a particular enterprise that may elect to use it in its training program. The industrial leaders in training programs will do well to direct the attention of the members of their conference groups to the fact that they will profit by relating the material to their own jobs. This task is by no means as difficult as some inexperienced leaders think. As a matter of fact, many of the problems in the different units of the same plant are as diverse as between plants. The press room and the trim shop in an automobile body shop illustrate these differences.

In up-grading supervisors the question is often raised as to whether or not men of different executive levels should be handled in the same group. This question cannot readily be answered. Individual differences exist among supervisors of the same level, as well as among supervisors of different levels. The senior author has with excellent results conducted training conferences where the plant manager sat in each conference, attending six different conferences each week on the same subject. This particular plant manager at the beginning of the conferences said in substance: "In this training program it is our desire to develop constructive thinking, as well as to impart additional information to our supervisory force, when additional information is needed. No man will be questioned outside of this room because of any opinion he may express in these conferences on controversial subjects. Should I ever in a moment of forgetfulness violate this promise, please remind me of the broken promise and I shall immediately apologize." For the first few conferences, discussion was slightly restricted by the presence of the manager. The manager on several occasions repeated his statement which was reproduced in the minutes of the meetings. Soon the reserve disappeared and the conferences were immensely successful both from the standpoint of the manager and his men. Some managers are not so forthright as the one referred to above and by all means should not depress the training program by their presence.

The question of the method or procedure to be used in conducting training programs is often raised. During the past twenty years the *conference method* has been emphasized, sometimes to a degree not warranted by the facts of the situation. The conference method is highly desirable when discussing questions concerning which the group has had experience, yet it is not suited to the presentation of new material. New material may be presented by the lecture method, by a combination of the lecture and quiz method, by the laboratory or experimental method, by the sound or silent movie, by the use of sound slides, by the use of slides with the lecture explanation, or by any combination of these. It is a mistake to make a fetish of any one system. Variety stimulates interest and meets the requirements of individual differences more than one set formula of presentation. In any event, the leader should carefully plan his work and supplement the content by a dynamic personality.

Should the supervisory training be conducted by the regular operating force or by a specialist, either within the organization or from the outside? There is little doubt that the ideal leader should be the regular line officer, provided he has the necessary training, ability, and time to devote to the task. Unfortunately, most operating officers do not have either the proper background or the time to conduct a detailed follow-up training program. Even though the line officers do not actually conduct the training program, they should be tied in with the administration of the training through master conferences or at least advisory committees; or it may not achieve what they would like to have it accomplish. In a large institution some of the executives may conduct their training programs, and the staff or outside specialist may conduct the others. If an outsider is brought in, he should be given counsel by the operating executives so that he can do the things that are desired. Frequently consultants from management firms or specialists from universities may be secured to aid or to conduct the training programs. Business firms have conducted training programs with success by the use of any of the foregoing leaders.

The authors wish to acknowledge with thanks the assistance given them by Mr. A. R. Kelso, Assistant General-Manager of the United States Cartridge Co., St. Louis, Mo.; Mr. O. W. Roberts, Director of Training, also of the United States Cartridge Co.; Major Albert Sobey, Director of the General Motors Institute of Technology, whose philosophy of management has influenced the thinking of the senior author; Professors S. C. Andrews, Frank Henry, and Chester Willard of Northwestern University, whose friendly counsel has contributed to the general approach. They wish to acknowledge their indebtedness also to the practitioners and authors whose works have both directly and indirectly influenced their writing.

The authors wish to express their special appreciation to the late Richard H. Lansburgh for granting permission to quote directly from Lansburgh and Spriegel's *Industrial Management*. Some of the discussions and ideas are taken directly from *Industrial Management*.

Wm. R. Spriegel
Edward Schulz

Evanston, Illinois
July 1, 1942

Contents

The Supervisor—
1   an Organization Man

Who Is a Supervisor? The National Labor-Management Relations Act in substance defines a supervisor as *any individual* having authority, in the interest of the employer, to hire, transfer, suspend, lay off, recall, promote, discharge, assign, reward, or discipline other employees, or having responsibility to direct them, or to adjust their grievances, or effectively to recommend such action, if in connection with the foregoing the exercise of such authority is not of a merely routine or clerical nature but requires the use of independent judgment [Section 101, Sub-section 2: (11)]. The Fair Labor Standards Act [Section 13(a)(1)] incorporates essentially the same definition. The supervisor *directs the work of others* and at least *has the authority to recommend hiring and to discharge or lay off, and must exercise discretionary power.*

A supervisor may be defined as *any person who is responsible (1) for the conduct of others in the achievement of a particular task, (2) for the maintenance of quality standards, (3) for the protection and care of materials,* and *(4) for services to be rendered to those under his control.* Men are, generally, responsible for things; they are primarily responsible for materials and equipment. On the other hand, the supervisor is primarily responsible for making things happen through the efforts of people. To those responsibilities of the men for materials and equipment, the supervisor adds the responsibility for the men. It is obvious that the supervisor's responsibility is chiefly for the relationship between the men and their work. The difference between the supervisor and his men is largely the difference between the responsibility for things and the responsibility for people. The

1

supervisor's emphasis is on the human factor: managing manpower and guiding it in the direction of getting things done and of achieving the desired objectives with maximum efficiency and due regard for the interests of all concerned.

Decision Making.   Judgment is the application of reason to experience in solving problems.   Only through the use of sound judgment can the supervisor expect to make the right decisions.   Alfred P. Sloan lists the following steps as essential in formulating sound judgments in the light of experience and reason: [1]

1. Get the facts.
2. Evaluate or weigh the facts.   (Organize them so that they are understandable and usable.)
3. Decide.
4. Let the decision be final, unless later evidence conclusively demands a revision.

Every supervisor who expects to win and to hold the respect of his men by well-considered decisions must learn to get the facts and must be certain to get them all.   The supervisor must study the facts and develop the skill of careful analysis.   Consideration must be given to the objective—what the supervisor wants to accomplish.   Finally, when the supervisor makes his decision based on the facts which he has carefully analyzed in the light of the end to be attained, his decision should be final.   Men watch their supervisor closely for two things: (1) snap decisions based on inadequate information, and (2) instability, resulting in decisions made today and reversed tomorrow.   Every supervisor should learn to apply automatically the steps listed above to each problem as it arises in his daily work.

Basic Supervisory Tasks.   Fundamentally the responsibilities of the supervisor may be classified under three main headings: (1) *planning,* (2) *organizing,* and (3) *executing* or *operating.*   "Planning is setting objectives, forecasting future conditions, and determining the future course of action and policies required to attain them." [2]   This definition applies primarily to top management.   Nevertheless the supervisor has a similar responsibility, but one more limited in scope.   The supervisor's planning is within the framework of company objectives and

---

[1] Adapted from the material developed for the General Motors Executive Training Program by the General Motors Institute, 1927.

[2] Lawrence A. Appley, "Management and the American Future," *General Management Series,* No. 169, American Management Association, New York, 1954, p. 11.

policies. The supervisor must plan the work of the department and of the men in an orderly manner, with due regard for the responsible relationship of one person to another, so that there is a minimum of friction and a maximum of production. *To organize* means that the supervisor establishes relationships between his men on an orderly basis and assembles his materials and equipment in such a manner as to maximize his production at a minimum of cost. The fundamental force behind the planning and organizing is the company objective and the particular assignment to the supervisor's department. *Executing* or *operating* means carrying out the plans within the framework of the established organization and company objectives. Operating requires *delegating* or deputizing, initiating action, and checking performance. To delegate or deputize means to give someone else the responsibility and authority to do something which the supervisor himself does not have the time or ability to do efficiently. The supervisor confers upon his subordinate the same authority and responsibility that he himself possesses, but within a more limited scope. It is important to remember that, even though someone else is deputized to do the task, the supervisor, in the last analysis, is responsible for getting it done. Executing also requires initiating action to get plans under way and checking to see that the performance is according to the plan. The executing phase of the supervisor's job is usually called *supervising*. *To supervise* means that the supervisor initiates action and follows up to see that the work he has organized and deputized is carried out and that the plans which have been made are put into effect on time and in the proper manner.

Many supervisors are reluctant to deputize or delegate. They hate to release any of their responsibilities to others. There are also a few who willingly give others responsibilities but never provide them with the necessary authority to get results. Delegation involves not only delegating responsibilities to others but also conferring the authority to carry out these responsibilities. Then there is the supervisor who delegates his responsibilities and authority according to a sound plan but fails to follow up the men to whom he has delegated the responsibilities. No supervisor can say "The responsibility is yours," and then forget it. The amount of follow-up will depend on the type of work and on the individual deputized. To supervise effectively demands the highest degree of leadership. Supervising calls for the building of morale, the development of cooperation, the use of proper instructional methods, the ability to discipline wisely, and above all a sound knowledge of human nature. Supervisors who are weak in delegating are usually also weak in organizing; they are unable to see their work in its broader aspects and to break it down into its details. In fact, proper organizing provides natural channels for delegating and fixing responsibilities.

What Can Be Delegated? The supervisor's responsibilities fall into three broad classifications: (1) those which cannot as a rule be delegated, (2) those which can be shared in part with others, especially subordinates, and (3) those which can be delegated to others, provided adequate authority is also given to the subordinate. Responsibilities that cannot as a rule be delegated include: (1) the personal responsibility for delegating (the supervisor is still responsible for the actions of his subordinate), (2) the maintenance of appropriate relations with other departments, (3) the requisitioning and planning of the training of an adequate work force (the actual training may be done by others, but the planning for the training remains the responsibility of the supervisor), (4) reports to superiors, (5) settlement of basic disagreements among subordinates, (6) the provision of proper tools, equipment, and materials (certain details may be delegated, but primary responsibility remains with the supervisor), (7) departmental morale, including a consideration of absences, tardiness, discipline, safety, and any activity that produces a satisfied work group, and (8) promotions and discharges.

The supervisor will need assistance in discharging most of the responsibilities listed in the previous paragraph as being primarily his personal responsibility. Those responsibilities which can be shared with others, especially subordinates, include: (1) preventing accidents, (2) maintaining quantity of production, (3) maintaining quality of production, (4) keeping down departmental costs, (5) training employees, and (6) encouraging cooperation and teamwork.

Responsibilities which can be delegated to others, provided adequate authority is also given, include: (1) proper use and control of materials, (2) provision of safe operating conditions and first aid, and reports of its use, (3) maintenance of proper records on which reports are based, and preparation of reports, (4) health and sanitation, (5) inspection and care of tools and equipment, (6) inspection and check on raw materials, (7) recording men's working time, and (8) maintenance of premises in a clean, sanitary condition. One fact cannot be overemphasized: when a responsibility is delegated, the supervisor must also delegate the necessary authority to carry out the responsibility.

One of the most reliable measures of a supervisor's leadership ability is the way in which he delegates. A real leader has the courage to delegate to others and the organizing ability to institute checks to see that delegated responsibilities are carried out according to plan. No supervisor stands alone. With his men he is a part of an organization made up of many supervisors like himself and many men, each as a group under a supervisor. The successful supervisor constantly considers his responsibilities in terms of (1) those which he can delegate whenever possible, and (2) the effect of his action on his own work, his men, and the rest of the organization.

What Is an Organization? *An organization is the structural relationship between the various factors or functions necessary to achieve the objective of the enterprise.* There are many definitions of organization but most of them emphasize either the structure and process or the people involved in getting things done. Lawrence A. Appley says: "Organizing is determining, assembling, and arranging the resources by function and in relation to the whole to meet the *planned objective.*" [3] Oliver Sheldon defines organization as "the process of so combining the work which individuals or groups have to perform with the facilities necessary for its execution that the duties, so formed, provide the best channels for the efficient, systematic, positive, and coordinated application of the available effort." [4] Another definition of organization often used is "the men in their various relationships in the enterprise." When successful organizations are studied, all are found to have certain common characteristics. The development of an effective industrial organization requires proper observance and application of a series of "fundamentals of organization."

The Fundamentals of Organization. The primary fundamentals of business organization deal with those phases of management which include policy formulation and organization structure. The operating fundamentals deal almost entirely with the operating phase of management. The primary fundamentals of organization may be summarized as follows: [5]

1. Regard for the aim and objectives of the enterprise.
2. The establishment of definite lines of supervision within the organization structure.

[3] Lawrence A. Appley, *loc. cit.*

[4] Oliver Sheldon, *The Philosophy of Management,* Sir Isaac Pitman & Sons, 1923, p. 32.

[5] William R. Spriegel and Richard H. Lansburgh, *Industrial Management,* John Wiley & Sons, New York, fifth edition, 1955, p. 4.3.

3. The placing of fixed responsibility among the various persons and departments within the organization.

4. Regard for the personal equation.

The operating fundamentals, which are also four in number, are:

1. The development of an adequate system.

2. The establishment of adequate records to implement the system and to use as a basis of control.

3. The laying down of proper operating rules and regulations within the established organization in keeping with the established policies.

4. The exercise of effective leadership.

The first of the primary fundamentals, regard for the aim of the enterprise, serves to tie the developed organization closely to the determination of major policies, which is the first of the three major tasks of management. Through the construction of an effective organization, major policies are followed in operations.

Regard for the Objective. The objective of the organization, when clearly kept in mind, provides a beam to be followed when pressures might otherwise lead in directions that are costly. When the organization structure is formulated with the objective in mind and all executives (including the supervisors) are thoroughly imbued with the soundness of the objective, this objective becomes a powerful element of control. Detailed instructions are not needed by a qualified group of executives who accept the company's objectives. Qualified men of "good will" do what is expected of them when they know what the objective is.

Let us consider the organization which is necessary to take care of the unusual situation of clearing of a railroad right-of-way after a wreck. All thought of cost is thrown aside, and an organization is constructed which has but one end in view, namely, clearing the tracks and letting the trains through at the earliest possible moment. Compare this to the organization necessary for the operation of a huge manufacturing plant which is to remain in existence for many years and whose activities are not only numerous but varied and must all be carried on with due relation to each other. The organization structure required to meet the emergency of the railroad wreck will be simpler and more direct than that required to carry on the work of the manufacturing enterprise. Length of life of the organization and desired speed of results are also important factors in the development of its structure. The organization structure must change when the organization's objectives change or when the conditions under which it operates change.

The Establishing of Definite Lines of Supervision. Every employee has a right to know to whom he is responsible and for what. This requires definite lines of supervision. In developing definite lines of supervision the executive will have to give careful attention to the fourth primary fundamental, regard for the personal equation. A lack of definite lines of authority will result either in an overlapping of duties or in gaps which are not taken care of. On an organization chart such gaps or overlaps may be thought of as *horizontal* and existing between the lines of authority which have been laid down, as contrasted to *vertical* gaps or overlaps that will occur if the third of the primary fundamentals, namely, the placing of fixed responsibility, is not adequately handled. Lack of definite lines of authority will result in dissension among whole departments of the organization, and therefore the personal attention of chief executives must be directed to the problems that arise.[6]

Definiteness of control through the establishment of lines of supervision implies the idea of *tapering authority*. It implies the development of a group of supervisors along this line of supervision, each one down the line having somewhat less authority in scope, and somewhat more direction of detail. The job boss, although he has control over a small piece of the business undertaking, is not charged with error if the undertaking has been wrongly conceived and has proved to be generally unprofitable.

At every step in the line of supervision there should be someone in charge. The organization structure should also provide for someone to take the place of the regular supervisor when he is not available because of vacation, illness, death, or resignation. In small businesses the desire to have a substitute for each executive sometimes has led to a surplus of executives. It is never profitable to carry this idea to the point where additional executives must be put on the payroll. This consideration is often a real one because, particularly in small businesses, there is often a wide difference in caliber between the executive head of a department and anyone else in his department. Lines of supervision should, as far as possible, permit specialization with all of its attendant advantages. Definite lines of supervision reduce conflicts, serve as a basis of promotion, facilitate budgeting, and improve cost control.

[6] See James D. Mooney and Alan C. Reiley, *The Principles of Organization,* Harper and Brothers, New York, 1939, Chapter III, for a scholarly discussion of the scalar principle.

The Placing of Fixed Responsibility. Standard practice instructions setting forth in detail the exact limits and responsibilities of each job and position are part of an efficient organization structure. It is sound procedure to *fix responsibility as far down in the organization as competence and the necessary information exist.* Definite fixing of responsibility has the following advantages:

1. Fixed responsibility acts as an incentive to a subordinate. This is particularly true in large organizations.
2. Fixed responsibility aids in the general speed-up of work. It immediately becomes possible to know to whom communications should be addressed or which executives should be called into conference on any particular topic.
3. Accurate placing of responsibility assists in developing discipline as a means of control.

When a man knows his exact responsibilities, he is in a position to concentrate his efforts on meeting the requirements of his position. This tends to promote a high morale since he receives full recognition for his achievements. It facilitates the evaluation of performance and serves as a strong stimulus to perform. Functional definition of the exact area for which an executive or worker is responsible is the third step in the *scalar principle.*[7]

Regard for the Personal Equation. Recognition of the dignity of the individual definitely influences the effectiveness of an organization structure. In developing lines of supervision and in fixing responsibility, it is necessary to consider the personnel which is available or can be made available. Men are of different values and work together in different ways. Merely assigning duties to men does not lead to the accomplishment of tasks, and therefore it is not always possible to draw organization charts and find men to fit them. The scientific manager will either train his men to meet the standards of the desired organization or will seek them on the outside. At a given time, however, compromises may have to be made.

Some enterprises with branch establishments have organized each branch in exactly the same way, having for each branch organization charts which are exactly the same. In some of the branches it will be found that everything is working smoothly, whereas, in other branches jealousies have arisen, dodging responsibilities is prevalent, and the organization seems to be generally ineffective. The main

[7] *Ibid.,* p. 14. Mooney and Reiley list leadership, delegation, and functional definition as the three factors in the scalar principle.

difficulty is that although the organization has been outlined, the lines of supervision have been drawn, and the responsibilities have been fixed, the personal equation—the abilities and limitations of individual men and women—has not been taken into account.

Proper consideration must be given at times to home conditions and outside worries. It is well enough to say that men and women should keep their social affairs outside the business, but, unfortunately, human nature frequently does not permit this. The habits and inertia of the personnel of an organization must be considered. For just this reason new organizations are easier to construct than old organizations are to reconstruct. The "efficiency man," who developed so much trouble for himself, frequently did so because he refused to consider the habits or inertia of personnel involved. They gave lip service to the suggested changes but did nothing about putting them into practice.

The Supervisor and Organizational Fundamentals. Every supervisor, as a matter of basic philosophy and attitude, should have due regard for the personal integrity and rights of others. Without this he cannot build the cooperation and morale essential to successful operation of his department.

Every supervisor should be familiar with the aims or objectives of the organization for which he works. Furthermore, he should be sold on them and enthusiastic to the extent that he can sell these objectives to the men under him. The supervisor constantly has to explain company policies to his men, and successful explanation is based in part on a knowledge of the aims of the enterprise. Even within his department, as the supervisor organizes and delegates the work, he must establish definite lines of supervision if the work is to be done successfully. It is also true, whether in the large organization or within a department, that a man cannot do a job well unless he has been assigned fixed responsibility and authority to do the work. The successful supervisor will also understand the reasoning that lies behind the assignment of responsibilities to him and to others and will scrupulously follow the lines of supervision in all his dealings with others. This demands a knowledge of the fundamental principles of organization and management and how they are applied in the organization of which he is a part. He must recognize that channels of supervision make for successful operation of the organization. The successful supervisor follows the same principles in setting up and operating his department as the management does in setting up and operating the entire organization. In every sense of the word, the supervisor in his department is operating a *little organization.*

Too many supervisors will not delegate their responsibilities, or, when they do, they fail to fix the responsibility definitely with detailed instructions and explanations. They also fail to accompany the delegated responsibility with the needed authority. Unless a man knows exactly what his duties are and how his work is tied with that of other departments, he cannot perform his duties successfully and to his fullest capacity. Most supervisors hope for advancement; they expect eventually to move up into the superior's position or to move to another company in a higher capacity. However, many a supervisor who has merited advancement has failed to receive it because there was no one to replace him. The wise supervisor, as part of his preparation for advancement, will train a substitute to fill his place when he moves up. Only the supervisor who is afraid of his own position and doubts his own ability and capacity will hesitate to train a substitute.

More and more the supervisor, provided with staff specialists, is becoming a manager of men, a specialist himself in handling men, in dealing with and guiding human effort. Much of this book will be devoted to methods and techniques of learning how to understand and handle men more effectively. The successful supervisor today must be a practical industrial psychologist, versed in guiding, developing, and controlling the actions of men. But his skill in his specialized field must be built on a sound foundation of knowledge—knowledge of his own organization, its objectives and pattern, its policies and methods; knowledge of his tasks of organizing, deputizing, and supervising; knowledge of his duties and responsibilities and their delegation. If he has the requisite knowledge and is highly sensitive to the need for recognizing the personal equation, he should succeed.

2   Essentials of Organization

The Supervisor's Need for an Understanding of Organizational Principles. A supervisor operates his department as an integral part of a larger organization. He is largely responsible for the organizational structure within his department. Even though the actual organizational structure may have been established by others, the supervisor is in a position to recommend changes if he can convince his superiors of the logic of his recommendations. With a firm background in organizational principles the supervisor is in a good position to influence the organizational structure of his division as well as that of his department. The supervisor may serve on committees as well as use committees to advise him in his department. He can better participate in committee work and use his own committees most effectively if he understands the uses and limitations of this organization device. Most supervisors hope to advance into better positions. A knowledge of organization fundamentals and principles is beginning to play an increasingly important part in the selection of executives today because as an enterprise grows and expands, its organizational problems intensify, and the supervisor who has the knowledge and ability to solve these problems is often selected to fill the higher position. Therefore, the forward-seeing supervisor will prepare himself by studying these organization fundamentals and principles and by analyzing them in terms of his own organization.

The Supervisor and the Essentials of Organization. The organization which is well constructed is characterized by the smooth flow of detail throughout the executive branch and by chief executives who are able to think constructively. Proper organization simplifies management in ways which are impossible in a business that is not well organized. Much of the criticism which has been leveled at certain methods of management in particular enterprises should be leveled rather at the faulty organization pattern of the enterprise. Through a knowledge of the essentials of organization the supervisor can: (1) appreciate the basic requirements of a successful organization, (2) see his place in the organization as well as the organization as a whole, and (3) develop an awareness that the same principles that are applicable to the larger organization are applicable to departmental organization, but on a smaller scale.

Organization reveals to the supervisor his relationship to the other divisions and units in the business. It is the structural relationship existing between the various factors in an enterprise. It is the structure within which the various factors operate to achieve the major and minor objectives of the institution. Sometimes the term organization is used to refer to the personnel functioning within a given structural setup or to the functioning unit as a whole. These two uses seldom cause any great confusion since the content of the sentence usually conveys the specialized meaning. The specialized use of the term organization is frequently clarified by such modifiers as factory, sales, engineering, or accounting.

The essentials of the executive process (in which the supervisor participates) are shown in Figure 2.1. Assume that the entire circle represents the functioning of the executives. The primary functions of the executive are planning, organizing, and operating. Planning is in terms of objective. Organizing is for the purpose of creating relationships that will minimize friction, focus on the objective, clearly define the responsibilities of all parties, and facilitate the attaining of the objective. Defective organization creates an unnecessary drag on the efforts of the members of a group striving to accomplish a desired result. A sound organization structure creates an atmosphere in which both personal and group satisfactions may be realized, cooperation is encouraged, morale and "the will to do" are substituted for detailed orders, and the group moves smoothly and resolutely toward its goal. Operating consists of initiating action according to plan within the framework of the organization structure and checking to see that the results conform to the plan and objective.

Responsibility is derived from the objective. Authority has its

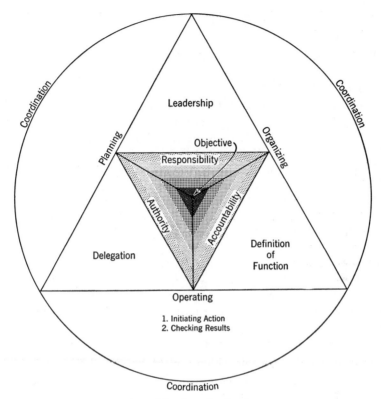

Figure 2.1. Executive functions.

base in responsibility. Authority [1] makes itself felt through leadership that is multiplied through delegation [2] and clarified by functional definition.[3] Accountability [4] is always associated with responsibility and authority. The triad is not complete until the recipient has rendered an account of his stewardship.

The all-pervasive element in the management process, acting through the organization to carry out a plan, is coordination. Coordination is achieved through direct action by the line, and the

---

[1] Authority is a right conferred by some higher power.

[2] Delegation is the process or act of conferring upon another the authority, responsibility, and accountability possessed by the conferring individual.

[3] Functional definition is the specifying and clarifying of the scope of the responsibility.

[4] Accountability is the state of being responsible. Accountability is discharged by reporting to higher authority on the carrying out of the responsibility.

assistance of the staff in advising, coordinating, and controlling in the name of the line.

Basic Considerations in Organization.   Organization carries out its purpose by determining the scope and limits of each individual or group of individuals in a business undertaking, together with their relationships and contacts with each other.   By a consideration of fundamentals and types of organization, an executive builds up a structure for his business, while the supervisor builds for his department a structure which is peculiarly suited to its needs.

The application of the fundamentals of organization will differ widely in two different businesses.   The size of a business, particularly, has an effect on the way in which the organization develops. On the whole, in the small business it is possible to develop essentially the same type of organization that may be developed in the large business except that the duties of several people in the large business will in the small one necessarily have to be combined.   In a manufacturing business producing a standardized product, the organization usually will be constructed differently than if the product is diversified.   The same amount of business may be handled with fewer chief executives if the product is standardized, because it is easier to delegate responsibility in such businesses.   Even the location of a plant or of the departments within a plant may affect the precise way in which the organization is constructed.   The effect of location on the personnel may demand this.

The primary fundamentals were discussed in the preceding chapter, which should be re-read at this point because it is essential that the supervisor know and understand the use of these fundamentals.[5] The primary fundamentals must be considered by the executive before he gives any appreciable attention to the operating fundamentals.   The primary fundamentals of business organization may be thought of as dealing with those phases of management that include policy and organization building.   The operating fundamentals may be said to be executive in character.   They aid in the application of the primary fundamentals to the business and may be thought of as dealing almost entirely with the operating phases of management. The operating fundamentals of organization include: (1) the development of an adequate system, (2) the establishment of adequate records, (3) the laying down of proper operating rules and regulations, and (4) the exercise of effective leadership.

[5] See Chapter 1. page 5.

The Development of an Adequate System. System is a strong instrument of control. Although system implies order in work, it does not necessarily imply economy. A procedure may be highly systematic but still be very wasteful. Balance is needed in the establishing of systems as well as in all other managerial activities.

System is a part of organization, not the whole of it. As an operating fundamental it helps to bind the whole mechanism of organization together. System is the existence of order and method in all parts of an undertaking. System implies a formalized procedure that is to be followed in the handling of standardized activities. It relieves the man at the head of the details of execution and is a bulwark that prevents the lines of authority which have been laid down from being overstepped. It insures that work will be brought to executives and supervisors with the preliminary steps completed so that it is ready for their attention, thus enabling them to apply their entire time to matters of maximum responsibility. When all factors in a business are moving in a regular and accustomed routine, the waste of time and effort involved in repeating the preliminary steps of the solution of any problem is avoided.

The "Exception Principle." System makes possible the practice of the "exception principle" in management. When the system is understood thoroughly by all of the members of the work group and followed as the accepted practice, the supervisor is freed to look after the exceptional situations. Frederick Taylor clearly expressed the use of the "exception principle" as follows:

> Under it the manager should receive only condensed, summarized, and invariably comparative reports [6] covering, however, all of the elements entering into the management, and even these summaries should all be carefully gone over by an assistant before they reach the manager, and have all of the exceptions to the past averages or to the standards pointed out, both the especially good and especially bad exceptions, thus giving him in a few minutes a full view of progress which is being made, or the reverse, and leaving him free to consider the broader lines of policy and to study the character and fitness of the important men under him.[7]

[6] The executive must exercise care not to have this editing process function in such a manner as to keep from him vital information about employee unrest and similar items. Sometimes his assistants think that he should not be bothered with such details, which, however, are often more important than other items reaching his attention.

[7] Frederick W. Taylor, *Shop Management,* 1911, p. 126, as reprinted in *Scientific Management,* Harper and Brothers, New York, 1947.

Through the operation of the exception principle all routine matters may be handled by the executive in a few minutes; thus he is enabled to devote his entire time to the more important matters which demand his personal attention.   He may devote more detailed consideration to the peculiar cases that do not fall under the routine.   In devoting his attention to these matters, he frequently correlates them and develops the points of similarity and difference among them, until they, too, are classified and routine and no longer may be termed exceptional.

Reports as an Aid to the Supervisor.   Most supervisors are "action-minded" and do not like reports.   A report in part discharges the supervisor's responsibility to his superior.   It is the completion of a task, the end of an assignment of work to be done.   Just as an order should communicate all information necessary for execution, so a report should contain all the data essential for the appraisal of performance.   A report should serve a really useful purpose.   Some men require the submission of reports which are of little practical value.   This situation must be avoided if reports are to be an aid to the operation of the exception principle; otherwise the reports will not be read and cannot serve as the basis for action.   The ability to prepare a report which covers all the necessary facts and at the same time does not waste space by the inclusion of nonessential details is evidence that the sub-executive has an understanding of his work, has completely thought through and analyzed the situations that have confronted him and, in short, has successfully mastered his job.   He is the type of person to whom more responsibilities may be given.

Business executives are constantly complaining about the quality of the reports of most of their subordinates.   Reports to executives should be concise, should give the facts and basic conclusions in the first few paragraphs, and there should then follow such elaboration and data as are necessary.   In a more comprehensive report, such as an economic survey, it is advisable to include *a summary and conclusion* as the first chapter of the report.   This section is somewhat more condensed than the summary at the end of the report, but it should include the important conclusions.   All information that is susceptible of comparative treatment should be so handled, so that the executive may see trends without having to look up previous reports or other older information.   This comparison may be accomplished by the use of graphs or comparable statistical data.   To be effective in the development of system, statistical reports must readily call the attention of the executive to unusual figures but should not draw his attention unduly to figures that may be considered normal. Organization reports may be periodic or special. Special reports are prepared on some unusual subject by special assignment. Periodic reports are presented regularly at stated intervals.

Adequate Records Help the Supervisor. The supervisor who burdens his memory with operational details is certain to handicap his effectiveness. When he wants the facts, he will not have them. Records should give the facts concerning the operation of the enterprise. Their preparation and use make possible the elimination of guesswork for management. Too few records are costly; too many records are possibly even more so. Record keeping should avoid "red tape." "Red tape" is of three general kinds: (1) too many records, including some unnecessary ones and duplicates made up by different departments, (2) too many forms to secure essential information which might be obtained on a smaller number by combining several, and (3) the unnecessary refinement of information. A multiplicity of forms results in frequent loss and the consequent absence of necessary information because one of many forms relating to a particular problem is not at hand. Forms should be constructed so that they are read easily, with the most important information standing out most prominently when the form is filled in. An integral part of keeping adequate records is to maintain them so that they are readily available when needed.

Many of the records that assist the supervisor most are compiled by other departments, such as the cost department, the inspection department, and the personnel department. The supervisor must recognize the need of records and learn to use them effectively in the planning and the management of the work in his department. Records may also be invaluable to the supervisor in handling his men, in his work of rating, transfer, and promotion, and in matters of discipline or dismissal.

It is a great help to the supervisor to consult his records from time to time to see how his department compares with other departments. This procedure enables him to find out just why certain problems are turning up. The supervisor must control his records, however, and not let them control him. He cannot supervise his department efficiently if he spends the majority of his time at his desk keeping records, although there are some which he must keep himself, especially those from which he rates his men and makes decisions on promotion, transfer, and dismissal.

Reports are valuable only to the point where the cost of their compilation is less than the savings which they will effect. Cost records usually justify the expense of collection. Proper cost analysis gives invaluable data on conditions demanding attention. All records should indicate trends. Like reports, records which do not give comparative information frequently are valueless. Certainly the records that include comparative information are far more valuable than those that do not.

Proper Operating Rules and Regulations. If the supervisor has developed his systems properly, they will include many of his operating rules and regulations. Operating rules and regulations define the scope of the application of system to the various portions of the lines of authority which have been built up. They provide methods for the utilization of the records. Generally accepted rules or regulations, either verbal or written, facilitate the delegation of authority and responsibility and permit system actually to work, because *the superior and the subordinate both have a definite concept of their respective duties and responsibilities.* Written rules and regulations may be general in nature, touching only the broad outlines of business policy, or they may be more detailed, taking the form of a "standing order," which may provide the exact method of performance of nearly every task in the business. In developing rules and regulations, care must be taken to insure that they are amended as conditions change and that they are not so detailed as to eliminate individual initiative. An operating manual exerts a stabilizing effect upon the organization and serves both as a guide to performance and a standard against which to measure accomplishment.

Proper rules and regulations minimize direct supervision and order giving and give stability and security to the group. Unless written rules are orally and intelligently interpreted at the time of their issuance and the spirit behind them is clearly defined, too often they will be observed according to the letter of the rules in situations where judgment should prevail.

Dynamic Leadership. Of all persons in the organization needing a dynamic personality the supervisor heads the list. Dynamic leadership is the cornerstone on which the entire managerial process rests. No company or service can rest on its laurels. Dynamic leadership does not come naturally to the great mass of officers, executives, and supervisors. It is achieved through the example and training provided by a few outstanding personalities. A dynamic leader can get results with defective organization structure. An ideal organization structure may become sterile in the hands of defective leadership. The operating executive spends most of his time administering the major plans of top management, organizing to effectuate the institutional objectives, and exercising supervisory control over his subordinates. His organization task, although equally important, is not the one to which he devotes the majority of his working hours. The task of supervision or leadership consumes most of his time. In carrying on this work, the executive, if he is capable, will at the same time provide inspirational leadership for his subordinates.

The exercise of dynamic leadership provides the lubrication which makes possible the functioning of the organization as a whole. The more nearly perfect the development of the organization, in other words, the more intricate the machinery, the more necessary is intelligent executive direction or leadership. The supervisor's success in organizing and supervising is largely dependent on his ability to deputize. Too many men insist on retaining all the authority and responsibility vested in them and as a result devote much of their time to details and desk work. The task of supervising demands that much of the supervisor's time be spent with his men. This is only possible if he is willing to select and train men to assume some of his responsibilities. Effective leadership implies the prior development of the primary fundamentals of organization. Without these, executive control involves one-man supervision of most of the details of a business, with all the attendant difficulties and dangers.

The supervisor should ever beware of developing the "strong man" complex. The so-called "strong man" is a man at or near the top who brushes aside the carefully developed lines of supervision or responsibilities which have been fixed and, through his own dynamic guidance, operates the organization or a large part of it. Such men are dangerous in long-enduring organizations because they tend to trample on the feelings and rights of others, destroy morale, and ordinarily, if they resign or die, cannot be replaced.

Managerial Characteristics in a Successful Enterprise. The supervisor is a part of the managerial team. As such he is a manager of a department and should be interested in the characteristics possessed by successful businesses. The basic factors or characteristics of an organization, which are essential if it is to function efficiently,

are (1) strong resourceful leadership, (2) clearly defined responsibilities, (3) a carefully selected, trained, and placed working force,
(4) standardized methods, (5) adequate cost and other records, and
(6) cooperation.[8]

Strong, Resourceful Leadership. The supervisor as the leader of
his department should recognize that resourcefulness and strength are
equally important. He must possess the ability to recognize problems
and meet them with sound solutions, taking decisive action to put the
solution into effect. As a leader the supervisor must develop foresight to anticipate the situation and plan in advance to meet it. As a
leader the supervisor must know the men and their capacities, his
department, and its operating problems. He must possess confidence
in his own ability, tact and self-control to win the confidence of his
men, and the ability to develop them into a hard-hitting, well-coordi-
nated unit to meet the demands of the organization in his department.
Leadership is essential in the largest organization and the smallest
department if they are to be successful.

Men who have climbed the executive ladder have possessed:

1. Technical competence for the job to be done.
2. Social competence—can get along well with people.
3. Wide acquaintance—know to whom to go to get things done.
4. Ability and willingness to delegate.
5. Ability to organize, in the light of the objective, to get things done.
6. Ability to plan to achieve the objective.
7. Dynamic leadership.

Clearly Defined Responsibilities. Clearly defined responsibilities
have been discussed as the third of the primary fundamentals of organization (p. 8). This need not be elaborated further in this paragraph other than to say that a successful supervisor has a right to
lead from a position of strength rather than uncertainty. He needs
the strength supplied by a clear definition of his responsibilities.

Carefully Selected and Trained Working Force. All executives
have a training function to perform. The closer the executive is to
operations, the greater is his responsibility for training. The industrial relations department, through selection devices such as interviews, tests, and verification of past employment, can only assist the
supervisor in the correct methods of training the man; it is up to the
supervisor actually to instruct the employee in the correct methods of

---

[8] The authors are indebted to material developed by the General Motors
Institute of Technology for this list of characteristics.

job performance. If the employee cannot readily adapt himself to the new work, it is the supervisor's responsibility to take such action as is indicated by the facts of the situation. Frequently only a transfer to another job is required. Sometimes it is necessary to discharge the employee. If the supervisor knows his organization, and understands the principles of the line and staff type of organization, he will recognize his responsibilities and at the same time avail himself of all the staff services of the industrial relations department. No organization is stronger than its weakest link, and this is true also of the supervisor's department. The strength of the department and organization in terms of manpower is based on successfully selecting, training, and placing employees. Many men are selected to fill positions for which they have no special training or aptitude. The successful supervisor takes such men and through training or transfers makes them efficient producers. However, this requires careful selection of the man by the personnel department and then proper placement and instruction of the individual by the supervisor.

Standardized Methods. "Standard" under modern management means a carefully thought out method of performing a task or carefully drawn specifications covering some phase of the business. Standardization does not imply perfection. The supervisor should constantly be on the lookout for ways and means of improving standardized methods. Standardized methods should be reduced to writing and should be clearly understood. They should be followed until they are improved. Their use takes routine and detail off the shoulders of the supervisor, providing for application of the "exception principle." Standardized methods are essential to advanced planning. The department operating under standardized methods performs its work smoothly and successfully. The necessity for adequate cost and other records has been discussed previously in this chapter, and the wide-awake supervisor is "records conscious" and uses them to their greatest advantage.

Cooperation. Cooperation implies the *willing* working together of individuals and groups. Cooperation within the organization accomplishes the following ends: (1) develops teamwork, (2) encourages suggestions, (3) improves morale, (4) facilitates production, and (5) eliminates waste. Cooperation on the part of the supervisor means the willingness to help out the next fellow whether he is one of his men, a fellow supervisor, or his superior. A friendly relationship between the supervisor and others is as essential to cooperation as is the confidence of others in his ability and willingness to aid them. Cooperation cannot be one-sided; the supervisor cannot expect cooperation unless he gives it.[9]

The Supervisor's Use of Organization Knowledge.   Organization is not an end in itself but a means of facilitating the achieving of the end.   A sound organization structure creates an atmosphere in which men's energies are released to work toward the objective.   An unsound organizational structure serves as a drag on the energies and emotions of a group.

The supervisor should be interested in providing the leadership that will facilitate the productivity of his department.   He must examine his own leadership, the records he maintains, and how he uses those records.   He must test the degree of cooperation in his department, his willingness to cooperate with others as well as his men's willingness to cooperate with him.   Are the responsibilities of his men clearly assigned, and has he delegated the necessary authority to carry out these assignments?   Are methods standardized?   How effectively are his men selected, trained, and placed?   All these are questions the supervisor can use to examine his success in applying the essentials of organization in his own department.

[9] For detailed discussion of cooperation, see Chapter 18, "Promoting Cooperation Between Men and Between Departments."

3 Types of Organization

Types of Organization. Organization types have emerged as an attempt to solve the problem of so arranging the factors of the enterprise as to achieve the objective. Organization structure strives to create an atmosphere in which friction is minimized and men's energies are released in productive and satisfying effort. The various attempts to create effective organizational structures have resulted in three distinct types, namely, the line organization,[1] functional organization, and the line and staff organization. Historically, the line type of organization, which was the first form to develop, was patterned after military and church types of organization since these existed long before industrial organizations came into being. In the line, or military, form of organization, the line of authority flows directly from the chief executive to various sub-executives in charge of particular phases of the business and from them to the men. Figure 3.1 illustrates the line type of organization in its simplest phase with authority and responsibility flowing directly from the president to the sales manager, works manager, and treasurer, and from them through the foreman to their men.[2] The principle of functionalization or

---

[1] The line organization is sometimes called the military organization or the scalar organization. The word scalar is especially expressive in that when applied to an organization it implies alike in kind but more limited in scope as responsibility is delegated to the lower levels.

[2] The term "foreman" is used rather loosely in industry. One company uses the hierarchy of supervision as follows: superintendent (of a division or branch), assistant superintendent, general foreman, foreman, assistant foreman, section chief, group chief (the lowest level of supervision). Another company of equal size calls its lowest level of supervision "foreman." The general foreman in the

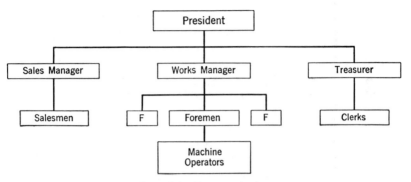

Figure 3.1. Line organization.

specialization [3] is a basic consideration in building an organizational structure.

The Line Organization. Any supervisor who has worked in a relatively small organization is most likely to be acquainted with the line organization. In this type of organization, responsibility and authority flow from the top to the worker in a direct chain. Save in the very small enterprise the organizational structure is one of departmental line organization. In the *departmental line organization* the various workers and supervisors are divided on a functional basis such as manufacturing, engineering, sales, and accounting. Line organization is direct, and the members know to whom they are accountable; it is simple and easily understood, flexible and able to expand or contract readily, strong in discipline through the fixing of responsibility, and capable of developing the all-around executive at the higher levels of authority. However, the line organization overloads a few key executives, encounters difficulty in getting the executives at the lower levels to grasp the need for coordination, makes little use of the principle of specialization, and requires a high type of supervisory personnel to carry the burdens imposed in the absence of specialists as advisors.

first company occupies about the same position as the superintendent in the second company. Other companies' terms, such as "supervisor" and "job master," designate their foreman. A foreman in one plant may be responsible for more men than a general superintendent in another plant.

[3] A function is any activity that can be clearly differentiated from other activities. Functionalism in top organization consists in the dividing of the enterprise into the organic functions of finance, sales, manufacturing, and sometimes engineering and personnel. Each of these broad functions may be divided into many minor functions.

Under the line type of organization well-rounded executives are developed. Decisions are easy to get, and there is no doubt about who is required to make them. There is a singleness of purpose, and responsibility is easily fixed. Each division is under the direction of one person who is held completely responsible for his department.

Supervisors who have worked under the line organization, however, will recall the disadvantages that they had to face. There is no specialized personnel available to meet the difficult technical problems which arise as the enterprise expands. The works manager cannot be expected to handle employment, purchasing, and engineering in addition to production, on which his chief interest must be centered. Too great a responsibility is placed on the department head, and too much is expected of him. The line organization is obviously at a disadvantage since it concentrates control in several key men and frequently is not prepared to replace any one of them if he is lost to the organization by resignation, by illness over a long period, or by death. Effective coordination between departments is unlikely under this form of organization. A major difficulty is encountered in determining the division of work which will form the major units of the enterprise. As the organization expands and develops, the deficiencies of the line type of organization become more obvious since line organization does not provide for balanced growth and development in an enterprise.

The Functional Type of Organization. Frederick W. Taylor's functional type of organization has only a historical interest since it is almost never found today save at the top echelons of a few very large enterprises. Even where it is used in these large organizations it is not in the pure form conceived by Taylor. The functional type of organization (illustrated in Figure 3.2) resulted from the realization that the responsibilities of the general foreman in the line organization were greater than could be adequately borne by the men

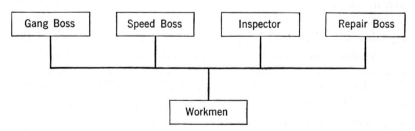

Figure 3.2. Taylor's functional organization.

available.   Under the functional type the solution was found in the functional division of these responsibilities among different foremen who were specially qualified.   Frederick W. Taylor employed eight functionalized foremen—four removed from the shop to the office to plan the work: (1) the route clerk, (2) instruction card clerk, (3) time and cost clerk, and (4) shop disciplinarian; four in the shop to help the men personally in their work, each foreman restricting himself to help only in his particular function: (1) gang boss, (2) speed boss, (3) inspection boss, and (4) repair boss.   It is obvious that this plan of organization resulted in confusion among the men in the shop, but out of it grew the staff principle and the merging of the line and the functional types into the line-and-staff type of organization.

The functional type of organization recognizes the principle of specialization as applied to the work of the supervisor and to management as well.   It does away with one-man control, dividing responsibility and authority and facilitating the development and maintenance of standards.

The disadvantages of the functional type of organization are obvious to the supervisor.   The organization pattern itself is difficult to put into effect and maintain.   It is hard to develop coordination under such a form.   Discipline is difficult to maintain because the employee is responsible to eight supervisors instead of only one. Since the responsibilities of the functionalized foremen are very nearly impossible to define and limit, confusion results.   Operations are complex, causing confusion and mounting costs.   Obviously the high degree of specialization fails to develop men who are well-trained and prospective executives.

The Line-and-Staff Type of Organization.   The line-and-staff organization is the old departmental line organization with staff specialists or staff departments added.   A distinguishing characteristic of a staff function is the fact that it is a service that aids the line organization in the performance of its major activities.   Nearly all of the staff activities at some time were performed by the line officers in small organizations.   The staff brings specialization to the assistance of the line organization.   Staff officers should ever remember that theirs is a service function even though they may be delegated certain control duties by the central line authority.   This recognition by the staff influences the attitude of staff people and such an approach promotes cooperation with the line.   Line officers and supervisors should recognize that management has assigned certain service functions to the staff as an aid to over-all efficiency of operations. This attitude on the part of staff officers will smooth the relationships between them and the line officers.

Figure 3.3 shows a simple development of the staff, with the advertising manager as an aid to the sales manager, the production control supervisor performing a staff function for the works manager, and both the personnel officer and the purchasing agent performing special functions for the entire company. In the manufacturing division of a business, the functional departments guide and to some extent control the foremen. The organization is so constructed that the foreman or supervisor can retain his one-man control over the men under him and at the same time can have his direct responsibilities reduced to a point within the range of accomplishment. The foreman's primary duty is leadership, and under this plan of organization he can better perform this function. The functionalized staff departments give technical operating information and orders to those in direct charge of the workmen. In the sales division of a business the functional staff departments do not direct the operating or sales activities but perform some specific staff function, such as advertising, which is of direct assistance to the line members of the organization in better performing their duties. There may also be functional staff departments in the financial division.

The staff departments are provided to make available specialized technical assistance to the executive, but the undivided authority and responsibility of the line type is maintained. The organization is made more flexible by the addition of the staff departments. Staff officers interested in the entire organization act as coordinators and encourage cooperation. The line-and-staff type of organization takes advantage of the principle of specialization; it also recognizes that some men are essentially "staff" men while others are "line" men, and if the organization is properly manned, those individuals best suited for staff work are placed in such capacities.

The maintenance of a proper balance in the line-and-staff relationship is not easily done. A strong line officer may dominate a staff man and thus fail to get a full measure of assistance from him. Similarly, a strong staff man may step out of his role and weaken the line man. The perfect organization is yet to be developed, but if the disadvantages in the line-and-staff organization are recognized, an effort to anticipate and overcome them can be made. Staff officers lacking in authority cannot enforce their decisions, and since they are not responsible for results, they may sometimes give advice rather carelessly.

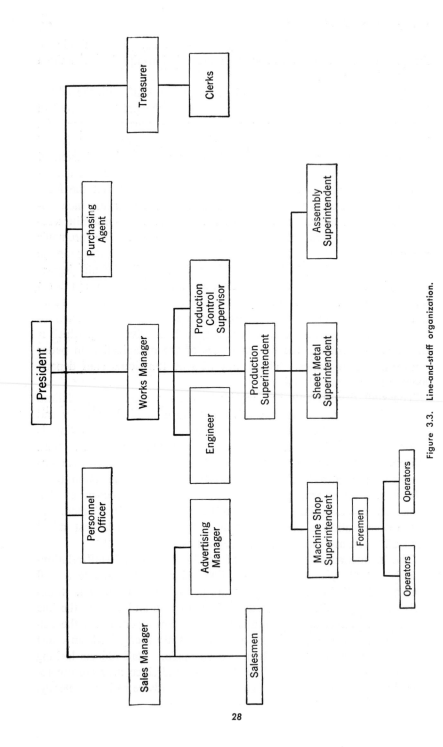

Figure 3.3.　Line-and-staff organization.

Again, the addition of staff officers may give men in the line an excuse for failure. Too often staff men have sound ideas but are unable to sell their method to the line man who is responsible for instituting the idea, and so it is never tried or, if tried, does not receive a fair test. Too often the line expects the staff members to do the line thinking, and the result is stagnation of initiative by the line officers. The following *do's and don'ts* might well be kept in mind by the line as well as by the staff men:

Do's and Don'ts for the Staff:

1. Do not give staff advice so that it will be taken as a line order.

2. Do not give staff advice without careful checking to make certain that it is right (it is dangerous to rely upon the line to catch the staff's mistakes).

3. Do your best to make full use of the line's intimate knowledge of actual operations (consultation with the line promotes cooperation).

4. Do not undermine the position of the line office (remember yours is a service to the line that is expected to help it do a better job).

Do's and Don'ts for the Line:

1. Do not pass the buck to the staff (you are responsible for operations).

2. Do not confuse advice with an order.

3. Make full use of the services that the staff can render (it is a gross waste of your time to try to work out details when there is a specialist whose functions are to help with such matters).

4. Remember that both you and the staff officer are working for the major service objective (each can help the other).

The staff may perform any of the following functions:

1. As a control agency in such departments as:
   1.1 Organization
   1.2 Cost
   1.3 Industrial engineering
   1.4 Standard practice or procedure
   1.5 Budget
   1.6 Personnel—wage administration, transfers, promotion, etc.
   1.7 Accounting
   1.8 Auditing
   1.9 Credit
2. As a service agency in such departments as:
   2.1 Research and development
   2.2 Engineering and construction
   2.3 Purchasing
   2.4 Statistics
   2.5 Traffic
   2.6 Tax
   2.7 Real estate

2.8   Insurance
2.9   Motor vehicle or traffic
2.10 Personnel—employment, restaurant, medical, etc.
3. As a coordinative agency in such departments as:
    3.1   Order and distribution
    3.2   Production planning and control
    3.3   Merchandise
    3.4   Personnel—transfers, wage administration, training, organiza-
          tion, communications with employees, and public relations
4. Advisory agencies in such departments as:
    4.1   Legal
    4.2   Economic
    4.3   Public relations
    4.4   Personnel—labor relations, training, transfer and promotion,
          public relations

The Use of the Committee.   The committee may be used in any
type of organization and at any level—from the board of directors to a
committee of workers striving to develop safety consciousness.   A committee may be attached to a line department or to a staff department.
It may be composed of any combination of line or staff men.   Committees may be divided into four general classes:

1. The committee which has full power to act (seldom found save at
the top management level).
2. The committee which has limited power but whose actions are
subject to veto (not used extensively).
3. The advisory committee.
4. The educational committee, the class or discussion group.

Supervisors are frequently members of committees.   They are usually aware of the time wasted by many committees.   A great many
people do not understand the nature of a committee.   To function as
a committee a group of persons must learn "to give and take" in their
deliberations until there is a meeting of the minds.   Committee action
nearly always is a compromise between various interests and viewpoints.   The best method of developing a proper group spirit is to get
men together.   Their jealousies and their distrust of each other can
be eliminated only by bringing them into close contact with one another.   The spirit of helping each other for the good of the enterprise
can best be developed in a conference.   The committee recognizes the
human factor, fosters the spirit of cooperation, implants the new ideas
of organization and its fundamentals in the minds of all members of
the organization, and gives everyone the contacts necessary to perform
his tasks properly.   On troublesome problems the committee secures
the advice of those best qualified to aid.   It stimulates these men to

give the company the best that is in them. The standing committees solve routine problems of operation but also investigate and advise concerning policy and organization development.

Securing cooperative efforts through committee action requires the recognition of the following cardinal principles of cooperation:

1. Consideration for the viewpoint of those persons who must execute the plan is essential.
2. Persons close to the details of operations may contribute constructive suggestions.
3. Plans will be more effectively executed when the participants thoroughly understand all the causal relationships and factors involved.

The advisory committee is one of the most common in industry. It usually suggests courses of action to the chairman, aiding him in reaching the decisions for which he is held responsible. He may accept or reject these recommendations, but normally matters will be threshed out and the decision reached will be practically final.

The committee is a weak control device and a poor substitute for proper organization in the first place. Committees are of great value as a means of coordinating the efforts of the departments which are represented. They are also of special value in broad policy determination. As a rule, a committee is not well adapted to the collection of facts or technical data. A member of the committee or an expert under the direction of the committee may collect the facts, and the committee may evaluate them or formulate a policy supported by them. Such a policy is likely to be more inclusive than a policy that is the work of a single individual. In order not to waste the time of the committee members the chairman should prepare an agenda that is sent to the members of the committee in advance of their meeting. If costs of committee meetings were accumulated, they would not be held so often.

The advantages of the committee rest on obtaining decisions or recommendations based on group experience. The use of the committee results in many excellent ideas and combinations of ideas; originating among men from different departments its use tends to facilitate seeing the organization needs as a whole; men of differing classes and levels tend to iron out their differences in viewpoint when serving together on committees (this is especially true of union-management committees); and the committee tends to promote greater interest, enthusiasm, and cooperation within the organization.

The committee strengthens the organization structure by promoting cooperation, facilitating coordination, giving stability and continuity to the organization policies, and rendering collective advice. The committee is an excellent educational device, serving as a method of educating and developing younger members of the organization. Many a supervisor has changed his point of view and broadened his vision of the organization and its problems by serving on a committee. Often a supervisor has turned a careless employee into a strong advocate of safe practices by placing the employee on a safety committee.

A committee may be used to advise on any phase of business activity from product design to plant layout or from finance to labor turnover. A committee may be used to aid in any of the functions of the staff: (1) control (the wage and salary committee), (2) advice (the safety committee), (3) coordination (the manufacturing committee), and (4) service (the purchasing committee and the personnel committee). The supervisor is generally informed regarding each of these four types of committees. He may serve on his divisional manufacturing committee or a safety committee. As an illustration of an active factory committee it might be well to consider the *manufacturing committee.*

The manufacturing committee may readily serve as an advisory, coordinating, and control instrument. This committee would include the *product engineer;* the *sales manager,* or the member of the production organization whose function is to effect liaison with the sales organization; the *head of the cost department;* the *general superintendent;* the *purchasing agent,* if purchasing is a major item; and the *director of manufacture,* who would preside over the committee's deliberations. Other men may be added to the committee when special items are considered. The production manager should sit in on the discussion of production schedules.[4] The director of personnel often is a member of this committee, as is the plant engineer if plant changes are being considered. The representative of the sales department need not sit in on the meetings of this committee where matters are being considered that do not directly affect sales. Other members need not attend its meetings when special items in which they are not interested are the major factors for consideration. A copy of the minutes, however, should go to every member of the committee. The secretary should not only preserve information concerning actions taken but also should straighten out many difficulties between meetings and have matters for the committee's attention in such shape that

---

[4] He is frequently a permanent member of the committee and often serves as its secretary.

it will be possible to get them out of the way in minimum time at the meetings.[5] The work of the committee may include:

1. Plans to change the product, including a consideration of new methods of design or new items to be marketed. The interplay of sales and production factors must be considered here.

2. Progress that has been made on changes already begun. This is important, for otherwise it will be found that new ideas which have been decided upon and partially put into effect can be totally forgotten in the press of daily routine.

3. Consideration of methods of cost reduction. Reports by committee members upon economies, decided upon in previous meetings and assigned to them to put into effect, might be included. In this connection, when work of a specific department is taken up, it is possible and advisable to have the foreman in charge of that department attend the meeting, whether or not he is regularly a member of the committee.

4. Coordination. A discussion of routine operation, the status of orders, causes of hold-ups, progress of manufacturing programs, and similar subjects.

Summary. The alert supervisor will recognize that his company organization is another tool at his disposal to make his work more effective. Although the supervisor must be an all-around man, he will face problems and will need to make decisions which require specialized assistance. He must know where to go for such help. The organization pattern set up by management is one of the methods it uses to develop coordination within the enterprise, and the supervisor is expected to cooperate to effect this coordination. But cooperation is based on knowledge, and, therefore, *the supervisor must know his organization.* The reason for reports and procedures, the "whys" of policies, and the authority and responsibilities of departments may be found in the organization and the principles that lie behind the reasoning on which it was developed.[6]

[5] See Paul E. Holden, Lounsbury S. Fish, and Hubert L. Smith, *Top Management Organization and Control,* McGraw-Hill Book Co., New York, 1951, pp. 59–73, for an excellent discussion of the uses and limitations of the committee. Every executive who uses a committee should read this section of the book.

[6] The authors are indebted to E. H. Anderson and G. T. Schwenning, *The Science of Production Organization,* John Wiley & Sons, New York, 1938, for many of the ideas contained in this chapter.

4   Interpreting Company Policies

The Supervisor and Company Policies. Just as the supervisor needs to understand the principles behind the development of an organization, so he needs to understand the fundamental principles on which policies are built. A knowledge of these principles will help him successfully to apply, interpret, and explain the company policies to his men. Today men have a habit of asking "Why?" and questioning the reason behind the policy. Therefore, the supervisor must be more than a parrot stating the policy; he must be able to explain the *why* of the policy, the reasoning behind it. Men are more inclined to accept policies, even if they do not like them, when they understand the reasoning behind them. Every supervisor should recognize the direct relationship between interpretation of the company's policies to the men and industrial morale. Much of the industrial unrest and employee dissatisfaction can be traced to failure of the men to understand the company's policies and the reasoning behind them. In larger organizations, the supervisor not only represents the company to the men but also the men to the management.

The men's ideas about the company, the management, and its policies are the result of their contact with their supervisor. What they think about the company is often the result of his influence on them. The supervisor is required to apply and interpret his company's policies in his daily work. In both their application and interpretation the supervisor must develop an awareness of his responsibility to the company and to his men. His responsibility to the company is to interpret its policies accurately and in the spirit in which they are intended. His responsibility to the men is to interpret accurately and impartially the company policies. Every supervisor must be familiar with the policies of his company and should understand the basic principles underlying these policies.

Some supervisors take the attitude that the rules of conduct and the procedures growing out of policies restrict their freedom and make their work routine, depriving them of the opportunity to make decisions. Actually the reverse is true, as the successful supervisor realizes. Policies, rules, and procedures make the supervisor's work easier —they are his guides to action. They steer his initiative and judgment into the correct channel. They serve to furnish him with the conclusions reached by others with more experience. They relieve him of making many routine decisions he would otherwise have to make, thereby freeing him for other work. In the last analysis, he must still use all his skill in formulating judgments and applying his initiative to interpreting and explaining policies.

Policies Defined. Business policies are related both to the primary and operating fundamentals of organization.[1] Policies are founded on the company's objectives and its organizational structure to achieve these objectives. *Business policies may be broadly defined as that body of principles or rules of conduct by which the aims of the enterprise are to be achieved.* Policies serve to point out the definite directions in which the organization moves as well as to coordinate the efforts of the various divisions. The supervisor must recognize, however, that policies are not a universal set of rules or laws which give him an explanation or solution for every difficulty or problem that may arise. They are a guide to him in charting his course of action rather than an exact pattern to be followed. When he meets problems the supervisor must exercise individual initiative and judgment to solve them, keeping his solution in harmony with the general company policies.

Types of Policies. Company policies may be classified into three main groups: (1) broad, general company policies, (2) operating policies, and (3) departmental policies. The broad, general company policies give definiteness and general direction to the activities of the company as a whole. These policies establish the basic principles which guide the management in the conduct of the business. To make these general policies effective there is needed a group of operating policies to designate the operating methods of the enterprise. These

[1] See p. 5.

policies determine the general procedure to be followed in such matters as production, engineering, purchasing, and sales. To make these major policies effective, departmental policies governing the actions in each of these divisions or departments are developed.

The supervisor should recognize the difference between a policy and a rule of conduct. A policy is more basic than a rule of conduct. Policies change slowly and seldom, whereas rules may be modified at more frequent intervals to meet temporary or changing conditions, as may the procedures used to put the policy into practice. Even though rules of conduct and procedures may be changed, it is generally recognized that these should be changed only when it is necessary to meet changed conditions.

Requirements of Business Policies. In order to be truly effective, *company policies should possess organic unity;* they must harmonize with each other. *Unity of purpose,* as expressed by its policies, should permeate the entire business. Sound business policies serve as a gyroscope keeping the company stabilized and on its charted course. If the personnel policies do not carry out the aims of the enterprise in the same manner as the broad company policies, they not only fail in their purpose but also will result in confusion. For permanence and as a basis for checking performance, policies, wherever feasible, should be put in written form. Over a period of time gradual, unintentional deviations from the policy may radically change a basic policy. This is especially true where the policies involve production standards which must be met. Every supervisor has the responsibility for following up to see that policies are maintained and that the interpretation is in accordance with the letter and the spirit of the policy as originally formulated.

The effectiveness of any policy depends largely upon its being carefully explained by the responsible leaders to all persons who are to carry it out. The supervisor is this key man to the great mass of workers. He must explain the policy *accurately,* that is, as it is worded. Changing a word frequently changes the entire meaning. It is also the supervisor's responsibility to interpret the policy in the *spirit* in which it was intended; he must get across to his men its intent, explaining the reasoning that lies behind it, giving the "why and wherefore." A policy cannot be issued as a top sergeant issues an order. Instead, the supervisor must explain it carefully, sympathetically, and in detail, until it is thoroughly understood.

A knowledge of company policies is as much a part of the supervisor's equipment as knowledge of his machines and tools. He himself must learn, understand, and be thoroughly familiar with policies so that he can interpret them clearly and impartially. *Clearly* means in language the men can understand, with explanations of the "why and wherefore" of the policy, the reasoning that lies behind it. *Impartiality* is the essence of putting across the policy to the men and means explaining it fairly, without emphasizing either the company's or the men's side. The supervisor must not only be sold on the company policy as of a given time, but must also *stay sold* on it. Unless he is sold on it, he cannot put it over to the men. They will sense his indecision and will not fully accept the policy. The supervisor should remember that one of the steps in building and maintaining morale in his department is the proper introduction, interpretation, and follow-up of company policies. When the supervisor is sold on the company policies and his men are in accord with them, the supervisor is well on the way to having a smoothly operating department with high morale.

Methods of Interpreting Company Policies. Any of the various devices for communicating with employees is a potential method of interpreting company policies. In part, these avenues of communication include:

1. Employee handbooks covering personnel policies in general, as well as special handbooks covering one subject, such as safety, pensions, and similar subjects.
2. The employees' paper, sometimes called the "house organ."
3. Union contract.
4. Bulletin boards.
5. Inserts in pay envelopes.
6. Training classes.
7. Suggestion systems.
8. Public address system.
9. Information racks.
10. Verbal explanations by the supervisor without the aid of booklets or printed matter, or in addition to the use of most of the devices listed above.
11. Union stewards or other union officials.
12. Letters sent to the employee's home. This practice tends to get the support of the family in interpreting certain policies.

Policies may be released in memorandum form or posted on bulletin boards. Meetings may be held to inform the men about a policy and to discuss it. The best way, when it is possible, is to bring the men together and give them the policy in written form and then, at that time, to discuss it while they have the policy before them. Many companies at the time of hiring give new employees a booklet containing the company policies, but, even if booklets are given to new employees, the supervisor should carefully instruct them to be sure that they understand the company policies and are sold on them.

Personnel Policies. It is highly probable that personnel policy interpretation and administration require as much of a supervisor's time as any other single activity. Personnel policies are those principles and rules of conduct that govern a company's relationships with its employees. Personnel policies apply to company officials as well as to supervisors and office and manual workers and are a fundamental part of the basic business policies that guide the organization in the achievement of its major objectives. The more clearly these major objectives are outlined, the more specific will be the personnel policies, both in statement and in operation. Personnel policies, like business policies in general, are dynamic; changing to meet fundamental changes, such policies nevertheless should possess a large measure of stability. In other words, business policies and personnel policies have an organic unity.

A successful business enterprise possesses organic unity of purpose. A weakness in any function weakens the entire organization. In the long run, personnel policies will not be sound unless the organization policies are also sound. The sound personnel policy avoids opportunism and is essentially stable, having due regard for the human equation. The objectives of an enterprise are naturally influenced by many considerations: competition, tradition in the particular industry, technological development, social approval, the prevailing attitude of labor, governmental controls, and the ideals of the entrepreneurs. In the light of our present business customs a sound personnel policy should in general have the following characteristics: (1) It should *recognize individual differences* as to capacities, interests, ambitions, emotional reactions, desire for security, etc. (2) It should *recognize the current trend toward group action* and a tendency to seek a voice in those phases of management in which the worker is vitally interested. (Management should not be blinded by collective bargaining to the fact that individual differences are important. An employee or a group of employees may feel as lost in a large union as when they had no formal recognition whatever.) (3) It should be *definite*. Ambiguity and uncertainty are destructive of plant morale. (4) It should be *stable, yet possess sufficient flexibility to meet changing conditions* and the varying needs of individuals. (5) It should be an *integrated part of other basic company policies.* The lack of organic unity results in confusion. (6) It should provide adequate *means for becoming generally known* and understood by all interested parties. (7) It should give *due regard to the interests of all parties,* the employees, the public, and the owners of the capital.

The Supervisor and Departmental Policies. The supervisor is primarily responsible for the formulation of any special departmental policies. In the establishing of departmental policies he should consult his associates and his workers. Consultive supervision promotes the acceptance of policies and is likely to avoid the pitfalls that may occur when due consideration is not given to the interests of all concerned. The departmental policies should evidence: (1) a recognition of the primary and operating fundamentals of organization, (2) due regard for working conditions and hours of work, (3) an ever-present consciousness of the need for safe practices, (4) a clear recognition of quality and quantity requirements, (5) a definite awareness of the need for cost control, (6) a recognition of the desire of employees for a fair wage, of management for a fair return on its investments, and of the public's desire for a quality product on a quantity basis at a fair price, and (7) an attitude of square dealing to men, to management, and to the public.

The supervisor, in developing the policies for his department, must always take into consideration the aims of the enterprise and regard for the personal equation. If his policies are contrary to either of these primary fundamentals of organization, the policy will not be successful. The supervisor must allow for the fixing of responsibility and set his policies within the framework of the lines of supervision. Policy formulation and interpretation demand effective leadership, and to carry out the policy the supervisor will have to establish an adequate system and provide for the necessary records. Every departmental policy must be balanced between the management and the men, fair to both. In policy formulation, the supervisor must be cost conscious, man conscious, and product conscious. Every policy developed within the department must be considered from the viewpoints of its effect on costs, how it will affect product quantity and quality, and its effect on the men in terms of their earnings, their hours, and their working conditions. Finally, the supervisor must know the basic company policies to be certain that his departmental policies will possess organic unity with the general company policies.

Factors to Consider in Interpreting Company Policies. The first factor to be considered in interpreting a company policy is a complete knowledge of the policy itself. Not only should the supervisor know the specific policy, but he should know how it fits into the total company philosophy. In case a given policy involves a change in a previous policy or general practice, the supervisor should know exactly what this change is. In explaining policies, he should seek illustrations that the employees will understand. Even when the new employee is given the company's policies in written form, the supervisor is still responsible for seeing to it that the new man reads and understands them. He cannot even be sure that the old employees remember and follow the policies that have been given to them. A major difficulty is encountered when the supervisor assumes that, because a policy has once been explained, it will always be followed, even when it is used only at infrequent intervals. The difficulty arises from the fact that men are inclined to remember only those policies which they use regularly. Those used only at rare intervals are likely to be forgotten. The group will change, and new men will come in over a period of time. The supervisor must constantly follow up and reexplain policies that are infrequently used. He should be certain that all basic company policies, all major policies, and all departmental policies that affect the men are clearly understood by each man in his department.

When the supervisor knows the company's policies so well that they become a part of his everyday thoughts and actions, then his department will have no trouble following them. Company policies are second nature to the successful supervisor; he must make them a part of his thought processes and an integral part of his attitudes and actions. If his reactions to problems are decisions based on the company policies, his department will never be in a state of confusion. The supervisor will find that personal instruction of the men will help when a particular point involving a policy is raised. It is not sufficient for the supervisor merely to decide and base his decision on the policy. He should explain the policy to the individual employee involved and see that the employee understands how the policy applies to the particular point raised. This personal contact with the men on policies will pay big dividends. Men like to know the "why" as well as the "what" of a decision. Explanation builds cooperation, increases the men's respect for the supervisor, and develops his leadership among them. It should always be remembered that face-to-face explanations of policies is the most effective manner of acquainting a work group with these policies.

The Supervisor Reports to Management. Policies should be stable, yet flexible enough to meet changing conditions. The supervisor can aid management in this respect by knowing his men, their desires, and their ambitions. He should be alive to changing conditions that give rise to new or changed policies. Knowing the men is not sufficient, nor is merely recognizing changing conditions. The supervisor must see that the information, together with the necessary facts, reaches his superior. Yet the supervisor cannot furnish this aid to management unless he understands management's policies and objectives. Only the knowledge of management's side plus the knowledge of the men's desires will make it possible for the supervisor's suggestions or recommendations to be sound. It is the supervisor's responsibility to harmonize the company policies with the work the men are doing and to keep management informed of the results. This is a dual responsibility —to the management to interpret its policies and to the men to see that they understand these policies, which results in both working in the same way and using the same method to accomplish the common objectives of the enterprise.

5 · The Supervisor— a Representative of Management to Men and Men to Management

The Supervisor's Position. For the past thirty years management has been striving to train the supervisor to be its representative. Practically every supervisory training program emphasizes this fact. The National Labor-Management Relations Act recognizes the foreman as management's representative, and under this Act management is not required to recognize a union of foremen. The supervisor not only *represents* management to the men but to the average employee the supervisor *is* the company. If he is a good supervisor, impartially representing both the men and the management, the company (so far as the workers are concerned) is a good one for which to work. Poor supervision, especially when it is overbalanced on the side of management, results in the men's rapidly coming to feel that the company is not a good place to work. The supervisor should also recognize the need for representing the men to the management. Since the supervisor is the liaison officer between the men and the management, he falls down in his responsibility to management if he does not keep it informed concerning the difficulties his men face and the way they feel. Unless he keeps the management informed, it does not possess all the information necessary to make sound decisions. Since the supervisor's personal success is largely determined by the performance of his men, he is also charged with the responsibility of looking after their interests. Every supervisor recognizes that in the final analysis his men make or break him. The importance of this dual relationship of the supervisor, representing the management to the men and representing the men to management, cannot be overemphasized.

Many industrial troubles between management and the men originate because each misunderstands the problems or difficulties faced by the other. The supervisor standing between management and the men is in an advantageous position to prevent such misunderstandings and to show each the problems and difficulties of the other. The supervisor serves both management and the men by clearly and carefully interpreting one to the other. It is possible that much industrial strife could have been avoided had supervisors as a whole clearly understood and carried out their responsibilities.

The supervisor must see that materials are available for his men, that men are available and trained for the various tasks, that work is performed according to specifications, that quality is maintained, that each man turns out the quantity of work expected of him, that the machines are in proper working order, and that the machines are operated in such a manner that they will have maximum life as well as give maximum output. It is not unusual for a supervisor in a large organization to have more men under his direct supervision than plant managers in small institutions. These supervisors are, in reality, general managers of their departments. It is true that the supervisor may have staff or functional assistance in performing many of his duties, yet such aids do not wholly relieve him of any of his responsibility.

A wise group of staff or functional officers will consult the supervisor in making many of their decisions. These staff officers relieve him of many of the details that he formerly had to care for, but he still remains an important person in the proper functioning of these specialized staff or functional departments. By being relieved of some of the details, the supervisor is enabled to exercise more effective *leadership* in his department. He is no longer required to be an ultra specialist in many things but he must still be an all-around leader. The supervisor still remains a specialist in one thing—the handling of men. Being the representative of management closest to the men, his one chief function as a specialist remains the understanding, guiding, and controlling of the men under his direction.

The Supervisor's Place in the Lives of His Men.   Many supervisors forget the tremendous part they play in the lives of their men. Both the earnings and position of the men under his direction are largely dependent on the supervisor and his actions. This is a serious responsibility, not to be taken lightly. Actions taken with respect to a man should be based on facts, and full consideration should always be given by the supervisor to the effects of his acts upon the entire group. Too often in considering wage increases or promotions the supervisor will quickly select several men and let it go at that. This often results in overlooking the most deserving and best-fitted men for the increases or promotions. Every supervisor should recognize that he should consider every man in his group in relation to every other man when taking action relative to wages or promotions. Every supervisor should remember men like to be led by a leader in whom they have confidence. The beginning of this confidence comes from the supervisor's position, but he must develop and maintain it through his actions. The fact that the approval of the supervisor is necessary for most promotions and wage increases gives him a vital influence on the economic lives of his men as long as they remain employees of the company. The supervisor plays an important part in the social and industrial lives of his men. Hired by management and representing it, he naturally assumes the prerogatives of leadership in the eyes of his men. Given this natural advantage the supervisor should make the most of it, *developing and building his capacity for leadership.*

The Need for a Balanced Relationship. It is perfectly natural for a man recently promoted from a work situation to a supervisory position to have his sentiments oriented more nearly in accord with workers than with the sentiments of management. Many supervisors remain tuned in to the "logics of sentiments" of the workers. Some supervisors who have been in that capacity for many years tend to forget the logics of sentiments of the workers and to think only in terms of the logics of management. Other men, without experience at the bench or on machines, will tend to lean toward management. Realizing these tendencies, every supervisor should study himself to avoid any bias and, in every action he takes, should try to square his actions with the basic policies of the company.

Frequently supervisors get out of balance. Sometimes a particular supervisor will lean over backwards to be on either one side or the other. Some supervisors attempt to sacrifice the men to the interests of the management; others are concerned only with the interests of the men and forget their responsibilities to management. When the supervisor gets out of balance either way, he is heading for trouble. To carry out his responsibility completely he will have to consider the interests of both management and the men. In the long run the interests of both are identical, but in the short run the interests may be different. For example, the men may demand a wage increase without considering the fact that production and sales do not justify the increase. After all, wages are paid out of gross income of the company, and, if they exceed a reasonable proportion of this figure, the excess must come out of capital or surplus. This leaves the men, if they insist on the wage increase, with the possibility of the company's going bankrupt and their being without a job. Many times when the short-range interests of management and the men are not identical, the supervisor is required to decide which interests are right from both the short- and long-range viewpoints and, siding in with that group, must strive to show the other where it is wrong. As a matter of fact the supervisor should also strive to give due consideration to the interests of the consumer. It is only when both management and the workers strive earnestly to give the consumer a desired quality product at a reasonable price that they can expect to secure continued patronage for their product.

In discharging his responsibility to management the supervisor is in a broad sense required: (1) to transmit faithfully managerial policies to the men, (2) to transmit the men's desires and aims to management (this is a dual function and the supervisor owes this to both the management and the men), (3) to get out the required production on time, (4) to maintain standards of quality, (5) to formulate plans and methods to increase productive efficiency, (6) to reduce all waste and scrap to a minimum, (7) to keep accurate records from which future actions can be guided, (8) to render reports as required. In a more specific sense the supervisor represents management in matters such as: (1) wages, (2) promotions, (3) assignment to a specific job, (4) safety, (5) layoffs and days worked, (6) recalls, (7) merit rating, (8) instruction on the job, (9) working conditions, and (10) providing inspirational leadership.

The Supervisor's Attitude Influences His Men. The worker's attitude toward the company during his early work experience with that company is almost entirely a reflection of his attitude toward his foreman. To the men, the supervisor is in a large measure the company. It is easy for the supervisor to forget this fact and to represent himself, his attitude, and his feelings, rather than the company. Modern management strives to develop a working force of satisfied employees, and, in general, policies are directed to this end. Only when the supervisor recognizes his responsibility to represent management impartially to the men and carries out this responsibility to his fullest capacity can the company expect to have satisfied employees.

The supervisor represents management properly when he interprets orders to the men clearly and simply, giving explicit information to the men about their work. When changes are made in methods, product, operations, or policies, the supervisor who is doing a good job in representing management will carefully explain to the men, as far as possible, all the reasons lying behind the change. It is always well to remember, in representing management, that the men not only want to know the *what* but also the *why* of the change in policy. The supervisor must set a good example, showing in his actions and his talk that he believes in the aims and the policies of the company and follows them as they are laid down. The supervisor who carries out the orders of management promptly and properly is setting a good example, leading his men and his department toward cooperation with other departments and coordinating his department's work with the larger operations of the company.

The supervisor of today will do well to remember that the work group has undergone a change during the past twenty years. The men are, in many cases, younger in years but more mature in outlook. They are definitely better educated. Twenty years ago the high school graduate seldom entered the factory. Today the high school graduate is found everywhere. The men are anxious to advance and with this in mind are studying their jobs, other jobs, the supervisor, and the company as a whole. Men today have a questioning attitude and seek the company and the work environment that they feel will satisfy them. In general they are open-minded and willing to be convinced, but they must be sold by facts. The success of a supervisor is largely determined by his ability to get the facts, to interpret these facts to his employees, and his ability to reconcile the interests of his workers with the objective demands in the total work situation.

The Workers Look to Their Supervisor. The workers look to their supervisor for direction and dynamic leadership. They expect their foreman or supervisor: (1) to provide adequate instruction in company policies, in correct methods of performing required operations, and in the next job ahead so as to prepare the men for promotion if a vacancy occurs, (2) to maintain satisfactory working conditions, such as cleanliness, order, safety, and an even flow of work, (3) to maintain discipline, (4) to promote cooperative effort and good will, (5) to represent the men to management, (6) to promote and transfer men impartially when the opportunity is present, (7) to rate the men fairly for the purposes of wage determination, (8) to encourage suggestions and give credit where credit is due, (9) to strive to fit each employee into the job for which his capacities are best fitted,

(10) to recognize individual differences, and (11) to provide inspirational leadership. A few persons may question item (3) above. Actually a work group prefers an orderly direction to the confusion that arises when discipline is lax. What they really like is positive leadership, with certainty of action when there is a violation of generally accepted regulations.

The supervisor or any executive may well consider his position in the light of the familiar symbol of Justice, holding in her hands a balance. The balance is weighted on one side with his responsibilities to represent his superiors (management) to his men, and on the other with his responsibilities to represent his men to management. The solution to every supervisor's problem resolves itself into keeping the scales in balance by meeting his dual responsibility both by representing the management to the men and the men to the management, fairly and equally.

The Supervisor Strives to Maintain an Attitude of Balance. Every individual has sentiments and biases arising from his experiences. In striving to discharge his responsibilities the supervisor should recognize his normal sentiments and sincerely endeavor to live up to both the spirit and the letter of his company's policies. Company policies are the product of the collective thinking of many persons and are likely to be broader than the biases of almost any individual. There are well-defined practices that the supervisor may follow in keeping to the middle path of balance between the men and management. These practices include: (1) avoiding prejudices and striving to develop a judicial attitude in all matters where there is a conflict in interests, (2) continuously studying his men, (3) knowing the company policies, (4) encouraging goodwill by manifesting it himself, (5) leading in teamwork, and (6) practicing loyalty.

Since the supervisor is a representative of management, he should exercise great care not to let his men feel that he is on their side at the expense of management. He may voice an objection to management when he thinks a particular action is not desirable; however, after management has considered all the factors involved, the supervisor should make management's decision his own, present it sincerely to his men, and not "pass the buck." It is recognized that management can be wrong. Such a situation places the supervisor in a tight spot. If the supervisor cannot conscientiously carry out management's policies, he should resign. The supervisor in his work with the men should work constantly toward developing in himself a judicial attitude. With practice he will find that being fair and impartial will gradually become a habit. Every successful supervisor knows his men well. This knowledge comes only through continued study of his men. Learning to know them is not sufficient, for over a period of time men change. Many a supervisor has said "But I thought I knew my men," when he should have said "I used to know them, but I stopped studying them." The actions of the supervisor toward his men and toward management and other departments determine the teamwork he develops in his own department. With the men, actions count far more than words. Every supervisor is under the spotlight, his men watch his every action, and unless he practices what he preaches, the men will note it and act accordingly. This is especially true in winning the loyalty of the men. *If one would have loyalty, he must first be loyal.*

The Supervisor Is More than a Referee. Like the referee the supervisor is supposed to be fair and impartial. Each must possess a judicial attitude and be constantly on the alert, ready to make a decision. The referee and the supervisor both stand between two groups, but the referee is representing neither—he is only present to see that each will do its part according to the rules of the game. The supervisor, on the other hand, represents both groups, a far more difficult position. The referee owes his allegiance to neither side, but the supervisor must be loyal to both.

The supervisor, unlike the referee, has a vital interest in the outcome of the struggle, for his position and future are involved. Although the supervisor interprets the rules and regulations, he also has a vital interest in seeing that they carry out the aims of the enterprise. The supervisor is a coordinator between two cooperating groups, and his vital interest is in promoting the common interests of both groups. The referee rarely interprets a rule; the supervisor may do so frequently but with discretion. The referee never considers the interests of both sides in arriving at a decision—to him one side only is right, the other is wrong. The supervisor looks at both sides, weighs the facts, and then makes his decision, which is often a compromise. The referee usually has certain hard and fast rules to follow, whereas the supervisor frequently has to follow tradition or policies and build his decision on the basis of them. The supervisor cannot consider himself only as a referee between the men and management. His is a greater responsibility: he represents both; he has a dual responsibility to represent one to the other to the end that all three—the supervisor, the men, and the management—work toward a common end, the achievement of the aims of the enterprise.

Factors Influencing the Supervisor's Position. Any executive should learn to *avoid the display of authority and favoritism*. A supervisor cannot function effectively unless he has *authority commensurate with his responsibility*. Try though he may, the foreman cannot be merely a counselor to his men. He is responsible and must at times take the full weight of the burden of decision making. To do this he must have the inherent authority to carry out the requirements of his position. With respect to authority the supervisor should have a guiding rule: *use it sparingly, display it never*. It is amazing how a little authority will go to a person's head, and many a young supervisor has stumbled because he immediately relied on his authority to carry him through a situation requiring leadership. A real leader rarely has to use his authority. Whenever a supervisor has to fall back on his authority to get something done, he may rest assured that his right to leadership is being questioned. When the supervisor leans back on his authority, he is waving a red flag before his men, and usually they will meet the challenge. Authority overused becomes useless as a supervisory tool. Authority has its place and may be used occasionally, but its place and use are rare. As a last resort, the supervisor will call it into play only when he has exhausted every other means and device at his control. The supervisor should not display his authority and should never hold it as a threat over the heads of his men. Its use, when necessary, should ordinarily be in the privacy of the supervisor's office with only the man on whom it is to be exercised present. When a leader has to take action involving authority, it should be on a basis of having to bear the responsibility for the action; hence he must make the decision when agreement cannot be reached. Most certainly this attitude is not one of weakness. The supervisor must lead from a position of strength, but this strength does not need to be offensive.

Many departments have easy and hard jobs, and low-rated and high-rated jobs, and overtime or emergency work may always be necessary. Without the slightest intention of playing "favorites" the foreman in assigning jobs may be accused of *favoritism*. In seeking to avoid the charge of favoritism the supervisor should set for himself the following guides: (1) impartially assign easy jobs, (2) impartially assign hard jobs, (3) impartially assign dirty jobs, (4) impartially assign clean jobs, (5) impartially assign emergency jobs, (6) impartially assign jobs requiring overtime, (7) always avoid any semblance of selection based on nationality, religion, politics, fraternity, age, or family relationships, and (8) keep adequate records as an aid in carrying out the avowed policy of impartiality. Consultation with his men regarding the establishment of procedures for doing the types of work that frequently lead to the charge of favoritism is often the best method for avoiding such accusations.

Cooperation with Other Departments. To receive cooperation one must give it. A willing attitude of helpfulness goes a long way toward inspiring the same response in others. There are a number of places where the degree to which the supervisor's willingness to cooperate will be watched by his men. Their cooperation with him will depend to a large degree on his cooperation with the other departments and with his own men. The supervisor cooperates with other departments in achieving quantity production, quality production, and in the lending and transfer of men. Mass production today demands complete cooperation between departments in the processing and moving of materials from department to department as rapidly as possible. Here the supervisor must see that as rapidly as his department finishes work on the product it is moved without delay to the next department. On the other hand, he must be certain that the material he moves passes inspection and will be satisfactory for use in the next department. Where there are staff departments working with the supervisor, such as production control or inspection, he must give them his fullest cooperation in making their work effective. Here again he is also cooperating with the departments which follow his, because these staff departments must service the product before it can leave his department. When unavoidable shortages of men occur or overloads on departments develop, the supervisor may be called on to lend men to other departments. In such instances the supervisor cannot send his least capable men, for, if he does, he can expect the same in return when it becomes necessary for him to borrow men because of shortage or trouble. The wise supervisor soon learns that he gets only what he gives, and that cooperation is a two-way process. When the men see that the supervisor willingly cooperates with other departments, they will usually cooperate with him.

Special Awards. The judicial use of special recognition is one of the tools of the effective leader. The giving of special awards serves as a strong incentive when these awards are made on a clearly demonstrable basis that is available to all persons meeting the requirements. This, of course, does not mean that every person who qualifies is given the same classification. For instance a helper may be qualified to hold the position in which he is only the helper. He will not be made the operator until a vacancy arises. In this case the recognition rests in promotion when there is a vacancy. Special awards may include: (1) wage increases for continued production above the average, (2) financial or other rewards for suggestions resulting in a constructive measurable saving, (3) preferred assignment to a particular job or machine, and (4) finally, recommendation for promotion to positions in higher wage brackets or with additional responsibility. The supervisor must be certain that the men, as well as the supervisor, recognize that the award is given on merit. These rewards should be used judiciously, however, and only after careful consideration of all the men who are eligible. Occasionally a supervisor has found, after it was too late to do anything about it, that the man he selected was neither the best nor the most deserving.

Full Responsibility Rests on the Supervisor. The ability to delegate is one of the measures of a real leader. However, there is one thing a leader cannot delegate: *his responsibility for delegating.* The supervisor is still responsible for the action of the person to whom he has delegated. He must assume the blame for mistakes as well as share the credit for success. Among the major tasks in his department is the responsibility of maintaining a balanced relationship in representing management to the men and the men to management. The supervisor cannot delegate the responsibility for representing both men and management. It is his and his alone; both management and his men hold him solely responsible for representing them fairly and impartially to each other. It is a major problem, one always present and never completely solved, yet the supervisor who fulfils this responsibility adequately is well on his way to success, both with his men and with the management for whom he works.

Some people, committed to class struggle between management and the workers, contend that a supervisor cannot represent both management and the workers; that he must be on one side or the other; that the trade union leader is the only one who can represent the workers. Such an attitude is wholly inconsistent with the facts of life as manifested by literally tens of thousands of supervisors who recognize the rights of both workers and management, as well as the responsibilities of each, if free enterprise and opportunity are to continue to exist in this country and other parts of the world.

Wants of Both the Worker and His Boss. Travis Elliott has expressed the wants of the worker and his boss as follows: [1]

---

[1] Adapted from Travis A. Elliott, "What the Bosses and Workers Want," *Personnel Journal,* March 1950, p. 372.

I Want a Boss

Who had something to do with hiring me and who wants me to work for him.

Who helps me when I am new to get acquainted with my job.

Who explains to me just what my job is—just what I am expected to do.

Who tells me frequently how I'm getting along—what I do well and what I don't do well—who shows me how to do better.

Who not only thinks of me for what I am but also for what I may become.

Who takes a personal interest in me and my problems.

Who listens to my ideas for making the job easier and better.

Who has something to do with my pay and does it when the time comes.

Who stands up for me when I am right.

Who is honest and four-square with me.

Who tells me about changes before they are made.

Who has a personal faith and confidence in me.

I WOULD DO MY BEST FOR A
BOSS LIKE THAT!

YOU WOULD TOO!

I Want a Worker

Who likes his job.

Who knows his job.

Who keeps himself physically fit.

Who wants to do a day's work for a day's pay.

Who wants to get ahead.

Who is always on the job unless excused.

Who is cheerful—not sullen.

Who works safely—with due consideration for himself and his fellow workers.

Who gets a bang out of a job well done.

Who tries to avoid waste and cut costs.

Who looks for a better way to do the job.

Who tells the truth; who is sincere.

Who gripes little and looks forward.

Who keeps a spirit of teamwork.

Who asks questions when he needs help.

Who is willing to face his personal problems squarely.

Who tries to put himself in my place now and then.

Who feels that his job is a privilege —not a right.

I WOULD GIVE A WORKER LIKE
THAT MY BEST!

YOU WOULD TOO!

6 Planning the Work of the Department

The Nature of Planning. Henri Fayol, the great French industrialist and pioneer student of organization and management, said that "if foresight is not the whole of management, at least it is an essential part of it. To foresee, in this context, means both to assess the future and make provision for it; that is, forecasting is itself action already."[1] Planning is the act or process of interpreting the facts of a situation, determining a line of action to be taken in the light of all of the facts and the objective sought, detailing the steps to be taken in keeping with the action determined, the making of provision to carry through the plan to a successful conclusion, and the establishing of checks to see how close performance comes to the plan. Planning is thinking ahead or thinking a thing through and requires a high type of constructive analysis. Good planning is not mechanical, but some mechanical devices may be used in planning. Unless the supervisor uses some type of effective planning, he will leave many things undone. It is a waste of energy for the supervisor to burden his mind with unnecessary details that can be taken care of by constructive planning. If planning is essential in the larger aspects of the enterprise, then certainly it is also essential in the smaller unit of which the supervisor is the directing head.

Planning is a prerequisite for the successful operation of a department. Without it the supervisor cannot possibly meet the requirements and standards of the company. The ability to plan is a technique every supervisor needs, and like other skills it comes only with

[1] Henri Fayol, *General and Industrial Management* (English translation), Pitman Publ. Corp., New York, 1949, p. 43.

long assiduous practice and cultivation. If unnecessary delays are to be avoided, unnecessary waste of material eliminated, effective use of machines and equipment to be realized, and manpower to be effectively utilized, planning is essential. Ability to plan is one of the essentials of leadership. *No supervisor is entitled to the confidence of his men unless he is willing to plan for them.*

Institutional Planning. Institutional planning sets up the procedures for attaining the major institutional objectives, divides the institutional activities into major functional divisions, such as finance, production, and sales, and provides for the development of the institutional budget. Departmental or divisional planning involves both the coordination of the work of the supervisor's department with the other departments within the organization and the smooth and successful operation of his department. Successful organizations, like successful individuals, are budget conscious. The supervisor assists in the institutional planning that is done by top management. He furnishes through records and suggestions the details that are needed for broad planning. For example, in the development of budgets the department supervisor checks the required manpower and labor costs, and makes recommendations on equipment capacity and suitable equipment available or needed for the work to be done. His advice may be asked concerning operating methods, such as shift rotation and the hours of shifts. Institutional planning comes down to the supervisor in the form of orders telling him what to do, but before the development of the institutional plan the supervisor has already told his superior what he can do with his present equipment and manpower. A reciprocal relationship must be present in all successful institutional planning, a two-way flow of ideas from the supervisor up to the management in the form of facts and recommendations and then from the management down to the supervisor in the form of policies, procedures, and orders.

Departmental Planning in Terms of the Primary and Operating Fundamentals of Organization.[2] Both institutional and departmental planning should be founded upon the *objectives of the enterprise.* Organizational objectives can be realized departmentally only if they are understood and a definite program is followed to achieve them. *Definite lines of supervision* within the department can be assigned only as the result of careful planning, if maximum results are to be obtained. Unless *responsibilities* are assigned only after careful planning, gaps

[2] See Chapter 1, pp. 5–6, for a statement of the four primary and four operating fundamentals of organization.

will occur, and everybody's business is nobody's business. Effective use of personnel must be planned, or the supervisor is likely to overlook the *personal equation.* Any system that is put into effect should be the outgrowth of careful planning. Coordination, the synchronizing force of all line-and-staff organizations, can be achieved only through careful planning. Effective coordination supported by *dynamic leadership* results in teamwork, or cooperation, and high departmental morale. Effective industrial leadership presumes careful planning supported by a dynamic force and the will to carry out the plan. Leadership does not come naturally to most people. It is not an innate quality but comes only after long, hard work. Leadership qualities can be developed by the supervisor, but only as the result of careful planning and long practice. *Effective records* are the result of planning, and the supervisor who installs *systems* and *records* without careful planning and research is likely to find them expensive and useless. Records are essential as a part of planning but should be developed to serve a specific purpose. Similarly, *operating rules and regulations* that are not planned are likely to be conflicting and subject to frequent change to make them workable. One reason planning pays dividends is that it minimizes change and tends to allow time to care for the emergencies that do arise. Planning facilitates the use of the "exception principle" [3] in management.

Phases of Planning. Since we are using *planning* to include the carrying out of the plan and the checking for conformance to the plan, it is well to define common terms used in production planning and control. Planning within the department or within the enterprise as a whole is made up of three major divisions: routing, scheduling, and dispatching. *Routing* is establishing the sequence or path to be followed by a piece of material to be fabricated or a task to be accomplished. *Scheduling* is the setting of the time when each operation is to be started and finished. *Dispatching* is the actual releasing of orders and starting of operations. Essential in the dispatching step is *follow-up* to find out if the work is accomplished, if it is done on schedule, what obstacles develop, and if there is a better way to do the work the next time.

Basic Aspects of Departmental Planning. The supervisor must plan the work of his department to cooperate with other departments, and to coordinate the work of his department with the whole institu-

[3] See p. 15 for a statement of the *exception principle.*

tional program. This coordination requires that the supervisor and his department should: (1) be able to handle work in the proper sequence as it is received from other departments, (2) be able to supply other departments according to schedule with worked materials that they ought to receive from his department and must have to carry on their work, and (3) help other departments, if emergencies or breakdowns occur, by taking a part of their work or by lending their men. Follow-up to see that the plan has been carried out according to schedule is one aspect of planning that is frequently overlooked. The plan may have to be changed because new conditions arise. Unless the supervisor follows up and is on top of his planning as it goes into operation, he cannot see that the necessary changes are made as they are needed with the result that delays occur and departmental efficiency decreases. Wise supervisors make due allowance for unexpected emergencies, such as machine breakdowns, absences of employees, or special rush orders. Rarely does a department operate at 100 per cent efficiency for very long. Therefore, the supervisor will plan for production at a rate which he knows he can maintain. Past experience gives the supervisor knowledge on which he can determine the productive capacity of his department. Hopes or expectations have no place in planning; only facts can be used as the basis of planning if the plan is to be successful. Good planning always allows for unforeseen emergencies and provides for alternatives which can be placed in operation should they be required.

Planning is not entirely a mechanical operation, although it requires the use of such mechanical devices as charts, planning boards, and forms. Effective planning must be predicated on a complete knowledge of the capacities and reasonably expected performance of the men, machines, and materials. Before any planning can be done, the supervisor must possess a complete knowledge of operating conditions. The supervisor must know his men and must keep on knowing them, because men change; their desires, interests, and capacities expand and contract as a result of new and changing conditions. Machines grow old or may be rebuilt. Machine capacities this year may not be the same as last year. Major processes change as do minor methods within the process. There are variables in materials even when they are purchased from the same source and to the same specifications. One time the materials will work more easily and therefore faster, and the next time they may cause trouble and result in the slowing down of production. These are all facts the supervisor must have at his fingertips before he can start his planning which results in the routing, scheduling, and dispatching.

A sound organizational structure within the department is a prerequisite to effective planning. This structure provides that responsibilities and authority are properly distributed and that the men in supervisory positions have *time to supervise*. Unfortunately, the supervisor is frequently the one most responsible for departmental delays because he is so overloaded with details that he simply does not have time for urgently needed planning, yet he will refuse to delegate these details to others. Many supervisors make the mistake of *too much personal doing* and *too little constructive planning*. If the supervisor is going to use his men and machines effectively, a great deal of planning will be required. Therefore, the wise supervisor does not overload himself with details but instead provides for the care of details by delegating them to others and by setting up procedures so that he has to attend only to the exceptions. Thus he frees himself to have time for the constructive planning that results in a successful department. Planning does not just happen; it develops only as the result of the supervisor's taking time out to do it.

Steps to Successful Departmental Planning. The planning pattern itself should be orderly and systematic in order to achieve the desired goal. The first step in planning requires the getting of the facts, which include the supervisor's knowledge of his men and of his equipment and an analysis of the job requirements. It has been said previously that the supervisor must know his men and know them well, as they are; this information is fundamental to him in every step he takes in handling the work of his department. Knowing his men the supervisor trains them to become what he wants them to be, both versatile and highly productive. No supervisor ever starts out with a group of men who are wholly satisfactory. Once he knows them and knows what they are, he then must train them to be what he would have them be.

In addition to knowing the capacities and interests of his men the supervisor must know his equipment exactly as it is. He must know what he needs better to meet the requirements demanded of his department. He must see that his equipment is properly maintained and his machines adequately tooled. The supervisor must analyze the requirements of the job he has to do. Knowing his men and his machines, he must train his men for the machines in terms of the work to be done. It may be necessary to adapt the machines to the work; it may be necessary to train the men for the adapted machines and the kind of work required. This requires planning for retraining of present employees or the securing and training of new men to staff the machines and do the work.

Having all of the facts as to men, materials, and machines, the supervisor then selects the men and equipment to meet the needs of each situation, plans a definite time schedule, and arranges to follow up the adopted plan of action. The planning of the definite time schedule involves the steps of routing, scheduling, and dispatching. The follow-up is necessary to determine whether or not the plan is working successfully, to meet the emergencies that arise, to adapt the plan to the changing situation, and to decide from experience what improvement can be made in the plan the next time the same work is to be done. The importance of the follow-up stage cannot be over-emphasized. The supervisor can only develop his ability to plan by constant practice and review of his planning. Likewise, improvement in his department's work can come only from benefiting by past experience so that each time the same work must be done again, it can be done more effectively, faster, at a lower cost, and with less effort.

The Effect of Planning on Production. When the causes of low production are examined, the major causes are usually found to include: material supply, equipment, power, improper instruction, untrained men, and deliberate restriction of output by the men. All except the last are the result of poor planning. When the supervisor lacks materials for his men, the fault lies either with his planning or the planning in the departments preceding his—or with the central planning department if one is in use. Frequently lack of materials is caused by the failure to requisition materials in time and in sufficient amounts to keep the men busy. Untrained men are definitely the result of inadequate planning. If the supervisor fails to see his needs in terms of men sufficiently in advance of needing them, it is obvious that he has failed to plan ahead. When the supervisor has materials on hand, has obtained his men in advance of his needs, and has trained them, only to find that faulty instruction has resulted in inadequate training, the fault again rests with the supervisor's planning—it is his failure to plan the proper type of instruction and to allow for sufficient time to put the instruction to work. Lack of proper equipment resulting in low production is largely due to lack of planning. It may be true that the supervisor planned for additional equipment or asked in advance for changes to be made in his equipment to adapt it to the new work and the management failed to fulfill his requests. Even when inadequate power is the cause of low pro-duction, ordinarily lack of planning is the basic cause, although that planning is the responsibility of the supervisor's superiors.

Planning and Morale. Men react favorably or negatively accord-ing to whether or not the department is run in an orderly manner. Poor planning or lack of planning on the part of the supervisor has the definite effect of lowering morale within the department. It makes little difference whether planning is totally lacking or just poorly done; men are interested only in results. The men lose confidence in the supervisor's leadership when they cannot be reasonably sure of their earnings per day or per week, or, for that matter, of their job. When poor planning results in a decrease in earnings, workers lose interest in their work, begin to lack confidence in their supervisor, and their loyalty to the company wanes. The final result will be high labor turnover, especially among the best men. In summary, poor planning results in lowered morale among the men, uncertainty as to their earnings, lack of confidence in their supervisor, lack of confidence in and loyalty to the company, and high labor turnover.

When planning is sound, equipment is in good condition, com-pletely overhauled and tooled, materials are plentiful, the men are trained, and their earnings are fair, they have confidence in and are loyal to their company and labor turnover is low. In other words, confidence is one of the essential ingredients in positive morale. Effective planning gives the workers confidence that their supervisor knows where he is going and how to get there.

Personal Abilities Used in Planning. Since planning requires "pre-vision," or looking ahead in terms of the present and anticipated facts, it is evident that planning requires analysis and the ability to project activities yet to take place. Planning requirements include: (1) the ability to see the situation as a whole, (2) the ability to break a prob-lem down into its elements, (3) constructive imagination, versatility, and resourcefulness which will result in the ability to convert old methods into new, (4) an impersonal analytical approach not dom-inated by personal prejudices, (5) the ability to measure the effective-ness of a given plan or procedure, and (6) the ability not to become so enmeshed in details that no time remains for planning.

Planning at the departmental level requires protracted mental effort and self-discipline. Planning should not be delayed for a more ad-vantageous time. If it is put off it is likely never to be done. By careful planning, it will not be necessary to put it off, for it will have been scheduled and taken care of accordingly. Planning begins with the supervisor's planning of his own time. Many supervisors say they have so much to do they lack the time to do it all. The supervisor in planning his own time should sit down and, using paper and pencil, should list all his duties, together with their relative importance and the time he needs for each. Then he should divide his working day or week into quarter-hour or half-hour sections. In each of these sections he should schedule one or more of his various tasks. If he needs more time than he has to carry out his tasks, he will have to handle this problem the same way he would a scheduling problem in his department, doing first things first and, if necessary, delegating some of his tasks to others. The supervisor should schedule himself on the same basis he uses in scheduling machines, that is, never scheduling 100 per cent of his time. He is better off to schedule himself at 80 per cent to 90 per cent capacity rather than 100 per cent. When the supervisor has trained himself to *plan his work and work his plan,* he is on the way to developing the ability to plan effectively. The supervisor must learn to think and work in an orderly fashion. When he learns to plan his own work and sees the advantages planning affords him, the next step in planning the work of his department will come naturally. The same principles apply and the same methods are used whether the planning is of the supervisor's time, departmental tasks, or institutional programs. The best way to find time for planning is to plan so that the time is available.

The Relationship of the Departmental Supervisor to Central Planning. In most of the large establishments, institutional planning and some of the departmental planning are handled by the central planning department. Such a procedure relieves the departmental supervisor of much of the clerical work involved when he does his own scheduling, routing, and dispatching. This merely gives him more time to concentrate on effective workmanship, new methods, instructions to his workers, quality, and those items for which he is best qualified. He still has a real job on his hands to distribute his time most effectively. Even where central planning is followed, many things, requiring close cooperation with the central planning department, can go wrong. That department helps him and gives him time to perform his tasks, but it does not relieve the supervisor of his responsibility to see that production flows smoothly.

7 Interviewing— a Skill Needed in Supervising

The Nature of the Interview. An interview is an exchange of ideas or opinions between two or more persons. In a true sense it is a purposeful exchange of ideas even though the actual meeting may not have been planned. The work itself is a combination of two words, *inter* + *view*. *Inter* means between or among. *View* means sight, or in some cases, attitude, such as "point of view." It cannot be emphasized too much that an interview is a two-way exchange of ideas, points of view, or getting and giving information. Even the information gathering interview involves the giving of the reason for the interview by the interviewer to the interviewee. If this is not done the response is likely not to convey the desired information. The giving of a command is not an interview. It is a one-sided relationship. Order giving may or may not be an interview. If an opportunity is given to the recipient of the order to ask questions to clarify the order itself and possibly its objective and other phases of the order it may be an interview.

The participants in an interview need not be equals in status, intelligence, skill, character, or any other characteristic. In case of a superior status of one of the participants the one occupying the higher status should recognize the equality of both in terms of the "dignity of man." The oft-repeated phrase that "all men are created equal" should be recognized by leaders in business in terms of equality in the sight of government and in terms of the dignity of the individual. Any other approach does not promote a successful exchange of ideas or information. An interview is not a mere social conversation, but its success is promoted when the same freedom of expression is encouraged.   An interview is a *purposeful exchange of information,* whereas a social conversation may be merely polite conversation.

Types of Interviews.   Practically every phase of business uses the interview as one of its most important tools.   A few of the uses of the interview include:

1. Employment
2. Introducing the employee to his job
3. Instructing
4. Any phase of operations, such as a discussion of specifications, quality, or quantity of work
5. Wage adjustments
6. Promotions, layoff, demotion, or discharge
7. Correction or discipline
8. Merit rating
9. Evaluation of jobs and job descriptions
10. Explaining rules, regulations, or procedures
11. Giving information of any kind about such matters as insurance programs, union contract provisions, safety requirements, production plans, vacations, or any other item.   (Of course, information may be given by other means than the interview.   It may even be given verbally by a supervisor without giving the employee a chance to ask questions, but the interview promotes clarification and acceptance.)
12. Sales, credit, and collections
13. Resolving grievances
14. Suggestions, research, development, design, or processes

This listing of interviews is based on the objective or on the subject matter of the interview.   Interviews may also be classified in terms of the method used: (1) the directed interview, (2) the patterned interview, and (3) the non-directed interview.   The *directed interview* is one in which the interviewer has specific items on which he wishes to get or to give information.   He may follow a series of questions or he may formulate his questions as the interview progresses but always with the same purpose in mind.   The *patterned interview* is one that has been worked out (usually with considerable care) in terms of a specific procedure to be followed, often with exact questions to be asked.   The questions may be memorized or they may be written and be read aloud by the interviewer.   Often the questions are so well known to the interviewer that a mere glance brings forth the entire question.   The patterned interview has the advantage of making certain that desired questions will be asked.   In the hands of a skilled interviewer the patterned interview may be conducted without the appearance of being stilted or formal.   This following of a pattern is helpful in training new interviewers.

The *non-directed interview* is not designed (as a rule) to get answers to specific questions but rather to permit the interviewee to talk about the things in which he is interested. This kind of interview is particularly helpful in permitting an employee to tell about his complaints and grievances. This kind of interviewing may also be valuable in any phase of relationships where specific answers or information are not sought. The famous Hawthorne Experiment of the Western Electric Company developed this technique.[1] In summary form, the attitude of the interviewer and the method has been well expressed as follows: [2]

1. Interviewer's attitude:
   1.1 One of interest and sympathetic curiosity.
   1.2 Quite as much interested in interviewing satisfied workers as those who are dissatisfied.
   1.3 An employee's interpretation of his own personal situation can only be changed by an internal or psychological change within the employee.
   1.4 An employee will take the necessary steps to correct a situation when he has clarified his thinking by talking over his problem in detail with the interviewer. This employee will initiate his own action and assume the responsibility for his acts.
   1.5 Any action initiated by the employee will tend to relate him to other people in the situation in question.
   1.6 The supervisor's relationship with his employees will be strengthened rather than weakened by the interviewing process.
2. Methods used:
   2.1 The employee is put at ease by the general surroundings and attitude of the interviewer.
   2.2 Strict confidence is guaranteed the employee in reference to anything he may say.
   2.3 The employee is encouraged to talk freely and to continue to talk until he is talked out.
   2.4 The employee is never interrupted while he is talking.
   2.5 The interviewer never argues with the employee or gives him advice.
   2.6 The interviewer strives to discover how the employee thinks and feels and why.

Essentials of a Successful Interview. Most interviews are conducted with relatively little preparation in advance. This may not

[1] See F. J. Roethlisberger, William J. Dickson, and Harold A. Wright, *Management and the Worker,* Harvard University Press, Cambridge, Mass., 1939, for a challenging description of the evolution of the non-directed interview. This book should be read by all supervisors.

[2] See William J. Dickson, "Understanding and Training Employees," American Management Association, *Personnel Series,* No. 35, pp. 4–18, for a discussion of this method.

cause any unfortunate results in those cases where the interviewer has had a wide experience in the field covered by the interview. On the other hand a failure to plan for the interview is frequently the cause of partial or complete failure. Every interview is influenced by the following factors:

1. The objective of the interview. Why is it being conducted?

2. The current situation out of which the interview emerges. This frequently involves a series of events or factors. In meeting the situation the company policies and the worker and group sentiments, and at times conflicting desires, should be kept in mind.

3. The interviewer. The interviewer brings to the interview his own background, attitudes, responsibilities, and skills. If he relies solely on his experience without having planned his interview it may be a success so long as it falls within the area of his background.

4. The interviewee. The reaction of the interviewee depends largely on his previous experience, his general attitude, and the demands he is making upon his present situation.

The Interviewer. The interviewer's success depends not only on his own inherent capacities and how he uses them but also upon the interviewee's ideas as to what the interviewer represents and his reaction to the interviewer's statements, attitudes, and general presentation. In other words the interview is an exchange between two or more persons. The reactions of each person influences the reaction of the other one. Each is influenced not so much by the real reactions of the other as by what he thinks them to be. A business interview frequently is an evolving social situation as well as an economic situation. It often reveals unanticipated things.

The interviewer brings to the interview several selves: (1) his real self, (2) the self he would like to have the interviewer think him to be, and (3) the self that the interviewee recognizes. To a substantial degree these three selves will be largely the same if the interviewer has a well-adjusted personality, has made careful preparation for the interview, has been clothed with the proper position and organizational support, and the interviewee is acquainted with the enterprise and its policies and procedures. This last statement, of course, presumes that the interviewee is also well adjusted and accepts in general the company policies and procedures.

It is very difficult for a supervisor successfully to achieve the desired objective in an interview if the interviewee does not think that he has the organizational authority covering the subject of the interview. For instance, if the employee thinks that the supervisor does not have authority to make an interdepartmental transfer, a discussion of such a transfer can usually only develop the employee's attitude toward or desire for the transfer. In such a situation, also, the employee's side of the interview will likely be different from what it would be if he thought his supervisor had this authority. The interviewee's attitude in an interview with his supervisor is usually colored by the fact that he recognizes that his supervisor can exercise authority over him. It is also influenced by his attitude toward all persons in authority. In view of this generally prevailing attitude toward authority the supervisor is handicapped in counseling in personal matters.

The Supervisor's Skill in Interviewing. No amount of reading about the advantages or disadvantages of any particular type of interviewing will take the place of actually planning the interview and carrying it out. The weaknesses in the area of interviewing by supervisors are: (1) their failure to interview when an interview should be used, (2) a failure to plan the interview as to time, place, approach, and subject matter to be covered. A failure to *interview at all* when it is needed arises from the pressure of other duties and a hesitancy to meet a man face-to-face to discuss unpleasantnesses or something that may lead to an unpleasantness. For instance, a man is laid off, and the foreman merely tells him that a reduction in force makes it necessary. This often is done when there is no intention of calling him back to a particular job such as being a motion and time study man. Another occasion when an interview is often dodged is at the time of the annual salary review. When a man is passed over because he is not entitled to a raise on a merit basis the reasons should be explained to him together with what he needs to do to earn a raise at the next salary review.

Most foremen do a fairly good job of interviewing their men on routine matters of operations. They also do a reasonably good job of instructing. Their biggest road blocks arise in the area of interviewing their employees on matters of a personal nature even though the items pertain to the work. Such items as working safely, low quality or quantity of work, absenteeism, tardiness, and wages are points of contact that are potential sources of friction. It is surprising how hesitant many supervisors are to discuss safety other than when they see a violation of the rules. Even in the face of an accident hazard some supervisors look the other way.

In planning the interview the primary requirement is to know exactly what is to be covered. It is an excellent idea to write the items down in an orderly fashion and check them off as they are covered.

Some successful supervisors show the list to their employees after all of the items have been covered. They may say "We have now covered each of these points. I am going to put this memo in your folder as a reminder when we evaluate each man's performance the next time. I hope that all of them will be on the plus side from now on." Of course, it is desirable to find something that is good, as well as the bad things, in planning an interview. On the other hand when an important item has to be covered there is nothing wrong with going straight to the point. The pleasant aspects can come at the end of the interview as an expression of hope that things will work out better from then on.

While the different kinds of interviews are often discussed as if they are never used together, in practice this need not be the case. Following a directed interview a supervisor may urge the interviewee to discuss any matter that he would like to talk about. It is not unusual in such situations for the employee to talk about almost any subject. The opportunity to talk about anything he wants to talk about may serve to release nervous tensions. However, the supervisor who has authority over a man is seldom so successful in conducting a nondirected interview as someone else who does not have authority over him.

The Supervisor and the Employment Interview. In those companies where the supervisor has the final approval of a new employee before hiring, he has a real responsibility for the employment interview. In most of these relationships the personnel department has done a thorough screening on those items that are not of a technical nature. In reality there should be an agreement between the personnel department and the supervisor as to the role each is to play, so that one will not blame the other for poor selection.

The supervisor should plan the employment interview with care. It may readily follow a pattern so that important items will not be passed over. With his experience as a background the foreman is in a better position to question a prospect on his job knowledge than the personnel interviewer. If the applicant is a beginner who has to be trained the supervisor should explore those areas that he has found to be important to success on the job. Some supervisors show the beginner the actual job so that he will not be disappointed later when he finds the work and the work environment different from what he had expected. If the employment interview causes the supervisor to accept the applicant it may readily become a part of the induction process. He can explain to the new man the wage plan, expected earnings, how long the average man takes to learn the job, vacation allowances, sick leave (if any), rules and regulations regarding reporting unavoidable absences, insurance programs, and other things of importance. It must not be assumed that a brief explanation at the time of hiring will complete the induction process. The employment interview is very important. When properly handled it reduces labor turnover. Everyone associated with employment should keep in mind W. V. Bingham's classic statement, "The functions of the employment interview are: to get information, to give information, and to make a friend." [3]

The Induction Interview and the Supervisor. The supervisor's exact role in introducing the new man to his work will depend somewhat upon the employment procedure. Where the employment department does all of the hiring, subject to a rejection by the foreman in case the new man cannot do the work, the foreman may not have seen the new man prior to his reporting for work. In this event the supervisor may have to discover the new man's background by an exploratory interview. (It is seldom that the employment department furnishes the foreman with such a complete record of the new man that he need only consult the record to get all of the information he needs before starting him to work.) This first interview with the new man sets the pattern for future relationships. During the initial interview the new man is entitled to be told the important things about his work, lunch periods, punching in and out for work (where required), the location of washrooms and the cafeteria as well as the first-aid department, the need for working safely, when to expect his first pay, the rotation of shifts (when practiced), overtime regulations, and anything else that a new man should know.

Of course, if the foreman has participated in the employment interview some of the items listed above will have already been covered. Even though they have been discussed earlier they should again be covered at a later date. For instance, group insurance may be available to the employee, but not until he has worked a probationary period. In this event he should again be reminded of the insurance when he is eligible. If the company has a union contract with a union shop provision, this must be explained to the new man both at the time of starting to work and again when the time arrives that

[3] W. V. Bingham, "The Three Functions of the Interview in Employment," *The Management Review,* Vol. 15, No. 1, Jan. 1926, p. 36.

he must join the union. There are so many things a new man must know that the supervisor should have a schedule of follow-up to explain later things that are likely not to be remembered. These occasions of explaining the privileges and regulations also give the supervisor a natural opportunity to talk with the new man. Frequent personal contacts make him feel at home, give him a feeling of belonging.

In addition to the routine procedure phases of the work the new man should be extended a cordial welcome into the department. In fact, making the new man feel welcome is more important than many of the items listed above. If he feels at home he will not hesitate to ask about things he does not know. The new man should be introduced to his fellow workers, the inspectors, the departmental clerk, the lead man, assistant foreman, or anyone else who may be responsible for his direction or guidance. If perchance the foreman is pressed for time and cannot give the new man the attention he deserves, he should tell him that he will talk with him later but at the present time he will have to turn him over to his assistant or an instructor. In this event the supervisor should make it his responsibility to drop by the new man's workplace as soon as he can to ask him how things are going. Later he should take time to talk with him personally. There is no substitute for the supervisor's personal attention to getting the new man properly oriented to his job.

The Instructional Interview. An entire chapter is devoted to the "Supervisor as an Instructor" (Chapter 11). We are here concerned primarily with the interview phase. Instructing in its simplest form includes:

1. Explanation
2. Demonstration
3. Further explanation
4. Asking the learner to tell the instructor what he has been told to make certain that he understands (this becomes the response aspect of the interview. He should be invited to ask questions)
5. In a complicated operation a further demonstration by the instructor (further answering of questions follows this demonstration)
6. Trial by the learner, correction, and further trials

The key to the instructional interview is a thorough explanation of each and every detail by the instructor and the encouraging of the learner to ask questions. This refers primarily to the first steps. As time progresses, encouragement is needed when the new man feels that he is not making the progress that he should. Learners nearly always hit a plateau where they seem not to be making the needed improvements. This is a critical period. When the instructor explains that this is to be expected, that others have had the same experience, that all that is needed is persistent effort, discouragement is translated into hope and determination.

The Disciplinary Interview. We are devoting all of Chapter 24 to the subject of "Maintaining Discipline." The disciplinary interview is one that is often avoided or put off to a later day when the offense is not a serious one in and of itself so far as the single occurrence is concerned. This type of offense includes: excess absences, excess tardiness, just getting under the wire so far as compliance with various rules and regulations is concerned, being below standard in quantity and quality of output. Serious offenses are usually met with dispatch, even though the supervisor may not like the difficult assignment. Regardless of the nature of the cause for the disciplinary interview it should:

1. Be carefully planned.[4] In an emergency situation it may not be possible to plan for the particular occasion, yet a recognition of basic policy considerations will sustain the supervisor and prevent his being impetuous.

2. Be impersonal and arise out of the needs of the situation. There is no place for vindictiveness or personal anger.

3. Be constructive, not punitive. The objective should be to correct, to avoid repetition, and to protect the interest of the company and of other employees.

4. Provide hope for the disciplined. This should be true even though the employee may be discharged. So long as an individual retains his self-respect and hope, there is a possibility for improvements.

5. Leave the disciplined with a feeling that after he has paid whatever penalty is required he has an opportunity to go ahead with a clean slate. He should be aware that a record is made of the event but only as a matter to be considered in the case of future infractions and not as further punishment.

The Interview Work Sheet. As stated earlier, the merit rating interview and the disciplinary interview are usually dreaded by supervisors. John J. Grela has said, "Talking to a person 'for his own good' is no fun for anybody under any circumstances. But that is what supervisors are expected to do when talking over employees' short-

[4] Proper timing is essential for the disciplinary interview. A "cooling-off period" often is required before a disciplinary interview can be carried out successfully.

comings with them after performance ratings." The *interview work sheet,* parts of which are reproduced below, will make the task easier provided 1A, 1B, 1C, and 4 have been carefully worked out in advance.

1. THE PROBLEM—Complete Sections A, B, and C before the interview!
   A. STATE PURPOSE OF INTERVIEW. "I'd like to talk to you about—your job, something you are doing" or "I have a problem on which I could use your help—cooperation," etc. NOTE PROBLEM HERE:
   Mary, I'd like to talk to you about your total work output. That is, the amount of work that you produce as compared to other girls in the department.
   B. TELL HIM GOOD POINTS. "There are some things you are doing well" or "You're valuable to—me, the company, because," etc. NOTE GOOD POINTS employee has, things he does or has done well:
   We've learned to like you here. You're very cooperative and you get along well with the other girls. Another thing I've noticed is that you are always willing to help out. Your typing has improved and I'm very happy about that portion of your work. In other words, I feel you can become a good member of our team here.
   C. TELL HIM WEAKNESSES. Have FACTUAL evidence available—show what is desirable. "I think you can do a better job than you are doing if" or "I would like to talk to you about what we can do regarding." NOTE THE FACTS AND CLEARLY STATE to employee:
   The problem is that at the end of each week you are below the other girls in the amount of work that you do. I've had to give some of your work to other girls so that we can finish our week's work. I've estimated that you are about 20 per cent behind. We schedule our work load on the basis of so many girls completing so many cards per week. You can understand the problem that develops when one of the girls falls behind. I realize that at times all the girls fall behind, but if it's several weeks in a row, then we have a real problem.

2. GET EMPLOYEE'S REACTIONS
   D. ARE THE FACTS RIGHT? "Do you agree that this is true?" or "Is that the way things are?" NOTE EMPLOYEE'S ANSWER. IF EMPLOYEE AGREES, GO TO STEP 3.
   Mary, what are your thoughts on it?
   Mary: I never realized that I was below any standard. I didn't even know I was expected to do so many cards each week. I think I do as much as the other girls and I know I work as hard as they do.
   IF EMPLOYEE OFFERS VALID REASONS OR NEW FACTS, CLOSE THE TALK FOR PRESENT AND LOOK INTO THE MATTER: NOTE REASONS. ARRANGE FOR ANOTHER APPOINTMENT.
   (Note: Mary did not offer valid reasons or new facts. She expressed her feelings and what she believed. Take next step.)
   IF EMPLOYEE DISAGREES AND HAS NO GOOD REASON, NOTE HIS STATEMENTS BELOW. Say, "I'm sorry but that is not the solution" or "Even

if you don't agree I feel we should take some action." GO TO STEP 3.

Well, I can't say you don't work as hard as the other girls, but I do know that I've had to assign some of your work to other girls, so that we could finish.

3. CONSIDER PROPER ACTION

E. GET EMPLOYEE'S IDEAS TO SOLVE PROBLEMS. "What do you think we can do?" or "What suggestions do you have?" If suggestion requires study or if new facts are given, close the talk and inquire further. NOTE SUGGESTIONS:

Just think for a few minutes and give me any ideas you may have on how we could get your production up to the standard. I would really like to have you solve the problem and I'll help you in any way I can.

Mary's comment: I don't know. I work steadily and seem to keep up with the others. I like the work pretty well. *Maybe I can transfer.* (Supervisor: I would rather not consider that now.) I suppose I could try to *distribute my work each day in a different way.*

If no suggestions, move on to Step 4-F. If his idea is not good "I'm sorry, but I don't think that would do." (However—go to Step 4-F.)

4. THE PLAN OF ACTION—HAVE A PLAN WRITTEN OUT before the interview.

F. IF NO IDEA OR AN UNWORKABLE IDEA: "Suppose we try this"— state plan of action.

Supervisor's plan: Ask Mary to jot down each day how much time she spends on each of the 4 major duties she has (the other girls spend 3 hours per day on cards to complete their quota).

Plan adjusted to Mary's suggestion: Suppose we try distributing your work and you keep an informal check list of the approximate amount of time you spend on typing, filing, pulling, and posting. Let's try it for a month. I'll tell you each week how you're doing, then we'll get together again. In the meantime, maybe I can help you organize. Please ask me whenever you find I can help.

G. IF EMPLOYEE ARGUES BUT HAS NO VALID OBJECTION: "I'm sorry but this is a real problem and I'll have to ask you to do this. . . ."

If employee has strong objections a modification of plan made under 4-F may be necessary. NOTE PLAN:

Mary agreed.

5. CLOSE WITH FRIENDLINESS—Be sure he understands exactly what you have suggested or that he understands what's expected of him. "Have I been clear?" etc. Make date for follow-up.

Restate the plan—"Now this is what we're going to do." Leave the employee with a feeling of assurance that you are trying to help.

6. FOLLOW-UP—If employee has improved in reasonable time, tell him

7. INTERVIEW SUMMARY NOTES: Mary used to spend time talking to girls in the next department. She has cut that down. She work

methodically and rather slowly, but is willing and will turn out her share as she gets adjusted.[5]

The Art of Listening. Many supervisors fail to make a success of their interviews because they really do not have an interview. In fact they lecture the interviewee but do not give him an opportunity to contribute his ideas. A substantial part of the success of many interviews arises from the fact that the interviewee is encouraged to express himself and the interviewer is an alert, interested listener. The interviewer encourages the interviewee to talk by his manifest interest in what he is saying. He not only listens to the words that are said but carefully interprets the interviewee's sentiments, emotions, and things that are not overtly expressed but easily implied by the things that are said. Many an interviewee has come away from an interview thoroughly satisfied when in fact the interviewer had done practically none of the talking but had been an attentive listener.[6]

Summary. The interview is used in practically every phase of business. It is not the sole method of getting information or giving information. In fact the interview is less reliable in securing some information than other methods; nevertheless, the interview is often used to supplement the information secured from other methods. For instance, psychological tests may readily reveal mental acuity more accurately than an interview twice as long as the time required to give the test. Nevertheless, finding out the degree of mental acuity is only one phase of the interview. The applicant's questions regarding the work can best be answered by an interviewer. No test can convince the applicant that the company is a good place to work. The interviewer can supply the human interest that is needed in hiring new employees.[7]

Interviewing is an art that can be acquired by most people who recognize its importance and are willing to put forth the required effort.

Successful interviewing requires careful planning in terms of its purpose or objective. It often pays to make brief notes of the topics to be covered, or else some of the most important items will be overlooked. Probably the supervisor's most frequent shortcoming is his

[5] John J. Grela, "Work Sheet Helps Supervisors Talk Constructively with Employees," *Personnel Journal,* April 1955.

[6] See F. J. Roethlisberger, William J. Dickson, and Harold A. Wright, *op. cit.,* pp. 271–291, for a challenging discussion of "the interviewing method."

[7] See W. V. Bingham, "Today and Yesterday," *Personnel Psychology,* 2: 949, pp. 272–274.

failure to use the interview when he should or his failure to interview at the proper time. There seems to be a hesitancy on the part of most people to sit down with their subordinates and to talk through with them their shortcomings. All too often this putting off of an unpleasant assignment when it should be performed leads to more difficulties later. In so far as possible, Walter V. Bingham's objectives for the employment interview should hold for all interviews, namely, "to get information, to give information, and to make a friend."

8 Discovering and Adjusting Grievances

What Is a Grievance? From an industrial standpoint *a grievance is anything in the work situation that the employee thinks or feels is wrong, unjust, or unfair so far as he is concerned.* The employee does not need to be right in his ideas or opinions. What is important is that he thinks or feels the way he does. Right or wrong, the grievance should be adjusted to avoid unfortunate consequences. Some grievances are based on some factual situation that can be determined precisely in terms of measurable items. Others are founded on some sentiment that may be very difficult to explain on a factual basis.

There are at least two types of grievances which the supervisor must be aware of. *Unarticulated* grievances arise out of the failure of the job to give the employee the satisfaction he desires. *Articulated* grievances are those which have developed to the point where there is open protest either to the supervisor or to fellow employees or others. Unarticulated grievances may be recognized by such employee actions as indifference and daydreaming, absenteeism, tardiness, irritability, and falling off in production or, in a learner, the failure to increase production in keeping with his progress and training. Manifestations of articulated grievances include, in addition to the above, gossiping, jealousy, active criticism and argumentation, increased labor turnover, carelessness in the use of tools and materials, untidy housekeeping around the workplace, loafing on the job, and poor workmanship.

The Discovery of Grievances. Since grievances have such detrimental effects on the happiness and productivity of workers, it is highly important that the supervisor be on the alert to detect them and remove the cause when he can. A soundly conceived organization with adequate delegation of responsibility does not run itself. It requires supervisory follow-up to detect deviations from the organization pattern and to adjust the deviations before they become truly destructive. Even the supervisor with a well-organized and well-equipped department and with carefully selected employees will meet with grievances among his employees. The supervisor cannot hope to eliminate every grievance, yet he can strive to reduce them to a minimum. It is essential that the supervisor be able to recognize grievances and their symptoms and also be prepared to handle them to the best of his knowledge and ability. It is therefore necessary for every supervisor to develop techniques and methods of discovering and adjusting grievances.

The supervisor should understand those basic urges which, when not satisfied in a reasonable degree, will result in discontent and develop into grievances. He must realize that a grievance may not be expressed at first but may manifest itself only in uneasiness or discontent. From the standpoint of group unrest, this is a very important stage. Finally, the supervisor should recognize that the alleged cause of an articulated grievance may not be, and often is not, the real cause of the grievance, but merely a symptom of a basic cause. It is just as essential for the supervisor to know and to understand the human side of his department as to know the mechanics of his equipment. Only when he has knowledge of what ordinarily lies behind grievances can the supervisor handle those that will develop in his department. Like every other job of the supervisor, to develop the skill of adjusting grievances requires time and practice.

Demands the Employee Makes of His Job. Every employee from the president of the company to the lowliest worker brings to his job certain expectancies and hopes that he would like to realize. Many of these are not directly related to the job but they definitely influence his reactions to it. The work situation occupies a large segment of an employee's life and cannot be separated from the demands he makes on life. To the extent that an employee's demands on life are satisfied inside or outside of his work life, the employee will likely be contented and seldom have a grievance. Some employees' demands on life are not capable of being realized. Such employees are likely subjects for personal slights, a feeling of being discriminated against, or are likely to display many other manifestations of poor personal adjustment. The desires that bring satisfaction to most persons include: (1) satisfaction of such physical needs as food, shelter, and clothing, (2) security against disease, accidents, layoffs, and old age, (3) recognition by fellow employees and superiors, (4) service, a feeling that what one does is worth while, (5) loyalty to persons, institutions, and causes, a feeling of "belonging," (6) craftsmanship, the desire to produce something tangible and of which one can be proud, and (7) the opportunity for advancement. While it is not expected that the supervisor be skilled as an industrial psychologist, he should strive to understand why people react as they do.

The Supervisor's Point of View. In detecting potential grievances and in handling those grievances that have reached the surface, the supervisor's success or failure will rest substantially on his point of view, his basic approach to man's actions, and his willingness to keep an open mind until all of the factors have been examined. Detecting unarticulated grievances requires constant contact, careful observation, a study of the employees and their work, and an understanding of those motivating forces underlying the actions of the individual and the group. *Know your men* is a first requirement of every supervisor before he can begin to detect and adjust grievances successfully. Danger signals arise and the supervisor must be on the alert to receive them. He must know the factors that lead to grievances and possess an understanding of human nature and how it works. The supervisor will find his knowledge of individual differences [1] especially valuable in handling grievances.

While grievances should be reduced or resolved as soon as they are first observed (when possible), the supervisor should not rush headlong into the situation without planning his solution and first getting all of the facts that are available. The supervisor must analyze the causes that lie behind the manifestation of a grievance. Is it plant conditions, is it due to conditions outside the job, is it the employee himself? What does the supervisor want to accomplish, what is his objective in terms not only of the employee with the grievance, but the department as a whole and the company as well? What is the best solution and what other solutions are there? Sometimes the easiest solution for the employee and the supervisor is not practical, owing to other conditions. The supervisor must understand the company policies, his department personnel, and the employee with the grievance before establishing his plan of action and determining what is the best solution. Many a small grievance has developed into

[1] See Chapter 9, p. 85.

a man-sized one, many an individual grievance has grown into a group grievance, because a supervisor has made a hasty analysis or none at all and, without all the facts and without a plan, has tried to settle the grievance of an employee. Many a grievance temporarily settled has created new ones because the supervisor did not have in mind a clearly defined objective designed both to settle the particular grievance and to avoid creating conditions among his employees that would lead to other grievances.

In handling any situation involving people it is highly desirable to keep in mind those factors that govern their reactions. Different individuals react in entirely different ways to similar sets of circumstances. The supervisor must recognize this fact and understand what the factors are that influence the action of the individual. It is easy to overlook the many factors and conditions that may be the basic cause underlying a grievance. What an individual is and why he acts in a certain way can be divided into four classifications: (1) what the individual *really is,* (2) what he would *like* to be, (3) what he would *like to have others think he is,* and (4) what *others really think* he is.

Figure 8.1 provides a schematic reference that may help the supervisor understand the reactions of an employee which otherwise may seem irrational.

A. Possible cause, either environmental or as stated by individual.

B. Individual's behavior or acts, which may not seem logical in terms of *A.*

C. Personal reference, sentiments, desires, etc. These account for the action *B.*

D. Social past of the individual. Sentiments, *C,* are largely a reflection of the past and the expectations of the present *E.*

E. Social present of the individual.[2]

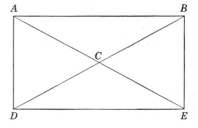

Figure 8.1.

[2] Adapted by permission from F. J. Roethlisberger, William J. Dickson, and Harold A. Wright, *Management and the Worker,* Harvard University Press, Cambridge, Mass., 1939.

The kind of person an employee really is depends on his sentiments, his beliefs, and his convictions. If an employee has certain
beliefs that have developed because of his religion or environment,
it will only increase the supervisor's problem if he tries suddenly to
change the man's beliefs. What an employee is depends on his past
experience, his present condition, and his future outlook. The kind
of work he has done and the supervision under which he has worked
have definitely contributed to molding his character. His contacts
with others outside his work, in his home and school life—all are
factors in the development of his character. The supervisor must
recognize this and analyze the employee before attempting to adjust
any grievance he may have or that may be developing. An employee's present condition, the job he is on, his outside life, are at
the moment making changes in the kind of person he is. His future
outlook, on the job, in his family life, and in his community affect
the kind of person he is and the way he acts and thinks. If he sees
a bright future ahead, he is less likely to develop a grievance than is
the man who sees little future prospects for advancement. Any unusual physical trait, such as height, weight, deformity, or birthmark
may have developed an inferiority complex that causes the individual
to react as he does. His health or the health of his friends may cause
excessive brooding that is manifested by a grievance. For instance,
if a worker's brother has had a bad experience arising from an allergic
condition caused by handling a given chemical the worker may complain about his working conditions even though he is not personally
affected in the least.

Not only must an aggrieved employee be studied from the standpoint of his present status—*what he really is*—he must also be considered in terms of *what he would like to be*. For instance, he may
have a strong desire to be recognized as a leader when neither management nor his work group so recognizes him. Again, the "lone
wolf" type of employee, when analyzed, is frequently found not to
be that kind of person by choice. His actions are often the result of
other conditions and the employee so characterized is frequently
found to be a person who would *like* to be one of the group. He may
have been rejected because of his violating one or more of the group's
sentiments, because of his membership in some minority group, or
even because of his lack of membership in a group such as a union.

An employee's actions can at times be understood in terms of *what
he would like others to think him to be*. Many an employee wants
his fellow employees to think of him as an entirely different kind of

person from the one he actually is. An employee will frequently go out of his way to impress others. He is anxious to have them develop a definite opinion about him. (Many people deliberately set out to sell themselves to others and in so doing create problems for the supervisor.) Not only must the supervisor consider the problem employee in terms of what he wants others to think of him, he must also consider *what the worker's fellow employees really think him to be.* Consideration of this viewpoint is essential because the employee is part of the group and the group will judge the solution of the grievance in the light of what they think of the employee. Frequently, the group knows the employee better than the supervisor does. The supervisor needs some of this knowledge of the employee before he can successfully detect and adjust grievances. It is all a part of knowing and understanding his employees. It is essential to know what the employee really is in order to understand his grievance and the conditions causing it. Understanding what the employee would like to be and what he would like to have others think him to be is necessary in order to choose the solution and to plan how to put it into effect. What others really think he is plays an important part in determining the objective or adjusting the grievance and the solution, because the employee is a part of a group of employees and the supervisor must realize that his objective and solution must be in terms of the group judgment as well as in terms of the employee's reaction.

Many a supervisor will spend hours analyzing the machinery in his department, studying or making drawings of machine parts and tools, yet he will spend only a few minutes with an employee settling what he thinks is some slight grievance. Factory machinery is easily adjusted and kept running smoothly compared with human machinery. There is no best way for determining and repairing man troubles and no one lubricant that will make human machinery run efficiently. Employees react in far more varied ways than do machines and are a great deal more difficult to understand. The supervisor must recognize the need for more intense study of his men and then follow up by actually studying them until he can more nearly anticipate their actions.

Steps to Be Taken. There is no one method of detecting and adjusting grievances. In most cases the following steps will prove helpful: (1) observing the employees and their work, (2) recognition of the factors that are danger signals, indicating difficulties, (3) analyzing these factors to determine causes, (4) selecting the most likely solution in the light of the objective to be attained, (5) planning the attack to put this solution into effect, and (6) putting it into effect.

Regardless of the care exercised in striving to motivate persons or in trying to adjust grievances, the supervisor must reconcile himself to an occasional failure. In other words, he must realize that we cannot always salvage all of our employees. Some persons make demands on their jobs that simply cannot be met. In such cases we should be reconciled to their quitting or even to our having to discharge them. However, such cases should be few. We can never escape the fact that such failures leave scars of unhappiness that we wish did not have to exist.

Observing the Employees at Work. Observations that are fruitful in detecting and resolving grievances include: the physical traits, the work performance, the group status, the social participation, the emotional stability, and the personal adjustment of the employee to his work situation. Among the physical traits the supervisor should observe in his employee are individual weaknesses or defects, individual superiorities, health, and any other unusual physical characteristics. In the work performance of the employee the supervisor will watch closely the quantity and quality of work as well as the uniformity of the work. Here the supervisor will regularly check the production records of the employee. The supervisor will observe the employee in the work group. He will watch how the employee fits into the group, the character of his job, personal characteristics that influence the group's attitude toward the employee, whether the employee is a leader or a follower, and whether others seek the advice of the individual employee. The supervisor will note the employee's participation in the group activities. Is he a "lone wolf" or is he a part of the group? What are the employee's desires with respect to the group—if he is a "lone wolf" would he actually like to be part of the group, is he an insignificant group member with the desire to be a leader? The supervisor will note how stable, emotionally, the individual employee is.

He will know if the employee is supersensitive, or if he is even-tempered. The supervisor will be familiar with the personal adjustment that the employee has made to his work situation. He will know something about the employee's past, the kind of positions held and the money earned. He will know the wage standards for the job the employee is now on and whether the employee has adjusted himself to his present wage scale. He knows whether the employee has been recognized as he expects to be and as his ability merits, and watches the employee's activity in making suggestions or criticism. The successful supervisor has all these keys at his disposal when he has carefully studied an employee. One or more of them ordinarily will reveal the solution to any grievances the supervisor may discover.

Recognizing the Danger Signals. The supervisor who is alert to the potential grievance will detect marked deviations from the normal performance of his workers. For example, a supervisor has carefully observed one of his employees. He knows that the employee is regular in his work habits, is always on time, and works steadily turning out work of uniform quantity and quality. He also knows that this employee is recognized by his fellow employees as a skillful worker whose advice is frequently sought by others, regarding both their work and their personal problems. The department is large and a number of new employees have recently entered it. This employee becomes grouchy and irritable; instead of frequently coming to the supervisor with small suggestions, he avoids him; he goes to the washroom more often than usual. Here the good supervisor will immediately detect the beginning of a grievance. The employee has not yet voiced it; he may not be sure in his own mind what the trouble is, but the storm signals are waving and the supervisor should dig in and search for the causes.

Identifying the Causes. Employee reactions are largely personal; relatively few employees are able to take an impersonal approach. This is the supervisor's job, and it takes a true executive to be able to keep the personalities out of the situation and take a really impartial view. Employees are almost entirely influenced by both the personal reactions of their associates and their supervisor. What the rest of the employees will think guides the individual employee's actions. As the supervisor has acted toward the employee, so will the employee react toward the supervisor. The supervisor must remember that the employee's sentiments and feelings are fairly stable over a considerable period of time. The supervisor's success is almost entirely dependent upon his ability to identify and understand these sentiments and feelings of the employee. It is not enough to set the employee straight on the facts. Sentiments are not changed by logic. On the other hand an analysis of the cause of the sentiment, and its identification, may lead to an understanding. Often a sympathetic listening to a complaint and a sincere attempt to understand it causes it to cease to exist without any formal change in the operating situation.

In Settling Grievances the Supervisor Must Look at the Total Situation. Company policies and the broader group attitudes must always be kept in mind in seeking solutions to a specific grievance The farsighted supervisor recognizes that precedents are easily established and hard to disestablish. He will recognize that although grievances must be adjusted on an individual basis the individual action has an influence on the group and must conform to the group's idea of fair play. Favoritism in settling an individual grievance merely substitutes a group grievance for the individual one. The supervisor must beware of any attempt to remake an employee but strive to bring about an easy and natural relation between the employee's mind and the series of circumstances that will make for willing cooperative action.[3] To be lasting, the solution to the grievance must strike at the cause. The current grievance may and often is merely a symptom of a more serious grievance. The supervisor will look beyond the current grievance to make sure he is getting at the source of the irritation. Many an employee is a chronic complainer. As fast as one complaint is settled, another arises. Here is a sure indication that the source of the trouble has been missed. There is something deep-seated to be attacked rather than a minor complaint. If the supervisor cannot discover the real cause, a referral to the employment office for a suggested transfer may be in order. For every difficulty giving rise to grievances one of two situations exists: (1) something is present that should not be, or (2) something is lacking that should be present. Either or both of the above may relate to the work, the employee, work environment, or any combination of all three.

Some Common Approaches. In handling real or imaginary grievances the supervisor should recognize the need for: (1) information or knowledge of the basic cause, (2) an explanation that must be made immediately, not weeks hence, (3) sympathy for the individual in particular and men in general, (4) reassurance that things are not as imagined by the aggrieved employee, (5) recognition of the personality and worth of the individual, (6) training of the employee

---

[3] Much of the material in this paragraph is adapted from General Motors Executive Training Program G-9, "Better Personnel Relations," Chapter IV. This entire chapter is influenced by this pamphlet published by the General Motors Corporation.

when needed, (7) help for the employee in facing the realities of the given situation, (8) solution for private problems, (9) a firm hand to give direct orders when needed, (10) replacement, at times—all men cannot be readjusted, (11) change of physical environment, (12) medical aid, (13) any combination of two or more of the foregoing.

The Planned Approach to Grievances. At best the striving to adjust grievances is a difficult and energy-consuming assignment. It is human to avoid such assignments, when possible, in the hope that time will bring about an adjustment. Actually time often does cause a temporary grievance to fade into the background with normally adjusted persons. To rely upon the passage of time to handle grievances is a serious error even though a very human one. Planning is required for the handling of grievances as in other major operating problems. Careful planning enables the supervisor: (1) to know what to do or say, (2) to know why it is to be said or done, and (3) to know how it is to be said or done. Planning that involves the *what, why,* and *how* will usually be successful. Few employees are fluent talkers. Many an employee has wanted to say something, but did not know what he wanted to say or how to say it. The good supervisor, as part of his technique of detecting and adjusting grievances, is a good listener.[4] Making it easy for the employee to talk contributes to both detecting and adjusting grievances. Planning reduces the likelihood of making a bad situation worse. It gives the supervisor an opportunity to select the time and place to make the adjustment. By careful planning the supervisor can devote his time to putting the plan into effect and will not be handicapped by attempting to solve a grievance without having prepared for it. In planning his solution, the supervisor has an opportunity to put his emphasis on securing the employee's desire to "buy" the program and not to feel that he has been "sold" something against his will. After the supervisor has carefully planned the approach to adjusting the grievance he should apply sound sales methods in putting the plan across. He will have due regard for the time and place to introduce the subject. He will show the advantages of the solution. He will get the employee to suggest the solution, if possible. "Face-saving" is important to everyone. He will give the reasons for the claimed advantage. Finally, he will secure acceptance,

[4] *Management and the Worker* by F. J. Roethlisberger, William J. Dickson, and Harold A. Wright, Harvard University Press, Cambridge, Mass., 1939, has provided the inspiration for much of the material in this chapter.

which will come easily if he succeeds in getting the employee to suggest the solution.

The Foreman's Role in the Formal Grievance Procedure. Some companies have a formal grievance procedure even though they have no union contract. Most companies having contracts with unions have such a procedure. In many cases it is spelled out in the contract. There is no absolute uniformity in the grievance procedure, but in the main the following pattern is followed:

1. The employee presents his complaints informally to his foreman. In the absence of a settlement the employee, with or without the assistance of the union representative (usually the steward), reduces his complaint to writing and files it with the union representative. The union representative files the complaint with the foreman. Many persons consider the reducing of the complaint to writing and its initial filing as being the first step in the formal grievance procedure.

It should be remembered that the union steward may accompany the aggrieved employee when he first presents his verbal complaint to the foreman.

2. When the union representative (with or without the complainant) discusses the grievances with the foreman it may be settled at once or the foreman may take the allowed time (usually two or three days) before filing his answer in writing. In the absence of an agreement the union representative files an appeal to the general foreman, division superintendent, or some other line officer. In some cases the appeal is filed directly with the personnel director or industrial relations representative.

3. The same general procedure is followed at this stage as in step 2. A hearing may be held at which the union is heard as well as the foreman. In case an agreement is not reached at this stage, management's representative gives its answer in writing and the union files an appeal in writing to top management or its representative, the director of personnel or the industrial relations representative.

4. Before the top management representative a hearing is held and detailed records are accumulated. In case of a failure to agree at this stage a final appeal may be made in writing to top management. If the union request is rejected by top management, some contracts provide that the case may be submitted to arbitration.

5. If the dispute is submitted to arbitration the decision is supposed to be binding on both parties. Management and the union may agree to submit a given grievance to arbitration even though there is no contract provision for the use of arbitration.

In any step in the grievance procedure the supervisor should support his actions or claims by factual data. This requires careful preparation prior to the action and the maintenance of adequate records during normal operations so that they will be available should a grievance arise.

9 Individual Differences, Group Attitudes, and Group Morale

A Tool of Leadership. One of the major assignments of the supervisor is to place his men in such a manner as to make maximum use of their special capacities. This use of the workers' abilities tends to increase their satisfaction in their work. Individuals differ markedly in capacities and interests. The recognition of these individual differences is a prerequisite of proper placement. The supervisor can strengthen and develop his leadership by: (1) recognizing the nature and extent of individual differences, (2) recognizing their influence on the actions of his men, (3) observing the increased effectiveness resulting from taking advantage of individual differences in getting work done, (4) understanding the nature and method of the functioning of group attitudes and morale, and (5) understanding the influence of the group attitude and morale upon individual members of the group.

Individual Differences. As materials differ, *so do individuals.* They differ physically, mentally, and emotionally. They differ in race and sex, in education and environment. There are many ways, great and small, in which individuals differ from each other. People have a wide range of I.Q.'s (intelligence quotients, i.e., scores measuring the mental ability and capacity of individuals), and although a skilled mechanic may be developed out of a man with an I.Q. of 90 as well as from one with a score of 110, as a rule, the time required and the methods used will be different. The supervisor may not know the I.Q. of his men, but he must, nevertheless, recognize the need for a different approach with different individuals. The supervisor who studies his men will develop the ability to measure them, their alertness, and their ability to learn, and in an operating sense will measure their mental capacities. Individuals are found to vary to a greater extent in mental and emotional differences than in physical differences. It is unusual to find a man twice as tall or heavy as another, but it is common to find persons with as wide or wider differences than two-to-one in mental capacities. The degrees of emotional stability and maturity are likewise found to vary tremendously among individuals.

People differ in sex, although these differences have been magnified out of all proportion and are not so important as we often think they are. Most of the differences in the performances of the sexes are differences growing out of training. Differences in the senses of sight, feel, touch, taste, and smell exist. There are many industries where some of these senses are very important assets to employees on certain jobs. The work of inspectors requires a high degree of the sense of touch and sight, whereas certain other occupations require a highly developed sense of smell. Everyone does not possess these senses to the same degree. Individuals differ in their susceptibility to disease and in their general health. Although one individual may be affected by a chemical present in the product being worked on, others may not be affected at all. The development during the past few years of a knowledge of allergies has shown distinctly that some individuals are highly susceptible to things that have no effect on others. The supervisor must be on the lookout for such instances and promptly bring them to the attention of the medical department. There are racial differences, but again these are not so great as once thought. Evidence collected and analyzed during the First World War indicated that racial differences are not so great as differences growing out of environment and training. Most of the racial differences thought to exist have arisen from our present social system.

One of the best examples of the physical differences among men is in height and weight. Individuals also differ in motor reaction and coordination, varying in their ability to coordinate the use of hands, eyes, and body in doing physical work. Many supervisors have had experiences both with those who just cannot coordinate, who are naturally awkward and require more than the average amount of practice, and with others who have coordination ability in a high degree. The supervisor will take these differences into consideration in assigning work and instructing his men.

Possibly the greatest single difference among workers that are able to stay on the job is the wide range of emotional maturity. From the standpoint of the supervisor, the lack or presence of emotional stability in individuals is exceedingly important. The supervisor will have men under him who are emotionally unstable. It will therefore be necessary for him to know what causes them to be upset so that, if possible, he may take steps to prevent this from occurring. Of course, it must be remembered that there is no place in modern industry for some severe cases of emotional instability. While the severe cases of emotional disturbance requiring institutional care are seldom found in the industrial situation, the employee who has the emotional index of the eight-year-old is not uncommon. Sadly enough, some individuals of high mental acuity and training are emotionally immature. Some of them hold doctorates from leading universities. Others are highly skilled mechanics. Regardless of their abilities such persons are problem children. Their feelings are easily hurt. Often an imagined grievance causes the offended person of immaturity to want to hurt the other person in return. Such persons are difficult to handle and often take a disproportionate amount of the supervisor's time. They are also in the vanguard in leading the opposition to anything that management may want.

Individuals also differ materially in mental maturity or maturity arising from education and work experience. Some men are old at thirty-five and others are young at fifty. The man who went to work when he finished high school is usually more mature at twenty-three than is the man who graduated from college before entering the industrial world. Much of the so-called mental maturity is related to the passage of time and the maturing and seasoning physically, socially, and mentally. The worker adjusts to his total environment and acts the part of an adult and is willing to assume the responsibilities that society expects of a mature person. He has outgrown the childish ways and does not sulk in his tent when he does not have his way (as does the emotionally immature adult.)

Making Use of Individual Differences. In dealing with employees the supervisor recognizes the advantage of placing employees so far as possible in terms of their *capacities* and interests. *One individual differs from another in those personal aptitudes, those special abilities with which he is equipped and which he is able to contribute to the company in exchange for his salary.* Some individuals have an aptitude for details and work well on job assignments requiring a large amount of follow-up, whereas others, full of enthusiasm but disliking the details, are best suited to get work started and to leave the follow-up of details to others.

Individuals differ in interest and motive and respond best to varying stimuli. The young man in the department who is just married is anxious to succeed and advance and will accept promotion, even though it may involve taking a chance, because it will increase his earnings and improve his standing among his friends. In contrast, the older employee who is more interested in job security may turn down a promotion which will involve more responsibility and the possibility of failure and discharge. The younger man will sometimes respond more readily to opportunities to learn and advance than the older man for whom other methods of motivation will have to be used. This last generalization regarding the older person's not being willing to take risks is generally true, but there are many exceptions. In reality attitudes toward assuming responsibility and taking risks are not solely a function of age. Some men at fifty start new businesses and become very successful. Other young men just out of college are very much interested in the pension system of the firm for which they go to work. The supervisor should study his men and not blanket them in categories on the basis of age.

Many a young man when he joins a company wants to follow the same trade as his father or brother and a year later, because of his outside contacts with men of his own age, will decide to attend evening school and follow a path to some entirely different occupation. This is true not only of younger men but also of older ones. The influence of membership in professional societies or trade unions will often work a slow but definite change in the interests of the older man, who last year was interested only in working his way up to the top and now is interested only in security and higher wages. *The same individual changes from day to day and from year to year in ability and interests, both in degree and kind.* The man who could perform an operation best a year ago frequently is not the best man in the department on that work today. Someone else has studied, worked hard, and surpassed him. Men who last year were interested in advancing into a more skilled occupation, such as from machine operator to machinist, later may be found to have changed their interests to office work, such as drafting.

Job requirements vary widely. *Different kinds of work require different personal abilities in the individuals who are to perform them.* The routine job in the department should be filled by the man who likes routine; the job requiring contacts with other departments, such as pushing production or chasing parts, should go to the man with persistence and personality, who talks well, likes people, and yet underneath has a tenacious streak with a determination to get things done. *The work in each position in a company changes as time goes on;* duties are added and taken away. Sometimes the change is negligible, sometimes it is great. In the measure in which it takes place, a similar change is likely to take place in the abilities and interests the work requires. The supervisor who has been in charge of his department for several years seldom realizes that these changes take place, since they often develop slowly and by small degrees. The speed with which the job is done may have changed, the tolerances may vary, the methods may have changed, in fact, it may even be done on a different machine or in a different way. Many a skilled machinist's job has been turned into a production job over a period of time and the man originally on it may no longer be fitted for production work, yet there is an ideal spot to use him in the tool room.

A failure in one job does not mean that the worker will fail in other jobs. *Granting equal ability, different kinds of work are best done by persons who temperamentally are particularly interested in them.* Many men have been failures at one type of work and outstanding successes at another. The answer usually is that the individual was not temperamentally suited to the work at which he failed. *Changes in environment have a tremendous influence on men.* This is true whether it is a change in the work environment or in the social environment of the employee. The social environment of an employee, his home surroundings, the people with whom he mingles, exercise a tremendous influence on personal and group efficiency. When an employee is transferred from one department to another with a change in supervisors, there is often a perceptible change in his production and attitude. It may increase if he has been unhappy in his previous situation and hopes for success in his new environment. When an employee is a "lone wolf" and shies away from other employees in the department, the result will frequently be noted in production. The lone wolf may work hard to compensate for his tendency to want to go it alone or he may be depressed and have a low production rate. The lowered production rate may be such that it will be necessary to transfer the employee to another department. Personnel men are now coming to realize the impact of social environment on industrial efficiency, and a few large companies are taking steps to attack this problem.

An individual who gives the outward appearance of being reticent may undergo a change and strive for new responsibility or promotion. He may derive his new interests from attendance at evening school where he associates with other young men who are ambitious. The supervisor should study the many combinations possible in social and work environmental changes in his employees which will affect their work and their relations with him.

Special Interests, Desires, and Abilities. Men differ as to the wages they desire and their reactions to overtime. Some men will try to earn all the money they can, but others are satisfied with a moderate wage and are more interested in other incentives, such as security and the type of work to which they are assigned. Some men will fight for all the overtime they can get, and others want to quit at the end of eight hours and head for home and their families. To these men, their home life is more important than the increase in the pay envelope resulting from overtime work. Men vary as to which shift they prefer. Most men like the day shift; others prefer to work the second or even the third shift. Frequently outside interests are found to be the reason for shift preferences.

Influence of Working Conditions. Some men prefer white collar work and will even accept lower wages rather than go into the factory. There are other men who like the atmosphere of the factory, the hum of the machines, and who have no desire for nor interest in "pushing a pencil." Under some conditions, such as when factory wages rise and white collar wages do not follow, but there are increases in the cost of living, white collar workers seek to move into factories, and during such times the supervisor will be wise to study the interests of his new employees and take advantage of any special abilities of these men. One may be found that will make a good production clerk, another can take the responsibility for record keeping off the supervisor's shoulders.

Educational, Mental, and Emotional Differences. Individuals differ in education and this influences the manner in which the supervisor will issue orders and give instructions to them. With a group most of whom never reached high school he will not resort to a typewritten notice on the bulletin board, or if he does, he will put it in the simplest possible language. He will make his instructions detailed and then explain them fully. The supervisor who has a group of youngsters fresh out of college can make his instructions shorter and more explicit, for he will find they will catch on faster since they have become accustomed to brief, concise instructions. Engineers and accountants will read long detailed reports and like them. Others may have to have information simplified and given in small doses.

The individual's mental acuity is largely a function of inheritance.

Little can be done about it other than to train the individual to use what he has to its maximum effectiveness.[1] Sometimes men are found who have latent possibilities that have been neglected or overlooked. Many an employee has been judged to lack backbone, yet when given additional responsibilities he shows determination and persistence which he was thought to lack. The capacities of many men are far greater than most supervisors realize. Although the psychological tests available cannot be used by most supervisors, yet one can play safe by not forming snap judgments or misjudging men on limited evidence of their performance on a single job. Some men like painstaking detailed work; others dislike details intensely. Some men prefer to work with the group; others want to work alone. Some men are anxious to be leaders in their group; others are natural followers. Some men are found who like to work with their hands; others want to work with figures or do clerical work. Some men want to create; others want to develop ideas. Some people are versatile and answer all the above descriptions and can do things they do not particularly like when the remuneration is sufficiently high to justify it. Some men who prefer to work with machinery have become successful salesmen, not because they like selling especially, but because they had versatility and were motivated by the money urge. Some workers, women in particular, may prefer office work and yet work in the factory because their pay is greater than they could earn in the office.

Emotional differences seem to arise from the functioning of the vital organs and habitual reactions acquired in youth. A reciprocal relationship seems to accompany stomach ulcers; the emotional disturbances intensify the physical difficulties, and the stomach disturbances seem to accentuate the emotional imbalance. Illness, when it becomes chronic, may have a definite effect on the work of men. Periodic physical examinations have done much to eliminate emotional disturbances, but they are not the entire cure. Anger when it occurs frequently may be the result of organic difficulties such as high blood pressure. Nervous disturbances lead to emotional differences between men that must be taken into consideration by the supervisor both in his own relations with his men and in the relations among the men themselves. A supervisor who has developed a reputation of being friendly and considerate of his men is in an advantageous position in handling men whose emotional biases tend to cause them to be problem employees.

[1] Special studies have cast a little doubt upon this statement, yet for all practical purposes it still holds.

The seasoned supervisor treats his men as if they were mature individuals even though he may recognize that some of them have not fully grown up emotionally and socially. The saying that human beings are like children is false, and following this belief will only lead to trouble. Some people never mature, but they are few, and the supervisor must single out such individuals and recognize the individual differences. The supervisor will find that just as he expects to be treated by his superiors so his men expect to be treated by him— given reasons for actions, receive explanations, be talked to as adults. Some people have emotional balance save in one particular item such as, for example, religion, unionism, or politics. When this subject is raised they will become unable to see any side other than their own. In these instances the supervisor who understands his men and recognizes their individual characteristics will avoid discussion of such subjects and will see that the other members of the group do likewise; otherwise the work of the individual and the whole department may be affected.

Causes of Individual Differences. Individual differences growing out of sex are basically rather slight but very real. Size and strength are important and every supervisor must beware of putting a woman on a job which is too heavy for her. Job analyses frequently bring out elements in a job which slow it down because of one operation that requires strength greater than a woman has, yet a woman will be found on the work. Jobs that involve reaching high shelves are best suited to men or else call for changes in layout. Most differences between men and women, however, outside of height, weight, and strength, are the result of social training. Age accentuates individual differences and may cause some of them. Middle-aged persons tire less easily but require longer to recover from fatigue. However, they have fewer accidents, they are more tolerant of both supervisors and subordinates, their greater experience gives increased wisdom, and they are more regular in attendance. In youth there is a tendency to learn quickly, but younger employees have more accidents. The younger men are less regular in attendance and have a higher labor turnover, but they are eager to learn and usually more willing to try new and experimental methods than are older men. The age group of fifty-five and over has fewer accidents than either of the other groups, but their accidents are more serious. Their physical strength is on the decline and their eyesight is more likely to be defective. They may possess high skills and valuable experience but may not easily adapt themselves to changes or to learning new skills. In the final analysis the effective age of an individual is indicated by his physical and mental condition, not by calendar years. A man is young or old in terms of his physical and mental conditions.

Ordinarily, physically small people mature earlier and develop coordination more rapidly than do large people. Flyweight boxers are not unusual at sixteen, yet it is rare to see a heavyweight boxer under twenty or twenty-one. The supervisor can use this factor to advantage in placing new employees, especially if they are youngsters just out of high school. Climate has considerable influence on maturity. There is also a relationship between age and emotional maturity; however, it is not so close a relationship as that of such other factors as environment, training, and experience.

Racial differences arise largely from factors other than race itself. This does not mean that by and large there may not be racial differences in a given community. Traditions, customs, social inheritance, and economic status definitely do produce individual differences. Chinese, Indians, Negroes, and others have all developed separate characteristics as a group. Men having a common inheritance are usually much more alike than unlike. Men coming from the same kind of environment or home background are likely to be similar in their characteristics. This is one more reason why the supervisor should inquire into and understand the background and social environment of his men, their interests and amusements, something about their home life, and the other kinds of work they have done.

Educational training not only intensifies individual differences, the nature of the training itself definitely influences the demands of the individual. The college-trained employee is likely to expect a higher paying job and leadership responsibility even though his particular training may not have prepared him for such responsibilities. On the other hand a person not having certain educational training may lack the confidence to assume leadership responsibilities for which he is qualified. Given two persons who receive identical training but who are not given an incentive to absorb the training, the differences between them at the end of the training period will be about the same as at the beginning. The same training will not increase the individual differences between men unless there is a strong incentive present and then the training will markedly intensify the differences. Unlike training for two men may account not only for different individual performances but also different attitudes. Two men given different training under different men may develop entirely different results. Some individual differences are natural and can be changed very little by training. This is especially true of some of the physical traits.

Detecting Individual Differences.   Physical examinations, standardized psychological tests, records of job performance, tardiness, absenteeism, accidents, and practically any deviation from the group standard may indicate individual differences.   Men pride themselves on their ability to judge individuals by their appearance and by the answers to a few questions asked and answered orally.   Scientific tests have shown how utterly unreliable this method is.   *No supervisor should rely entirely on his personal ability to size up men by interviewing or talking with them.*   Standardized tests that have been developed, tried out, and verified are available today and many supervisors know that their employment department is using these tests. The successful supervisor will use the facts or scores from these tests as part of his information about his men.   The supervisor may not be able to interpret these scores but the testing department can interpret them for him, thus giving him more information about his men. *Actual job performance is the best method for measuring individual differences but only on the specific job.*   Too often, performance on one job will result in a man's selection for another job on which he does very poorly.   A supervisor would not ordinarily take a man who has done a good job as a machine operator and make him a production clerk without determining if he has the ability to handle figures and records accurately, if he has the educational background for clerical work, if he is skilled in or has the capacity and willingness for cooperation with others.   Yet how often do we see a man promoted from a good setup man or operator to assistant foreman without any check to see if he has the qualifications for supervision!

Records recall to the supervisor facts which he may have forgotten; they give him an over-all and detailed picture of his men.   They are one of the most revealing tools the supervisor has in detecting individual differences in his men.   Records may include time cards, production records in terms of quantity and quality—even broken down by hours, attendance, accidents, earnings if the employees are on piecework or incentive wage plans, and merit ratings.   The foreman owes his men the consideration that their records entitle them to.   He cannot discharge this responsibility unless he compiles records in such a manner as to reveal the facts.

Consideration of Individual Differences.   *Men differ in nearly all respects, yet they have many things in common.*   These differences are a matter of degree and detail. Successful placement of men should involve consideration of individual differences. *Mental and emotional differences are considerably greater than physical differences,* and in modern industry they are immeasurably more important. *The traditional methods of detecting individual differences are not reliable* and more accurate aids to sound judgment are available. One of the greatest deterrents to the use of known techniques is the commonplace attitude on the part of each man that he is a good judge of human nature. *Not all differences between men can be eliminated by training.* As a general rule men can best be handled on an individual basis and whenever possible the supervisor should handle his men as individuals. Moreover, when individual adjustments are neglected the individual grievance may readily become a group grievance with all its complications and difficulties. *Individual differences require careful consideration in the development of constructive discipline.*

Recognizing Individual Differences in Handling Operating Situations. A good supervisor nearly always can handle one of his men and win his point with the man, but when he tries to handle his men as a group, the group may have several individuals in it who are each as alert as the supervisor and collectively can talk him down. Different members of the group are likely to talk at the same time, argument may result, and the point at issue that the supervisor wished to make with his men is lost. Many a supervisor has called a group meeting and after it was over spent more time straightening out the results growing out of the meeting than the time it would have taken him to contact each of his men individually. The advantages of handling men on an individual basis far outweigh the disadvantages. When the supervisor talks to his men as a group he loses the advantage of using the individual differences of each man to put across his point.

Increased production needs often present a challenge to leadership. If the supervisor handles his men on an individual basis he will explain to each man the requirements and the reasons behind them and then use the incentive best suited to that individual's characteristics to stimulate him to increased output. His explanation to each may vary, his instructions certainly will, and his methods of discipline and measures of winning cooperation from each individual may also vary. The supervisor who knows his men, recognizes their individual differences, and applies this knowledge in handling them individually will seldom resort to the old-fashioned methods of supervising his group. This does not mean that there are not occasions where meetings with his group are successful, but such occasions are the exception, difficult to handle, and must be planned carefully in advance, as will be shown later in this chapter.

Effective training starts with the individual's current status. It is usually a waste of time to assume that each person needs the same training. The supervisor can improve his instruction and training of his men if he will tailor them to the differences in his men. Any training program that does not take into consideration individual differences will meet with little success.

Recognizing mental differences is not enough; the supervisor must use them to his and the company's as well as the individual's advantage. Industrial conditions today bring these mental and emotional differences to the surface more rapidly than in the past. If the supervisor does not recognize this and handle them properly, outside organizations will move in and the supervisor's problems of handling these differences will be increased.

Modern industry often provides staff aid for the supervisor. He can ask for assistance from the personnel department in solving difficult problems involving social maladjustment. Problems that he recognizes as over his depth he must refer to the personnel department. If instead he just overlooks them, eventually he will have to face them as group problems rather than as the problem of only one individual. With his knowledge of the work in his department and the requirements of each position, together with a knowledge of the individual differences of his men, their capacities and interests, he should be able to place each man successfully on the work for which he is best suited.

In a Group, Man Is More than an Individual. A group is ordinarily thought of as a number of individuals. Actually the group differs in many ways from its individual members. To handle group problems successfully and to use the group as another tool in effective departmental operation the supervisor must understand group attitudes and group morale as distinct yet integral factors in his department. The group has a tremendous effect on the human relations problems in industry. In terms of modern society *the group takes precedence over the individual.* Historically the group or tribe had priority and only recently has the individual been recognized. The doctrine of the individual's rights and of the individual as a separate political entity is comparatively recent historically.

Practically all the characteristics that distinguish man from animals are transmitted by the group and it is doubtful what type of individual would exist in the absence of the social group. The individual is born into a group, lives with a group (although not necessarily the same group) all his life, and dies as a member of a group. The normal man has a group or gregarious instinct and is happiest when part of a group.

Men frequently turn down positions which are promotions because it means they leave a group of which they are a part. *The group changes more slowly than the individual and possesses more stability than the individual.* It takes much longer to change the habits and customs of the group than it does to change those of an individual. In fact, groups will frequently continue to act in certain ways long after individual members of the group have tired of the particular action. The group's stability is affected and increased because the group is more permanent than any individual. One individual drops out and another is added, but the major part of the group continues unchanged.

The individual is influenced by three groups of which he is ordinarily a part. He is influenced by his family group, by the social group of which he is a part, and by the industrial group with which he works. If the industrial group is motivated by strong incentives it will move toward the company objectives in an orderly fashion. If the supervisor can transmit the company objectives to the group so that these objectives become group objectives, quantity and quality can be achieved with the minimum of supervision on his part.

The worker is influenced positively or negatively by his work group. When the group is contented and productive, the individual will tend to improve his work and bring it up to the group standard, but the individual who is of a dissatisfied group will likewise rapidly become difficult to handle. The group is sensitive to the grievances of the individuals forming it, and group movements will spring out of the personal and frequently petty irritations of its members. The individual is influenced by the group not only in his work but also in his opinions and ideas. The employee's opinions of his supervisor, the management, and the product he helps to make or sell are influenced by what the group of which he is a part thinks and says.

A group possesses characteristics which are peculiar to it and which are more than the sum total of its members' characteristics. The action of a mob is usually much greater than the aggregate desires of all the individuals making up the mob. A group is more emotional than its individual members. The group can be led more easily than the individual and is much more susceptible to suggestion than almost any individual in the group. The group is slower to start, harder to stop, and its inertia is greater than the sum total of the inertias of the individuals who compose it.

When strongly stimulated by the group the individual will often rise to heights above those to which he can reasonably be expected to rise when operating on his own. This has been illustrated time and again by acts of patriotism during wars, and outstanding performances by average athletes who rise to unexpected achievements in a single game. The individual under the influence of the group is effectively controlled by group restraints as well as inspired by group incentives. The individual will rarely go contrary to group desires or mores, yet with the group as an incentive he will frequently surpass himself in output and effort.

Group Behavior. A mob illustrates how the purpose of a group influences the group's action. It is rare when a group has gathered to commit an act contrary to law that it is deterred from carrying out the intended action because of individual objections. Even though as they gather, their minds are not made up as individuals, the influence of the group welds them together to carry out the group action. During labor disturbances the group actions which result in damage to buildings and machinery as well as personal injuries to the combatants can definitely be traced to the purpose of the group's assembling rather than to the desires of the individuals before or as they assemble. *The purpose that brings the group together influences the action of the group.* Of course it may not be strictly accurate to say that the group itself has a purpose when committing atrocities. What actually happens is that leaders incite the mob to frenzy by exhortation or other means and the members of the group participate in actions that they would not perform as individuals. The well-defined industrial group under effective supervision and motivated by a strong incentive will move toward its objective in an orderly manner. The supervisor who has developed in his group a strong discipline based on a knowledge of the aims of the enterprise and who has created a desire to gain those aims has nothing to worry about, for then the group purpose will guide the individuals that are a part of it, so that each accomplishes his task efficiently.

Companies that develop strong slogans have found them useful, and the supervisor will do well to utilize slogans, preferably those suggested by his men, as tools of supervision. A successful slogan must appeal to the group sense of unity—that of belonging. Recall the chant of the section gang on the railroad. With the singing the group in rhythmic action concentrates the energies of its members and accomplishes more than the gang could ordinarily accomplish. *Well-chosen slogans tend to unite the group sentiments and to direct the group efforts toward the objectives associated with the slogan and sentiment.*

Fads and fashions that harmonize with the group's sentiments and emotions tend to influence the group's actions along the lines manifest by its sentiments. These fashions can influence the thinking and actions of the group to a high degree. The only way to control such action on the part of the group is to replace the fashion or idea with another. The effectiveness of this replacement will be based on the worth of the idea, the manner in which it harmonizes or clashes with the sentiments of the group, and the open-mindedness of management to recognize the need for intelligent substitution of new ideas to replace old and harmful ones. No management can combat a group idea or objective with another that the group recognizes as unsatisfactory. The supervisor should remember that a perfectly sound idea may be rejected if the group thinks there is an ulterior motive behind it. The most successful way to introduce a new idea is to let the members of the group think it is their own, original with them, and to permit them to make it their own with the supervisor's efforts in the background. The supervisor and management, in developing an idea to combat an unhealthy one that has developed, must remember that the substitute must harmonize with the ideals of the group. Some managements and many old-line supervisors too often forget these last two points: the source of the idea and its acceptability to the group. No new objective as a replacement of bad practices is likely to succeed unless it meets these two tests.

Group Action Often Irrational. Group action is largely motivated by custom and sentiment. While sentiment may be associated with the noblest acts of man it is seldom the product of reason; in fact, it is often irrational. Group action is usually influenced by emotional feelings of oneness or opposition. When an individual becomes part of a group he is more likely to follow his emotions than his common sense since the group merges the individual into it and becomes the unit. An idea or statement once taken up by the group grows in force as it circulates and develops. A man relates a personal grievance against his supervisor to another. As it is passed on from one member of the group to another the grievance develops. Group influence on a grievance magnifies it out of all proportion to the original facts. As the story is repeated by the members of the group, it is twisted until the original facts are lost and it becomes eventually a jumble of distortions. This action found in group behavior tends to perpetuate desirable traits as well as undesirable ones and the supervisor can use this trait of the group to good advantage since *he must only sow the proper seeds and the action of the group will do the rest. When the supervisor has won the group over to his side the group members are his strongest supporters.*[2]

Care in removing individual reasons for complaints and preventing undesirable ideas and actions from starting will protect the group from becoming contaminated with unhealthy ideas and fashions. Great care must be exercised in the elimination process or the grievance will not be eliminated but will only spread. Preventive medicine is more effective than remedial medicine. Even though irrational, group behavior is more continuous than individual behavior; the group is more dependable day in and day out and this is a stabilizing influence. While the supervisor will make every effort to handle his men as individuals, striving constantly to avoid antagonizing the group, he should recognize the advantages of the group, and guide it into productive channels.

Methods of Promoting Group Action. It would be impossible to overemphasize the influence of group action in the life of civilized man. The group under the influence of a demagogue produced Hitler's Germany and Mussolini's Italy. To a lesser degree such tactics produce completely irrational industrial situations. In striving to direct group action, force only begets force and only requires more supervision to obtain compliance with the order; it leaves the group sullen. Force upsets the group emotionally and requires more force to sustain the action. This circular effect in itself becomes destructive. The supervisor, when tempted to fall back on force to win his way, should remember that force is effective only in the presence of the source of the force. Usually the supervisor should grant reasonable requests arising from individuals and the group. When it is not possible to grant the request, all the facts involved in the re-

[2] See F. J. Roethlisberger, William J. Dickson, and Harold A. Wright, *Management and the Worker,* Harvard University Press, Cambridge, Mass., 1939, pp. 255–269, for a classical discussion of sentiments.

jection should be given. It is wise to remember that partial facts promote rumors but that the whole story will usually put the group at ease. The troublemaker should be removed from the group but only after every attempt has been made to adjust him. Great care must be exercised in his removal, for unless the supervisor is extremely careful when removing one troublemaker he will create two more. Sometimes in bad situations that never should have been permitted to develop, whole groups have to be broken up by transfers. The supervisor must prevent the development of groups on the basis of nationality or religion, since such grouping often leads to trouble. The supervisor must seek a balance in his group, men of different ages, religions, and nationalities, and fraternal orders making up the group.

It is essential that groups be constantly studied for the detection of discontent. While groups tend to be stable, the ambitious leader is an ever-present threat to group serenity. Such a leader preys upon the group's sentiments by attacking some constituted authority. He nearly always will get a small following. He often makes promises he can never deliver, but this does not restrain his influence. The supervisor should study his group of employees to determine what are their objectives and should then direct his efforts to the best of his ability toward helping them to reach their objectives. Too often the supervisor labors under the delusion that the primary objective of his men is more money, and, since he cannot increase wages as he thinks they wish, he lets them go their way. Actually their objectives and desires may be far different, ones which he is equipped to satisfy, but since he lacks knowledge he fails to take the action within his power which would tie the group to him. No supervisor should ever permit himself to forget that it is his men who make him what he is and that they can destroy him with ease. Without them behind him he is helpless; with them behind him he is a success.

The Supervisor
10   and Mental Health

Emotional Factors.   The importance of emotional factors in influencing the behavior of men and their effective functioning in any situation has long been known to professionals in the various fields of human relations, but only in relatively recent years have consistent attempts been made to apply the principles of mental health on a large scale.   Despite the publicity given to such dramatic diseases as poliomyelitis, heart disease, and cancer, mental illnesses constitute the nation's number one health problem.   Neuropsychiatric patients occupy about one half of the country's one and a half million hospital beds, and millions more of our fellow men lead unhappy or ineffective lives because of emotional maladjustments of one type or another.

The Supervisor and Mental Health.   A disproportionate amount of the supervisor's time is consumed by a few employees.   A substantial number of these "problem" employees have problems of their own that they have not been able to handle within the framework of collaborative organizational requirements.   They are maladjusted or suffering from poor mental health.   The supervisor's responsibilities in relation to the mental health of his men are perhaps less well defined than most of his other duties, but they are none the less important.   The skilled and effective supervisor can do much to promote the mental health of his men, while the inept supervisor sooner or later will have an adverse effect on their mental health—particularly on those men who are especially vulnerable to psychological stresses.

Relatively few studies of industrial employees have been sufficiently extensive so that reliable estimates can be made of the number of workers with significant emotional problems. Estimates run all the way from 3 to 10 per cent of workers as having suffered from milder forms of emotional difficulties. Russel Fraser reported substantially higher percentages than these. His report showed that women have a higher ratio than men. This may perhaps be due to the fact that woman's traditional role has been in the home, and only recently have women worked in industry in large numbers.[1]

Reports indicate that from 60 to 80 per cent of all separations or dismissals from the job in industry are due to social incompetence, while only 20 to 40 per cent are the result of technical incompetence.[2]

Marked differences may occur between different work groups as to the incidence of employees with emotional problems, but the differences seem unrelated to the type of work, whether the workers are unskilled or skilled, their level of income, education, social standing, or position in the business hierarchy. Emotional problems affect workers, supervisors, executives, teachers, lawyers, doctors, engineers, ministers, scientists, and others alike.

In the industrial setting, we are primarily concerned with the individual's effectiveness in doing his specific job or in functioning as part of the organization. Among the personnel problems which frequently result from emotional factors are the following:

1. Reduced productivity
2. Excessive tardiness and absenteeism due to illness
3. Excessive absences for personal reasons other than illness
4. Antagonism toward regulations and authority
5. Excessive complaints and grievances
6. Increased employee turnover
7. Friction between fellow workers
8. Withdrawal of individuals from the group
9. Alcoholism
10. Accidents

Mayo's Classic Illustration. Elton Mayo, one of the greatest students of the influence of feelings and emotions in industrial relationships, described the resistance to his seeking union support for extending facilities for adult education in Australia as follows:

[1] See Russel Fraser, *Incidence of Neurosis among Factory Workers,* Medical Research Council Industrial Health Research Board Report No. 90, H. M. Stationer's Office, London, 1947, p. 4.

[2] Harold A. Vonachen, "Medicine in Industry," *Journal of the American Medical Association,* Vol. 157, No. 18, April 30, 1955, p. 1592.

Usually the more moderate and responsible union members sat in the front rows; the back rows were the haunt of those who represented the irreconcilable extreme left. Before long it became evident that six men were the nucleus of all the most savage opposition. In the course of many years, I came to know these six men well. The extreme party changed its name many times . . . but whatever the change of name or doctrine, it was always the same six who led the opposition at union meetings or spoke from soap boxes in the public parks. The fact that I came to know them personally made no difference to their platform attitude to me or to the university: but on other occasions they would talk freely to me in private. This enabled me to place on record many observations, the general tenor of which may be summarized as follows:

1. These men had no friends except at the propagandist level. They seemed incapable of easy relationship with other people; on the contrary, the need to achieve such relationship was for them an emergency demanding energetic effort.

2. They had no capacity for conversation. In talk with me they alternated between self-history and oratory which reproduced the compelling topic—revolution and the destruction of society.

3. All action, like social relationship, was for them emergency action. Any idea of routine participation in collaborate effort, or of the "ordinary" in living, was conspicuously absent from their thinking. Everything, no matter how insignificant, was treated as crisis, and was undertaken with immense and unreasoned "drive."

4. They regarded the world as a hostile place. Every belief and action implied that society existed not to give but to deny them opportunity. Furthermore, they believed that hostility to be active, not merely inert; they regarded everyone, even their immediate associates, as potentially part of the enemy forces arrayed against them.

In every instance the personal history was one of social privation—a childhood devoid of normal and happy association in work and play with other children. This privation seemed to be the source of the inability to achieve "ordinary" human relationships, of the consequent conviction that the world was hostile, and of the reaction by attack upon the supposed enemy. One of the six drifted into the hands of a medical colleague with whom I was accustomed to work on problems of adaptation. Thus was established a clinical relation of confidence in his physician. He discovered that his medical adviser was not at all interested in his political theories but was very much interested in the intimate details of his personal history. He made a good recovery and discovered, to his astonishment, that his former political views had vanished. He had been a mechanic, unable to keep his job although a good workman. After recovery he took a clerical job and held it; his attitude was no longer revolutionary.[3]

[3] See Elton Mayo, *The Social Problems of an Industrial Civilization,* Graduate School of Business Administration, Division of Research, Harvard University, Boston, Mass., 1945, pp. 25–27.

Examples such as this, although extreme, are not rare. More frequent, however, are situations where emotional problems are expressed more subtly.

Mental Health and Emotional Maturity. The supervisor should have some concept of what mental health is, not only because it gives him some guideposts by which he can evaluate himself, but also because it gives him some criteria for evaluating others.

Mental health may be defined in many ways. It implies emotional maturity, and a simple definition of emotional maturity is the ability to work, love, and play effectively without conflict. Dr. William Menninger in his instructive booklet, "Self-Understanding," goes beyond this and states that you are emotionally mature to the extent that you find greater satisfaction in giving than receiving, form satisfying and permanent loyalties in give-and-take relationships, use your leisure time creatively, contribute to the improvement of your home, school, community, nation and world, learn to profit from your mistakes and successes, and are relatively free from fears, anxieties, and tensions.[4]

A similar but more detailed list is given by Dr. Maurice Levine under the following headings:

1. Ability to be guided by reality rather than by fears
2. Use of long-term values
3. Grown-up (adult) conscience
4. Independence
5. Capacity to "love" someone else, but with an enlightened self-interest
6. A reasonable dependence
7. A reasonable aggressiveness
8. Healthy defense mechanisms (self-punishment and blaming others are examples of unhealthy mechanisms)
9. Good sexual adjustment with acceptance of own gender
10. Good work adjustment [5]

Personality and Personality Development. The term personality is a rather inclusive one which refers to the entire individual, the way he thinks, feels, and acts, the way he gets along with others, and the way he adjusts to his surroundings. These are the unique characteristics that distinguish each of us from everyone else.

The proverb that giant oaks from tiny acorns grow refers to men

[4] William C. Menninger, "Self-Understanding," *Better Living Booklet,* Science Research Associates, Chicago, 1951, p. 48.

[5] Maurice Levine, *Psychotherapy in Medical Practice,* New York, Macmillan, 1942, p. 268.

as well as trees. Remarkable changes occur between the birth of the helpless infant and its emergence as a mature adult capable of taking his place in society and giving rise in turn to new offspring. During this process of growing up the individual's personality develops as his body grows.

Although the individual's physical characteristics and his intellectual endowment are determined to a large extent by heredity, during the process of growing up the individual is subjected to an infinite number of environmental influences which help shape his personality. The years of infancy and early childhood are of extreme importance in personality development. The most important figures in the life of the infant and child during these years are his parents. Their attitudes toward the child—as expressed in the way they feel about him, the way they touch him, the things they do to and for him, and the things they say to and about him—determine to a large extent what sort of person the child will be when he grows up. It should be emphasized that attitudes toward a child over a long period of time are far more important in the child's development than are the isolated, emotionally charged events which are so often depicted in the movies.

Basic Needs, Anxiety, and the Unconscious. The needs of the newborn infant are relatively simple. The baby needs the love and affection of its mother, a certain amount of tactile stimulation (babies need physical contacts), food, and protection, but little else. As the baby grows into the child and as the child becomes the man, however, both his physical needs and his psychological needs become infinitely more complex.

These needs are variously referred to as basic urges, drives, motivations, and instincts, and they are classified in various ways by various authors. Dr. Fritz Redlich, June Bingham, and Jacob Levine, in their highly amusing and instructive book *The Inside Story: Psychiatry and Everyday Life,* discuss the basic urges "boiled down to an essential and inclusive three: 1. The urge to be safe and protected (security and dependence). 2. The urge to master the world (aggression). 3. The urge to unite with others (love and sex)." [6] Under these three headings can be listed nearly all of our common needs such as food, water, shelter, clothes, work, love, sex, the desire for children, the desire for adventure, the need to explore, the drive to compete, the need for self-expression, the desire to belong, etc.

[6] Fritz Redlich, June Bingham, and Jacob Levine, *The Inside Story: Psychiatry and Everyday Life,* Alfred A. Knopf, New York, 1953, p. 46.

All behavior has some meaning or purpose in the individual's attempts to maintain his psychological and physiological equilibrium within himself and between himself and his environment—an equilibrium in which basic needs achieve maximum gratification with a minimum of pain or anxiety.

Some of the basic needs mentioned above are very primitive or barbaric, and they would conflict seriously with the environment if they were expressed directly. All basic drives arise in the unconscious. Drives which are socially acceptable are allowed to come into the conscious and to be expressed directly. Drives which are not socially acceptable cause anxiety when they threaten to come into consciousness. In the unconscious, however, unacceptable drives can be handled in two other ways. They can be channeled into behavior that is acceptable and thus be expressed indirectly, or they can be converted into a variety of symptoms.

The importance of unconscious factors in determining human behavior cannot be overemphasized. Dr. William Menninger compares the unconscious with the nine tenths of an iceberg which is submerged: "All that we are aware of about ourselves and others is contained in the one tenth which appears on the surface." [7]

Normal People Are Not All Alike. Variety is stimulating, and it would be a dull world indeed, if we all looked alike, acted alike, thought alike, and in other ways were carbon copies of each other. Fortunately it is not thus. People with widely differing abilities, temperaments, and interests are every day leading happy and effective lives.

One of the greatest temptations of people who work with others is to judge others by their individual standards of behavior and of values. Each of us has his own way of handling problems, and what may work for one person may not work for another. We should not substitute our likes and prejudices for more objective evaluations of others as measured by the criteria of maturity already discussed. Many men can work together very effectively who are not temperamentally suited to like each other but who have mutual respect for each other's ability.

Because men vary so greatly in their personalities, they also vary greatly in the jobs for which they are best suited. Out-going personalities who like to meet people and who are persuasive tend to make good salesmen. People who are orderly and like to do things according to routine often make good file clerks, bookkeepers, or accountants.

[7] William C. Menninger, "What Makes an Effective Man?" American Management Association, *Personnel Series,* No. 152, p. 24.

Unconscious drives frequently are important in the individual's choice of his vocation. Sometimes the choices are unwise and only accentuate basic conflicts, but often the vocation may provide a satisfactory and socially useful expression of unconscious drives which otherwise might be unacceptable. For example, unconscious aggressive drives become productive in the work of carpenters, butchers, or surgeons. Persons with unconscious needs to be taken care of (dependent needs) are often led to careers in social service, teaching, nursing, or medicine where they take care of others.

What Is Maladjustment? Many different terms are used to refer to those of us with emotional maladjustments. Unfortunately there is much confusion over the terms, since some people use the terms only in a very general sense, while others have something quite specific in mind when they use them. Then, too, some of us, because of our own prejudices, feel that the terms carry unfortunate connotations which actually they should not carry. The important thing is not the label or epithet which is "put on" the individual, but rather the understanding that he is unhappy or sick as evidenced by his particular difficulties or symptoms.

Among the terms used are maladjustment, mental illness, nervous sickness, emotional disorder, functional condition, and personality disturbances. Some persons use these terms almost interchangeably, while others use mental illness to refer only to psychiatric patients who require hospitalization or whose illnesses are otherwise easily recognizable, and they use the other terms to refer to the milder or less obvious maladjustments.

Emotional maladjustment and mental illness can be defined in many ways. One rather inclusive definition is that emotional maladjustments or mental illnesses are any disturbances in the individual's personality or adjustment pattern which cause him persistent inner discomfort, persistent difficulty in getting along with his fellow men, or persistent difficulty in adjusting to society. This definition includes the grossly disturbed and maladjusted as well as those who appear to get along well but who are really torn by inner conflicts and anxiety.

From the definitions of mental health and maladjustment or mental illness which have already been discussed it should be apparent that no clear-cut boundary or dividing line exists between the two. They should be considered as being at the two ends of a continuum—such as a rainbow—with various degrees of mental health and maladjustment existing on the continuum between the two extremes.

People who are maladjusted or people who are mentally ill are human beings just like ourselves (although we sometimes do not treat them as such), and the problems they have are essentially the same as those of more healthy persons. The essential difference is that they have been less successful in solving their problems.

Manifestations of Emotional Problems. The manifestations of emotional problems are so varied and so many that it would be impossible to discuss them adequately in even the space devoted to this entire chapter. Symptoms range from difficulty in concentrating, loss of appetite, difficulty in sleeping, headaches, "butterflies" in the stomach, nervousness, overeating, and daydreaming, to mention only a few, to obsessions, delusions, hallucinations, very bizarre behavior, assaultiveness, and even suicide.

Whether or not a given bit of behavior is a manifestation of an emotional disorder or mental illness, and thus a symptom, depends largely on how effective it is in helping the individual make a successful adjustment to his environment. Thus in certain parts of our society a few drinks are quite acceptable, but in an alcoholic even a single drink might be a symptom if it were to lead to a spree which would interfere with the individual's home life or work.

The same basic urges may express themselves in the senseless doodling of a normal person on a telephone pad, the bizarre drawings of a disturbed hospital patient, or the masterpieces of an artist. In the hospitalized patient the behavior is a symptom. In the normal person the behavior is a harmless way of releasing tension. In the artist the behavior is creative and contributes to our culture. The same basic urge in an engineer or an architect might lead to a new automobile or a new building to add to the material welfare of society.

Mental Health in Industry. In some ways it would be ideal if personnel departments could hire only those persons who are completely emotionally mature. Under such circumstances, however, we would probably not have enough workers to run our factories, and many workers who are highly productive might be left without jobs. At the time of hiring it is actually very difficult to predict how the prospective employee will function on the job. Certain personality inventory tests are helpful in detecting some applicants with personality disturbances which are potentially more incapacitating, but they require trained personnel to interpret them, and at best they have some limitations. The Humm Wadsworth Test, the Guilford-Martin Personnel Inventory, and the Minnesota Multiphasic Personality Inventory are three well-known examples of such tests which have been used in attempts to measure temperament.

The employee's effectiveness on his job can be influenced greatly by emotional factors relating to his personal life or to his job situation or to both. Sources of stress at home include financial problems, wives (or husbands) or sweethearts, marital difficulties, in-laws, children, schools, illnesses, religion, neighbors, politics, world affairs, military service obligations, and many other things.

At work the employee is subjected to many other stresses. The industrial situation is a constantly changing one. Layoffs occur, men are fired, jobs are changed, production schedules change, new products or new models are put into production, fellow employees come and go, company contracts change, opportunities occur for advancement, rivalries develop, unions organize or compete for members, supervisors change, company policies change, new plants open, etc. All this takes place in a setting where men work together under a supervisor doing a job for a complex organization.

Work and Mental Health. One of the important factors which determine an employee's functioning on the job is his attitude toward work. Earlier in the chapter the ability to work was one of the criteria given for emotional maturity. We ordinarily spend about half of our waking hours at work, and it is important to understand the various things work may mean to different people. To nearly all of us work means a way of earning a living, but to most of us it usually means something more.

To some, work is something distasteful that is to be avoided whenever possible. To others, it is something uninteresting that must be tolerated. To still others, work is both one of life's challenges and one of life's satisfactions. To some, work is an end in itself. Still others find work the only escape from an otherwise intolerable existence. These attitudes toward work are sometimes conscious and sometimes unconscious. Many who accept the necessity of working are unaware that deep down they secretly would rather be taken care of than work themselves. Various unconscious and conscious feelings about work are often reflected in behavior on the job. Some men are always restless and dissatisfied and agitating for change. Others always seem to resist change even though it might be for their own betterment. Only a few are able to discriminate and make decisions based on the merits of a situation. Unfortunately this is as often true of executives and supervisors as it is of employees.

In an emotionally healthy person work is stimulating, creative, and rewarding. But work is just a part of his life—not his entire life. The healthy worker has a family, friends, and a place in his community, and it is not an accident that the best workers and best supervisors are also active in civic affairs, club groups, fraternal organizations, and the church. To some men, however, jobs are substitutes for the satisfactions which healthy family and social relationships bring. Such men are prone to make demands on their jobs which are difficult to satisfy. They may work very hard, but they frequently do not make good leaders, and they may resent not receiving recognition and advancements which they feel they are due.

In the paragraphs which follow, several types of problems that occur frequently in the industrial setting will be discussed, as well as some of the things which supervisors can do to promote the mental health of their men and to deal with those of their men who have emotional problems.

The "Touchy" or Overly Sensitive Employee. One of the problems more commonly encountered by the supervisor is the "touchy" employee who is overly sensitive to any actions or remarks which might reflect upon his worth as a person, his ability, or his functioning on his job. We meet such persons every day both at work and on the outside. These people tend to imagine slights when none are intended, or they magnify or misinterpret or see some special significance in the decisions of the supervisors or the actions of their fellow employees.

Such individuals are usually quite insecure, and they have an exaggerated need for the approval of others to maintain their self-esteem. When such approval is not forthcoming in large doses, they feel rejected. Some become overtly hostile and complain openly, but others do not say anything, but instead pout or become petulant and withdrawn. They may become inefficient, and some may even subtly undermine the effort at hand. These individuals require constant reassurance of their value as persons and of their value to the organization. Very frequently these persons do not have the outside sources for social satisfaction described above.

The repetitive nature of the work on many modern assembly lines unfortunately may contribute to such problems, since it may limit the worker's contacts with others while at the same time it gives him opportunity to brood over the slights which he has imagined. If the individual's personal relationships are more satisfactory both on the job and off, his fantasies or reveries while doing repetitive work will tend to be more pleasant. He will use the time to plan constructively what he will do when he finishes work. Rest periods have more significance for their social value than for reducing physical fatigue.

The "Problem" Worker. Certain employees seem to come to the attention of their supervisors far more often than others. They seem to have more complaints and grievances, more excuses, more special requests, poorer production records, more absences, more differences with their fellow workers, and more accidents, and they change jobs more often. The pattern for the individual worker varies greatly.

"Problem" workers such as these have a variety of emotional conflicts which prevent their gratifying their basic needs in healthy ways. Their common characteristic is that they tend to live out their conflicts and express them in their relationships with their environment and the others in the environment. Mayo's example cited earlier in this chapter represents an extreme, and although such extremes are not infrequent, less dramatic and more subtle expressions of difficulties are far more common.

The supervisor of necessity must deal with the overt behavior, but if he understands that the overt behavior is the result of the worker's unconscious conflicts, he is in a better position to deal with the situation in a constructive manner. "Problem" workers tend to be very provocative in their behavior—particularly in their relationships toward authority. The natural tendency of those who are provoked is to retaliate, but retaliation only accentuates the problem. The supervisor who recognizes that the provocative behavior is the result of the worker's conflict and not a reaction to him personally, will be less threatened by the "problem" worker. If he is patient and a good listener, the sensitive supervisor may even be able to develop an understanding of the worker which may help the worker or at least minimize the worker's difficulties on the job.

Absenteeism. Emotional problems are estimated to cause from one-quarter to one-third of the absences from work.[8] Only a small portion of this absenteeism is contributed by employees with disorders that require hospitalization or medical treatment. The bulk of it is due to problems associated with difficulties and dissatisfactions in interpersonal relationships both in the worker's outside life and in his situation on the job itself.

Studies in reducing absenteeism show that departments with the best developed group solidarity have the lowest rate of absenteeism.

[8] Russel Fraser, *loc. cit.*

Group solidarity is usually associated with a leadership that is basically employee centered.[9] In such groups the worker has a very real sense of belonging. Relationships in such groups tend to provide healthy emotional satisfactions as well as a means for meeting economic needs.

Accident Proneness. Every observing supervisor is familiar with the fact that certain employees have accidents repeatedly, while others work year after year at similar or even more dangerous jobs with perfect safety records. The same persons who injure themselves repeatedly also seem to have difficulties in other areas.[10] They have more sickness absenteeism, and they visit dispensaries with minor complaints more often than the average employee. They also seem to have more difficulty with their bosses and fellow workers, and "they seem to suffer a disproportionate share of life's misfortunes generally."

To show that accidents do not happen entirely as a matter of chance, Dr. Gerald Gordon reported: "A recent study of 3,000 occupational injuries incurred over a two-year period in one of our plants showed 100 per cent of the injuries had been incurred by 35 per cent of the total plant population and almost half of these were distributed among a 7 per cent group who had between two and six injuries each for the two-year period. Sixty-five per cent of the employees had not reported to the dispensary with so much as a scratch." [11] The 7 per cent group of repeaters cannot be accounted for on any chance basis.

Among the personality traits commonly mentioned in the literature in relationship to accidents and accident proneness are the following: aggressiveness, anger, frequent conflict with authority, lack of attention to job at hand, attention getting ("show off") tendencies, boredom, tendency to take chances or risks, competitiveness with inability to bear being outdone, discontent, distraction, excitement, guilt feeling, hostility, being in a hurry, impulsiveness, faulty judgment of speed and distance, domination by strong drives to overcome opposition, love of power, unconscious need for punishment, unwillingness to accept monotony or routine, neurotic tendencies, being easily offended, overactivity, rashness in action, rebelliousness, restlessness, and resentment.[12]

[9] See Elton Mayo, *op. cit.,* p. 107.

[10] See Gerald Gordon, M.D., "The People Who Get Hurt," *Safety News,* Vol. 69, No. 2, February 1954, p. 20; see also James A. Dirkwood, "The Mind Behind the Accident," *Safety News,* Vol. 68, No. 6, December 1953.

[11] See Gerald Gordon, *op. cit.*

[12] Leonard E. Himler, "Psychological Factors in Industrial Accidents," *Michigan Business Review,* Vol. VI, No. 2, March 1954, p. 12.

Alcoholism. Industry's interest in alcoholism comes from loss in productivity due to the decreased efficiency and absenteeism that result from excessive drinking. Studies at Yale indicate that the use of alcohol causes the problem drinker in industry to miss twenty-two working days a year. The problem drinker loses an additional two days a year more than other employees for other illnesses, and he has twice the number of accidents.[13]

Recognizing the problem of alcoholism, the Consolidated Edison Company of New York in 1947 began a treatment program for problem drinkers which eventually led to the establishment of the Consultation Clinic for Alcoholism at the New York University Bellevue Medical Center in 1952. Since then a number of other companies have made use of the clinic's services, and the results have been encouraging.[14]

Much prejudice still surrounds alcoholism, but the public is gradually accepting the fact that alcoholism is an illness. The first step in the rehabilitation of an alcoholic is the recognition of the fact that drinking is a problem. Much still needs to be learned about alcoholism, but the earlier that drinking is recognized as a problem the greater the chances for rehabilitation. The alcoholic should be encouraged to seek medical treatment from a physician or clinic specializing in the problem of alcoholism. Another resource in aiding the problem drinker is Alcoholics Anonymous. The supervisor, together with the plant physician, can be of real help to the worker in recognizing the problem as early as possible and in then following through and obtaining assistance from both of these sources.

The Art of Leadership. Probably the most important factor contributing to the maintenance of good mental health among the men in industry is good leadership. The art of leadership is something which is quite intangible and difficult to define, and it is something which we tend to take for granted when we have worked with a good leader for a prolonged period of time. The importance of the art of leadership becomes more apparent, however, whenever we attempt to analyze the difficulties that a poor leader can cause for himself, his men, and his organization. Leaders are not all alike. First of all, the leader should be a person who gets along with other people, and he should be a person who has healthy and constructive ways of handling

[13] Harry Levinson, "Consultation Clinic for Alcoholism," *Menninger Quarterly*, Winter Issue, 1955, p. 15.

[14] *Ibid.*

the normal everyday problems of his own life. Secondly, the leader should be a person of above average competence. He need not necessarily be more intelligent and/or more skillful than all of his men. He should furthermore have a realistic understanding of his own strengths and limitations—both as to the technical aspects of his job and as to his ways of getting along with people.

These qualities are important, but they are not enough. The leader should have a general knowledge of the structure of the entire organization, and he should have a specific knowledge of both the formal and informal structure of that part of the organization in which he works. The leader must understand his role in the organization and he must have healthy respect for those above him, a healthy respect for himself and his role in the organization, and a healthy respect for the men under him. With the proper respect for all concerned the leader will have a much easier time in exercising the authority which his position demands. The leader should also have a feeling of responsibility toward both those above him and those under him in the organization.

The chief characteristic which distinguishes the good leader from the non-leader is his ability to deal constructively with problem situations. In a very real sense this is the subject of this entire book. The good leader should not only be temperamentally suited for problem solving, but he should also have an understanding of the general principles and specific techniques for handling both the technical problems and interpersonal problems which he will encounter. The good leader must be able to evaluate realistically the strengths and weaknesses of those with whom he works, and he should be able to foresee the consequences of his own decisions and actions as well as those of others. Actually the reason things seem to run so smoothly under a good leader is that he is foresighted enough to see potential problems before they arise and thus really to prevent the problems from ever actually developing.

Last but by no means least, the leader must be human, but he must also be fair and impartial in the exercise of his authority over his men. The leader heads a unit that has a job to do, and he must deal with many things which his men may do which do not contribute to the job at hand or which interfere with it. Discipline and criticism are responsibilities that the leader cannot escape even though he might often like to. The challenge for the leader is to handle these problems constructively rather than destructively. The task is made easier if the leader has respect for his job, himself, and his men, and if he feels that the job is worth doing well. The leader's goal is increased effort and better performance. If the leader respects the man, if the leader makes the man feel that he is accepted and wanted both as a person and as an employee, if the leader makes the man feel he is capable of doing a better job, the worker will profit and feel "I've learned something new that will help me do the job better," or "I'll try a little harder." A certain number of failures are inevitable, but the leader can at least have the satisfaction of having tried a constructive approach. Matters of tardiness, absenteeism, rule violations, and other disciplinary problems are best handled early when constructive help can remedy the situation rather than late when the problem has advanced to the point where some drastic action is necessary.

The Supervisor's Own Mental Health. The supervisor is a human being who has the same needs as anyone else, and he faces the same everyday problems of life. His position of leadership may help to satisfy some of his needs to master the world (see above under "Basic Needs, Anxiety, and the Unconscious"), but it also puts him in situations of particular stress. The supervisor's responsibilities to management and his responsibilities to his men are discussed elsewhere in more detail, but it should be mentioned here that these dual responsibilities may subject the supervisor to conflicting pressures. The supervisor wants the cooperation, approval, and respect of his men, yet at the same time he wants the cooperation, approval, and respect of his superiors. One is hardly more important than the other, and the supervisor must satisfy both groups, while at the same time reconciling both real and apparent differences between the two. To do all of this, it is necessary for the supervisor to be secure as an individual, so that he will not make excessive demands on his job and so that he can handle the responsibilities of the job without experiencing undue stress. The supervisor should not bring his problems from home to work with him in the morning, and he should leave the cares of his job at the plant when he goes home in the evening. He should have healthy outlets for his aggressions and healthy sources of satisfaction for his needs for security, love, and affection in his relationships at home in his family, at church, in various fraternal, social, or civic groups, or in other recreational activities.

What the Supervisor Can Do. Problems of mental health which the supervisor will encounter tend to fall into three groups. First, there is the largest group of employees who ordinarily adjust very well and who are generally healthy emotionally, but who under stress and in times of crisis need support. The supervisor can be a great help to these employees at such times just by being understanding and by accepting them as friends, although such employees will usually readily find the support that they need in their fellow workers and in their friends outside of the work situation.

Second, there are those employees who have emotional problems or personality disturbances that are significant enough to cause them to be unhappy or uncomfortable or to decrease their effectiveness in working or in getting along with others, but that are not sufficiently incapacitating to cause them to seek guidance or professional help. This group is of most significance to the supervisor, since it includes most of the men who are minor troublemakers or "problem" workers in other ways. Again the supervisor can do much by attempting to understand and accept these men and by respecting them as individuals who have a contribution to make to their families, their jobs, and society. If the supervisor is successful in winning the respect and confidence of this group, he is often in a position to encourage the ones who need counseling, guidance, or treatment to seek it. Skill in making original referrals in many cases may determine whether or not the counseling or treatment can be effective. The man who is sent to a counsellor or psychiatrist with the feeling that the referral has been made because his supervisor wants to get rid of him has far less chance of profiting by the experience than a man who is referred with the feeling that his supervisor respects him and considers him to have worth-while potentials and thus to be worthy of receiving help.

Third, there is the group of employees who have or have had emotional illnesses of such magnitude as to require psychiatric treatment in a hospital or as an out-patient. Too often we condemn these people for being weak, and we fail to understand that they are sick. Even some of us who pay lip service to recognizing that they are sick indicate our prejudices by our actions. Some people ask, "Why should we have anything to do with these people? Won't they always be sick?" The answer to the latter question is "no." Many persons who are hospitalized with the major psychoses recover and are able to return to their jobs and to being productive members of society. Such people who have recovered often feel quite insecure about the attitudes of others when they first return to work. Supervisors can do much in preparing the other men for their return and helping the others accept them back as members of the group. Former patients do not want to be treated differently. They want to be treated like everyone else. The matter of their past illnesses should be treated in a matter-of-fact way. It should not be hushed up like a scandal nor should an issue be made of it. If the former patient wants to talk about his illness, let him, but do not be too inquisitive about it. Interest can be shown more appropriately in the ex-patient's present situation. The response to a simple "How are you?" or "How are things going?" will usually give a clue as to whether he wants to talk about himself or not.

The Art of Listening. Of all the qualities which help the supervisor in his working with others, perhaps the most important is the ability to be a good listener. The nature of much of the supervisor's work requires that he initiate many of the contacts and that he do much of the talking. Listening is an art which comes more easily to some than to others, but it is one which can be cultivated. Being a good listener requires a sincere interest in the other fellow and plenty of patience. We all desire the respect and approval of others, and we are complimented when someone listens to us attentively and respectfully. A worker is similarly complimented when his supervisor listens to his opinions or complaints or simply his observations on the state of the weather. An opportunity to ventilate complaints often relieves emotional tensions sufficiently so that no further action is necessary.

Frequently complaints are registered or questions are asked about something quite different from the real issue at hand. Men often test their listeners by disguising what they are driving at rather than by revealing it. If the supervisor is an understanding listener and if he does not feel the compulsion to express his own opinions, the worker may feel comfortable enough to begin talking about what is really bothering him. The real problem may be something relating to the job situation or something quite unrelated, such as a personal problem.

The good listener makes use of certain techniques which encourage the other person to talk. Among these are a quizzical raising of the eyebrows, a questioning "Oh?" or "How's that?" or a request for more information or an elaboration.

One of the more difficult things for a listener to do, but an important one, is to make the speaker feel accepted and respected without actually agreeing with him or approving what he says. It can be accomplished in most cases, however, if the listener feels secure, if he is interested in the other person, and if he respects the other person. It takes two to make an argument, and the listener can disagree without arguing. Often questions are asked or statements are made in such a way as to provoke rejection. The good listener is not caught by such traps, but rather tries to find out what is behind the provocative behavior.

Listening is of value because it offers the speaker an opportunity for emotional catharsis or ventilation, but it does have its limitations when working with persons with deep emotional problems. If the problems which the worker presents get worse instead of better, if they become more frequent, or if the worker seems to get no benefit from talking about his problems or becomes more upset, it is then probably time to seek help from someone who has specialized training in treating persons with emotional problems. The plant medical department or personnel office may offer some such services, and if they do not, they usually can be of assistance in referring the worker to the resources that are available elsewhere in the community. Even in these cases the supervisor who is a good listener has an important role, because he is the person who is in the best position to advise the worker to get the specialized help which he needs. The worker who feels his supervisor understands and respects him can accept such advice, whereas the worker who feels his supervisor wants to get rid of him will only resent it.

11 The Supervisor as an Instructor

Instructing as an Executive Function. A major function of an executive is the directing of the efforts of others in achieving the objective of his enterprise. The higher the executive in the organization, the less personal directing he does. Nevertheless, at almost any level of the executive process there is some personal supervision of others. Almost invariably a person who directs the efforts of others is required to do some instructing. Of course, this statement presupposes that the executive is really qualified for the position that he holds. An executive at the level of the factory manager, sales manager, or chief engineer has a substantial amount of instructing to do if he is really a developer of men.

Figure 2.1, Chapter 2, portrays the executive process. It will be recalled that the executive, in directing the efforts of others, is required to plan, organize, and supervise. Since he cannot possibly do all of the planning himself, one of his responsibilities is to get his subordinates to do their share of the planning. This often requires meticulous care and training. Even when the chief executive works out the details of a reorganization he usually has a training assignment in order to get his subordinates to accept it and to put it into effect. Merely drawing a new organization chart does not mean that the prescribed structure will function as set forth. It is in his supervising function that the maximum training effort of the executive is called for. This is especially true when a new subordinate is added to his staff through the creation of a new position or through promotion or through being hired from the outside to fill a vacancy. The training requirements are even greater when a man is brought in from the outside than when he is promoted from within. This is especially true in relation to company policies. The executive may have assistance in this training, but some of it rests squarely on his shoulders. In a very real sense *training is a vital phase of leadership.*

The Importance of Instructing. The supervisor is responsible as an instructor because effective instruction is: (1) a vital factor in the training of new men, (2) an integral part of introducing new orders, specifications, and procedures to the organization, and (3) a means of upgrading the regular work force to insure the adoption and maintenance of work standards. The degree and extent of the instruction which will take place in the enterprise depends largely upon: (1) the character and complexity of the enterprise, (2) the static or dynamic state of business in general and the specific enterprise in particular, (3) the extent of labor turnover within the organization, and (4) the rate of expansion or growth of the particular business (or it may be the rate of retrenchment). If the supervisor is to delegate with certainty, either one of two conditions must be present: there must exist an organization already trained and indoctrinated in the company's policies, processes, and procedures, which presupposes successful earlier instruction, or careful training must be provided to accompany the delegation of responsibility or issuance of instructions. In a continuing organization, instruction as a part of delegating is a function that must constantly be performed from the president down to the lowest ranking employee. Whenever the supervisor delegates a person to perform a task for which the supervisor is responsible and gives that person the authority to carry out the assignment, he should check to see if the person is qualified to carry out the assignment. He must determine any qualifications that are lacking and give the individual the necessary instruction along with authority to perform the task. Underlying successful delegation by the supervisor is the need for careful and detailed instructions when he delegates authority so that the delegated task will be performed in the most efficient manner.

To supervise requires more than mere follow-up to see that functions are being properly performed. Men will be found who fall somewhat short of the desired work standards. Pointing out the deficiency to a man is not sufficient in many instances. It often becomes necessary to instruct him in the correct method of performing the work. It costs money to hire men, and under unemployment compensation it also costs money to let a man go. It is the supervisor's responsibility to hold the labor turnover to a minimum and instruction is an effective tool in carrying out this responsibility. As an instructor, the supervisor must analyze the man's requirements, know the right way to do the work, and teach the employee the proper method until it is learned and he is producing work of the required quality and quantity. Old methods are frequently replaced by new and better ones which: (1) may be developed by one of the men, (2) may be discovered by the supervisor in his regular line of duty, and (3) may result from research by the methods or research department. In any of the three foregoing situations it is necessary for the supervisor to bring to all his employees the benefits discovered by the few. This requires instruction, sometimes difficult instruction, because it involves getting men already doing work one way to change over to a new work method.

Efficient production is often the result of detailed instruction properly followed up. Production and instruction cannot be separated. Production is to a large degree dependent on the quality of instruction. Poor instruction or lack of instruction is reflected in unsatisfactory quantity and quality production. Lack of instruction is also reflected in low morale. Without adequate instruction the supervisor is unable to interpret company policies to the men. Table 11.1 illustrates the relationship between production and instruction in the supervisor's work of handling his department.

TABLE 11.1

A Comparison of the Supervisor's Instructional and Production Job *

Object	Finished product	Instructed workman
Knows	Nature of product to be turned out	Nature of work to be taught
Analyzes	Details of parts and processes to be assembled and the sequence of operations	Details of operations or steps involved in the instruction job
Determines	Order in which parts are to be assembled and the sequence of operations	Order in which steps should be taught to be learned most readily
Puts across	Assembly of parts and performance of operations to get the finished product	Instructional job step by step according to a plan
Checks	Finished product	Ability of the workman to perform his job

* Adapted from material developed for the General Motors Executive Training Program by the General Motors Institute.

The Absorption Versus the Planned Method of Learning. There are two general approaches to instruction, the absorption method and the intentional method. Instruction by absorption is the way many employees learned their jobs in the past, namely, by being put on their own to sink or swim. Sometimes an older employee was assigned to take an interest in the new man, but usually the new man learned for himself by trial and error, by watching others and asking questions, since there was no special incentive for the older employee to teach the new man. Purposeful instruction is the planned method of training new men. In the ideal situation every step in learning the job by the new employee has been planned in advance. Modern techniques of instruction are employed and utilized to their fullest extent. The learner is given every opportunity to develop as rapidly as possible and is encouraged at every step.

The supervisor has several duties when he actually meets his responsibility for instruction. (1) He needs to know the nature and extent of instruction (this again requires that the supervisor know his men, their capacities, and their present skills). (2) He must plan to have the great bulk of the detailed instruction (in a large department) carried out by instructors trained for this specific purpose. In the small department the supervisor will have to do the instructing himself and in the large department he must follow up the instructors, at times controlling and actually giving instruction himself out of his experience. (3) He must know the principles of good instruction and be able to train his instructors in them. He must also supervise and follow up the instructors' work to see that they apply these basic principles of good instruction. The instructional job is on a par with the production job. In fact, production costs may be excessive unless the instructional job is properly performed. Follow-up of the instruction is an essential part of good supervision. Many supervisors overlook the importance of instruction or even if they do see the need for it they leave the job and its follow-up to others, when it is definitely the supervisor's responsibility. Since production is dependent on the quality and quantity of instruction, every supervisor should recognize the need for instruction, the principles of instruction, the planning required in instruction, and the follow-up that is always an essential part of every responsibility.

Some Observations on Instruction Principles. There are certain basic attitudes and approaches to instructing. While details in a particular situation may readily vary, the fundamentals remain the same. An instructor should convey to the learner an attitude of patience, painstaking effort, and good will. Such an attitude tends to become reciprocal and results in establishing a feeling of mutual confidence between instructor and learner. The instructor should have clearly in mind a specific objective for the individual lesson. Unless this objective is definite there will be much wasted time and effort. Every instructor should carefully break down the particular subject or task into its instructional factors. (Often this will already have been done for the supervisor or his instructors, but, if not, he must do it himself or have it done under his supervision.) These instructional factors should be arranged in their logical *learning sequence* for teaching purposes, and then to insure effective results a plan should be developed to present each step. The supervisor will often find that the logical teaching sequence varies from the order in which he learned the job. It is essential that he rely not only on his past experience but also that he analyze the job and the method of teaching it in order to find the one best way to instruct the learner. Occasionally this best way is to teach the easy parts of the work first, irrespective of where these parts come in actual job performance. If the job has been broken down into its elements, the determination of the logical learning sequence is facilitated.

The bringing of the learner up to the required standard should be kept in mind at every step in the instructional process. The instruction has a specific purpose. All experiments in the instructing should be conducted with the objective of shortening the learning process, its improvement in terms of the quality of the product, and the giving of increased satisfaction and confidence to the learner. *Instruction is a tool used by the supervisor for the purpose of improving and increasing production.* The time devoted to instruction of employees can only come from one place, out of that ordinarily used for productive purposes. Every part of a man's work day which is devoted to instruction must be fully utilized to the end of developing that man into a more effective producer. This end can only be accomplished when the instruction is planned in advance, each lesson is part of a broad plan, and the proper methods and techniques are used with the objective of the particular lesson in mind. When he has staff instructors to assist him, the supervisor must be certain they are using sound methods to the same end of increasing production in terms of both quantity and quality.

There has been a great deal of discussion as to whether speed or accuracy should be stressed in the early stages of instructing. The answer is not a simple one. If the motions are the same at both the slow and fast speeds the use of a slower speed in the beginning does not require learning new motions when the speed is increased. Gilbreth found a different set of motions used when laying brick at a high rate of speed than when working at a slower rate.[1] In such a case, if at all practical, the learner should work at high speed. Naturally, certain operations may involve so much expense in terms of the cost of the product being worked on and the cost of the equipment being used that the emphasis will be on working at the speed that will minimize the breakage of equipment and spoilage of the product. Usually this is at a speed lower than the one to be used when the learner has mastered the machine operations.[2] Whether he must be his own instructor in his department, must supervise learners from a vestibule school as they adapt themselves to actual production when they are assigned to his department, or must supervise staff instructors in his department, the supervisor will find he can carry out his responsibility for instruction more effectively when he understands the problems and methods of instruction.

Steps in Teaching. Practically every supervisor who occupied a supervisory position during World War II is familiar with the little card that he carried around in his pocket on which were listed in concise form the steps of "How To Get Ready To Instruct" and of "How To Instruct." For the benefit of persons who have not used these cards, both the front and back of one is reproduced below:

These cards are a boiled down version of the famous work by Charles R. Allen, *The Instructor, the Man, and the Job* (1919). The steps listed below are another version of essentially the same teaching process. These steps are primarily the ones to be followed in teaching a skill such as operating a typewriter, a factory machine, or an assembly operation. It must not be thought that the mere learning of the words and phrases will cause the instructor to follow the words in practice. Until these steps are incorporated into his thought processes and attitudes the instructor will continue to instruct as he has been accustomed to teach. "Teachers tend to teach as they were taught when they learned the operation and not as they have been

---

[1] See William R. Spriegel and Clark E. Myers, *The Writings of the Gilbreths,* Richard D. Irwin, Homewood, Ill., 1953, p. 59.

[2] See E. F. Wonderlic and Carl Iver Havland, "Principles and Methods of Industrial Training," American Management Association, *Personnel Series,* No. 47, 1941, p. 12.

HOW TO GET READY TO INSTRUCT

Have a Time Table—
how much skill you expect him to have, by what date.

Break Down the Job—
list important steps.
pick out the key points. (Safety is always a key point.)

Have Everything Ready—
the right equipment, materials, and supplies.

Have the Workplace Properly Arranged—
just as the worker will be expected to keep it.

Job Instruction Training

TRAINING WITHIN INDUSTRY
Bureau of Training
War Manpower Commission

KEEP THIS CARD HANDY
GPO   16—35140-1

HOW TO INSTRUCT

Step 1—*Prepare the Worker*
Put him at ease.
State the job and find out what he already knows about it.
Get him interested in learning job.
Place in correct position.

Step 2—*Present the Operation*
Tell, show, and illustrate one IMPORTANT STEP at a time.
Stress each KEY POINT.
Instruct clearly, completely, and patiently, but no more than he can master.

Step 3—*Try Out Performance*
Have him do the job—correct errors.
Have him explain each KEY POINT to you as he does the job again.
Make sure he understands.
Continue until YOU know HE knows.

Step 4—*Follow Up*
Put him on his own. Designate to whom he goes for help.
Check frequently. Encourage questions.
Taper off extra coaching and close follow-up.
16—35140-1

If Worker Hasn't Learned, the Instructor Hasn't Taught

Front of Card   Back of Card

Figure 11.1. The Job Instruction Card.

taught to teach when considering sound principles of learning." This fact is witnessed on all sides. The supervisor should constantly look for and practice good teaching methods.

1. *Explain to the employee the nature of the work,* the hazards to be avoided, the value of the equipment and product, and the use of special tools, specifications, and gauges. Giving an introductory over-all picture of the work to be done pays dividends because then the employee learns the operations more rapidly.

2. *Demonstrate the work* with the learner in the position, as nearly as possible, that he will be in when he performs the same operation. Although very important, this is often overlooked, and the instructor will frequently place the learner on the opposite side of the machine or work bench. The first demonstration may well be at normal production speed. The second demonstration should be performed slowly enough for the learner to see each step of the operation in detail, and the relationship of each operation to its succeeding operation. The *why* of each operation should be explained as well as the *how.*

3. *Let the learner do the job himself.* After the learner has had ample opportunity to familiarize himself with the details required, he should be allowed to make his initial trial under the direct guidance

and supervision of the instructor. It has been proved scientifically that the desired skill will be acquired more quickly if the learner from the beginning completes the entire operation at standard production speed. From a practical standpoint, however, this is seldom possible where the value of the equipment or material is high, since scrap and breakage under such a procedure are excessive.

4. *Correction by the instructor* should accompany the initial trials as well as later work. This correction should be carried out both by suggestion and demonstration.

5. *Follow-up* is essential not only during the early part of instruction but also as the learner progresses, in order to avoid the formation of bad work habits. The instructor must teach the one best-known method, and he must see to it that the beginner learns this standardized method of operation.

Retraining. In a continuing organization every supervisor is faced with the necessary retraining of old employees that results from the changing work situation. The conditions giving rise to the need for retraining are several. (1) Technological changes may abolish the job on which an employee is working, and the company may wish to retrain rather than discharge him. (2) An employee, because of illness, accident, or incapacity due to age, may no longer be able to carry his share of the task he performed when in normal strength. (3) Depression or cyclical variations in production create conditions where, in part, employment stabilization may be achieved by having a versatile work force capable of performing more than one job. (4) Some employees are engaged in a confined phase of a particular task and lose their all-around skills in their particular trade. Retraining is often necessary to keep active their all-around skills as a reserve in case of need. The same principles of good instruction apply in retraining old employees that have been found successful in training new employees. In retraining, however, one additional factor is involved— the ability of the supervisor to sell the old employee on the need for retraining. The new employee is anxious to learn his new work and in training a new employee the supervisor starts with a person willing to receive instruction. The old employee frequently is not so willing to be retrained. This presents another instructional problem to the supervisor. If the supervisor knows his men well, has their confidence, and is recognized as a leader among them, then this problem will not arise or can be resolved in conference with the old employee who needs retraining.

Types of Training. The more common types of training methods include: (1) on-the-job training, (2) off-the-job training, (3) company training schools where subjects other than manual skills are taught, (4) safety instruction, (5) apprenticeship training. *On-the-job training* takes place in the department on the equipment where the employee will work. Instruction may be given by an old employee who is experienced in the work to be taught, by the supervisor, by a special instructor, or by the understudy method. Many supervisors depend on an older, experienced man who has some ability as a teacher to break in each new employee in the department, yet here the supervisor must follow up the progress of the learner and the methods used by the older employee in his instruction of the new man. Few supervisors, unless they are natural-born teachers, carry out their responsibilities for instruction as they should, either because they lack time to instruct their men or because they have never studied the principles of instruction. Instructing is a specialized skill that cannot be acquired overnight. Every supervisor, even though he has staff instructors, should know and be able to practice the correct methods of instruction. Successful supervisors are usually good instructors and regularly devote a part of their time to instruction. In large companies staff instructors are frequently provided, but this does not relieve the supervisor of his responsibility for instruction; he must still follow their work. The understudy method, where a new employee is assigned to an old employee to learn the work, also requires frequent follow-up by the supervisor.

The *vestibule school* provides a place to teach new employees away from the turmoil of the production floor. It frequently is adjacent to the main production area. This type of training was popularized during World War I and again used extensively during World War II. It is especially suited to mass training of semiskilled operators. Its advantages include: (1) more efficient use of the instructor's time and skill, since the trainees are more conveniently located and under closer supervision, (2) regular production is not impeded by learners as is true in on-the-job training, (3) the general atmosphere is more favorable to learning, since there is not so much confusion to the beginner unacquainted with machine production, (4) emphasis can be laid upon the phases of the work where the learner is weakest, without disrupting production, (5) instructors should be more highly skilled as instructors since the principles of specialization enable the organization to take better advantage of the instructor's time, and (6) vestibule school training is well adapted for training regular employees for promotion when used after regular work hours. Among the most common disadvantages of the vestibule school are the following: (1) with the passage of time, there is a tendency for equipment and methods of the vestibule school to lag behind the shop equipment and methods, (2) the vestibule school tends to underemphasize the time element in the performance of a task, definitely an unrealistic situation, and (3) an adjustment period is required when transferring the learner to the shop. Despite these disadvantages it may be used to advantage by companies needing a large number of quickly trained employees. Some companies today are finding means to overcome the disadvantages of the vestibule school. They have worked out a combination of vestibule school and on-the-job training that appears to be successful. Every supervisor expecting to become an effective instructor can well afford to study the instructional methods and techniques used in the vestibule school.

Other Methods of Training. Apprenticeship training as it is practiced today is a combination of on-the-job and off-the-job training designed for training young men to become skilled craftsmen. This type of training covers both mechanical and classroom work and ordinarily lasts several years. Many companies operate schools for their employees in subjects other than the manual skills. These schools, usually under the direction of the training department or personnel division, give employees an opportunity to take courses in blueprint reading, drafting, designing, other engineering courses, accounting, and other subjects. Recently some companies have developed courses for prospective supervisors which include discussions of human relations problems, production problems, and labor relations. Supervisors may attend these courses to provide themselves with up-to-date information to enable them to do a better job of supervision. Employees in their department may be selected for such courses, and when this occurs the supervisor must be on his toes to see that he practices the same methods and techniques of supervision taught his men. Safety is an additional responsibility of the supervisor and will be discussed at length later. It must be noted here, however, that when the supervisor is instructing his men in safety practices, he follows the same principles of instruction used in other training he gives his men. Some companies have libraries which are well supplied with books and magazines that relate to their processes and products. A few companies maintaining such libraries are the Goodyear Tire and Rubber Company, Aldens, Inc., Burroughs Adding Machine Company, the

National Cash Register Company, and the Detroit Edison Company. These libraries are more likely to be used by engineers and technical people than by workers in the shop. Some industrial libraries are not open to the rank-and-file workers. In fact, relatively few factory foremen use them. However, they should be used extensively by supervisors. Some companies have technical magazines that are circulated among the supervisors by the library or more frequently by the personnel departments.

Some companies have developed correspondence courses that are run by the educational departments in the personnel division. Most of these companies are multi-plant operations. A number of them have small plants or branches. These correspondence courses may cover almost any phase of the work. Other companies encourage their employees to take correspondence courses with commercial correspondence schools or with the extension divisions of universities or colleges. Correspondence courses have merit, but the number of people who have the staying qualities to complete them is relatively small. The experience of company operated correspondence courses shows that more people finish their correspondence courses than those taking them from outside correspondence institutions.

The Learning Process. A great deal of research in the learning process has been conducted by schools of education and departments of psychology. Entire courses are given in this area in colleges. These basic findings have value for the supervisor. A few of these findings are as follows:

1. The learning rate of a skill is not constant. Plateaus develop when learning progress is charted and these plateaus differ with different jobs and among different learners, yet they appear to follow a general pattern. The supervisor must recognize this fact in his instruction work, especially encouraging beginners when they reach a plateau stage in their progress.

2. From a strictly learning standpoint it is desirable to learn the operation as a whole in the sequence that will be followed when the proper skill has been acquired. In actual practice this may not be feasible. The learning sequence, in order to avoid excessive scrap and learner discouragement, should follow the principle of going from the less difficult to the more difficult, even though in the beginning the instructor may have to perform certain intervening operations himself. When the supervisor must act as his own instructor in his de-

partment, this requires him to analyze the work to be taught and to plan his instruction carefully.

3. Motivation influences the rate of learning and performance. A strong incentive definitely influences the rate of learning. This incentive may take several forms; financial incentives are most effective, but the supervisor may well employ other incentives in his instruction of learners. These include competition, recognition, and ratings.

4. There seems to be a definite pattern that is followed by most learners. The work of the average learner progresses from a high degree of inaccuracy to a high degree of accuracy. The speed at which he works is slow at first but increases as he learns and practices. Every learner at the beginning is hesitant, and this hesitancy is founded on a lack of confidence. The learner's confidence in himself and his ability to do the job develop as he gains speed and accuracy. It is found that the learner's progress in developing accuracy and speed, and in overcoming his lack of confidence, parallel each other. When the work to be learned involves a large number of operations, the learner should familiarize himself with the simple operations first and progress gradually from becoming proficient in a small number of operations to becoming proficient in many operations, some of which may be simultaneously performed with both hands.

5. Instruction is a continuous process; there is no completion point at which it can be cut off. The learner may fall into improper methods by getting away from the standardized method he has learned. New techniques are developed in which the older employee must be retrained. Instruction is also required when it is necessary to train old employees in the handling of new materials on regular equipment. Finally, there is instruction of men for upgrading to more difficult work or greater responsibilities. Instruction must be followed up regularly by the supervisor. Follow-up is essential both to make sure proper methods and techniques are used (where the supervisor has staff instructors available) and to plan for revised and future instruction.

What the Supervisor May Expect from Proper Instructing. Instruction is an integral part of the supervising process. Effective training contributes to: (1) a reduction in labor turnover, (2) a reduction in material waste, (3) a reduction in the learning period, hence a reduction in instruction costs, (4) a reduction in wear and tear, as well as machine breakage, (5) increased quantity and quality production, and (6) improved morale and institutional pride. These advantages from instructing the new man and retraining the older employee are realized only when the proper procedures are followed and when everyone associated with training carries his full share of the load. Instructing is not a side line to be handled during spare time from other operating responsibilities. It is an operating responsibility. To the extent that it is properly carried out, other aspects of supervision are reduced. For instance, scrap reduction is frequently a direct result of effective instruction in the cause and cost of scrap. Quality standards almost invariably are raised when the importance of quality is clearly made known to the workers. This information is given them through follow-up instruction in addition to the initial training.

Safety and good housekeeping are also products of proper training. While the employee is learning his job the supervisor should see that he learns the safety rules and regulations of the department and those practices designed to protect him and his fellow employees. The average new employee does not have good housekeeping habits and is not waste-conscious. Each of these factors should be emphasized as part of the instruction process. It is much easier to drive home the importance and value of a clean workplace, of conserving materials and taking proper care of the machine and tools, when the employee is new than after he has become an "old-timer." Safety, good housekeeping, and waste control are habits which can be formed during the instruction stage.

12   Introducing the New Employee to His Job

First Impressions Are Lasting. Many supervisors have been on their jobs or with their companies so long that it is not easy for them to realize how a new employee feels. A gruff statement or minor neglect causes a new employee to wonder what he can expect from his new job. The new employee naturally wants to make good. He wants to like his new job and associates. The foreman is the symbol of his expectations. If he is considerate, shows the new man the things he wants to see, introduces him to his fellow workers with the same courtesy he would use in a social gathering, the new man's confidence will be strengthened. Such memories are not easily erased.

Every supervisor faces the responsibility of handling the new men hired to work in his department. Proper introduction to the job bridges the gap of turning an ill-at-ease new employee into a confident and interested veteran. Many organizations make painstaking efforts to select the best qualified man for a position. Tests of various kinds are utilized, personal interviews are used, references and recommendations are checked, and considerable expense is incurred in hiring a new employee. After the employee is hired he is sent directly to a supervisor who frequently puts him to work immediately. This is as it should be. A man is usually anxious to get started. It is the care and genuine interest manifested by the supervisor and the fellow workers that will count in such a situation. *First impressions, irrespective of their reliability, usually are lasting.* Frequently an employee who seems to have great promise fails to make good or even quits. Very often the blame rests not on employment methods but on the induction or lack of induction methods which follow the employment process.

A certain amount of anxiety is common to all new employees. The majority of people who work for others are to a greater or lesser degree afraid of their superiors, yet as a general rule, the line supervisors fail to recognize this attitude in the new men who enter their departments. This is due in part to the fact that the new employee knows little or nothing about the company, its policies and methods, the work he is being hired to perform, or his opportunities for advancement within the organization. Few supervisors realize how little confidence new employees have in themselves, the effect of their lack of confidence on their efficiency, the bearing it has on developing their attitudes, and how it may result in a lack of morale. As a matter of fact, many employees harbor a real fear of the work and of their own ability to perform it. The supervisor's objective in introducing every new employee is to develop the employee into a satisfied worker-in-his-work unit. In order to accomplish this objective the supervisor must recognize the need for a carefully planned and detailed procedure for the introduction of new employees, and the necessity for a constant and regular follow-up until the objective of a well-balanced satisfied worker has been achieved.

Feeling at Home.[1] Until the new employee acquires a "feeling of belonging" he will not have been securely inducted into his new work unit. The factors necessary to produce a satisfied well-balanced worker include: (1) a balance in interests, capacities, and opportunities, (2) confidence in himself, (3) training to meet the demands of the job, (4) knowledge and understanding, and (5) a feeling of belonging and loyalty. *The supervisor is responsible for developing every worker-in-his-work unit into a well-balanced, satisfied employee.* There are three aspects of the employee which must be considered in adjusting him to his work situation, namely, his interests, his capacities, and his opportunities. Interests refer not only to his present desires and ambitions but also to those submerged and vague yearnings of the individual. By capacities is meant the abilities, both present and potential, possessed by that employee. Opportunities include not only chances for advancement but also opportunities to exercise capacities and satisfy interests. The supervisor should strive to balance the capacities, interests, and opportunities of his men, both old and

[1] See Walter D. Scott, Robert C. Clothier, and William R. Spriegel, *Personnel Management,* McGraw-Hill Book Co., fifth edition, New York, 1954, Chapter 2, for a detailed discussion of the worker-in-his-work unit.

new, since the employee who is out of balance can lower the morale and production of an entire department.

Confidence is a function of a feeling of security, a knowledge that one has the capacity to meet the physical requirements and that one is accepted as an individual. Many new men have misgivings as to acceptance and at times the ability to perform. They worry about their ability to adjust themselves: (1) to their job and the standards required in the work, (2) to the group of employees with whom they will live and work for eight or more hours a day, and (3) to the requirements of the particular foreman. Building the new employee's confidence in himself is one of the first steps which every supervisor should take in introducing a new employee to his department. *New employees frequently lack full confidence in the company.* The supervisor has a selling job to do, for the company is on trial as well as the new employee. If the employee is not satisfied he will quit and look for another position provided conditions are favorable, or in times of depression he may stay on the job but never become fully productive. Although the supervisor should not oversell the company and the opportunities it offers new employees, he should show each new employee that the company policies are sound, that the company is sincerely interested in him, and that it will provide him with training and an opportunity for advancement consistent with the requirements of the company. Men want to be proud of their company, to have faith in its policies, and to be able to defend its standards of wages and its management. Men like to boast to their friends and family about the company for which they work.

Too often the supervisor takes it for granted that the new man came to work for the company because of the company's reputation. To a limited extent this attitude is warranted, yet to make a temporary attitude permanent requires careful planning and follow-up. To foster the favorable attitude the new employee has toward the company the supervisor should tell the new employee about the company, its history, its policies, and the opportunities it offers, without exaggeration but with personal confidence in what he says. The supervisor, in discussing opportunities, may readily point out the security the job offers. Although this is not always possible, because of conditions and circumstances beyond the company's control, the supervisor should make each new employee feel that he is secure in his job, that his job will not be subject to the whims of subordinates or others but will depend only on his satisfactory performance and the continuance of work.

Initial Instruction as a Part of the Induction Process. The induction process begins in the community where the company's reputation and traditions are well known. The employment interview is in fact a very important phase of inducting the new employee. Induction in its most effective sense begins when the new employee actually starts to work under the careful and sympathetic guidance of his instructor. The supervisor may or may not, in person, do the instructing, but he is personally responsible for seeing that the instructing is properly carried out. Instruction or training is most effective if it is given when and where it is needed. The new man should not be given all his training at the beginning, but he should be given the essentials that he needs to get started and additional instruction when and as he requires it. Training is a continual process for both new and old men. Well-trained men usually are satisfied, contented employees, whereas inadequately trained men are frequently discontented. Each new employee, as a part of the introduction to his job, should be given this knowledge and an understanding of his place in the organization as well as the work that is required of him. The supervisor should see that the new employee knows the company objectives and policies, that he is familiar with the rules and regulations under which he works, and that he realizes the meaning of the traditions and customs of the company. *Satisfied employees are always found to have a feeling of belonging, which is the foundation of loyalty to the company.* Old employees contented with their employer and job are found to have this feeling of being a part of the company. It is their company and they are proud of it and its product. With this feeling men are loyal to their company and their supervisor.

Excess Costs for Failing Properly to Start the New Man on His Job. If the supervisor does not carefully plan and thoroughly carry out his program in introducing new employees, he will encounter the following results: (1) increased labor turnover, (2) increased hiring costs, (3) disappointed and disgruntled employees, and (4) an unnecessarily long adjustment period. There are two points at which labor turnover is very high: one is the first day an employee works and the other is the time when he is being transferred from the training period to actual operation. The extent of this turnover is partly dependent on the effectiveness of the supervisor's introduction of the employee to the job. More men quit the first day than at any other time. It is expensive when a man is hired and works only a short time before quitting. Hiring costs are considerable when it is realized that they include the costs of interviewing, checking references, physical examination, putting a man on the payroll, and training him, as well as the wages paid him in excess of his productivity during the training period.

It is not unusual for the hiring and training cost for a new man to be as high as $300. Should he quit before becoming a productive worker this is a complete loss. Proper induction procedures and training reduces the quitting rate of new employees. The employee who quits is disappointed and disgruntled and will talk about his unsatisfactory experience among his friends and neighbors. Departmental employees will be dissatisfied because of the increased burden they must carry temporarily and the delays in departmental production resulting from being understaffed. Even though the employee does not quit, the fact that the supervisor has not inducted him properly leads to an unnecessarily long adjustment period. When the new employee is thrown at his work, figuratively speaking, and expected to stick, he will make many mistakes and learn incorrect work habits which are difficult to break.

Getting the New Man Off to a Good Start. Convincing the new man that he is to be an important man on the company team begins in the employment office even before he is hired. Every applicant is entitled to the same consideration in the personnel department that he would receive if he were a customer of the company. Many companies forget that applicants may later become buyers and treat the applicant with an utter lack of courtesy. The supervisor has an important role in making the new man feel that he is "wanted." (Every normal man wants to feel that he belongs, that he is "wanted.") Obviously in order to do this successfully the supervisor must be sold on the company himself and be familiar with the company's objectives, policies, rules and regulations, customs and traditions.

When the personnel department has done its job properly the new employee will have had a goodly number of things explained to him, such as wages, general working conditions, company policies, union relationships (if any), and the basis of promotions. But the supervisor must be certain that the new employee has been so informed and reassured and that the new employee understands the policies of the company. The supervisor must follow up to make certain first, that the new employee was given these facts in the personnel department and second, that he understands them clearly. If the new employee is vague about the answers to these questions it is the supervisor and his department that pay the penalty. Many companies devote a great deal of attention to their salesmen and little or no attention to the employees in their production departments. Yet in the community the best salesmen for the company product and the company as a good place to work are these same production employees, who greatly outnumber the sales force. They influence many persons in their community who may be either potential buyers or prospective employees.

The Relation of the Personnel Department to the Induction Procedure. The importance of the personnel department, not only in hiring but also in inducting new employees, cannot be overemphasized. The new employee gets his first impression of the company at this point and first impressions are often lasting. The personnel department is the best qualified department to induct the new employee into his new position, up to and including the actual job, giving him all the information he needs to start him toward becoming a well-balanced, satisfied worker-in-his-work unit. The personnel department, because of its position, can show the new employee the relationship of his particular job to the enterprise as a whole, pointing out to him his place in the organization and how he contributes to the objectives of the enterprise. Many a man lacks interest in his work because he does not see where his job fits in with the other operations. The personnel department should define the terms of service to the new employee, telling him about hours of work, shift rotation, overtime, holidays, sick leave, absences and tardiness, wages, pay period, pay day, deductions from wages, insurance, vacations, and other information contained in the published personnel policies, rules, and regulations. In the personnel department the new employee should be given an accurate description of the duties and responsibilities of his job. Job descriptions when available are very helpful. The new employee should be shown the opportunities for advancement, and promotion charts, if available, are definite indicators to the new man that his company will give him promotion opportunities in line with his capacities.

A substantial number of large companies operate a formal induction program when they are hiring a number of people. Some of the items covered and explained in an induction program may include the history of the company, description of the company products with their method of manufacture and their uses, the organization of the company and its industrial relations policies, employee service activities, company plant and departmental activities, the importance of safety, and job routines. Sound slide films, movies, conferences, and lectures led by various departmental representatives, tours, displays, bulletin boards, and booklets may all be used. The cost of such programs and the personnel required to handle the work are minor considerations in comparison with the results obtained. Such programs create a good first impression, start the new employee off well sold on his company, with a foundation on which loyalty and morale may be built.

A portion of the outline of the indoctrination procedure of the Clark Equipment Company, Buchanan plant, is given below:

1. Personnel Department Orientation Interview—Built around Employee Handbook:
    1.1 Job title
    1.2 Department
    1.3 Rate of pay; starting rate, automatic raises, incentive, etc.
    1.4 Shift starting
    1.5 Lunch period
    1.6 Quitting time
    1.7 First aid facilities and their importance
    1.8 Safety program
    1.9 Parking
    1.10 Employee's responsibility as a good worker
    1.11 Attendance
    1.12 Plant rules
    1.13 Inform employee regarding vacation, pension plan, holiday pay, Christmas party, annual picnic, Clark News
    1.14 Employee also informed on joining union in 30 days, 3-month probationary period, bidding on jobs, finger printing
    1.15 Consultation with foreman advised
    1.16 Personnel department willing to assist at any time
2. Safety glasses, safety shoes
3. Safety film   (See Figure 12.1)
4. Employee returned to supervisor. The supervisor explains:
    4.1 The rate of the job
    4.2 The shift
        4.21 Starting time
        4.22 Lunch time
        4.23 Quitting time
    4.3 Importance of regular and prompt attendance
    4.4 Importance of good workmanship
    4.5 Personal tools
5. Probationary rating card forwarded to supervisor for appraisal 15 days prior to the expiration of an employee's probationary period

Many companies overlook the importance of the personal escort for the new employee to his place of work. This is not a job for an errand boy. Since first impressions are lasting the escort should be a person especially assigned to this work. The new employee may ask ques-

Courtesy Clark Equipment Company

Figure 12.1.   New employees viewing a safety film during the induction procedure.

tions of importance that require clear-cut answers.   In large organizations it may be a considerable distance from the place of employment to the department where the new employee will work and during this trip the escort can begin to build interest in and loyalty to the company in the new employee.   He should be able to answer questions about the company, its products, its policies, and even about the department to which the new man is assigned and the job on which he will work.   In some companies the supervisor goes in person to the employment office to escort the new men to his department, taking advantage of this opportunity to talk with his men as he walks back to his department.   In other cases a well-informed departmental clerk may go to get the new men.

The Supervisor's Responsibility.   The supervisor may be assisted in inducting the new employee by representatives of staff departments, personnel, and safety, but these departments are merely facilitating agencies with the real responsibility resting in the line where it belongs.   If the personnel department only hires men and is unable to induct them, the responsibility for introducing them then rests entirely on the supervisor.   When the personnel department not only hires but also partially inducts the new men, then the supervisor's job consists of follow-up and training.   After a follow-up of the induction program of the personnel department to make certain the new man understood what he was told, the instruction and training of the new employee begin. Whatever the method used to introduce the new man to his job, the supervisor must be sure he gets started properly. During the hiring period, many of the things told the prospective employee go in one ear and out the other, for his mind is on getting the job, not on what he is told about the job. The supervisor will find it a safe procedure to review with each new employee his wage rate, increases, pay period and pay day, hours, shifts, holidays, absences, and industrial relations policies. The next step in the introduction process then is to acquaint the man with the department, its work and operations, his job, and the instruction and training he will receive. The wise supervisor will point out the washroom, show the new man the location of the time clock and how to operate it, see that he knows where the lunchroom is and that he meets some of his fellow employees. Many supervisors see that one of the old employees takes the new man to lunch the first day.

Safety training is essential in the early stages of the induction process and must be diligently followed up. The new employee should be introduced to the safety rules and regulations. This may be done by the safety department as part of the induction program or it may be done by the personnel department, but again the supervisor is responsible for seeing that every new employee knows and understands the safety practices of the company and of the particular department in which he is employed. Too many supervisors let the new man pick up the safety rules for himself, from the bulletin boards, a company safety booklet, or from the other employees. Every supervisor owes it to his men, to himself, and to each new employee to instruct his new employees carefully in the safety rules and regulations and to be certain they are understood and will be followed.

The actual job instruction may or may not be done by the supervisor. It is the supervisor's responsibility, although he may delegate it, to give the new man instructions in and training on the work to which he is assigned. When the supervisor has used the right method of introducing a new man to his department and the departmental morale is high, he can ordinarily see that the new employee is introduced to several old employees and let them carry on the introduction and instruction process. Even though someone else may actually do the instructing the supervisor may profitably drop by the new man's workplace within the first few hours to ask him how things are going. At this time he may show him how to do something that may be causing him trouble. The worker likes to be instructed by his supervisor.

The introduction of new employees need not be a lengthy process;

the introductory interview with the new employee need not take more than ten to fifteen minutes. The supervisor is interested only in getting acquainted with the new man, reviewing or giving him essential information about the department and his work, and beginning to win the man's confidence. Then the supervisor will normally turn him over to a trusted employee who is capable of completing the introduction and carrying out the instruction program. The supervisor, however, must follow up new employees just as he does his other responsibilities. Really to learn to know the man he must contact him frequently, especially during the first weeks of his employment.

The role of the supervisor in the induction of new employees is well illustrated by a quotation from Thompson Products, Inc., Supervisory Manual, as follows:

INDUCTING NEW AND TRANSFERRED WORKERS

Remember, more than anything else, a new employee wants the respect, approval and friendship of his boss. A foreman or a supervisor can make a friend of a man or woman for life simply by steering them through adjustment periods in a friendly, sympathetic manner.

GET WHAT INFORMATION YOU NEED FROM THE PERSONNEL DIVISION

Always keep in mind that employment interviewers select the new worker for employment at Tapco because they believe he will fit into the Thompson Products Organization, and that he has a good work attitude.

1. Check with the Employment Office and find out what is known about the new employee's work habits, character and background.

2. Check the employment records of transferred workers starting in your group. This is important.

3. Be sure that all new employees meet the Divisional Personnel Manager or Personnel Supervisor.

ORIENT THE WORKER

1. Explain the department's function and the part he is expected to play in the department.

2. Check with the worker to be sure that he understands the rules and regulations which affect him.

INDUCT THE NEW WORKER INTO THE GROUP

Introduce the new worker to one of the leading employees in the group who will help him get acquainted.

Guide the new worker carefully during the 60 day probationary period. Help the worker capitalize on his good traits and to correct bad ones such as failures in punctuality, orderliness, starting work promptly, putting in a full seven and one-half hours, etc. Compliment the worker who has dexterity, and try to make the best use of his abilities by using him where he is best fitted. Observe the new worker's ability to get along with people, and compliment him for it. Try to place him in a group where close teamwork is essential.

Help the worker avoid friction points, and minimize unfavorable traits. Encourage the timid worker to mix with his associates, and tone down the over-aggressive person.

Tactfully try to eliminate offensive personal habits such as profanity, spitting, B.O., etc.

Some persons believe it is a mark of friendship to borrow tools, where the opposite is true. Encourage workers to buy their own tools as soon as possible.

Encourage good housekeeping. Failure in this respect leaves a bad impression of both the employee and the department.

CHECK UP ON THE PROGRESS OF THE NEW WORKER

1. End of the first day—make sure the worker has locker facilities. Knows how and where to ring time card and trailer card. Knows location of rest rooms, cafeteria, parking lot, etc.

2. End of the first week—Be sure to let the worker know how he is getting along. Be sure he has met the General Foreman, and that he is familiar with the department rules. Check to find out if the worker has any questions to ask.

3. End of the 30 day period—Tell the worker that you are putting through his 30 day raise. (Effective on Monday preceding the end of thirty day period.) In the case of an exceptional employee, don't wait 30 days before taking this action.

4. End of 60 day probationary period—If the new worker measures up to the requirements of the job, approach him and tell him he has officially become a member of the team. If the new worker does not measure up to the requirements of the job, now is the time to release him to the Employment Office.

The Sponsor System. The sponsor system has merit in getting the new man off to a good start and ties the sponsor into the management team. One man in each department, selected because of his personal interest in people, handles all new employees. This person carries through the introduction and instruction program after the foreman has initially interviewed the new employee. The sponsor sees to it that the new employee meets his fellow employees, accompanies him to lunch, and aids him in making the minor adjustments so essential to new employees. The sponsor may also be the instructor who trains the new man in the duties of his position. This method avoids the pitfalls that may arise through the new employee's contacting disgruntled employees early in his experience with the company.

The Need for Follow-up. Follow-up is as essential in dealing with new employees as it is in promoting safe practices or in maintaining quality. After a certain period of time the new employee may receive an appointment card from the personnel department for a follow-up interview. In some companies the new man receives a personal letter from one of the top executives welcoming him to the company and giving him some specific and interesting information about the company, its products, and its policies. The supervisor will want to check on the man's progress in learning his work, on his understanding and practice of the safety rules and regulations, and on his familiarity with company policies. When the supervisor delegates the responsibilities for the introduction and instruction of new men, he must not forget that he cannot delegate his own personal responsibility for delegation. The supervisor's follow-up will include checking both the man to whom he delegated his responsibility and the progress of the new employee. Nothing is more stimulating to a new employee than to have the supervisor, whom he met the first day of work, stop by to say "hello" and inquire about his progress. On the other hand, no supervisor can learn to know and understand his new men unless he does follow up and talk to them frequently. Certainly every supervisor, after introducing the new man to the job, will want to follow him up the next day, the following day, at the end of the first week, and again at the end of the second week. He should want to know what difficulties and troubles the new man is encountering and whether he is adjusting himself to the work and to his fellow employees. Follow-up on the part of the supervisor not only builds the employee's confidence in the supervisor but also will frequently catch minor grievances before they begin to grow.

When the supervisor follows up new men he can talk to them either in his office or at their workplace. Frequently the latter is more convenient but certainly the former is the more effective. Talking to the man in the supervisor's office means the supervisor will have the man's undivided attention. He is more likely to be frank with the supervisor and the interview will be less hurried. The introductory interview and these follow-up interviews will reveal to the supervisor certain characteristics common to new men. The new man is perplexed and often fearful. He is meeting strange people as well as strange work and methods. He is anxious to succeed and he may do things that evidence over-anxiety to do the job well. He will frequently have doubts as to his progress and a major reason for the follow-up by the supervisor is to relieve these doubts. Every supervisor who will remember when he last started a new job and how he felt, and who plans his introduction of new employees accordingly, will find that he has taken a long step forward in turning a new man into a well-balanced satisfied worker.[2]

[2] For a further discussion of this subject, see Walter D. Scott, Robert C. Clothier, and William R. Spriegel, *op. cit.,* Chapter 2, "The Worker-in-His-Work Unit," and Chapter 19, "Introducing the Worker to His Job."

13

The Supervisor and Motion and Time Study

What Is Motion and Time Study? Frank Gilbreth, its founder, defined motion study as "the science of eliminating wastefulness resulting from using unnecessary, ill-directed and inefficient motions." He defined time study as "the art of recording, analyzing, and synthesizing the time of the elements of any operation, usually a manual operation, but it has also been extended to mental and machinery operations." [1] This definition of Gilbreth's is still a good one, with the possible elimination of his emphasis on its manual aspects. Time study is an accurate analysis of the time required to perform an operation or some part thereof. A time study may be made without a motion study but it is better to have the motion study precede the time study.

A careful motion analysis of an operation may be made without an accompanying time study; however, a careful timing of the operation after the motion study is desirable. The timing of an operation provides time standards that are valuable in measuring the performance of the workers. These time standards also provide a desirable base for wage incentive systems. The careful motion analysis will indicate the best method of performing the operation. It may require a new layout or new equipment. When all of the conditions indicated by the motion study (including the training of the operator) have been met, most of the advantages have been realized. The timing of the revised operation merely completes the study and provides the desired time standards.

[1] Frank B. Gilbreth, *The Primer of Scientific Management,* D. Van Nostrand Company, New York, 1914, p. 8.

The Supervisor's Interest in Motion and Time Study. Dr. Lillian Gilbreth, the cofounder of motion and time study, has said:

It is essential that supervisors know about motion and time study. Questions will be brought to them. They should know the answers. It is hoped that they not only know about, but believe in motion and time study—for this belief will be passed on to the workers, consciously or unconsciously.

The supervisor who looks upon his job as helping his workers turn out the quantity and quality of work expected, will find his knowledge of motion and time study a *plus* on his job. In time the supervisor is certain to question his own methods of doing his work. This will lead to increased efficiency in performing his own duties. A supervisor's knowledge of motion and time study increases his technical proficiency as well as his appreciation of the problems in human relations.[2]

A supervisor's primary responsibility is the directing of the efforts of his men in getting out production. Studies have shown that the supervisors who are employee oriented in their attitudes get out more production than the ones who are production oriented. Some enthusiast may readily misinterpret this observation to mean that the supervisor need not be especially proficient in methods of production. Nothing could be further from the facts. Workers like to have their supervisors interested in them as individuals, but they also want their supervisors to help them as individuals to do their jobs more efficiently. The employees know that the only basis for their pay is production. They like to follow a leader who knows how to do the job and to show them how it can be done better and more efficiently. (Of course, they do not expect the general foreman to be an expert in each job he supervises.) A supervisor's knowledge of the basic principles of motion and time study enables him to improve the layout of the workplace, to locate hand tools advantageously and suggest changes in the location of controls on the machines, to simplify operations, to minimize walking, to locate material and parts more conveniently, and to be a real teacher and consultant to his men. When a supervisor can do these things for his men and convince them that he wants to help them in their work, he is certain to be accepted in a real sense as their leader. Such a foreman is employee oriented in the truest sense.

Although the supervisor need not be an expert motion and time study man, he should be familiar with the techniques and procedures of motion analysis and taking time studies. Space will not permit our describing the fine points of motion and time study. The supervisor

[2] In a letter to the author, 1954.

can readily learn these from any standard text in the field. He can also get instruction from the time study men in his plant. Most time study engineers would consider it a compliment to have a supervisor ask them to explain the details of: (1) the preliminary study, (2) the motion analysis, (3) the actual taking of the time study, and (4) the making of the needed changes suggested by the analysis. Since the supervisor has an intimate acquaintance with all of his jobs he is in an excellent position to make use of the motion study even though he may not always have the time to take a detailed time study.

A trained motion and time study engineer's basic trait is an inquiring attitude of mind. He accepts practically nothing as being the best possible method of doing a particular task until he has systematically explored the possibilities of doing it by a simpler or easier method. In a very real sense he is scientifically oriented. When a supervisor begins to look upon every operation as providing an opportunity for improvement he will have acquired the most important phase of becoming a motion and time study man. The employee oriented foreman practices consultive supervision by interesting his workers in improving their individual operations.

The Supervisor's Questioning Attitude. The progressive supervisor does not go through his daily routine questioning every act, order, and instruction from his superiors; neither does he constantly question his men. The person whose acts are constantly being scrutinized is himself. He constantly questions the operations for which he is responsible, not out of a feeling of frustration or insecurity, but from a sincere desire to find a better way. Such a supervisor usually has his own work well organized. He attacks one job at a time and devotes enough concentrated effort to look at it in its entirety from many angles. Naturally he should analyze the most important phase of his responsibilities first, the one that is most likely to result in the greatest saving. He is not lured to make a 50 per cent saving on a $10 per day expense and to ignore a possible 5 per cent saving on a $1000 per day item.

The supervisor who recognizes that no operation approaches perfection applies the six-way test to each operation that he seeks to improve. He asks:

1. *What* is being done? What is the purpose of the operation?
2. *Why* is the operation performed at all? Is all of the operation necessary? Could the part be modified so as to eliminate the necessity for this operation?

3. *Who* is doing the work? Could modifications be made so that a person with less skill could do it?

4. *Where* does the work need to be done? Is this the best place to do it or could it be done more economically elsewhere?

5. *When* should the work be done? Could it be done more cheaply earlier or later?

6. *How* is the work being done, assuming that it should continue to be done here and now according to present specifications? Can the principles of motion analysis show improvements to be made in handling the parts, the machine and tools being used, or the motions in performing the operation? [3]

A Check List for Work Simplification. Herman A. Straus, Supervisor of Work Simplification at Servel, Inc., in a speech before the Industrial Management Society (1950) presented a thought-provoking list of things to be considered before making a motion and time study. This list could profitably become a part of the working kit of the supervisor who would improve his operations. This list includes the following items:

Material

1. Can cheaper material be used without impairing quality?
2. Can lighter gauge material be used advantageously? Heavier?
3. Can part be made from offal?
4. Can standard stock parts be purchased?
5. Can some use be found for scrap and rejected parts?
6. Is it received in the most economical length? Size? Weight? Shape? Finish?
7. Is it utilized to the fullest extent?
8. Should we change from "make" to "buy," or from "buy" to "make"?

Design

1. Can part be eliminated completely? Partly?
2. Will it help to change tolerances? Specifications?
3. Can it be changed to make fabrication easier? Cheaper? Reduce scrap?

Sequence

1. Is every operation necessary? Can part of it be eliminated?
2. Is every operation performed at the right time? Place? In the right way?
3. Is plant layout the best that can be obtained?
4. Can operations be combined? Separated?
5. Is it economical to use conveyors to move materials?
6. Would change in lot size help?

[3] Adapted from the Motorola Corporation's manual, *Finding Better and Easier Ways to Work,* 1949, p. 9.

7. Can inspection be made a part of operation?

8. Can operations be performed while material is in transit?

Tools, gauges, equipment, and workplace

1. Is the machine the best type for the job? Can it be improved? Is it in good condition?

2. Is it running at the right speed?

3. Would it be economical to make it automatic?

4. Are the machine controls conveniently located for the operator? Are they easy to use? Are they safe? Can they be made automatic?

5. Must the operator continue holding controls after the machine starts for safety's sake or merely because controls are made that way?

6. Is material received and disposed of in suitable containers? Delivered to point of use? Any unnecessary handling?

7. Are tools and materials pre-positioned and in proper sequence for use?

8. Is it necessary to clamp part? If so, are clamps quick-acting?

9. Is it easy to locate parts in the fixture?

10. Can an automatic feed be used?

11. Is disposal automatic?

12. Are tools and fixtures the best that can be designed for the job?

13. Can combination tools be used?

14. Are proper gauges quickly available? Easy to use?

15. Can parts be made in multiple? One at a time? With another part?

16. Is workplace satisfactorily illuminated? Heated? Ventilated?

17. Is workplace properly laid out?

Operator

1. Can he perform his work either sitting or standing?

2. Does he do unnecessary positioning? Holding? Reaching? Bending? Turning? Walking?

3. Is he properly performing the job? Would further instructions help?

4. Will it help to change to a taller operator? A shorter one? A more dexterous one?

5. Is material handling by operator reduced to a minimum?

6. Are both hands productively occupied?

7. Is the work balanced between the two hands?

8. Can work now being done by the hands be relieved by foot devices? Automatic devices? Holding jigs? Indexing fixtures?

9. Are operators on similar jobs using the same methods?

The Supervisor and Job Methods Training. Tens of thousands of supervisors were trained during World War II by the twin programs of the War Man Power Commission, Job Instructor Training (JIT) and Job Methods Training (JMT). These programs were excellent but so short that they soon were forgotten unless they were followed up by higher supervision or refresher courses. The famous little cards that were common sights in the pockets of supervisors set forth in dramatic form the steps to be followed in improving methods. In substance these cards on "How to Improve Your Job" read as follows:

Step 1.   Break the job down into its elements
   1. List all of the details of the job exactly as it is now being done
   2. These details should include
      2.1   Material handling
      2.2   Machine work
      2.3   Hand work

Step 2.   Question every detail of the present method
   1. Answer each of the following questions:
      1.1   Why is the operation needed
      1.2   What is its purpose
      1.3   Where should it be done
      1.4   When should it be done
      1.5   Who is best qualified to do it
      1.6   How is the best way to do it
   2. Question the
      2.1   Appropriateness and suitability of the product design, materials, machines, equipment, tools, workplace, and layout
      2.2   The effectiveness of the safety practices and housekeeping

Step 3.   Develop the new method
   1. Eliminate any detail that is not needed
   2. Combine operations or details when practical
   3. Rearrange operations, layout, and workplace
   4. Simplify necessary details
      4.1   Make the work easier or safer
      4.2   Pre-position materials, tools, and equipment in the proper order and place
      4.3   Use gravity-feed hoppers and drop-delivery chutes
      4.4   Use jigs and fixtures for holding work
      4.5   Have both hands doing useful work
   5. Work out your ideas with others
   6. Write up your new method

Step 4.   Apply the new method
   1. Sell your plan to the boss
   2. Sell the new method to your workers
   3. Get final approval from all concerned on safety, quality, quantity, and cost
   4. Put the new method to work; use it until a better one is developed
   5. Give credit where credit is due

The Supervisor and the Preliminary Motion Analysis.   The supervisor should be consulted by the time study engineer prior to making the preliminary motion and time study. In the first place the job as it is being performed at that time may be one for which changes have already been ordered. It would be embarrassing for the time study engineer to recommend changes that already were being planned. Further, he should have the advantage of the previous thinking in doing the analysis that he is undertaking. In addition to the help the industrial engineer will get by having access to all of the previous planning and thinking on the job the supervisor's attention will be directed to the job. It is not unusual for the supervisor to make suggestions for revising an operation when he discusses it with the time study man during the preliminary survey. Occasionally the time study man, when he is hard pressed for time, may suggest to the supervisor that he study the job before the motion and time study is made. In this event he would go to another assignment, merely dropping by the department to discuss the progress being made by the supervisor or to give suggestions.

Later when the time study man returns to make his detailed study he will make an accurate record of its status as it is, note suggested changes planned by the supervisor, and begin his work from that basis. Naturally, full credit will be given to the supervisor for his work. Often the supervisor will call on the industrial engineering department for help in analyzing jobs and the timing of these jobs. The relationship is one of cooperation.

Advantages to Be Secured through Motion and Time Study. The advantages of motion and time studies, which include the preliminary studies, may be listed as follows:

1. Time standards are established that may be used as a basis for setting incentive rates or for setting goals that may reasonably be expected from the workers. (Unfortunately, there seems to be a tendency for workers to work substantially below their capacities when they know *that management does not know how much work should be done.*) Even where there is no deliberate restriction of production, positive standards that are known serve as incentives or goals to employees. When workers know what is expected of them this knowledge becomes a steady pull to make the standard.

2. Carefully established standards resulting from motion and time study exert a salutary influence upon the general morale of the employees, particularly when the savings are shared with the employees.

3. Motion and time study analysis frequently results in changing methods of performing operations and in the devising of more efficient production procedures or safer and less fatiguing operations. While increased productivity is nearly always an objective, reduced accidents or fatigue are also desired goals.

4. Motion analysis frequently suggests improvements in equipment or tools. If the suggested changes are not easily made on the machines in

current use they may readily be incorporated in new machines that may be purchased.

5. The detailed motion analysis and time study provide a record from which job specifications for employment use may be made. These records are also available in case the particular job may be discontinued for a time and later be started up. The job operation card with the accompanying standard times is made from these records.

General Rules to Follow in Trying to Improve an Operation. Experience has shown that certain general rules or procedures when followed increase output and minimize fatigue. Briefly these are:

1. Finger, hand, arm, and shoulder movements require the least effort and time according to the following order:
   1.1   Finger motions only
   1.2   Fingers and wrist motions
   1.3   Fingers, wrist, and forearm
   1.4   Fingers, wrist, forearm, and upper arm
   1.5   Fingers, wrist, forearm, upper arm, and shoulder

2. Hands and arms should be moved in opposite directions and at the same time in so far as practical. This synchronizing of movements promotes balance, reduces concentration and attention required, and facilitates learning.

3. Tools and materials should be so located in front of the worker as to minimize the distance to be moved. (See Figure 13.1 for vertical and horizontal distances and areas.)

4. All tools and materials should be in a definite and fixed place. By so placing them the worker can automatically locate them with a minimum of attention and effort.

5. Where possible use gravity feed bins for material and drop delivery chutes for the finished part.

6. The hands should be relieved of all work that can be done better by the feet or that can be done by the feet while the hands are otherwise in use.

7. Jigs, fixtures, and other holding devices free the hands for productive use.

8. Pre-position tools and materials where possible.

9. Parts should be made in multiples when possible. Gang milling and drilling illustrate this procedure.

10. The use of quick acting clamps and ejectors reduces handling time.

Taking a Time Study. It is suggested that the supervisor study the technical aspects of taking a time study in any standard text on the subject or in some text on industrial management.[4] Space will permit only our showing a representative time study sheet (which is largely

---

[4] See Ralph M. Barnes, *Motion and Time Study,* John Wiley & Sons, third edition, New York, 1949; also William R. Spriegel and Richard H. Lansburgh, *Industrial Management,* John Wiley & Sons, fifth edition, New York, 1955, Chapters 18–21.

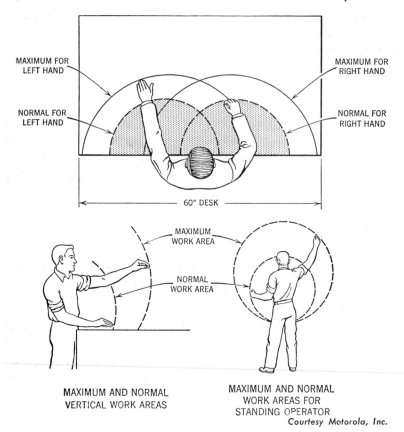

Figure 13.1. Chart showing work areas for most efficient operations.

self explanatory) and a decimal stop watch. Figure 13.2 is a typical decimal stop watch. The large face has 100 divisions. Each division represents 0.01 minute. Figures 13.3 and 13.4 show the front of an observation time study sheet and its back. Figure 13.3 records the elements being observed and the actual observed times. The R-readings are the continuous readings and the T-columns represent the difference between the two continuous readings or the time for the particular element.

At the bottom of the observation sheet is a summary of the readings and computations. It will be observed that abnormal readings are cancelled and not counted. For instance in the first column, "Pick up new casting, place into fixture, tighten two screw clamps," the reading 30 is cancelled. The number of readings in this column that is used is 9 instead of the 10 taken. The totals of T divided by the number of readings gives the average for the observed T's. In column 1 this average selected time is .187. When the rating factor is applied to this time (.95 in column 1), the elemental base time is secured (.187 for column 1). The next recording at the bottom is the number of occurrences per unit (occurr. per unit); for column 1 it is 1. However, for the last column ("Get new box of castings—25 pcs. per box") it is 1/25. This figure divided into the elemental base time gives the base time per unit (.187 for column 1).

Courtesy Ralph M. Barnes, "Motion and Time Study," John Wiley & Sons

Figure 13.2. Stop watch.

Figure 13.4 summarizes the data from Figure 13.3, gives the detailed specifications of the operation and computes standard time per unit, the standard units per hour, and the piece rate. It is essential that complete records be made of time studies should they be used at later dates.

Standard Time Data. The supervisor may not be called upon to figure the time for his jobs, but he should be familiar with the nature of standard time data when the motion and time study department uses them. By using standard time values for operations the time study man may compute synthetic time standards without actually timing the job. There are at least two kinds of synthetic time studies: (1) those built up from time studies of similar operations in the plant using those elements that are common, and (2) those built up from basic body movements for which time values have been established. A substantial number of companies have built up over the years basic data from which they may estimate the time for new operations having the same basic elements as previous operations. When careful data covering various elements have been accumulated, these data may be used in establishing synthetic time values for similar operations. All that is necessary is to construct a detailed operation sheet for the task and select the appropriate elemental times for each element from time

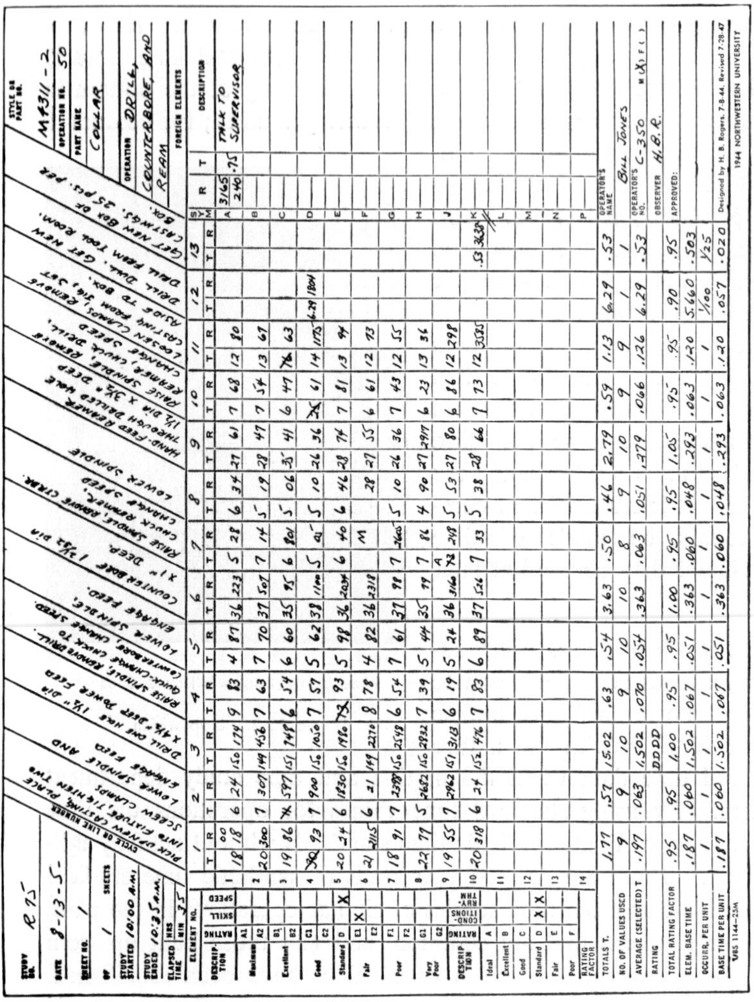

Courtesy H. Barrett Rogers and Claude George

Figure 13.3. Observation side of time study sheet. For convenience, the watch readings shown in the R columns may be recorded in pencil. The subtracted times shown in the T columns, as well as all other calculations and identification data, should be recorded in ink for permanency.

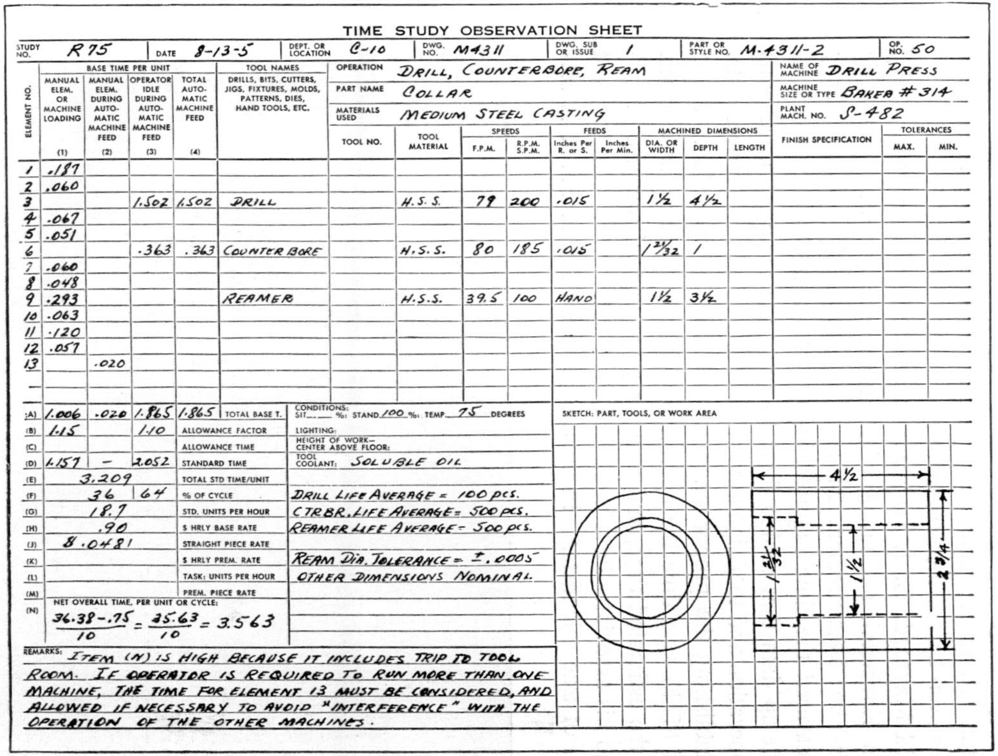

TIME STUDY OBSERVATION SHEET

STUDY NO. R75 | DATE 8-13-5 | DEPT. OR LOCATION C-10 | DWG. NO. M4311 | DWG. SUB OR ISSUE 1 | PART OR STYLE NO. M-4311-2 | OP. NO. 50

OPERATION: DRILL, COUNTERBORE, REAM
PART NAME: COLLAR
MATERIALS USED: MEDIUM STEEL CASTING
NAME OF MACHINE: DRILL PRESS
MACHINE SIZE OR TYPE: BAKER #314
PLANT MACH. NO. S-482

ELEMENT NO.	(1) Manual elem. or machine loading	(2) Manual elem. during automatic machine feed	(3) Operator idle during automatic machine feed	(4) Total automatic machine feed	Tool names	Tool no.	Tool material	Speeds F.P.M.	Speeds R.P.M. S.P.M.	Feeds Inches per R. or S.	Feeds Inches per Min.	Dia. or width	Depth	Length	Finish specification	Tolerances Max.	Tolerances Min.
1	.187																
2	.060																
3			1.502	1.502	DRILL		H.S.S.	79	200	.015		1½	4½				
4	.067																
5	.051																
6			.363	.363	COUNTER BORE		H.S.S.	80	185	.015		1 21/32	1				
7	.060																
8	.048																
9	.293				REAMER		H.S.S.	39.5	100	HAND		1½	3½				
10	.063																
11	.120																
12	.057																
13		.020															

	(1)	(2)	(3)	(4)	
(A)	1.006	.020	1.865	1.865	TOTAL BASE T.
(B)	1.15		1.10		ALLOWANCE FACTOR
(C)					ALLOWANCE TIME
(D)	1.157	—	2.052		STANDARD TIME
(E)	3.209				TOTAL STD TIME/UNIT
(F)	36	64			% OF CYCLE
(G)	18.7				STD. UNITS PER HOUR
(H)	.90				$ HRLY BASE RATE
(J)	8.0481				STRAIGHT PIECE RATE
(K)					$ HRLY PREM. RATE
(L)					TASK: UNITS PER HOUR
(M)					PREM. PIECE RATE

(N) NET OVERALL TIME, PER UNIT OR CYCLE: $\frac{36.38-.75}{10} = \frac{35.63}{10} = 3.563$

CONDITIONS: SIT.___%: STAND 100 %: TEMP 75 DEGREES
LIGHTING:
HEIGHT OF WORK-CENTER ABOVE FLOOR:
TOOL COOLANT: SOLUBLE OIL

DRILL LIFE AVERAGE = 100 pcs.
CTRBR. LIFE AVERAGE = 500 pcs.
REAMER LIFE AVERAGE = 500 pcs.
REAM DIA. TOLERANCE = ±.0005
OTHER DIMENSIONS NOMINAL

SKETCH: PART, TOOLS, OR WORK AREA

REMARKS: ITEM (N) IS HIGH BECAUSE IT INCLUDES TRIP TO TOOL ROOM. IF OPERATOR IS REQUIRED TO RUN MORE THAN ONE MACHINE, THE TIME FOR ELEMENT 13 MUST BE CONSIDERED, AND ALLOWED IF NECESSARY TO AVOID "INTERFERENCE" WITH THE OPERATION OF THE OTHER MACHINES.

Courtesy H. Barrett Rogers and Claude George

Figure 13.4. Write-up side of time study sheet (back of Figure 13.3), showing the method of calculating the standard allowed time for the operation, as well as data essential for future use of the time study for comparisons and the development of standard time data. The sketch may be freehand and should be sufficiently complete to show the shapes and dimensions directly associated with the operation.

values already established for similar work. The total of the elemental times, when adjusted for allowances for fatigue and other conditions, gives the operating time allowed for the operation. The use of synthetic standard times enables the production department to plan its schedules even before the first piece has been produced.

Harold Maynard, G. J. Stegemerten, and John L. Schwab, of the Methods Engineering Council of Pittsburgh, have developed their Methods-Time Measurement, MTM as it is popularly known.[5] They have measured the time required for the elemental body movements and built up data that enable them to study the required movements for an operation and to assign time values for each of these movements, thus establishing the proper standard time for the operation. Some users of MTM also time the operation with a stop watch as a check against the estimated time, and also for psychological reasons. Maynard and his associates have published their data, which is in the best tradition of true scientists.[6] In addition to the value of MTM in set-

Courtesy Texas Instruments

Figure 13.5. A work simplification class in session.

[5] See Harold B. Maynard, G. J. Stegemerten, and John L. Schwab, *Methods-Time Measurement*, McGraw-Hill Book Co., New York, 1948.

[6] See *Factory Management and Maintenance*, Feb. 1948, pp. 98–104, and Aug. 1950, pp. 84–91.

ting standards it is used in connection with methods improvements. It tends to develop a motion consciousness in the analyst which leads almost inevitably to methods improvements wherever MTM studies are made.

In general the steps in using established time values for elemental body movements are as follows:

1. Separate the operation into its basic elements.
2. Separate each operation element into its therbligs, or elemental body movements.

    2.1   If two or more body movements are executed simultaneously, the time required for the longest therblig is controlling.

    2.2   In some cases simultaneous body movements do not have the same time elements as each movement does when executed alone. This difference must be allowed for in computations. (MTM has worked out these situations more completely than in any published data known to the author.)

Courtesy The Frank G. Hough Co.

Figure 13.6. Supervisors participating in a four-session course in motion and time study techniques

3. Assign time values for each therblig in each operation element.

4. Total the time values for each therblig in each operation element.

5. Add allowances for fatigue and similar conditions to determine the required operating time.

6. It is not necessary to apply a leveling factor when MTM values are used. The MTM values are for the average man working under normal conditions at an average speed.

The supervisor is not expected to be an expert in synthetic time studies. Nevertheless, he should be acquainted with the principles behind them. By understanding the method of building up synthetic time standards he is in a position to explain them to his men. All too often some supervisors join their men in complaining that standard times are too short when in fact they have little reason for their stand other than the complaints of some of their workers. The supervisor should support his men when they are right and try to explain to them their mistakes when they are wrong. A clear understanding of the principles of motion and time study helps a supervisor do his job. (See Figure 13.5.) It would be excellent training for a supervisor if he could have six months' to a year's actual experience in the motion and time study department. He would acquire skills and a way of analyzing jobs that would contribute a great deal to the solution of many of his operating problems. A few companies give their supervisors short courses in the basic principles of motion and time study (see Figure 13.6).

14

Wage Administration and Merit Rating

The Nature of Wages. Wages include all of the remuneration that the employee receives for his work. This remuneration is made up of *money wages* and *fringe benefits*. Fringe benefits consist of all benefits that the employee receives, such as pensions, workmen's compensation, insurance policies paid in part or entirely by the employer, the employer's part of the social security tax, hospitalization and medical care charges paid by the employer over and above that part that would otherwise be a charge to the employer as a cost inherent in the work hazards, any contributions to mutual benefit associations by the employer, cafeteria costs absorbed by the employer, and any other costs such as those for recreation, and educational activities not directly contributing to worker efficiency. In addition to fringe benefits there are three kinds of wages that must be considered: real wages, monetary wages, and intangible wages. *Real wages* are wages in terms of the goods and services that may be bought with the money received as wages. A man's real wage may differ widely from his monetary wage. *Monetary wages* are the actual dollars and cents that the man receives or that are credited to him in his pay envelope. The money withheld by the employer for income tax and social security taxes is a part of an employee's money wages even though he never sees it nor thinks of it as his. *Intangible wages,* the third type, include those services, such as good schools, good drinking water, sewers, and garbage collection, found in the community where the employees live. There are many plants that must pay higher monetary wages to offset the lack of such advantages to the men they employ. *The most important wage, however, is the real wage.*

When comparing wages in one period with another or in comparing wages in one community with another it is important to distinguish real wages from monetary wages. From the standpoint of the man and his standard of living, the real wage is the vital factor. The real wage is measured by the goods and services that can be purchased with the monetary wage. The monetary wage is represented by the actual monetary units which the individual receives. A man who receives $90 per week and has to pay $80 per month rent for a home, with other living costs proportionately high, is in a relatively worse position than another who receives only $50 per week and pays $40 per month for rent with other living costs correspondingly low. Most executives have recognized this situation, but many labor leaders have either refused to recognize it or failed to comprehend its significance. The intangibles are also important. Many a man will take less in his pay envelope when better living conditions and good schools are available.

The Supervisor's Interest in Wage Administration. Although wages are not the sole concern of employees, they do serve as a focal point of many grievances and the rallying ground for much of the labor-management strife, particularly during contract negotiations between unions and management. The well-informed supervisor will know the vital factors that are included in wage administration: output, going rate in the community, cost of living, and the relationship of wages in one job classification to those in another. He must understand the factors that are sometimes raised in connection with wages, such as the needs of a particular employee, length of service, seasonal or steady work, and the ability of a particular company to pay a higher scale. Each supervisor should have:

1. A sound economic background of wage determination including a thorough operating knowledge of job classification and rating
2. A knowledge of the details of the wage system used in his department and the ability to explain it to his employees
3. The ability to rate his employees in terms of those items that are pertinent to their wages (the rating of employees is desirable in selecting employees for transfer and promotion even though the wage system may not be tied into the rating)

The supervisor should know both his company's wage plan in detail and the performance of his men in relation to the company standards. Nowhere is it more important that the supervisor maintain a balanced relationship between the two parties involved than in his handling of wages. It is only natural for the men to seek higher wages;

yet every management is interested in holding costs within reasonable limits, and in most organizations wages are a major factor in these costs. The supervisor must exert all his leadership, remain impartial, and base his every action on facts gained from knowing his men, as well as reflect in his actions both the viewpoint of management and the needs of his men, always keeping as his objective the fundamental aims of the enterprise. Wages are a frequent source of irritation unless great care is exercised not to overlook the equities of all concerned. Slight errors must be corrected at once, and the supervisor must be prepared to meet wage grievances with prompt actions and full explanations. Employees today are better informed than in the past, and the supervisor must understand and be able to explain to them the reasoning that lies behind company policies on wages. *The supervisor's responsibility for wage administration is an excellent illustration of the part he plays in representing management to men and men to management.*

No supervisor can fully understand and meet his wage problems unless he has a grasp of the principles underlying wages. Such knowledge not only enables him to understand his own company's wage policy and to explain this policy to his men, but also furnishes him with the necessary background to meet successfully the wage problems among his men. Much of the current effort of management to teach basic economics to employees is related to an attempt to show the relationship of wages to other costs and to selling prices. The bases of wage payment for a given job classification are: (1) time, (2) output, and (3) quality in relationship to time and output. Thus, men are paid for the time they work or the hours they put in, for the amount of work they produce or the number of parts, or for the combination of what they produce and the time in which they produce it, in terms of the quality of the work. Of course, the specific amount of money paid for the time worked is related to the expected earnings for the time spent or the wage level. The primary basis of any wage is *time;* it was the earliest unit on which wage payments were based. Fundamentally output also is based on time because even under piecework in the original setting of the rate a man is paid for how much he can do in a given amount of time. Of recent years wage incentive systems have been developed that combine the output and time bases for wages in terms of standards set for quantity and quality. Wage plans vary from company to company and many different types have been developed; every one, however, developed originally out of one of these three fundamental bases of wage payment.

The "Satisfactory Wage." It is practically impossible to establish criteria for determining a "just" or "fair" wage because of the ethical and philosophic implications of these terms. Business must go on and it is not necessary to get agreement on a "fair" or "just" wage; hence the term "satisfactory wage" is used. From the point of view of the working man in the United States *a satisfactory wage must either be high enough to maintain the American standard of living or must be the market rate of wage payment, whichever is higher.* Management in general would subscribe to this statement of the just wage with the proviso that it is the competitive market rate, not one established by a noneconomic means.

Presumably, regardless of the productivity of the individual, there is a point below which wages must not go, so that the individual and the persons dependent on him may survive. This is seemingly the lower limit of a satisfactory wage, but in particular cases even this lower limit must presumably be undercut if, for the moment, the industrial establishment in question is to survive. Of course, there may be some question as to the desirability of a particular company's survival if its efficiency is so low that it must pay wages below the subsistence level in order to survive. On the other hand industry is under no obligation to pay every worker, regardless of his low productivity, a wage sufficiently high to enable him to support his family. His family needs may be entirely too great for his economic ability. In this case the caring for his family may be a community responsibility rather than his employer's.

A satisfactory wage is one that is at least as high as the going rate in the community where a man lives. It may also be defined as the rate that enables a man to maintain his standard of living. Ordinarily the most satisfactory wage is the higher of these rates. Any time a plant pays wages lower than those paid by other plants in the community discontent will be found among its employees. Similarly, rates that fail to provide men with sufficient income to maintain their standard of living cause trouble. The concept of a standard of living must be considered in terms of group standards of living, not those of any one individual. Generally speaking, when men's wages provide them with sufficient money to maintain a satisfactory standard of living there is not much likelihood of labor trouble. It should be noted that specific standards of living vary from community to community and therefore wages vary also. Since it is the real wages that are important, monetary wages must vary whenever living costs vary.

For a wage to be satisfactory it must meet the requirements of the workers, management, government, and community, yet not result in excessive costs to the consumer. It is obvious that management's viewpoint of the cost of the product and the price for which it can be sold, together with the financial structure of the company, must be taken into consideration in the determination of wages. If wages are set at a level which raises the cost of the product above the cost of products with which it competes, both the wage earners and the management suffer over a period of time. One of the best examples of what happens when wages reach too high a level is the anthracite coal industry where wages were increased without consideration of the consumer or competing products with results ultimately tragic both to men and management in many segments of the industry. On the other hand, if wages do not meet the approval of the men, management will not be able to secure enough men to produce its products. Those men who do go to work for the company will be dissatisfied and labor turnover will be high. Transfer from one job to another is a condition found particularly when business is on the upswing. When jobs are difficult to find, men may be temporarily satisfied with work that does not pay wages they consider adequate, but as soon as business conditions improve those same men seek other jobs, and the resulting increased turnover and training of new men bring higher labor costs. It is obvious that in the long run company policies, including wages, must meet with the approval of the community in which the plant is located and in which the men live. Wages are an integral part of the personnel policies of the company and therefore should meet the standards of the community viewpoint or men will be difficult to get and to hold.

Businesses engaged in interstate commerce must meet the minimum wage standards established by the Fair Labor Standards Act and the Walsh Healy Act. Also, many states have minimum wage regulations as well as maximum hours regulations for women and children in particular. The theory behind such legislation is that individuals by themselves are not strong enough to represent themselves successfully in the labor market and as a result they are likely to be exploited by selfish and shortsighted managements; therefore it is the government's responsibility to step in and prevent such conditions from arising. Another argument advanced for governmental regulation of conditions entering into personnel policies is founded on the popular conception of the need for governmental action to equalize competition in submarginal situations. In actual practice these theories do not always work out, and evidence indicates that wage policies of farsighted managements with enlightened personnel policies are usually far above minimum standards set by the government.

It would satisfy man's urge for justice if we could specifically determine exactly what each person's contribution were to industry, thus enabling industry to pay each man his just wage. The contribution of an individual or, in other words, his "productivity," has never been satisfactorily measured under our present industrial system, and it is questionable whether it can be measured. Our whole life is so complex, and the relations of one person to production are so inexact, that it becomes practically impossible to determine the exact extent to which he or she has added to the goods of the world. Before the inauguration of the factory system it was more nearly possible to arrive at some concept of the productivity of an individual, but the factory employee of today is performing only a small part of the production of the article on which he is working. The machine on which he works and the building in which he is employed have not only been furnished and designed by the employer and the management, but have also, in the first instance, been created by others. A knitter working on a complex knitting machine contributes much to the production of the finished product that comes off the machine. The question remains, however: "How much of the production is made possible by the men in another factory far removed who made the knitting machine?" The economic theory of marginal productivity is helpful in theoretical discussions, but it is difficult to apply on a large scale to changing industrial conditions. Our idea of justice in the abstract must be tempered by practical considerations in its application to social conditions.[1] In view of the total situation it is preferable to use the term "satisfactory wage" and thus avoid trying to do something that seems impossible in a practical sense.

Wages and Federal and State Taxes for Social Security, Workmen's Compensation, and Unemployment Compensation. The viewpoint has been advanced that the social security program, with its old age annuities, affects wages. The supervisor should be certain that his men realize that the amount deducted from their pay checks goes to the government to provide for old age insurance and that the money paid by the company, in addition to the deduction from the man's check, goes for the same annuity and is in a sense a part of wages.

[1] See Frank C. Sharp and Philip G. Fox, *Business Ethics,* D. Appleton-Century Co., New York, 1937, pp. 181–194, for an interesting discussion of the ethics of a fair wage.

Taxes for workmen's compensation and unemployment compensation are in the same category. These wage costs may run as high as six per cent or more in many cases. The supervisor should explain these items to his men. They enter into the cost of the product just as much as the direct money wages paid to the worker.

The Relationship of Wages to Other Factors. Wages are often related to other factors such as total income from sales, seniority, employee suggestions, and profit sharing (where practiced). If the supervisor fails to see and understand the effect of company income on wages it is not likely that the men under him will recognize and understand what an essential tie-up there is between company income and wages. The average man will ask for wage increases regardless of the company's profit-and-loss statement and unless the supervisor is informed on the status of the company finances and understands the relationship of wages to income and then in turn can explain them clearly to the man's satisfaction, there is likely to be trouble. The supervisor is not always to blame; too often management has not kept him informed. This is an ideal subject for supervisory conferences shortly after January first and July first of each year. Many managements today are mailing to the employees a simple breakdown of the financial statement sent to its stockholders, explaining to them exactly where wages fit into the financial picture. Some of these reports divide up the total income from the sales dollar as if it were a pie, showing the part that goes for wages, materials, interest, dividends, depreciation, taxes, and that kept in the business for expansion.

Some persons relate wages in part to length of service. Seniority, as such, will be discussed at length in a later section,[2] but it should be noted here that many companies follow a policy of automatic wage increases to employees, at least when these employees are in the early stages of employment, and then use merit and promotion as the basis of wage increases in the latter stages. Civil service administrations in the federal and state governments have been the greatest advocates of automatic wage increases based on length of employment. There is some doubt whether length of service in and of itself should be a cause for wage increases. Where length of service, however, increases the knowledge and value of the employee and results in his advancement then, of course, there is no question as to the justification for increasing wages.

[2] See Chapter 16.

Suggestions are sometimes recognized by giving wage increases to the person making an accepted suggestion. Undoubtedly such rewards at times not only lead to a greater interest in the suggestion system but also result in suggestions which are more likely to be of value to the company. In most cases, however, it is better to pay the man a flat sum for his suggestion, even though it is a substantial one, than to add the amount to a continuing wage.

Characteristics of a Sound Wage Plan. A sound wage payment plan recognizes the requirements of the job. This requires that it be based on job analysis and job rating [3] and that wages be set only after detailed knowledge has been developed concerning the basic requirements of the work. *Output* must be recognized as another basic element in a satisfactory plan, whether the wage plan is based on piecework, day rate, or an incentive plan. It will consider *versatility* where versatility is required on the part of the man on the job. The *cost of computation* is a factor that should not be overlooked, yet often is, especially where the wage payment plan involves elaborately computed bonuses. There is also a need for a *predetermination of labor costs.* Management must know what the product will cost before it is made, and therefore the wage plan should be so designed that it can furnish such information to the company. The wage plan, if it is going to be satisfactory to the men, will take into consideration the length of the training period. If it is necessary for a man to spend three or four years learning his job, he is entitled to a higher rate of pay at the end of the training period than the man who is on a job that requires little or no training.

Special hazards to the employee's health or life should be taken into consideration, if these are present. Where the job places unusual or undue *responsibilities* on the employee, such as working on a machine using valuable tools or working with expensive materials, it is only natural that his wage will be somewhat higher than that of other men who are working with less expensive tools, machines, or materials. Unusual or *extreme working conditions* will ordinarily call for higher wages. Illustrations of such jobs include those involving work done under very wet, dirty, or extremely hot or cold conditions. Another characteristic of a satisfactory wage plan is that it is *readily understood by the employees.* Some wage plans fail miserably in this respect, and

[3] See Walter D. Scott, Robert C. Clothier, and William R. Spriegel, *Personnel Management,* McGraw-Hill Book Co., New York, 1954, Chapter 11, for a detailed discussion of this subject.

the more complicated the method of computing wages, the greater difficulties supervisors will face in explaining and administering wage policies. This is one of the chief criticisms directed at so-called incentive and bonus plans. Men like to know what their earnings will be, and when the wage plan involves complicated calculations in the payroll department the men have no idea what their pay envelope will contain until they open it. When companies operate under group bonus plans or complicated piecework arrangements there is the additional burden placed on the supervisor of being able to understand the plan and explain it clearly to his men, pointing out wherein the plan has advantages to the men that outweigh its disadvantages. Generally speaking, there is a trend toward the simplification of wage plans since the overhead costs of elaborate payroll department computations are eliminated and the men are usually more satisfied.

Another characteristic that is being incorporated in many wage policies is that of providing automatic increases for employees from the bottom of their wage range to the middle or even the top. It is desirable, however, to prepare job analyses, to make a careful study of job rating, and to be sure that employee rating is used as part of the wage plan, before the automatic increase plan is put into effect. Taking care of automatic wage increases in the hourly and sometimes even in the salary brackets is one of those responsibilities delegated to the personnel department. No supervisor should feel that the use of automatic increases deprives him of any of his authority over wages. Instead it relieves him of much of his detail work and he is still left with control over the wage situation in his department through merit rating. It is a perfect example of the application of the exception principle in which the supervisor has a procedure to follow which operates automatically; he is required to act only in the exceptional cases. It frees him to take care of other and more important responsibilities.

The Supervisor, an Interpreter of Wage Systems. Although the supervisor is not responsible for developing the wage plan, he is management's representative in interpreting and administering wage plans. He is usually responsible for determining the employee's status within a given job classification and setting the rate within the wage range. Frequently he is solely responsible, and almost without exception it is he who originates the initial rate increase. Many employees today are well informed on wage systems and the economics of wages. The older men who have worked for a number of different companies have had experience under a variety of wage plans but the younger employees today are better educated than they have been in the past, with the result that if the supervisor cannot explain the reasoning behind his company's wage plan in sound economic terms he will lose the respect of some of his men. Sound wage economics are essentially common sense and are summed up in the statement that satisfactory wages are those that are in general satisfactory to the management, the men, the community, and the government. Each must have its interests considered fairly but not to the detriment of the others.

The supervisor is the logical man to explain sound economic wage relationships to any of his employees who may hold false theories of wages. The supervisor in studying the wage system for his own department may make suggestions for improvements. These suggestions, of course, must be checked with management and against company policies and must move up through the proper channels before any changes can be made. Wage discussions possess possibilities of far-reaching results. Wage levels and scales by their very nature must be determined by management, or at least by management in connection with the representative of the workers. Of course, in the long run the consumer pays both wages to the workers and dividends to the owners, provided management can keep costs low enough to compete with other manufacturers and sell his product.

The Supervisor and His Departmental Wage Plan. If a man is dissatisfied with his wages and feels an injustice has been done, the supervisor must not only check the correctness of the amount with the payroll department but must also be able to explain to the man how it was determined. The supervisor must also understand the provisions for increases due his men under the wage plan. There is nothing that will cause a supervisor to lose face with his men faster than overlooking opportunities to give them increases to which they are entitled. He must understand these provisions and be able to explain them to men who do not come under the provisions or who cannot meet the requirements for increases. He should know whether the provisions are based on length of service, on output, or on some other factor. Where they are based entirely on the quality of the work turned out by the individual, and it is the supervisor's responsibility to recommend increases where he feels they are deserved, an additional burden is placed on the supervisor not only to know his men and the work they produce but also to lean over backward to see that his decisions are fair and impartial. Again wherever possible the supervisor should rate his men, using either those forms in use by the company or his own notebook as an aid in determining the men who should receive salary increases. The supervisor must also be familiar with the overtime provisions in the wage policy. He must be familiar with the procedure for putting through rate increases and know the relationship of a man's rating to his wage level. With the close control that governmental agencies exercise over wages today it is to the advantage of every supervisor to be thoroughly familiar with the laws administered by these agencies and their relationship to the wage policy of his company. He will find that this knowledge will often assist him in explaining to his employees the reasons behind company wage policies and will prepare him to protect his company against unintentional violations of these statutes.

The supervisor's responsibility is a dual one; most managements want their employees to get every cent that is due them, but the employees cannot expect the wage level to be increased beyond limits that will affect the selling price of the product. The supervisor must see that every employee gets the highest wage to which he is entitled and at the same time should assist management to keep the wage factor in the cost of the product within competitive limits. Inequality in wages is the breeding place of unrest, and favoritism in wage administration on the part of the supervisor weakens leadership and causes labor trouble. Wages are a major source of grievances and the supervisor will find that if he meets his responsibility for wages fairly and squarely, both from the viewpoint of management and that of his men, he will be well along the road toward developing leadership of the highest degree.

The supervisor is responsible to management for developing a sound background in wage theory and a thorough understanding of the company wage system. He must faithfully interpret the wage plan to the men and assume full responsibility for carrying it out without "passing the buck" to top management in an attempt to gain favor with the employees. He is required to see that output corresponds to the standard expected for a given wage. The supervisor is responsible to management for seeing that merited increases within the classification scale are put through when due. Fundamentally every management that *shows due regard for the personal equation* is as anxious as the men themselves to see men who deserve it earn more money. On the other hand, the supervisor owes it to management to see that proper records are kept, that wages are in line with the procedures of the wage plan, and that forms are properly executed so that other departments which share in the responsibility for wage administration, such as payroll, accounting, and personnel, can be properly informed. The supervisor's responsibility to the men in wage administration is first and foremost to recognize merit and to see that wage increases are put through in keeping with the company's scale and when they are due; then to see that accurate records are kept of all the factors that affect wages so his decisions are based on recorded facts instead of memory, thereby insuring that his attitude toward wages and his men is impartial and fair. He is responsible for seeing that all errors are corrected promptly. A twenty-five-cent shortage in an employee's pay envelope is a source of discontent that will be magnified out of all proportion to the amount involved. The supervisor owes his men a clear explanation of the wage system of their company and the reasons for it. He also should strive to see that they are sold on the wage plan in use. As with every other company policy the supervisor must see that the men understand and are satisfied with the wage policy.

Rating Employees. Ratings have been developed for all levels of employees, from men on the machines through supervisors, and including executives. Many companies tie their rating plans to their wage increase policy and ratings are also frequently used as one factor in selecting men for promotion. Ratings have been found valuable to some companies as a factor in determining the order in which men are to be laid off when work is slack, and recalled as business picks up. They can be especially valuable when used to establish an employee's rating within a given job classification scale. Ratings are not completely scientific, but they provide a method of obtaining objective evaluations of men although rating methods have not yet completely eliminated personal opinions. Every supervisor should recognize that the ratings of his men are only one factor to be considered in any decision he may make. The object of the rating form used by the supervisor is to enable him to consider his men on the basis of those factors which cannot be directly measured. It is easy enough to measure from available records the attendance of his men, the quality, and the quantity of the work they do. He does not have records, however, which measure the enthusiasm of his men, their loyalty, their dependability, their attitude toward the company, their fellow employees, and themselves, and their emotional stability. Periodic ratings will enable the supervisor to eliminate casual impressions or prejudices which he may have.

The rating, when shown to the employee or when he is told where he stands in relation to other employees, will point out his weaknesses and wherein he can improve himself, thereby providing a goal toward which to work. The use of ratings will tend to give the men a feeling that they are getting a square deal and that management is regularly informed about them; furthermore, the men recognize that the supervisor must define his opinion of them in writing, and that management is interested both in their ratings and in the accuracy with which the supervisor rates them.

Factors Used in Rating Employees. In most merit rating plans the employee is rated on three broad aspects of his work: performance, ability, and institutional value. Those items concerning performance which the supervisor may find on rating forms include quality of work, quantity of work, stability, and accuracy. Such items as job knowledge, versatility, and promotion possibilities fall within the ability group. The items which may be classed under the heading of institutional value include attitude toward fellow employees, attitude toward supervisor, loyalty, initiative, and cooperation. A rating form is of the greatest value for the items of ability and institutional value, since these are essentially intangible qualities, difficult to measure, yet of definite value when measured. The ordinary rating forms will not carry all these items worded precisely in this way, but they will as a rule include somewhere between four and ten items on each of which the men are rated individually. The rating forms are then scored and the result is a more accurate picture of the employee than any personal opinion of the supervisor. The value of the rating rests on the fact that the supervisor must look at each employee and rate him on each of the items. Too often when ratings are not used, the supervisor will let one particular trait of an employee overbalance his opinion of the man. For example, an employee may have a tremendous fund of enthusiasm, and, although he rates high in that particular quality, it may be found when a rating form is used that he is low in initiative, loyalty, job knowledge, and other items. His rating score would then be somewhat lower, although without the use of the rating form the supervisor may have considered the man very valuable because of his high degree of enthusiasm.

Methods Used in Merit Rating. There are some techniques which a supervisor must use if he is to rate his men effectively. First, he must understand the items on which he is rating his men. There must be agreement between himself and other supervisors as to the meanings of these items and the standards to be used. Where records are not available and the supervisor is relying on his own impressions, he should refer to his contacts with the men as recorded in his notebook and use this information for his ratings. Every supervisor should beware of ratings based only on recent impressions and he must endeavor to rate on the basis of a judgment formed over a reasonable period. It is very easy to rate a man low on an item because he has been below standard on it only recently, but the supervisor must look back over a period of time to see if it has always been true or if it has only happened once. The value of the supervisor's using his notebook to record his contacts with his men and his impression of them at regular intervals is a part of rating his men. Skill in rating does not come easily and is not by any means a simple operation. The supervisor will find his rating will improve as he rates his men a second and third time. Time is required to do a proper job of rating. The supervisor should check on ratings to make sure he has not over-rated or under-rated his men, and that he has not rated them all the same on any one factor. Where the rating form involves rating the men on a number of different items, the supervisor should *follow the practice of rating all his men on one item at a time before moving on to the next*. After all, the object of rating is to rate the men one against the other and this is the best means of achieving this purpose.

Use of Merit Rating in Wage Administration. The use of ratings eliminates to a large degree any unfairness or partiality in the supervisor's action on wage increases and promotion. Where an automatic wage increase policy is in effect, ratings provide the control exercised by the supervisor to prevent increases where the worker is not up to average performance. Periodic ratings by the supervisor are of value to the personnel department when men are being considered for transfers or promotions. The supervisor will find that if he is required to rate his men he will be forced to learn to know them better and to study them more closely. Only through regular contacts with his men and recording these contacts in his notebook can the supervisor do a good job of rating. Many companies find that it is valuable for the supervisor to discuss a man's rating with him. This gives the supervisor the opportunity to point out individual weaknesses in order to bring about improvement and better preparation for advancement.

Summary. A supervisor at times finds himself in a frustrating position. He has worked hard at collecting data on which to rate his men, has explained their status, and then must stand aside and see low producers get a substantial raise as a part of a union-negotiated wage increase for everyone.   In such cases there is little that the conscientious supervisor can do.   As a good team man he recognizes the facts of industrial life and carries on.   Like all other good leaders *the supervisors must have a high frustration tolerance.*

Wage administration is an integral part of the supervisor's work. He cannot delegate it to a subordinate.   The use of rating in connection with meeting his responsibility eliminates much of the guesswork in appraising the men and also tends to eliminate inequality and discontent.   When rating is tied into job analysis and job classification, it tends to eliminate inequality within the job.   It gives men an opportunity to improve themselves and requires the supervisor to understand his men and know their work.   As in so many of his other responsibilities, the supervisor must represent both men and management, keeping in mind the company's wage plan and rating methods and his men's performance in relation to the company's standards.   When he thus faithfully discharges his responsibility both to management and his men his wage administration will be more equitable and more satisfying to all concerned.

15 The Supervisor and the Suggestion System

What Is a Suggestion System? A suggestion system is a procedure, usually formalized, for securing from employees ideas that will increase productivity, the quality of work or product, or employee satisfaction in his work; that will improve the product as to design, new uses, maintenance or service, or improve the processes, layout, or working conditions; that will reduce the cost of the product or service or increase its service or satisfaction without proportionately increasing its cost. A suggestion system is primarily cost, product, and profit centered yet it may as a by-product result in improving employee relations. Unless employee relations are in a fairly satisfactory condition it would be unwise to inaugurate a suggestion system. Two other definitions of a suggestion system are worthy of consideration. "A suggestion system is a means of getting from employees ideas which will contribute to greater efficiency, higher quality of product, reduced costs, and better working conditions." [1] "A suggestion system is a formal definite procedure established by employers to solicit ideas from employees; to provide the machinery to appraise, accept, or reject; and if accepted, to insure use of the ideas." [2]

History of Suggestion Systems. The history of suggestion systems has been one of starts, discontinuance, revivals and again discontinuances, successes and failures. Not all of the systems have started

[1] See Charles C. Gibbons, "The Supervisor and the Suggestion System," *Personnel,* Jan. 1948, p. 284.

[2] National Industrial Conference Board, "Suggestion Systems," *Studies in Personnel Policy,* No. 135, 1953, p. 6. This is an excellent study.

and stopped. The following companies had early starts, as indicated by the dates after their names, and are continuing their systems today:

Yale and Towne Manufacturing Company (1880)
National Cash Register Company (1894)
Eastman Kodak Company (1898)
Bausch and Lomb Company (1898)
General Electric Company (1905)
Westinghouse Electric Company (1910) [3]
Western Electric Corporation (1910)
United Shoe Machinery Corporation (1911)
Public Service Company of Northern Illinois (1911)
Public Service Corporation of New Jersey (1915)
Philadelphia Electric Company (1915)
Stromberg-Carlson Company (1917)
Firestone Tire and Rubber Company (1918) [4]

World Wars I and II gave new emphasis to the inauguration of new suggestion systems, as did the boom period of the 1920's. Since World War II there has been a continued interest in suggestion systems. Many have been started and others have been discontinued. Their records of success seem to be greater today than before World War II. The National Association of Suggestion Systems, an aggressive association of suggestion supervisors and others interested in tapping the potential energies and ideas of workers, was founded in 1942. This association holds annual meetings and publishes the *NASS Quarterly*.

The origin of the National Cash Register Company's suggestion system, as reported by H. F. Heil, is worth quoting:

Back in 1894, John H. Patterson, founder of the National Cash Register Company at Dayton, Ohio, while going through the foundry, recognized a man who formerly worked for him in the coal business down in Jackson County, Ohio. Surprised to find him working on the job of cleaning castings, he asked the employee if he tried to win promotion by bringing himself to the attention of his foreman. Mr. Patterson, during their talk, asked him if there was anything he could see that should be changed.

"Lots of them," the employee replied, "but there's no use in my making any suggestions. The foreman would take all the credit."

Back in his office, Mr. Patterson pondered over the matter and then remembered a similar example. Some months before a foreman came to him with a new invention. It looked like a good improvement.

"I am much obliged to you," Mr. Patterson said. "Did it take much of your time?"

"Oh, no," the foreman replied. "I worked on it at home at night."

A few months later, Mr. Patterson discovered the foreman was **not** the

---

[3] National Industrial Conference Board, *loc. cit.*
[4] *Management News,* Vol. 19, No. 5, May 31, 1946.

originator of the idea. One of his employees came up with it and showed it to his foreman who took the idea to Mr. Patterson as his own invention.

Thinking over these two experiences, Mr. Patterson decided then and there to try some plan whereby these ideas could be brought directly to the attention of management with the guarantee that the employee receive proper credit.

Thus the NCR Suggestion System was born and the start of a channel of communication designed to reap many benefits for both the Company and its employees.[5]

Objectives of a Suggestion System. As indicated earlier, suggestion systems are designed to solicit ideas from employees in order to increase efficiency, improve the quality or design of the product, improve the physical working conditions, or increase the personal satisfactions of the workers in their work. The improving of human relations is a laudable goal but the effectiveness of the suggestion system in this area is open to question. Persons making suggestions often think that the suggestion is worth much more than the award given for it. Admittedly the suggestion system does provide an additional avenue for "blowing off steam" for disgruntled employees who want to tell management about something. For communicating there are more effective devices than the suggestion system save in the case where the employee does not have to sign his name but merely tear off a stub. Of course, the disgruntled employee could write management an anonymous letter telling of his complaints. In a few such cases a man may suffer from a feeling of guilt should he mail an unsigned letter registering his suggestion, usually a disguised complaint. This same man may preserve his self-respect by putting the same suggestion through the Suggestion System and tearing off a stub that does not require a signature.

The primary objective of the suggestion system is to reduce costs, increase efficiency, improve the quality or design of the product, and reduce waste or human effort to do the job. In other words, the chief aim of the suggestion system is to promote the primary objective of the enterprise, profits through service. The fact that the primary objective of the enterprise is profits through service does not in any sense rule out the importance of collateral service objectives which nearly always contribute directly or indirectly to increased efficiency in achieving the primary objective. Anything that the use of a suggestion system may contribute to improving human relations is certainly all to the positive side of the ledger. The suggestion system

[5] H. F. Heil, "NCR Suggestion System," *NASS Quarterly,* Spring 1954, p. 3.

does show that management is interested in the ideas of the employees. However, unless the supervisor really supports the suggestion system most employees will not use it. Great care has to be exercised in making awards to avoid negative morale factors. It is often difficult to convince many employees that they have been paid all that their suggestions were worth. In spite of the difficulties involved in turning a suggestion system into a strong builder of desirable human relations, it is a useful management tool and may with positive leadership promote such relations.

A well-known manufacturing company, in the Conference Leader's Manual for its Suggestion Plan, sets forth its objectives as follows:

1. To improve operating efficiency
2. To increase production
3. To cut costs
4. To make some jobs easier to do
5. To stimulate employee's interest in his and other jobs
6. To generate alertness on the part of workers

Later in the manual it is pointed out that items 5 and 6 certainly improve human relations.

Operating the Suggestion System. In launching a suggestion plan it is important to have support from top management. This should be given in the form of a written statement sent to all supervisors and at least posted on the bulletin board for employees to read. In a plant having a union contract it is also desirable to get the support of the union. Unions often are neutral in their attitude toward the suggestion system. At times they may be antagonistic when the suggestions eliminate jobs. Following the initial announcement it is often desirable to have conferences with the supervisors to explain the objectives of the suggestion system and also to indoctrinate them in its value to them and to the company. It is especially important to let the supervisors know that it is no reflection on them for their men to make suggestions. In fact, it is one measure of the leadership of a supervisor to be able to encourage his men to make suggestions. In a very real sense the supervisor is the key man in making a suggestion system productive. The best method of getting the employees interested in making suggestions is through their supervisor.

Figure 15.1 shows the flow chart of the Frigidaire Corporation suggestion system. Figure 15.2 is the suggestion form used by Aldens. Each company has its own special suggestion form. Often the general rules governing the submitting of suggestions and the basis for awards

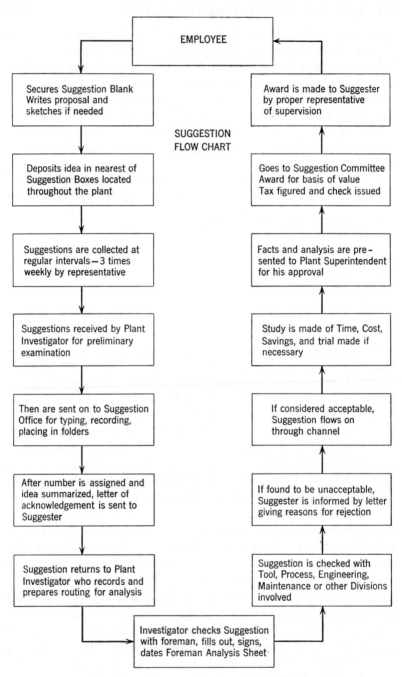

EMPLOYEE

Secures Suggestion Blank
Writes proposal and
sketches if needed

Award is made to Suggester
by proper representative
of supervision

SUGGESTION
FLOW CHART

Deposits idea in nearest of
Suggestion Boxes located
throughout the plant

Goes to Suggestion Committee
Award for basis of value
Tax figured and check issued

Suggestions are collected at
regular intervals — 3 times
weekly by representative

Facts and analysis are presented to Plant Superintendent
for his approval

Suggestions received by Plant
Investigator for preliminary
examination

Study is made of Time, Cost,
Savings, and trial made if
necessary

Then are sent on to Suggestion
Office for typing, recording,
placing in folders

If considered acceptable,
Suggestion flows on
through channel

After number is assigned and
idea summarized, letter of
acknowledgement is sent to
Suggester

If found to be unacceptable,
Suggester is informed by letter
giving reasons for rejection

Suggestion returns to Plant
Investigator who records and
prepares routing for analysis

Suggestion is checked with
Tool, Process, Engineering,
Maintenance or other Divisions
involved

Investigator checks Suggestion
with foreman, fills out, signs,
dates Foreman Analysis Sheet

Figure 15.1. Flow chart of a suggestion system in the Frigidaire Corporation.

are printed on the back of the suggestion form. This is a good idea since the person submitting the suggestion cannot later claim that he did not understand the rules. An occasional form has some such statement as the following, just before the place for the signature of the employee: "I have read the regulations printed on the back of this form and am submitting this suggestion in accordance with these rules." Sometimes these rules state that certain types of suggestions are not acceptable, such as items that are proper subjects of collective bargaining. In other instances a rule may cover the length of time that a suggestion is effective. For instance, a suggestion may have a life of only one year from the date of being submitted. To keep it alive the suggester is required to resubmit the suggestion. The reason for this type of rule is the fact that a suggestion may at a given time be rejected because its costs are not justified at the time in terms of the volume of production. Two years later the production may be increased to such an extent that a methods man may put into effect the exact suggestion or a modification of it.

One of the points of friction in administering a suggestion system is the later use of a suggestion that was formerly rejected. The man who recommends the later use may not have any knowledge of the original suggestion. This fact does not change the feelings of the employee who initially submitted the original suggestion that was legitimately rejected at the time of its submission. In fact, management may never be aware that such a suggestion was formerly submitted. The man making the suggestion may keep his peace but nurse a feeling that his suggestion has been stolen from him. This possibility necessitates careful record keeping on all suggestions. In spite of records a similar development may emerge without the researcher's knowledge. This fact alone is justification for having a time limit on the effective life of a suggestion.

Another point of friction similar to the one above may arise when an employee makes a suggestion similar to or the same as one that is currently being worked on in the methods department, the research department, the plant layout department, or some other division charged with the responsibility for improvements. In such an event the employee making the suggestion should be taken to the department and be shown the notes, blueprints, and other records pointing out specifically the dates on each so that he will know that his suggestion really is not a new idea. In this event the suggester may be given a token award. In any event he should be given a note ac-

Aldens

EMPLOYE SUGGESTION SYSTEM

№ 22559

I suggest ______________________________

I believe my idea will:

Increase Production ☐ Improve Service ☐ Improve Methods ☐ Reduce Costs ☐ Prevent Waste ☐

Improve Quality ☐ Prevent Accidents ☐ Or will ____________

№ 22559

While it is not necessary to sign your name, you may do so if you wish. Signing your name will help the Suggestion Secretary to get in touch with you if more information is required or if there is an award to be paid.

Submitted by ____________

Clock No. ________ Dept. ________ Date ________

Regarding ____________

Referred to ________ on ________ Reply Rec'd ________

Reviewed on ________ Apprv'd ☐ Rejected ☐

Award ________ Notified ________ by ________

All Suggestions for which an award is made become property of the company

*1061

DO NOT DETACH

TEAR OFF THIS STUB AND SAVE IT!

Thanks for your suggestion! Remember the more ideas you turn in, the greater your opportunity to win awards. Watch for notice of action.

SAVE THIS STUB

№ 22559

Figure 15.2. Aldens' suggestion blank.

knowledging the merit of his suggestion, thanking him for making it, but telling him that it was being worked on at the time he made it.

One of the most pertinent aspects of keeping suggestions coming in is the promptness with which they are processed. Not only should the suggester be promptly notified of the receipt of his suggestion, he should be advised from time to time of its progress, in case it is not promptly accepted or rejected. Suggestions should be collected from suggestion boxes at least once a week, preferably twice a week. It is also highly advisable that the foreman of the suggester's department stop by the employee's workplace and commend him for making the suggestion. The personal touches in connection with a suggestion system lend support to the desirability of having employees sign their suggestions rather than merely tear off a numbered stub to be kept until the number is posted on the bulletin board telling of its disposition. Of course, some employees may hesitate to sign their suggestions for fear of fellow workers' criticisms or from fear of the foreman's disfavor. To provide for these rare situations (it is hoped) it is advisable to provide both for the signature and the numbered stub so that it may or may not be signed, depending upon the feelings of the particular employee.

Who Is Eligible? At the time of setting up the program, management should give careful attention to the eligibility for making suggestions. It is common practice to make the following persons ineligible to participate in the suggestion system:

1. Foremen and department heads
2. Research and methods personnel, including industrial engineers
3. Members of the planning departments, including production control
4. Members of the patent department
5. Members of the advertising department (not always included)

In connection with eligibility, certain unusual situations arise, such as:

1. An employee who has filed a suggestion is promoted to a position in which he is no longer eligible. Usually he would be entitled to receive the award for his suggestion if it is accepted.
2. A suggester is laid off, retired, discharged, granted a leave of absence, or dies. Usually he or his estate receives the award.
3. An employee is called to duty with one of the Armed Services. Usually he is entitled to receive the award. If he were in a classification ineligible to receive an award while he was working he may not be eligible to receive an award if the suggestion is submitted soon after he left for duty. On the other hand a suggestion submitted a year later might be

considered for an award provided the company was not making regular payments to him (an occasional practice) to make up the difference between his service pay and his company salary.

Some companies urge their supervisors to make departmental improvements. One company pays an annual award of $500 to the foreman who has made the most outstanding contribution to methods improvement during the year. This company makes the presentation at an annual dinner. Occasionally a company gives special recognition to the foreman whose employees make the most suggestions that are accepted during a given period. In order not to give a large department special advantage this figure may be one expressing the ratio of the total number of accepted suggestions to the average number of employees on the payroll for the period. At least one company encourages methods improvement by its employees by making a moving picture before and after the improvement, including the employee or employees in the picture. In many of these attempts to recognize the suggested improvements, the fact that management does recognize and approve the employees' efforts is as important as the amount of the award or the method of recognition.

Awards for Suggestions. It must not be inferred from the statement above about the importance of recognizing the individual suggesters that cash or other material awards are not important. Some employees at all levels in the organization are "money hungry." These individuals tend to measure their importance by the money paid them for work or anything else they do. They do not have a very strong sense of responsibility to the company or anything else associated with their work situation. They are self-centered but would be highly indignant should anyone call them selfish. These people are frequently highly vocal and likely to be leaders in trying to get more and more for themselves but almost never are in the foreground of giving more of themselves for any common goal unless the goal is to get more for themselves. Fortunately this group is in the minority, but their influence is immeasurably greater than their numbers. Some foremen and others not eligible to receive awards belong to this group. There have been instances of their having workers make suggestions rather than taking the initiative to put them into effect themselves as a part of their responsibilities.

The other side of this question is the fact that management should be willing to pay for suggestions that reduce costs, increase quality, or add to the profits of the company. Nearly all companies do pay

for such suggestions. (See Figure 15.3.) The actual amount varies
with the individual company. One of the highest amounts paid by any
company is fifty per cent of the first year's savings from the suggestion. This particular company estimates the year's savings, deducts
the cost of installing the suggestion, and divides the amount by two.
The employee is then paid half of his share of the estimated saving
when the suggestion is put into operation. At the end of the year a

Courtesy The Frank G. Hough Co.

Figure 15.3. Congratulating a winner of a suggestion award.

recomputation of the saving is made and the employee is paid whatever amount is still due him. The most common award seems to be
ten per cent of the tangible savings for one year. One large company
gives ten per cent of the savings in the second month to the person
making the suggestion and divides another ten per cent of the savings
for one month among all of the persons working on the operation,
provided the saving arises from a reduction in labor cost. Some
companies have a limit on the award in some such amount as $750,
$2,500, $5,000, or even $10,000. Usually the lower limit on the
award is $5.00. Some companies have different classes of suggestions
for which there are different awards. These different awards may
apply to the person making the suggestion or to his fellow workers who
may share in the award. It is possible to find reputable companies
that have almost any combination of the systems of awards mentioned

above. The most important phase of paying for suggestions is promptness, followed by a reputation of dealing equitably with all persons.

Results from the Operation of Suggestion Systems. It is impossible to generalize about the success or failure of suggestion systems. Judged by the fact that some successful companies have had suggestion systems in continuous operation for more than fifty years it would seem that under proper conditions of leadership they are a success. On the other hand the mortality rates of suggestion systems would indicate that there are real problems involved in getting desired results from a suggestion system.

There is no question but that the successful operation of a suggestion system requires a lot of executive attention from men who are already hard pressed to take care of their operating responsibilities. Not only are foremen tied into the success of a suggestion system but so are higher line executives. Even when the suggestion system pays off in terms of improvements, would not the time and effort expended on it be even more productive if spent on these same problems directly rather than through the medium of the suggestions from employees? There is no clear-cut answer to this question. Unless the suggestion system is a vital part of other progressive managerial devices the effort exerted may readily be more productive if spent in other areas. Most certainly enough time and effort should be devoted to the suggestion system to make it effective or it should be closed out, if in existence, or it never should be started.

When the suggestion system is an integral part of effective operating management and human relations it seems to pay good dividends. The by-products of successfully operating a suggestion system may often be almost as important as the direct savings. Suggestions may help identify persons of constructive imaginations. It would be a serious error to promote a man to a supervisory position solely on the basis of his accepted suggestions. Many persons with fertile imaginations and the ability to make constructive suggestions are sadly lacking in other desirable leadership qualities. A substantial number of constructive and positive suggestions emerge through a properly operated suggestion system. There may be positive morale building aspects to the operation of the suggestion system. (Of course, negative results also may be present.) Large numbers of successful managers believe firmly in the operation of suggestion systems. They are one phase of industrial democracy. They require time and effort, but these two items are the essence of successful management regardless of the particular system being used.

The success or failure of a suggestion system frequently rests upon top management's attitude and willingness to pay the costs inherent in its operation. While the personnel department may be in charge of the over-all administration of the program, the support of engineering and operating personnel is required. The suggestion program will prosper almost in direct proportion to the willing support given by all parties.

16 Transfers, Promotions, and Discharges

The Maintenance of a Dynamic Work Group. In the maintenance of a dynamic work group within a department new men must be hired and trained, transfers must be made in order to make most effective use of men, promotions are required to fill jobs above the lower levels as well as to offer opportunity for the present workers, and finally a discharge may be in order when a worker is unable or unwilling to meet the requirements of the job. In a large enterprise men come, spend a number of years at work, and pass on of their own accord, or are forced to retire because of age or health. A work group is constantly maturing, growing old, and being renewed by younger men. Sound management requires that these various stages be kept in balance.

Inherent in the task of supervising is the responsibility of transferring, promoting, and discharging employees. Nowhere does the supervisor exert power over the economic and social life of his employees to a greater extent than in his selection of men for promotion and transfer, or in his decision to discharge men. In his exercise of the responsibility for transfers, promotions, and discharges, a supervisor must get all the facts. Snap judgment has no place in the picture when the supervisor is promoting, transferring, or discharging men. It is easy to promote a man, but if he turns out to be not entirely satisfactory it is often difficult to demote him. In any case, an unwise promotion creates an additional problem. The supervisor also suffers in the eyes of both management and his men, and the men's confidence in him decreases when he makes many unsatisfactory promotions.

The transfer is a most valuable tool in maintaining balance in the work force within the department as well as aiding in proper placement of the workers. Many a man, unsatisfactory in one position, has been transferred to another and has been saved to the company in which he later developed into a valuable employee. The importance of getting the right man for the right job frequently makes transferring a necessity. In times of a labor shortage especially, it may be necessary to try out a man on several jobs before he is properly fitted. Discharges are nearly always unpleasant. Most supervisors shrink from taking the action frequently called for in work situations. The supervisor should be sure of his ground and have a complete record before he moves to discharge a man. Many a supervisor has cost the management time and money as a result of discharging an employee without careful consideration of all the factors involved. When all the facts are in and there is no other way out, the discharge should be made as courteously as possible but none the less with firmness. There is no place for anger or recrimination in a discharge.

The Place of the Personnel Department in Promotions, Transfers, Demotions, and Discharges. The personnel department is a staff department serving the entire business as a central agency for all personnel records, a clearing house for transfers between departments, employing new personnel, and many other activities related to the personnel function. If the alleged personnel policies are really to work, promotions should go to the best men even though they come from another department. The personnel department is the one agency that can best keep a constant lookout for men in all departments. Records are essential in reaching decisions and in carrying out this responsibility. The supervisor should use the help of the personnel department in reaching his decisions, but the responsibility for the decision is the supervisor's so far as his own department is concerned, and he must accept this responsibility before the management and the men. This is one of the many places where the spotlight shines on the supervisor, and he can make few mistakes in promotion, transfer, or discharge, or he himself will be marked for similar action by the management.

Conditions Giving Rise to Transfers. Transfers may arise from either a contraction or an expansion of the business. As production increases and new shifts are opened, the supervisor may have to transfer some of his men to the new shift to staff it in part with experienced men. Transfers may arise as a result of a shortage of skilled men in a department where skilled men are required to fill vacancies. Transfers may develop out of the need in one department for men with special skills when these men are available somewhere else in the organization.   Sometimes transfers are made to correct improper initial placement of new employees.   Health hazards are another major cause for transfers.   If a supervisor sees that a man is endangering his health on a particular job, the supervisor should take immediate action to transfer the man.   Interests of employees change and men will themselves ask for transfers to other work in line with their changed interests.   It has already been noted that the work of a particular position may change.   Frequently the man hired for the position is at first satisfactory, but, through no fault of his own, he can no longer handle the work.   This situation may require a transfer of the man to a new position.

Types of Transfers.   The two main classifications of transfers are: (1) those made for the convenience of the company and (2) those made for the convenience of the employee.   Of course, there could be a third class in which the convenience of both the company and the employee is served.   This type is a happy circumstance but does not happen too often.   Transfers for the convenience of the employee arise from: (1) personal illness, health, or an accident, (2) illness in the employee's family, (3) personal preferences as to shift, hours, and days worked, (4) special desires of the employee.   Many employees because of age, injury, or health can no longer do their regular work, yet are still valuable to their company.   An employee, because of illness in his family, may request assignment to a shift other than the one he is on.   An employee may develop a special desire to learn a trade, to improve his social status by moving from the factory to the office (this is especially true of women employees), to attend evening school, or to adjust a personal situation such as the clashing of personalities between the employee and his supervisor or with other employees.   Transfers from one department to another, one position to another, or one shift to another will frequently be required. A supervisor should be on the alert to meet these situations when possible.   Transfers for the convenience of the company arise from: (1) a shortage of men in a particular department, (2) a shortage of a particular skill or ability among the employees, (3) the desire to balance production on various shifts, (4) an effort to correct defective placement or defective adjustment of employees (this is also to the advantage of the employee), and (5) an attempt to increase versatility of the employees as an aid in stabilizing employment.

The Supervisor's Responsibility for Transfers. Within the department the supervisor has the primary responsibility for all transfers. Naturally he is concerned with meeting his operating responsibilities. Transfers frequently enable him to meet his production requirements. Of course, the supervisor also is obligated to assist his men grow in versatility and skill. Transfers assist in this training program. The supervisor also uses the transfer to take care of his men who may no longer be able for health reasons to perform certain tasks. The man may have incurred injury outside his work since he was hired and a physical examination before a transfer is frequently advisable. The supervisor will want to check the past employment record as well as the record of the man with the company. It is important to review the wage rate changes the man has received before making or recommending transfer for him. The records of the personnel department are available and valuable to the supervisor in these important decisions.

Transfers also may become a positive tool in supervision. If a supervisor expects his men to come to him with their requests for transfers, he will have to show them by his actions that he will not stand in the way of their advancement. When a supervisor finds a man in his department going through the personnel department for a transfer without having first consulted him, he should recognize it as a danger signal that he is not fulfilling his responsibility in regard to transfers. He should not hold this against the man, however, but strive to merit the confidence of his men so they will feel free to consult him.

Special Problems Arising from Transfers. Regard for seniority must be observed in transfers or trouble is certain to arise. There are three types of seniority: (1) job within the department, division, and plant, (2) departmental, divisional, plant, and company wide, and (3) super or special seniority such as that claimed by union officials. In some companies, a man transferred loses his departmental seniority but maintains his company seniority. In other companies, if he is transferred from one type of work to another, his seniority is based on his job. On the other hand, in some companies a man is permitted to transfer his departmental seniority. The procedure will depend on the individual company's policy, but the supervisor must expect to encounter questions on seniority in connection with transfers. The question of earnings will frequently arise when a transfer is under consideration. Where the transfer is for the convenience of the company, a problem of the rate on the new job arises. Will the man work at the beginner's rate as does a new employee? If the transfer is at the employee's request, is the answer to the previous question the same? If the transferred employee can come up to production standards sooner than a new employee, must he remain at the beginner's rate as long as a new employee would? Sometimes in order to get an employee to consent to a transfer, especially for the convenience of the company, wage concessions may be made. A special learning rate is frequently paid to an employee on new work when he is transferred from another position or department. In companies where promotions depend in part or entirely on seniority, the transferred employee may lose his job seniority in his old department yet maintain his seniority for promotional opportunities.

There may be very special types of applying seniority. For instance in one automobile accessory manufacturing plant a man holds his seniority on a job basis departmentally, divisionally, and plant wide. In case of a layoff, if he is the youngest man of the particular classification in the plant he will be laid off. After being off of the job for one work week (assuming that he has more than five years seniority) he can claim plant-wide seniority on any job in the plant that is held by a man of less than five years seniority provided he can qualify to perform the job in a seven-day training period.

Transfers between Departments. The personnel department is primarily responsible for interdepartmental transfers subject, of course, to the approval of the supervisor. The personnel department is the direct representative of the management and is not especially interested in any particular department except to see that men are so placed that their capacities will be used to the greatest benefit of all concerned. Because the records are available in the personnel department, its representatives can select men with desired qualifications in the shortest time. It is a violation of good organization for one supervisor to deal directly with another supervisor's men who may be seeking a transfer to the first supervisor's department. To do so is almost certain to result in ill feeling between the supervisors. The personnel department exists to solve such problems and should be used. When a supervisor is approached to transfer a man to another department, he should consider both the man's opportunity in the new department and the needs of his own department. The supervisor has a responsibility to every one of his men not to stand in the way of their developing their capacities to the fullest extent, and also to the company to see that each man's services are most effectively used. It is a reciprocal relationship and should always be viewed from the standpoint of the greatest advantage both to the company and the men.

A request for a transfer may originate from either the company or the employee. The employees' interests and their capacities must be matched against the position that is vacant. Finally, records of transfers are necessary. These records originate in the department from which the transferred employee comes and are approved in the department to which he is transferred; they pass through the payroll department and end in the personnel department. At times the personnel department may originate the records. The record-keeping phase of transfers is important to all the parties concerned and must not be overlooked by any of the parties involved.

Promotion. A promotion implies a present or expected increase in pay which would not be realized on the old job, or it may involve an increase in social status such as going from the factory to the office or from machine work to inspection. It frequently results in increased responsibilities and recognition and usually is followed by an increase in rank and pay. Sometimes promotion brings only some special privilege such as not having to punch a time clock. There are many who advocate promoting men from within the organization when openings occur rather than hiring new men from the outside. Justice to old and faithful employees requires giving them opportunities to advance when opportunities develop. Promotion from within improves morale and loyalty and should result in increased productivity. Promoting men decreases hiring costs and unemployment compensation costs. The reduced hiring costs, however, may be more than offset by increased training costs when promotion takes place at a level considerably above the lowest rank. One promotion starts a chain of promotions that results in having to train a number of men instead of one new man hired from the outside for the one vacancy. Nevertheless, the increased training cost may well be justified since it develops a versatile work force, maintains good morale, and enhances the reputation of the company.

Blind following of the "promotion-from-within policy" as a fetish is not justified by the facts of industrial experience. As a matter of basic policy the company should seek the best man for the job when considering the total situation. Provided men of the proper potential have been hired the best man is likely to be within the plant but not necessarily so. The soundest policy in selecting employees for new positions has been found to be: *secure the best possible man for the job from within the organization if he is available, but from the outside if a better man is available there.* The result of this policy is that the men in the organization are kept on their toes because they know that promotion will come only if merited on a competitive basis. Promotion from within, wherever possible, increases morale and loyalty, provides a more versatile working force, and leads to employment stabilization. It is advisable, however, to bring in new blood from the outside periodically and the policy just mentioned brings this result. Promotion solely from within, if constantly followed, is likely to result in an inbred organization, a scarcity of new ideas and methods, and eventual stagnation.

Bases for Promotion. Promotions may be made on the basis of merit, seniority, or a combination of merit and seniority. Seniority as a basis for special privilege is as old as recorded history and appeals to the masses very strongly. Some organizations use seniority as the sole basis for promotion—the man oldest in the job getting the promotion. In other organizations, merit is the sole basis of promotion—the man who has done the best work getting the promotion. Finally, many organizations have worked out a basis of combining merit and seniority to select men for promotion. This plan requires merit ratings, accurate and complete personnel records, and supervisors who understand and conscientiously rate their men at regular intervals.

Logic is against seniority as the sole basis for promotion. Company experience with seniority as the sole basis of promotion seems to confirm the logic of using merit as the major criterion. Seniority as the sole basis for promotion places a premium on service in terms of time alone and tends to destroy initiative. Obviously it places a heavy burden on the personnel department in terms of the original hiring. Merit alone as a basis for promotion raises objections from men who have been employed with a company over a period of time and are inclined to feel that ability alone should not control, but that service with the company should also be taken into consideration. Merit alone as a basis for promotion may affect both departmental morale and loyalty. The conflict between promoting on the basis of merit vs. seniority is a battle of sentiments. Workers' distrust of management inclines them to feel that they are protected only by seniority. Management's regard for productivity, the logics of costs, predisposes it toward merit. The two sentiments sometimes get close enough to operate by agreeing on a combination of merit and seniority. On the basis of a combination of merit and seniority, with seniority prevailing when merit is equal, the only disadvantage again is the fact that the best man available may not be selected, for the simple reason that the best man may not be within the bargaining unit or the organization, hence he cannot be promoted. If a company does follow a plan of filling all positions above the lowest level from within, however, the last plan is the most satisfactory both in terms of bringing results and of being acceptable to most of the men. The company gains through the use of merit and the employees, at least in part, have their seniority recognized. This plan, however, requires effective use of merit rating and a capable personnel department with detailed records readily available. It is one thing to announce a policy of promoting from within and quite a different thing to carry this plan into effective operation. Such a program requires careful planning and the establishment of adequate procedures to become effective.

Responsibility for Promotion. Top management is basically responsible for policies on promotion. In order to make itself effective top management delegates to its representatives most of its operating responsibilities. The supervisor is a representative of top management and plays a major role in promotions within the department. The training of his men and his understanding of their strong points and their weaknesses, as he corrects the latter and develops the former, are responsibilities to be met by the supervisor. Impartially and accurately rating his men and bringing their abilities and capacities to the attention of the management are also essential functions of the supervisor. The supervisor is accountable for recommending men for promotion, for the selection of men qualified for promotion, and for recognizing the necessity for the management, in carrying out the aims of the enterprise, to fill positions with the best qualified men. The supervisor who pushes his men, even when they are not the best qualified for the promotional opportunity, has lost sight of his major responsibility to management. The supervisor who plays favorites in his ratings and selections likewise is not fairly and squarely meeting his responsibility as a supervisor. The successful supervisor trains and develops his men so that when openings occur and his men are qualified to fill these promotional opportunities, he has them ready and management informed as to their capacities.

Interplant or interdepartmental transfers are major responsibilities of the personnel department in cooperation with the supervisors and other executives. The complete records of the employee under consideration for promotion are available in the personnel department. The supervisor through ratings and individual comments has made his opinions a part of the employee's records. The personnel department's records include the performances of the individual employees, their interests and capacities, scores made on various tests, physical examination reports, and their progress through the company in terms of positions held and wage changes. These records must be so filed that they are readily accessible in finding men with special qualifications to fill a specific position.

Some organizations through their personnel departments set up promotion charts, showing the new employee how his job is a part of the line of promotion and what positions above his own are open to him. Other organizations operate an understudy system by which men are trained for positions to which they are promoted as openings occur. Such a method of filling openings with understudies results in the company's usually having capable men ready to step into positions as these positions become vacant. The wise supervisor will develop an understudy for his position, bringing the man along carefully, instructing him in the duties and responsibilities of the supervisor's position. The supervisor will likewise develop understudies for the key jobs in his department in order that he may have someone ready to fill vacancies.

The three-position Gilbreth plan of promotion was devised by Frank Gilbreth, the founder of motion and time study.[1] This plan regards each man as occupying three positions in the organization which are considered as changing constantly in an upward spiral. These positions are: the position the man last occupied in the organization, the position he occupies at present, and the position he will next occupy. In the first position the man is teaching the person who took his place, in the second position he is doing the work of his present job, and in the third position he is being instructed in the next position for which he is being prepared. Thus the man is at the same time an instructor, a worker, and a learner.

The Discharge. *The policy in many organizations today is that the supervisor may discharge an employee only from his department.* In principle this policy is sound; when all concerned carry it out in good faith few, if any, serious disciplinary situations arise. The personnel

---

[1] See *The Writings of the Gilbreths,* edited by William R. Spriegel and Clark E. Myers, Richard D. Irwin, Homewood, Ill., 1953, pp. 260–267.

officer handling such cases must use great tact to obtain maximum results. The supervisor is jealous of his reputation and so is the employee. Both parties are anxious for a chance to save face. Each man desires not to lose status in the eyes of his associates. It is essential today that the supervisor recognize the need for the exercise of care in the event of discharge. Frequently, however, discharges are not necessary and a transfer of the man to another department or other work will save him to the company and eliminate costs that otherwise would be necessary. An examination of the causes of discharge will reveal many situations where this is true.

Causes of Discharges. Experience with and an analysis of discharges reveal that the major cause is character traits. Personality factors play a leading role as a cause of discharges. Emotional immaturity frequently provides a stumbling block to a worker's adjusting to the work situation. This problem arises among highly skilled workers and highly educated scientists as well as workers at the lowest levels. It is the quirks of personality and character that lead to the largest number of discharges. A lack of cooperation, laziness, absenteeism, tardiness, and dishonesty are the chief causes of discharges. The supervisor should study his men for signs of the beginning of these character traits and should attempt to nip them in the bud by working with the individuals and showing them how to avoid discharge by changing their ways.

If the supervisor has made every effort to change the attitude of the employee and he is definitely hampering the work of the department, the only recourse is discharge or at least a transfer to another department. Many companies have certain rules and regulations which when violated call for discharge. These rules usually are for the protection of the lives of other employees or for the protection of the good name of the company. Lack of capacity of the employee to fill the position for which he was hired is another cause for considering discharge. When the employee has received training, and yet cannot meet the production standards set for his work, he must either be discharged or transferred to another department for which he is suited. When no other position is available he will have to be discharged. Illness leading to incapacity to perform work or an accident resulting in a permanent injury are other causes for discharge of the employee, although this is not discharge in its ordinary sense. A shortage of work and definite knowledge that there will not be enough work to keep the regular force busy are other causes for a permanent layoff. Actually some of these causes will occur very rarely. If hiring is properly done incapacity to perform the work will seldom arise, although it may develop later after the man has been with the company for a period of time. If the new employee is properly introduced to his work and informed on company policies, rules, and regulations, he is not likely to violate those which result in discharge.

Procedures in Discharges. Above all things the supervisor should avoid any claim that disciplinary action leading to the discharge is due to the man's union affiliation. A written record should be made at the time of discharge, setting forth the reason for discharging the man. Whenever possible, this record should be supported by witnesses and evidence, if available. The charges on which the discharge is based should be consistent or the employee may be reinstated over the protest of management and receive back pay for the time he was off the job. When the offense is one other than a serious violation involving the safety and welfare of the company and others, the employee's record and previous ratings should be consulted before discharge. The supervisor should be permitted to discharge from his department only. Final discharge from the organization should be made only after a conference of the employee and a representative of the personnel department. Discharges always have definite effects on the morale and attitude of the men under the supervisor. The supervisor who uses the discharge only as a last resort but then does it firmly and in line with the policies and procedures of his company will retain the respect of his men. The men frequently recognize the need for the discharge of an employee before the supervisor does, and failure of the supervisor to act promptly will only hurt him in the eyes of his men. Undeserved discharges, however, will lower the confidence of the men since they are likely to know all the facts of the case and are able to evaluate the supervisor's action.

Demotion. Large numbers of supervisors and executives use the discharge rather than demote a man. Discharging a man is often the easy way out whereas demoting him raises problems which the supervisor may not wish to face. Nevertheless, there are certain advantages in demotion as opposed to discharge. When a man has been with the company for some length of time, the company has an investment in him which is thrown away when he is discharged. A machine is rarely junked, it is rebuilt. Men can be rebuilt, but it takes effort and care especially on the part of the supervisor. He must handle the demotion in such a way as to help the man "save his face," and when considering a demotion should attempt to get the man to suggest the change himself. This can often be done if the supervisor will recognize in advance the need for a change in status for the individual. The supervisor must, however, know the *capacities* and *interests* of the individual well enough to select a job that he can fill successfully. There is no reason for making a demotion which later has to be followed by another. Frequently a demotion and transfer can be effected at the same time.

17 : Safety and the Supervisor

Safety—An Attitude. As a rule accidents do not merely happen. They are caused by someone who did not think that it could happen to him. Of course, in a few cases an individual is hurt by the carelessness of someone else, such as the innocent worker on an adjacent machine who is injured by a flying piece that was not properly clamped in his neighbor's machine. These cases are rare in comparison with the injuries to the individual caused by his own negligence. Safety contests, safety talks, and instruction in working safely are valuable tools in getting workers to work safely; however, accidents take place at the point of operation. The actual workplace is the focal point of truly effective safe working practices.

Until the entire supervisory work force and each individual worker at work looks upon working safely as his individual responsibility, needless accidents will continue. Working safely can become truly popular, and it can give the worker a feeling of satisfaction equivalent to or greater than that derived by the "show off" who takes a chance and gets by with it. When an individual who cuts corners and fails to use the safety guard learns that his fellow workers frown upon his carelessness he will not be so prone to defy the regulations. When the entire work group looks upon working safely as both a group and individual responsibility, then the group can be regarded as being "safety minded." When an entire company manifests a safety attitude the record speaks for itself (see Figure 17.1).

The supervisor sets the pattern in practicing safety. When a new machine fixture or conveyor is turned over to him he will carefully check it for potential hazards and insist that all reasonable safety

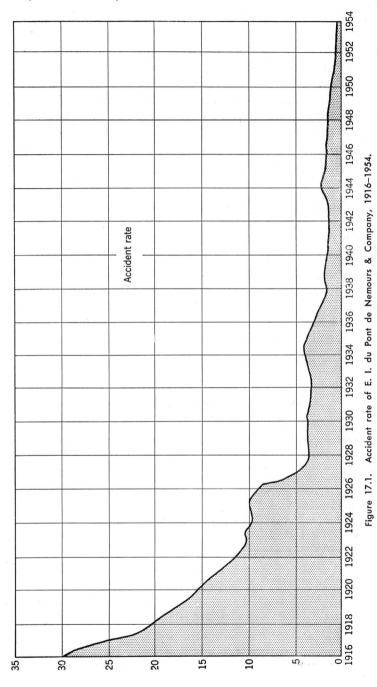

Figure 17.1. Accident rate of E. I. du Pont de Nemours & Company, 1916–1954.

guards be provided. In instructing a new man the supervisor will make certain that all guards are in place before he begins his instruction. He will not run the machine without the guards and then tell his employees to use the guards. Accidents in industry take place at the point of operations. Eternal vigilance is the price to be paid for developing and maintaining a safety attitude. When the supervisor at all times demonstrates by actions and words that he expects his men to follow rigidly safe working practices they will become imbued with the desire to work safely. One or two slips by the supervisor in setting an example may easily undo a year's efforts at promoting safety.

The Causes of Accidents. The breakdown of the *unsafe acts, personal causes,* and *mechanical causes* shown in Table 17.1 indicates definitely the responsibility of management for proper selection, training, and discipline of employees, as well as management's responsibility for removing most of the mechanical causes. The 20–80 ratio of accident causes has often been misinterpreted. In most of the cases, had either the mechanical factors been right or had the employee been working safely the accident would not have occurred. This fact shows that most of the accidents could have been avoided either by

TABLE 17.1

Causes (by Percentages) of Accidents *

Unsafe Acts		*Personal Causes*	
Unnecessary exposure to danger	26	Lack of knowledge or skill	48
Improper use of unsafe tools	16	Improper attitude	31
Non-use of safety devices	15	Bodily defects	3
Unsafe loading or arrangement	10	No personal cause	18
Operating at unsafe speed	7		100%
Working on moving equipment	6		
Improper starting or stopping	5	*Mechanical Causes*	
Other unsafe acts	2	Hazardous arrangement	34
No unsafe act	13	Defective agencies	18
	100%	Unsafe apparel	15
		Improper guarding	9
		Improper light or ventilation	2
		No mechanical cause	22
			100%

* Source: National Safety Council, *Accident Facts*, 1939 Edition, p. 19.

proper mechanical care or by the employees working more carefully. By management's approaching the problem from both angles, a few metalworking companies have better safety records than department stores. It can be done. The National Safety Council reports that 87 per cent of all work accidents involve some unsafe act, and that 78 per cent have some mechanical or material cause. In approximately 80 per cent of the unsafe acts, some definite personal cause was responsible. Mechanical causes accounted for about 20 per cent of the total accidents.

A serious problem arises at times when workers on an incentive wage system ignore safety regulations even though the allowed time takes into consideration the safe practices. An occasional safety device has been improperly engineered, thus placing an unnecessary burden on production. Figure 17.2 shows a unique device for protecting the worker from injury by the press. Careful engineering may change a hazardous operation into a safe one and increase production at the same time.

The Responsibility for Accidents. It is fashionable to blame the supervisor for all industrial ills. In fact, the individual worker is primarily responsible for most accidents. This statement is predicated on the assumption that the foreman has done his job of properly instructing the worker in safe working methods and has provided him with reasonable safeguards against injury. This viewpoint of the worker's responsibility for his injury is realistic when looking at his suffering and the loss to his family.

From management's viewpoint the supervisor is responsible for the accidents in his department. The supervisor represents management in instructing in safe working practices and in seeing to it that workers follow these practices. Management expects the supervisor to enforce safe working rules in exactly the same sense that he maintains quality standards. In a tough-minded sense the supervisor is supposed to teach his men how to work safely, strive to lead them in the practice of safety, but enforce penalties for a failure to work as instructed. Most of the supervisor's leadership is of a positive nature, yet there may be times when penalties are called for. An accident is an unnecessary cost in most cases just as excess scrap is a needless cost.

Accident Costs. It is very difficult to determine the exact costs of accidents. Data on the direct out-of-pocket costs of insurance are readily available as well as on all the direct costs of guards, the safety director's salary, and such items, but the indirect costs of accidents

Courtesy Hazatrol Corporation, San
Francisco, California

Figure 17.2. Safety guard. Radioactive material in wrist bands provides constant signal
that locks press instantly if operator's hands are too near. White tubes jutting out from
the press are the signal-detectors. They are connected to a control box and a fail-safe
timer.

are very difficult to measure.[1] There is also an additional cost that cannot be figured, namely, the added labor turnover arising from employees leaving when the accident experience is high. Practically every large company in the United States has a formally organized safety program. All of them have a vital economic and social interest in safety, even though a few may carry on their work through the regular line organization. A bad accident rate may run into a substantial cost per capita. To reduce this rate is to reduce costs. The total costs of injuries average at least five times the sum of compensation paid, plus the medical expenses. For instance, if compensation paid was $200 and medical expense for the same accident was $100, the total cost to the employer, when figuring every factor, would be approximately $1,500.[2]

Safety and the New Employee. The new employee not only has the additional strain of trying to adjust to his new associates and environment, he also has to learn a new job. If this is his first industrial employment he may never have had any experience in the type of work that he is beginning. To this type of employee nearly everything is new. Such an employee places a special responsibility on the supervisor to see that he is given detailed careful instruction in safe practices. Nothing should be taken for granted. This type of new employee may readily injure himself seriously if not properly instructed. The accident rate is higher among new employees than among skilled workers in spite of their eagerness to learn and willingness to observe safety regulations. Many of their accidents arise from awkwardness, but many others arise from a lack of skill and improper training.

Assuming that the new employee has emotional stability, his attitude toward working safely is likely to be acquired from his supervisor and his fellow workers. If safety is deeply imbedded in the consciousness of the work group the new employee soon acquires the

[1] See H. W. Heinrich, *Industrial Accident Prevention,* McGraw-Hill Book Co., New York, 1950, pp. 50–52, for his discussion of the 4 to 1 ratio of indirect costs of accidents. The 4 to 1 ratio was found to be too high by Rollin Head Simonds in his doctor's dissertation, "The Development and Use of a Method for Estimating the Cost to Eight Producers of Their Industrial Accidents," Northwestern University, 1948. He found the ratio "to be between 1.6 to 1 and 2 to 1, certainly not much over 2 to 1; however, the companies were weighted in the averaging." See also Rollin H. Simonds, "Estimating Industrial Accident Costs," *Harvard Business Review,* Jan. 1951, pp. 107–118.

[2] See Roland P. Blake, *Industrial Safety,* Prentice-Hall. New York, 1953, pp. 22–29.

same attitude. Of course the reverse is true. If the "old-timers" chide him about the use of safety guards he is likely to ignore their use as soon as he feels that he can do so without being hurt.

Safety and the Old-timer Who Is Placed on a New Job. The long-service employee is not likely to be given the same detailed care and instruction in safety as the new employee. Not only is he often not given the same careful instruction, he is even more likely to hesitate to ask questions when he should. Such a man may easily hurt himself when he would not if he were properly instructed. The "safety mind-edness" on the part of the supervisor should manifest itself in assigning "old-timers" to new jobs just as effectively as when training new men. The "old-timers" working on a new job have more accidents than experienced men on the same job.

The Maladjusted Employee. In Chapter 10, "The Supervisor and Mental Health," the unstable worker was discussed in considerable detail. Here, our interest in the maladjusted employee is the influence of this maladjustment on accidents. Fortunately most people have achieved a fair measure of adjustment to their total environment. Relatively few people are really unhappy in their work. On the other hand individuals who are usually going along on an even keel may have disturbances arising in the work situation that upset their normal equilibrium. The basis of the difficulty may be something outside of the company. For instance, a worker's son may have fallen in with some teen age gangsters and robbed a gas station. His thoughts are not on his work and he makes a series of mistakes. His foreman calls these to his attention or even lays him off for a week. While he is in this emotional state the worker's attention slips and he loses a finger. Under normal conditions this worker would not have had the accident. His foreman may not have known of the son's difficulties. This worker was not maladjusted in the usual sense, but under the circumstances he was in no condition to operate the machine.

In other situations certain employees (substantially more than we are willing to believe) simply have not come to terms with the realities of modern industrial life. They are immature. So long as things are going smoothly for them at work and at home they get along fairly well. Nevertheless, these persons are likely to be highly sensitive to the slightest criticism, jealous of their prerogatives, suspicious of the motives of others, and in fact not willing or able to assume their full share of contributing to the group effort. They are making greater demands on their work situations than their associates, including their supervisors, may reasonably be expected to make. A few of these persons may be highly productive when working alone or with others who are willing to tolerate or to cater to their excessive demands. When these supports are not forthcoming they brood over imagined injustices and are injured because of inattention to their work. It is not unusual for these people to be absent more than others or to suffer from violent headaches. Many of them are accident repeaters.

In either of these two groups the supervisor may reduce the number of accidents if he is fortunate enough to recognize the situation and provide the needed counsel and guidance. In the case of the man disturbed by outside factors the supervisor may not know of it until after the accident occurs. If he is fortunate enough to know prior to any accident he may encourage his troubled employee to redouble his efforts to work carefully, telling him in a sympathetic and understanding way that special care needs to be given when one is under an undue strain. In the case of the person who has really not matured a few supervisors possess that rare skill in counselling which enables them to point out to these people that they are the ones who are not carrying their share of cooperative effort, that they are not acting as grown-up men. This is a slow and painstaking process. However, some supervisors accept these people as a special challenge and do a remarkably good job with them. Unfortunately, most supervisors are so hard pressed with their other duties that they cannot or will not find time to try to make the effort. Other supervisors find it difficult to approach a consultive interview with their problem employees. Their hesitancy is understandable. The assignment is not an easy one; neither is it always successful. On an occasion when the author was commending a supervisor who has enjoyed remarkable success in helping maladjusted workers get on their feet he received the following reply: "If you knew of the many times I have failed you would not think that I have had much success. I have learned one thing, however. These people need help. I would like to be the one to help them. I am willing to be rebuffed by many in order to help a few."

Training Employees to Work Safely. There is nothing special about training employees to work safely. It is merely proper training. There are no special techniques or methods that are of major importance other than the ones used in the regular training of the employee how to do his job. Of course the instructor needs to recognize that training in safe practices is an integral part of the training process. To overlook any phase of the training is a serious error. The safety aspects may readily be overlooked in the concentrating on the "how" of the production requirements. There is one other phase of training in safety and it is an eternal requirement. When the new employee is making real progress, the supervisor should not assume that his job in safety is over. This is the time he should drop by his trainee, commend him on his progress and ask him to demonstrate the safety requirements. This type of approach is more effective than committee meetings, posters, contests, or practically any of the popular devices, helpful as they may be.

Safety Contests. Safety contests awaken team spirit in emloyees and tend to keep the group aware of the need for working safely. They probably have as much effect on the supervisor as on the men. These contests call to the attention of the supervisor one of his responsibilities that should ever be on his mind but one that may be slighted under the pressure of other duties. For instance, the safety minded supervisor usually has the good intention to talk with each worker during a certain period about his safety record and the importance of safety to everybody (Figure 17.3). He means to do it but sometimes just does not get around to doing it. The safety contest may readily be the real impetus to his finding time to do what he promises himself to do.

Courtesy Frigidaire Corporation

Figure 17.3. Foreman talks safety with an employee.

Workers also derive group pride from a record of safety as publicized by thermometers, clocks, bar charts, and the many other devices used. Figure 17.4 shows a dramatic method of calling the safety performance to the attention of an entire division or factory. Ofttimes a similar but smaller board displayed in a conspicuous place in each

Figure 17.4. Clock records lost time accidents each month.

department is an effective method of recalling the importance of safety to all employees. When a department has achieved a good record a spirit of keeping up the good work is developed.

Enlisting Employee Cooperation—The Safety Committee. The safety committee may be used at any managerial or operative level. It has a valuable place as an all-company institution. Such a committee may be composed solely of management representatives or (where there is a union) it may include union members. Committees are valuable instruments for giving advice and for securing cooperation in carrying out the advice given. Top-level committees have their major advan-

tage in developing an awareness of the need for attention to safety at
the work level, the only place where it really counts. Figure 17.5
illustrates a meeting of the plant manager with an all-factory safety
committee.

Committees at the department or division level get closer to the point
of operation and are likely to have a more direct effect on the safe
working practices of the employees. Some companies have found
it advantageous to rotate the membership on these committees, thus

Courtesy Frigidaire Corporation

Figure 17.5. Plant manager's safety meeting.

involving as many men as possible in the safety movement. Some
committees of workers or their representatives make inspections of their
departments and render reports on their findings. These, of course,
are of primary importance in terms of getting the workers to work more
carefully or in pointing out unguarded hazards that need attention.
Any reasonable effort to develop and maintain a safety consciousness
on the part of a work force is justifiable. Committees seldom run
themselves entirely divorced from interested leadership. At the departmental level this leadership nearly always is directly or indirectly
provided by the supervisor. The more he remains in the background
as a sympathetic counselor, the better.

Safety Guards. Figure 17.6 illustrates an effective point-of-operation punch-press guard. Other types of guards pull the worker's hands
away from the descending tool.

Courtesy General Motors Corporation

Figure 17.6. Basket guard for punch press, Ternstedt Manufacturing Company, Detroit. (See handle for feeding parts into press.)

The loss of eyes could easily be avoided by the use of goggles. Goggles should be fitted by someone skilled in fitting glasses. This person should appreciate what constitutes a fitted goggle, so that the wearer may, in addition to obtaining protection from the eye hazard he is compelled to encounter, be given the assurance of a feeling of security and comfort. Proper clothing for the worker is almost as important as the guarding of machines. Safety garments tend to induce a safety attitude. Accident prevention by making floors and walk-ways safe is a big factor in reducing the industrial-accident toll. A study by the National Electric Light Association indicates that more than one-third of all falls occur on the level and on stairways, not from poles, scaffolds, or other equipment.

The Supervisor's Place in Organizing for Safety. Figure 17.7 portrays the safety functions in a well-organized company that strives to enlist everyone's efforts to reduce accidents. It will be observed that the foreman occupies a key position. Safety is not one man's job; safety is everybody's business.

Summary. The safety role of the supervisor is primary in the struggle to eliminate waste and human sorrow and suffering. On a humanitarian basis, if for no other reason, supervisors should be proud of their opportunity for service. The achievement of accident reduction in American industry has been summarized as follows:

1. The accomplishment of numerous firms in every major branch of industry proves that disabling injuries can be reduced to a figure that closely approaches elimination.

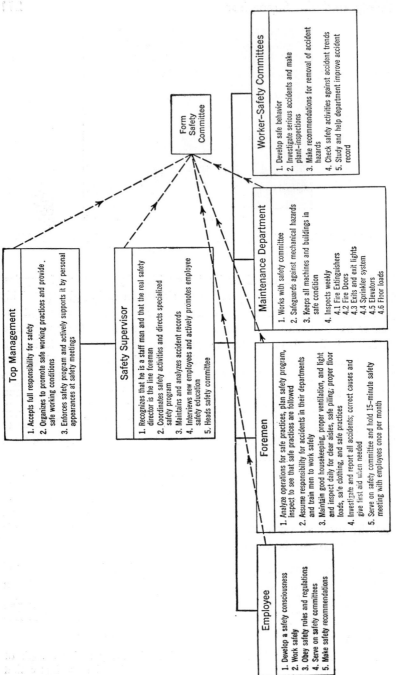

Top Management

1. Accepts full responsibility for safety
2. Organizes to promote safe working practices and provide safe working conditions
3. Enforces safety program and actively supports it by personal appearances at safety meetings

Safety Supervisor

1. Recognizes that he is a staff man and that the real safety director is the line foreman
2. Coordinates safety activities and directs specialized safety program
3. Maintains and analyzes accident records
4. Interviews new employees and actively promotes employee safety education
5. Heads safety committee

Employee

1. Develop a safety consciousness
2. Work safely
3. Obey safety rules and regulations
4. Serve on safety committees
5. Make safety recommendations

Foremen

1. Analyze operations for safe practices, plan safety program, inspect to see that safe practices are followed
2. Assume responsibility for accidents in their departments and train men to work safely
3. Maintain good housekeeping, proper ventilation, and light and inspect daily for clear aisles, safe piling; proper floor loads, safe clothing, and safe practices
4. Investigate and report all accidents; correct causes and give first aid when needed
5. Serve on safety committee and hold 15-minute safety meeting with employees once per month

Maintenance Department

1. Works with safety committee
2. Safeguards against mechanical hazards
3. Keeps all machines and buildings in safe condition
4. Inspects weekly
   4.1 Fire Extinguishers
   4.2 Fire Doors
   4.3 Exits and exit lights
   4.4 Sprinkler system
   4.5 Elevators
   4.6 Floor loads

Worker–Safety Committees

1. Develop safe behavior
2. Investigate serious accidents and make plant–inspections
3. Make recommendations for removal of accident hazards
4. Check safety activities against accident trends
5. Study and help department improve accident record

Form Safety Committee

Figure 17.7. Safety functions.

2. It pays to do so.

3. The expenditures required are relatively small.

4. Some degree of hazard is associated with every form of activity; therefore, the highest degree of accident elimination can be achieved only by careful, painstaking attention to safety in every form of activity carried on in any given establishment or undertaking.

5. Accident prevention does not rest upon involved theory or special technical skill. Instead, it depends mainly upon safety mindedness by management and men. Safety mindedness may be defined as "the ever-active attention to safety in every detail of each day's work."

6. If properly applied, the knowledge and resourcefulness possessed by every industrial organization, large or small, is adequate to bring its safety performance into accord with best practice and keep it there.

7. Any management, regardless of the size of the establishment, type of industry or undertaking, or financial condition, can eliminate the majority of its work injuries.

8. Each injury results from the combination of a physical hazard and human error. The correction of either will usually prevent the injury, but top safety performance can be had only by eliminating or reducing every physical hazard to the maximum degree practicable and, in addition, using every feasible means of controlling all work habits and practices in the interest of safety.[3]

Working safely is the result of effectively carrying out (on the part of both workers and management) of a positive attitude toward safety. Low frequency and severity rates manifest themselves in low production costs. Hazardous jobs usually carry a higher rate of pay than safe ones. Before a given job is given a higher rate of pay for its hazardous nature, every reasonable effort should be exerted to eliminate the hazard.

[3] *Safety Subjects,* Bulletin No. 67, U.S. Dept of Labor, Washington, D. C., 1948, pp. 5–6.

18 Promoting Cooperation between Men and between Departments

The Need for Cooperation. One of the basic desires of people brought up in the culture of the English-speaking countries is the desire for group acceptance. Cooperation is a manifestation of group and individual acceptance. The thoughtful executive is keenly aware that *his success is in reality group success*. Effective action in his department is to a considerable extent dependent on the cooperation of his men. Planning alone is not enough; cooperation is essential to translate the planning into action to obtain maximum results. Although a supervisor may drive his men and secure blind obedience in turning out some work, if he is to utilize their capacities to the greatest extent, he must have their cooperation. Ability to develop and maintain cooperation within the department is one of the attributes of positive leadership.

Not only does a department head need the cooperation of his own employees, he also needs the cooperation of other departments. The cooperation between departments is a reflection of the cooperation between the heads of these departments. The production department, to meet the production standards set for it, must have cooperation from the maintenance department, from the departments preceding and following it in the production line, from the materials supply department, and many other departments within the organization. Essentially the same methods and the same approach may be employed to win cooperation from other departments as are used to secure the cooperation of the men within the department.

What Is Cooperation? Cooperation is a term in such common use that one seldom stops to examine its true meaning. "Co" means *with* and "operation" means *doing;* therefore, cooperation means "doing with." Too often men seeking cooperation think of it as meaning doing for. Cooperation refers to the *act of working or operating with someone,* not the act of working for someone. The *with* of cooperation implies willingness, whereas the *for* does not necessarily mean willingness and may even imply coercion or force. Cooperation is not given for the asking; it can arise only out of situations that give satisfactions to the individual and the group. Many a supervisor sets out to win cooperation, overlooking the fact that the way must first be paved. The characteristics essential to cooperation include: (1) a common purpose, (2) recognition of the mutuality of interests, (3) working together to achieve that common purpose, and (4) submergence of individual interests at least temporarily to achieve the greater group objective.

A recognition of the mutuality of interest in attaining a common purpose is the real basis of the integration of interest from which cooperation naturally flows. Too often the supervisor overlooks the need for showing his men that they are part of the organization and that the purpose of the organization is also their purpose. The supervisor should interpret company policies impartially and completely to the men and then follow up to see that there is a continued and complete understanding by his men of the company policies in relationship to the purpose of the organization. The interests of the men, the supervisory force, and the management are the same in the long run. All three groups succeed or fail together. Much of the trouble between management and men during the past years can be traced to the failure of both to recognize that fundamentally their interests are the same. Since the supervisor is management's representative to the workers, he is the most logical person to develop a recognition of the common purpose and the mutuality of interest of management, the workers, and the consumers. The act of cooperation involves submergence of individual interests, temporarily at least, in order to achieve a greater institutional objective. The individual, whether the supervisor or one of the men, must recognize that his long-range interests are paramount, and it may be necessary for him to sacrifice his short-range interests at times for the sake of the ultimate objective. Sometimes *operating with* means doing it the other fellow's way. When this way means achieving the common purpose and when the interests of both are the same, doing it his way or submerging one's ideas in his method produces cooperation.

Cooperation requires *knowledge, identification,* and *action* on the part of the individual. He must first know the common purpose, then he must identify himself with it, and finally he must take action to make the common purpose a reality. The supervisor must not only know the purpose but also see that his men know it. He must show them that he is identified with it and that they are also. It is relatively easy for the supervisor to get a man to work *for him* but what counts is having the man willingly work *with him.* The man who only *works for him* will work only when the supervisor or his representative is around; the man *working with* the supervisor will work just as well when the supervisor is away. The third condition necessary to cooperation is the act of doing the thing that is recognized as what should be done. This is something more than blind obedience; it is action with both parties working together intelligently and effectively, each contributing his own ideas and methods to achieve the common purpose. Cooperation is the act of *working together willingly and intelligently to achieve a common purpose.*

Cooperation Is Essential. What *coordination* is to the formal organization, *cooperation* is to the informal organization (see Figure 2.1). The informal relationships contribute a great deal to the smooth functioning of the formal organization. Earlier in our book we have said that *organization is not an end in itself but a means to the end; sound organization creates an atmosphere in which the energies of the employees are released so that the enterprise moves slowly but resolutely toward its goal.* This type of operation requires a high measure of both *cooperation* and *coordination.* Cooperation in industry is essential because of the interdependence of individuals, departments, groups, companies, industries, areas, and even nations. Our entire economic life is dependent on the principles of specialization, and cooperation is inherent in specialization. If it were possible for one man to perform all the operations in the processing of a raw material into a finished product, cooperation would not be so important. The degree of cooperation necessary between the farmer and the employees in the factory is obvious. The principle of specialization is not new, but the broad application of it has come only recently and its recognition and use demand effective application of the principles of coordination and cooperation. Through cooperation individuals as a group are capable of accomplishing far more than they could accomplish individually.

The Individual's Role in Cooperation. Anyone who has observed very small children at play recalls how their desires frequently dominate their actions and how they often ride roughshod over the rights of others. We also are familiar with grown-ups who have never outgrown their youthful ways. They are immature. As an individual, man possesses certain urges that are competitive rather than cooperative and it is necessary to learn to submerge these desires to the common purpose. When he learns this the individual will find his work progressing a great deal more smoothly. Contacts between men and management are successful only to the degree that both sides submerge their short-run interests, recognize the common purpose and their mutuality of interest, and cooperate by working with each other. The original basis of cooperation among men was self-preservation, and from the primitive tribe down to large-scale industry today experience has taught that the self may be extended and more satisfactions in goods and services may be realized through cooperation, especially within certain broad areas of human effort, than through unbridled strife or competition.

While competition characterizes many of the actions of individuals, group association is also one of the basic urges of man. Under proper conditioning men derive pleasure from cooperative effort when the results satisfy their wants. Cooperation appeals to the gregarious instincts of men.

Group Cooperation. In Chapter 9 we discussed the nature of individual differences and group attitudes. Among savages the stranger is a common enemy of the tribe. The group has priority over the individual and as such has acquired certain traditions and customs that change slowly and exert a profound influence on its members. Therefore, the supervisor cannot expect cooperation from his group when his actions or requests run contrary to the group traditions and expectations. Group action is seldom a reasoned action but one arising out of a total situation and is definitely influenced by such factors as emotions, sentiments, customs, traditions, physical environment, physical conditions of members of the group, suggestions that harmonize with some other strong influence, and a feeling of oneness. Group pressure may aid the supervisor in getting an individual worker to conform to an accepted standard. On the other hand the group's own standard may be immeasurably lower than what may reasonably be expected and it may exert pressure on an individual to keep him from working up to management's standard. By a careful study of group action and individual differences a supervisor can increase his effectiveness in developing cooperation.

Winning Group Acceptance and Cooperation.   Integrating the interests of management and the workers is the soundest basis for promoting group acceptance of a given action or standard.[1] The supervisor must make it easy for his group to identify its interests with those of management. He must show them by word and action that his interests and their interests are the same. The supervisor must find the easy way, not the difficult path for the men to follow in identifying their interests with his. He must recognize that fundamentally men like to work together for a common purpose because it satisfies their gregarious instinct. The successful supervisor takes the attitude that his men want to work with him, not that they are antagonistic to him, his interests, and the company's interests. Men like to be led by a leader whom they respect and whose leadership is in harmony with group ideals. When the supervisor drives his men he is taking the hard way of accomplishing his departmental objectives. Driving men upsets them and often runs contrary to group attitudes and objectives. Leadership recognizes and takes advantage of the group attitudes to win and develop cooperation. A group will subordinate some of its desires so long as it has faith in the integrity of its leaders and the leadership of these men does not require too much sacrifice of group objectives. The supervisor who is a strong leader can get the group to submerge some of its interests but has to be careful not to ask too much or attempt it too rapidly. When the supervisor can show the group that doing the job his way and working with him will accomplish the group's basic objectives, then the group will cooperate.

Specific Factors in Promoting Group Cooperation.   Satisfactory working conditions are an essential factor and the underlying foundation of cooperation, for without these continued cooperation cannot develop. Lighting conditions must be correct, proper heating and ventilation must be maintained. Steps must be taken to meet fatigue and monotony in the work of the individual and the group. Some companies have increased production by playing recorded music at certain periods during the day, and also by introducing rest periods at appropriate times. The supervisor who sees that his equipment is maintained in good condition, that tools and materials are available in the right quantity when needed, and that the work is planned and carried through on schedule will promote cooperation.

[1] See Henry C. Metcalf and L. Urwick, *Dynamic Administration,* Harper and Brothers, New York, 1940, p. 71.

Causes of Employee Attitudes. An individual's attitude is conditioned by his present personal situation, his social situation, the work situation, as well as his past and expected future in relation to these various situations. An unreasonable action by an employee can usually be explained by a past experience as it touches on a present problem. Faced with a reprimand for poor work a new employee may react in a specific way because he sees in his new supervisor the same type of individual as his last supervisor whom he disliked. His attitude is thus affected by his past environment. The employee who has been the victim of kidding during the lunch hour may have developed a sullen attitude that comes out in his contact with his supervisor. How often the description "he got out on the wrong side of bed" is applied to an employee. This is only another way of saying that the personal situation controlled the attitude of the employee. Unsatisfactory home affairs condition the attitude of many an employee. Similarly, the social life of an employee affects and may control his attitude toward his work and his supervisor. The man who spends the evening with friends who are making more money, or who hold more responsible positions than he, may go to work the next day with a chip on his shoulder because of his lack of prestige in the eyes of his friends. These factors may become interwoven with each other, developing a complicated attitude pattern. The schematic arrangement in Figure 8.1, page 77, illustrates the various factors that enter into the reactions of an individual.

Frequently the surface cause of an employee's actions is far removed from the real cause. Often the employee himself will blame his actions on causes that are not the real ones. In many cases the employee does not realize what the real cause of his action was. It may be based on some incident that happened far back in his past employment experience. The supervisor should constantly study and endeavor to understand his men not only as employees but also as individuals. No supervisor who thinks of his men as similar to machines will get far since the human being is a very complicated personality and must be studied as such. Man's mental and emotional reactions are even less predictable than his physical reactions.

A Reflection of the Supervisor's Attitude. The relationships among men are very sensitive. It is difficult at times to say which action is cause and which is effect. The supervisor's attitude is basically influenced by the attitude of his men. The contrary statement is true —the men reflect the attitude of their supervisor. The supervisor's attitude is either a magnet to attract the cooperation of his men or is a repellent that promotes competition and antagonism. It is rare indeed that the supervisor's attitude is neutral. To attract cooperation the supervisor's attitude must be based on absolute honesty and impartiality, supported by the strength of knowing the requirements of the job, having carefully planned the program with a positive approach to the men. A positive yet understanding attitude begets acceptance of leadership, which is a prerequisite of cooperation. Relatively few leaders take the time to analyze their own attitudes. Self-analysis is highly advantageous for the leader who sincerely desires to increase the cooperation in his department. The sample check list on pages 221–222 is an excellent aid in self-analysis.

General Factors That Influence Cooperation. A recognition of individual differences as related to the workers' *desires, capacities,* and *interests* strengthens the leader's hand in promoting cooperation. Internal cooperation within the group is a forerunner of the group's cooperating with the supervisor. *Personnel management is a major function of management* and a high degree of recognition of the personnel needs by the supervisor is a prerequisite of developing cooperation in his department. Little courtesies and considerations are the foundations upon which loyalty is built, and out of loyalty comes cooperation. Courtesy to men and women employees is one sure step toward winning their cooperation. Both employees and supervisors almost universally subscribe to this principle of "square dealing" but difficulties arise in putting it into practice. "Square dealing" does not mean exactly the same treatment for every employee but rather the appreciation of the same honest approach to the situation in the light of the individual differences. All solutions should be based on the company's policies. Uniformity of interpretation and impartiality in administration are important, yet they do not require identical treatment in each case. To apply this principle with equity is a test of real leadership.

The effective supervisor avoids "wishful thinking" and conducts himself so as to create conditions that promote cooperation. *Difficult problems are seldom solved on the spur of the moment, as they arise, but are resolved by the application of principles and procedures that have been worked out in advance.* A real leader knows where he is going and how to get there. Men like to follow a leader when they recognize that he is headed in the right direction. Effective headwork will eliminate much footwork. *Cooperation,* like loyalty and morale,

Check Sheet for the Supervisor *

Check each question—add others if important		Yes	No	What should be done
Is there anything in the job conditions that would hinder rather than help the worker to give creative coopera- tion?	1. Equipment? 2. Condition of equip- ment? 3. Layout of work- place? 4. Flow of material? 5. Fatigue—spread of work? 6. Fatigue—length of work period? 7. Lighting? 8. Temperature? 9. Ventilation? 10. Cleanliness? 11. Safety? 12. Rate on job? 13. Hours on job? 14. ? 15. ?			
Is lack of organiza- tional information hindering the worker in cooper- ating?	1. On machine repair? 2. On tool repair? 3. On safe practices? 4. On shop rules? 5. On wage policy? 6. On policy as to hours? 7. On grievance pro- cedure? 8. On seniority? 9. ? 10. ?			
Is a lack of job skill hindering the worker in giving full cooperation?	1. Not accurate? 2. Lack of uniformity? 3. Low in quantity? 4. Unsafe workman? 5. Lack of job knowl- edge? 6. Unfamiliar work? 7. Lack of ability? 8. Lack of experience? 9. ? 10. ?			

* Adapted from material developed for the General Motors Executive Training Program by General Motors Institute.

Check Sheet (Continued)

Check each question—add others if important	Yes	No	What should be done
Is there anything in the worker's attitude that is hindering rather than helping him to give cooperation? 1. Toward the company? 2. Toward the supervisor? 3. Toward the other workers? 4. Toward any *one* person? 5. Toward wages, hours? 6. Toward type of work? 7. Toward future possibilities? 8. Toward job security? 9. Toward suggestions? 10. ? 11. ?			
Is there anything in the supervisor's (MY) attitude that hinders rather than helps others to cooperate? 1. Toward the company? 2. Toward my job? 3. Toward other foremen? 4. Toward workers? 5. Prejudice against anyone? 6. Favoring anyone? 7. Resent suggestions? 8. Too impatient? 9. Interested in helping others? 10. Willingness to learn? 11. ? 12. ?			

is a by-product of satisfactory relationships. Satisfactory relations grow out of planning, planning the work of the department so that it flows smoothly, and planning the supervisor's own program so that he has time to study and to know his men as well as to give them an opportunity to learn to know him.

Men are "feeling" as well as "thinking" individuals. Both the group and the individuals of which it is composed are often guided by their sentiments and emotions rather than by their minds. Because the supervisor tries to think through his problem, basing his action on logical conclusions, he cannot expect his men to do the same when the logic of the situation runs contrary to the group standards and traditions. The logic of a situation may point clearly to full production, thus eliminating the restriction of output, yet restriction may still be practiced. The wise supervisor will prepare himself for reactions from his men that are based on feelings and emotions rather than cold logic. While recognizing that the influence of the group may be against him at times, the supervisor will remember that the group would rather be *with* him than *against* him provided he creates conditions favorable to cooperative effort.

The confident leader operates from a position of strength, not hesitancy. He has all of the accoutrements of his position, such as titles, organizational recognition, and support, but even more important he has a dynamic outlook. Leadership is a dynamic force that may be marshaled from many directions. Supervisors with widely varying personalities develop it as part of their supervisory equipment. In every instance one thing is present, namely, the dynamic element. Dynamic leadership means having power or strength to achieve as the result of a singleness of purpose and an integrated personality. The supervisor as a leader should be physically alert as well as mentally alive. A part of the dynamics of leadership is adherence to *purpose*. This demands that the men be thoroughly trained in the requirements of their work and that constant follow-up takes place to determine the need for retraining. Recognizing the common purpose also requires constant indoctrination of the men in company policies.

When the supervisor makes it possible for his men to get out their production on time and up to standard he is forging a tool that brings cooperation. Men willingly cooperate with their supervisor when they know that he does everything in his power to provide them with adequate tools and equipment, adequate materials and an even flow of production, that he recognizes them as individuals and gives credit where it is due. The supervisor who sees that his men get the credit due them for the work they do and the ideas they develop will take a long step toward gaining their cooperation. Supervisors who have won cooperation from their men are men who use authority sparingly and display it never.

Example Is Stronger than Words. Willing cooperation encourages cooperation in others. Actions tell the story more effectively than words. The supervisor who is successful in winning cooperation from his men seldom criticizes an individual in the presence of others. It should be remembered that planned instruction is not criticism and should never be given as such. The supervisor should avoid criticism of others, especially his associates and superiors. Men like to say of their supervisor: "He always has a good word for the other fellow whenever it is possible." *A good practice to follow is to say nothing about a man if it is not possible to say something good about him.* A good supervisor *never shirks a task no matter how unpleasant it is to perform.* He never puts off a difficult task, but does it with dispatch and gets it over with. At times disciplinary action may be necessary. *The strong leader expects high performance of others* and sets an example by a high level of performance himself. Self-discipline precedes the discipline of others. The supervisor must discipline himself by planning his work and working his plan. Men watch their supervisor to see if he conducts himself toward his superiors as he expects them to conduct themselves toward him. A strong sense of "followership" begets willing acceptance and cooperation when the supervisor is cast in the role of the leader. Every executive below the level of the chairman of the board of directors is both a follower and a leader.

19 Reducing Absenteeism and Tardiness

Kinds of Tardiness. Tardiness may be defined as the reporting for work later than the designated time to begin work. Various companies interpret this being late in various ways. Some few companies do not consider an employee tardy unless he is at least two to five minutes late. Most companies interpret tardiness literally. If the employee reports for work after the official time to go to work he is considered tardy. The actual recording of the being late may be the time punched on the time card (when one is used), the ringing of a bell or gong that indicates it is time to begin work, or any other method such as the supervisor's personal check.

Tardiness may also be defined as a temporary form of absenteeism having reference to the employee's arriving at his workplace late. Absenteeism consists of an employee's absence from his regular task regardless of the cause. Absenteeism and tardiness, although related, can best be understood if each is analyzed separately. There are two types of tardiness, unavoidable and avoidable. *Unavoidable tardiness* arises from conditions over which the employee, in the exercise of reasonable care, has no control. *Avoidable tardiness* arises from negligence on the part of the employee. Whether an employee's tardiness is avoidable or unavoidable, it is necessary for the supervisor's departmental organization to possess sufficient flexibility to absorb the shock of unexpected tardiness. Tardiness is one of the difficulties for which the supervisor can plan in advance, anticipating its occurrence and being prepared to take it in stride to avoid the otherwise probable losses. One of the best preparations for meeting tardiness is a versatile work force with employees trained to handle two or more jobs in the department.

Causes of Tardiness. Tardiness is caused by a number of factors, such as: (1) accidents, (2) sickness, (3) personal difficulties, (4) transportation, and (5) unsatisfactory adjustment to the work situation. Accidents to the individual, either in the plant or outside, are frequent causes of tardiness. Accidents to members of his family or others may also result in tardiness. Sickness of the individual, of members of his family, or of others, also is a cause of tardiness. Personal reasons are often the cause of men being tardy; household or home duties may delay them and such duties frequently cause the tardiness of married women or widows. Excessive intemperance is another cause of tardiness. Oversleeping, due to excessive fatigue, is still another. Departments working overtime frequently see an increase in the number of late employees. Discontent either with the job or in private affairs is a major cause of tardiness; the employee simply doesn't care whether he is on time. Frequently the first manifestation of discontent or a grievance is tardiness. Transportation delays, breakdowns and accidents, and inclement weather are other causes of tardiness.

A study of the causes of tardiness usually reveals that most employees are prompt, that the majority of tardiness is chargeable to a relatively small segment of the total work force. Of course, this statement would not hold for the tardiness arising from a breakdown in transportation or from a blizzard or intense storm. The supervisor should not be particularly alarmed by an occasional tardiness. A flat tire or an excessively long freight train across the road may occasionally cause an individual to be late.

The Supervisor's Responsibility in Relation to Tardiness and Absenteeism. Almost all research that has been conducted into the causes of tardiness and absenteeism ascribes to the supervisor a leading role in its reduction. "Our findings indicate that absenteeism is actually very closely tied in with over-all industrial administration. . . . Irritating uncertainty, irregularity, and confusion in the factory are likely to be important causes of absenteeism." [1] This same study clearly showed that in the three plants studied, the record of least absenteeism was held by the company that had for years concen-

---

[1] See John B. Fox and Jerome F. Scott, *Absenteeism; Management's Problem,* Graduate School of Business Administration, Harvard University, Bureau of Business Research, Boston, 1943, pp. 26–27.

trated on training its supervisors to be alert to the "human relations" problems.

A more recent study of absenteeism by the National Industrial Conference Board, *Studies in Personnel Policy,* No. 126 (1952), "Controls for Absenteeism," devotes an entire chapter to supervision. It points out the fact that "the supervisor's influence is paramount" and discusses the various methods the supervisor can use in reducing absenteeism under the headings of "right attitudes," "right contacts," "follow-up," and the use of "records." Like every other problem that the supervisor faces and must solve to bring his department up to maximum operating efficiency, he must (1) recognize the kind and extent of tardiness and absenteeism and the economic losses that result, (2) analyze the causes of absenteeism and tardiness and discover ways and means of reducing each to a minimum, (3) distinguish between necessary and unnecessary absenteeism and tardiness, and (4) develop techniques for meeting the work situation arising from tardiness and absenteeism. Many supervisors fail to recognize the important effect of the actions of their employees on both departmental operations and employee attitudes. Considerable economic loss may result from continued absence or tardiness of employees.

Economic Losses Due to Tardiness. There are both direct and concealed losses from tardiness. When an employee is late in a plant operating two or three shifts it is frequently necessary to hold over a man from the previous shift at time-and-a-half pay to operate or maintain equipment and continue production. On one-shift operations tardiness results in production loss on a given machine with attendant excessive overhead costs. Delays in handling and processing material occur because employees are late to work and consequently slow up the movement of work from their department to the next department. Frequently delays in meeting production schedules down the line result from the tardiness of men in departments where the work originates. When men are late other employees must do their work, and since a new employee is not entirely familiar with the work, excess scrap and breakage occur. Not only may waste occur from the use of a new man to replace the tardy man but the man who comes in late frequently rushes to make up his lost time and causes scrap or possibly an accident.

Tardiness may create additional reports for the supervisor to handle, time-keeping difficulties, and later explanations of the reasons why employee pay checks are less than they expected them to be. These indirect losses in themselves are small, but added together over a period of time they amount to considerable sums. In addition to these losses there are intangible losses growing out of employees' forming bad habits, out of the development of unsatisfactory attitudes, and out of the reduction of employee loyalty and morale. Of course the tardiness may also be in part due to the low morale of the worker. The supervisor must take time to adjust production and assignments at the beginning of the shift at a time when other work demands his attention, which when delayed, results in other losses.

Means of Reducing and Caring for Tardiness. Firmness with genuine understanding has proved effective in most cases of tardiness. There are legitimate reasons for an employee's being late. When the facts show that the reason is legitimate, the supervisor might say "I am sorry that the accident occurred," or whatever the cause was. An unreasonable attitude on the part of a supervisor toward first offenders may result in employees' taking the day off when otherwise they would be only a half-hour late. Accurate records should be kept even of unavoidable tardiness. When accidents to employees are the most frequent reason for tardiness, the supervisor can intensify the safety program. Accidents in the home are also frequent causes of tardiness. Where illness of employees causes tardiness, the supervisor will do well to check working conditions, heating, ventilation, and possible poisons in the air. He should check the time cards to determine if the tardy employee may be fatigued from too much overtime work. The supervisor may also send the employee to the medical department for a check-up or recommend a visit to the family physician. When the cause of tardiness is personal the supervisor faces his most difficult task. Here is one of the many problems the supervisor is equipped to meet only if he knows his employees well and has their confidence. The best attack on this cause is a frank talk with the offender, emphasizing the burden that the employee's tardiness places on his fellow employees.

In securing the facts regarding tardiness the supervisor may be surprised to find that the tardy person never looked at his tardiness from the standpoint of its effect on others. In the talk the supervisor can emphasize the need for teamwork in the department, pointing out that the success of all the employees depends on the successful operations of each individual employee. It is necessary for the supervisor to point out to an employee immediately and emphatically the need for temperance if the lack of it is a cause for tardiness. Many supervisors explain to their tardy employees the need for making an allowance for minor delays by starting a few minutes earlier. If tardiness arises from discontent the supervisor must immediately take steps to determine the reasons for the discontent and try to eliminate them. As has been said previously, grievances must be nipped in the bud and the causes eliminated. A supervisor should recognize that in certain cases there may be personal requirements that are legitimate but which, nevertheless, cause tardiness. Handling tardiness affords a real opportunity for the supervisor to exercise leadership and at the same time really to adjust personal situations.

Since tardiness may be unavoidable the supervisor must be prepared to meet it. Some of the methods include holding over an employee from the previous shift and paying the employee overtime, transfer of an employee from some machine or operation from which he can be spared temporarily, the use of understudies or trainees, the use of a "flying squadron," and occasionally the carrying of excess employees in the department to take care of emergencies arising from tardiness or absenteeism.

Special Methods of Handling Tardiness. The cure adopted by the supervisor depends on the policies of his company and the individual involved. The supervisor should state the company policies and explain why they were formulated in such a manner. The supervisor must recognize that frequently the employee during the talk may not give the real cause. It is necessary to check into the reasons for the tardiness and try to ascertain all the facts. Many companies dock employees for tardiness as, for example, fifteen-minute pay deduction for any tardiness up to fifteen minutes, thirty-minute pay deduction for tardiness ranging from fifteen to thirty minutes, etc. Another device is not to permit the employee to participate in the group bonus for the half-day when the tardiness occurred. Frequently records of tardiness are maintained and used in computing sick leave, vacations, and even profit-sharing bonuses. Some employers reward punctuality by adding a percentage in the form of a bonus to the employee's pay for the pay period. It is doubtful, however, if it should be necessary to reward men for being on time. One method found successful is the system of making all late-comers report to a certain gate, having the men on entering sign a slip which must be countersigned by the supervisor and then sent to the paymaster. Some companies remove time cards from the time clock rack and require a special report to be made out. Bulletin boards have been used successfully to list the names of all persons not tardy for a period of time, or, in the reverse, to list all those persons who have been tardy over the same period of time. Contests can be used to good effect, with shifts, departments, or groups competing with each other and the giving of publicity or rewards to the winners. The supervisor can keep records of tardiness and let it be known that these records are considered in the case of layoffs, wage adjustments, and promotions.

To correct tardiness the supervisor must realize that the cause, whatever it is, must be removed. Too often the supervisor fails to realize that his attitude and his lack of leadership may be the real cause. Tardiness in a department is one of the indications of poor leadership and the supervisor should beware when it begins to become frequent. In the final analysis tardiness may be the outgrowth of a lowered morale or weak discipline.

Tardiness Leads to Absenteeism. Absenteeism consists of an employee's absence from his regular task regardless of the cause. It may be classified in the same way as tardiness, namely, avoidable and unavoidable. In addition there is absenteeism by agreement, such as leaves of absence, vacations, and other special privileges arising out of an employment contract. Absenteeism is just another form of extended tardiness. Tardiness often leads to absenteeism. When the supervisor bears down too hard on tardiness it will tend to increase absenteeism.

Loss Caused by Absences. Some well-managed companies have kept records of time lost by employees as a per cent of scheduled hours for many years. The record of one of these companies shows an average lost time of about 4 per cent over a period of 30 years. From 1920 to 1930 it was nearly 5 per cent. From 1930 to 1941 it was slightly less than 3 per cent. From 1942 to 1951 it averaged more than 4 per cent.

The survey by Grant W. Canfield and David G. Soash of absenteeism in Los Angeles, covering 219 firms, showed an over-all absentee rate of 2.8 per cent. Excluding the exempt salaried employees (managerial, professional, and technical) this survey showed a 3 per cent absentee rate. This survey specifically excluded all absences of less than 4 hours and those due to industrial accidents, authorized leaves of absences, and vacations. "Generally speaking, the absentee rates for 'non-exempt' office employees were lower than for 'hourly' shop employees and, as might be anticipated, the managerial, professional, and technical 'exempt' had the best record among the three employee groups. In support of another widely accepted assumption, absence rates among female employees were found to be generally higher than among males." [2]

Absenteeism causes a loss both to the employer and to the employees. The losses to the company in terms of production include those which normally result from the absence of an employee and those in other departments caused by holding up production somewhere along the line. The losses arise also from the discontent of other employees who find themselves in unusual situations because of the absence of an employee. Idleness of equipment and machines contribute to the losses, and impaired discipline and control also increase them. The cost of carrying extra men may also be considered a debit. Possible losses may be sustained from lower quality when an inexperienced employee replaces the regular operator. There is an increased possibility of accidents and damage to tools and equipment arising from the inexperience of a new employee. It is necessary for the supervisor to devote his time to placing another employee on the work of the absentee, and the time of the supervisor is valuable. If men are used from other shifts on overtime the additional pay constitutes a loss. Many of these are indirect costs but added together may amount to a considerable sum, especially when multiplied by the number of absentees. A recent survey of absences in Los Angeles showed that the cost per employee in the Los Angeles manufacturing industry was $125 per employee. This was based on the 3 per cent average rate found in the survey.[3] Others have estimated that the cost to the company for each day's absence is equal to from 1 to 2 times the loss to the employee in wages.[4]

The losses to the absent employees include his wages, the possible loss to the group from the presence of a new man who pulls down the production of the group, possible loss to employees in a subsequent operation arising from a shortage of work in process on which to continue, accidents to the new man replacing the absent employee, and possible discontent on the part of the employee who is transferred to take the place of the absent employee. This same discontent may hold

[2] Grant W. Canfield and David G. Soash, "Presenteeism—A Constructive View," *Personnel Journal,* July–August 1955, p. 94; see also National Industrial Conference Board, *Studies in Personnel Policy,* No. 126, 1952, p. 6.

[3] See Grant W. Canfield and David G. Soash. *op. cit.,* p. 96.

[4] See "Reducing Absenteeism: A Three Step Program," *The Management Review,* July 1955, pp. 433–434.

for the employees who double up to carry the additional load of the absent individual.

It is very difficult to compute the total cost of absences from work from a national standpoint. Vacations with pay are a direct cost to the employer. It may be argued that employees benefit from these vacations and therefore produce more than they otherwise would when they are on the job. In view of the forty-hour week this would be difficult to prove in cases other than those in which the employee had a health problem. Vacations do have social value and probably can be justified on that ground alone. They also in all probability reduce the time that would otherwise be taken off by employees for visits to relatives or just for travel. Absences due to illness are one of the social costs of sickness. This figure may readily be more than $1,000,000,000 when it is recalled that our gainfully employed are in excess of 60,000,000. Management can do little about the costs arising from absences from illness other than to provide a healthful working environment, adequate medical facilities, and health education. The place where something may be done is in the case of absences due to the employee not wanting to come to work—the morale cases.

Causes of Absenteeism. As indicated earlier, absenteeism is caused by sickness, vacations, personal reasons related to the family, personal business and similar matters, as well as morale factors, some of which are distinctly of an emotional nature. It is estimated that 10 per cent or even more of the population has emotional disturbances at times that may not require them to be absent from work but may readily be the cause of their absence. Unmarried women and single men, in general, lose less time than married men or married women because of sickness and accidents. Men in general lose less time than women. Sickness and accidents cause more absenteeism among widowed or divorced men and women than among married men and women. These statements are generalities and certainly do not apply in specific cases. Young women seem to lose more time than women of twenty-five years or older. The probable answer is that they do not take their responsibilities at work so seriously. They also have more social life and are likely to be more fatigued. It is so easy to report ill when in fact it is only tiredness from the dance the night before. This is especially true when the employee is on a salary and allowed time off for illness. Young men under 22 also have more than their share of absences. There is more absenteeism on Monday than on any other day and it decreases daily until Saturday when absenteeism increases slightly among men.   The same is true for women except that the increase begins earlier in the week.   The causes of absenteeism are similar to those for tardiness with the addition of absence due to death in the employee's family, private business, occasional days off for fishing, hunting, football games, etc.   The findings of the research by Dr. Norman Plummer and Dr. Lawrence E. Hinkle covering 50,000 women and 25,000 men of the New York Telephone Company, as summarized by the American Management Association, are given below:

1. In any given year, absenteeism is concentrated in a small segment of the work population.   About one-third of employees have perfect attendance records; the other two-thirds have absenteeism; of these, the top one-third causes 75 per cent of all absenteeism.   About 45 per cent of absenteeism is caused by a group forming only 10 per cent of the company's total work force.

2. That group of employees which shows the highest absentee rate in the first years of service has the highest average absentee rate throughout the entire period of service.

3. The percentage of absenteeism has increased over the 30-year period covered by the study—1923 to 1953—despite improvement in general health.

4. The absentee rate for women is approximately twice that for men, despite the fact that women generally enjoy better health and live longer. Nervous disorders account for 10 times as much absenteeism among women as among men.

5. Economic as well as emotional factors cause the high absentee rate among women.   Women have generally less concern about attendance, since, as a rule, the woman is not the household breadwinner.   Moreover, supervisors tend to follow different standards for justifying the absence of women and of men.

6. A study of 20 long-service employees in the lowest-absence group and 20 in the highest yields a recognizable profile of the absence-prone employee.   She was found to be generally unhappy, discontented, and resentful.   She had few friends and drew little sustenance from the group in which she worked.   She was easily frustrated.   She reacted to transfers with distaste and complaints.   As a rule she was not liked by associates and supervisors, because she was unfriendly and complaining.   On the other hand, the low-absence employee was generally a happy, "outgoing" person.   She adapted well to change, was well-liked by her associates, and saw her job as her career.

Among the remedies for cutting absenteeism suggested by the study are:

Identify the high-absence segment by keeping accurate attendance records and having careful interviews with employees during health exams.

Medical examinations should rule out organic disease but should consider each illness in terms of past background to find out whether there is any history of chronic and repetitive disease having to do with the reactions of the particular person to the situations and stresses of life.

Sometimes, in extreme cases, separation from the payroll may be the only solution. Generally, however, proper counseling—and, sometimes, firm discipline—seems to be a sound approach to the problem of the high-absence employee.[5]

Company Policies toward Absenteeism. One survey [6] showed that the time before absentees are dropped from the payroll is as follows: immediately, 3 per cent; three days, 10.1 per cent; five days, 3.9 per cent; one week, 13.1 per cent; two weeks, 12.8 per cent; one month, 9.8 per cent; end of pay period, 1.2 per cent; after investigation, 20.8 per cent; no standard policy, 25.3 per cent. The same survey shows the penalties for absenteeism are: none except loss of pay, 47.1 per cent; subject to layoff, 10.9 per cent; subject to discharge, 28.3 per cent; first warning, second layoff, third discharge, 3.8 per cent; must report to supervisor, personnel office, or other official before returning to work, 1.6 per cent; loss of seniority after three days, 1.1 per cent; loss of vacation rights, 1.6 per cent; no standard policy, 5.4 per cent. A later survey by the National Industrial Conference Board shows that 1.7 per cent discharge immediately without warning for unauthorized absences, 16 per cent discharge after 1 warning, and 50.7 discharge after 2 warnings.[7]

Some companies require an employee to clear through the medical department after an unexcused absence or one involving claimed illness. Others require all persons to clear through the personnel department after an unexcused absence. If illness is claimed the personnel department would refer the employee to the medical department for clearance. There are other methods of handling absenteeism: attendance reward bonuses may be used; penalties may be imposed or men may be docked in excess of the time lost, especially for bonus work. Absentees may be made conspicuous by posting departmental or, occasionally, individual records. Many companies find a method involving competition and publicity successful in controlling absenteeism. Supervisors *may keep careful records and emphasize the im-*

[5] "Industrial Relations News," *The Management Review,* June 1955, pp. 377–378.

[6] National Industrial Conference Board, *Studies in Personnel Policy,* No. 23, 1940, p. 13.

[7] National Industrial Conference Board, *Studies in Personnel Policies,* No. 88, 1948; also, No. 126, 1952, p. 49.

portance of the records in determining wage increases, promotions, and layoffs.

In the final analysis the same methods are used to control absenteeism and tardiness. Emphasis is usually concentrated on the personal contact of the supervisor with the offending employee. Only through an interview can the supervisor get at most of the facts to determine the cause of absence or tardiness. One method of measuring the degree of morale and the quality of leadership in a department is by analyzing the numbers of employee absences and tardiness. Every supervisor can measure the quality of his own leadership fairly well by periodically analyzing the absentee and tardiness record of his department. The supervisor who knows his men, recognizes their individual differences, handles their grievances promptly, is firm but consistent in discipline, will normally have a lower absentee rate than that prevailing in the community. It must be remembered that outside influences over which the supervisor has little control also have a part in absenteeism. Also certain internal factors, such as a 45- to 54-hour week, nearly always contribute to a higher absentee rate. These long work weeks would seldom be followed save in emergencies. However, an emergency situation may cover a long period during a war economy.

20

Producing and Measuring Quality

Quality Defined. Quality can be defined only in terms of the desired characteristics of the article or service. From this standpoint *quality is the sum of a number of desired related characteristics such as shape, dimensions, composition, strength, workmanship, adjustment, finish, and color. The essential element in quality is not cost but conformity to established standards.*[1] The measure of quality is the standard set for the product. Any deviation from this standard is a variation in quality but is not a true gauge from the manufacturing standpoint. *Standards of quality are norms to be achieved and absolute quality as a standard is attainable only at great expense. Relative standards or standards with acceptable deviations are the measures of commercial quality.* The aim of production is to attain the "bull's-eye" of the standard, not the outer ring of tolerance. The supervisor who is interested only in keeping within the tolerances will have far more complaints in his department than the supervisor whose men strive to meet the specified standard.

Quality control, to most operating persons, means the same as inspecting to see that quality standards are met. To some persons *quality control* refers to the use of statistical devices for charting actual quality as determined by inspection. It is better to use the term *statistical quality control* to indicate the activities associated with these techniques. The *statistical quality control* function may be a separate unit from actual inspection; it may in a very few cases be the big

---

[1] See William R. Spriegel and Richard H. Lansburgh, *Industrial Management,* John Wiley & Sons, New York, fifth edition, 1955, Chapter 10, which has been quoted freely in this chapter.

division of which inspection is a department; or it may be a department of the inspection division reporting to the director of inspection. Some of the most effective statistical quality control operations are handled as a staff function, reporting directly to the plant manager and acting independently as a service group to the related activities of design, engineering, production, and inspection. Figure 20.1 graphically portrays the inter-relationships of the various departments with the inspection department.

Who Establishes Standards for Quality? The engineering department in the main establishes standards of production, supported by the advice and recommendations of the sales, purchasing, and manufacturing departments. The purchasing department advises the engineering department regarding the practicability of a given standard for materials or purchased parts. The manufacturing department assists the engineering department with data on the possibility of producing the desired quality at a given cost. Although the engineering department establishes the quality standards it must rely on the facts it develops in the laboratory plus the information available to it on materials, production methods, production costs, and available equipment to reach its conclusions. In the long run the consuming public by its approval in buying or by its refusal to buy sets the standards for commercial quality. The sales department, the part of the organization closest to the consumer, recognizes and interprets the consumers' desires and passes them on to the engineering department.

Whose Responsibility Is Quality? *Within his department the supervisor is responsible for producing and measuring quality.* In a line-and-staff organization the supervisor is aided by his assistants, his setup men, his machine operators, and others, each responsible in his respective sphere, but all answerable to the supervisor. In many organizations staff departments such as engineering and inspection also assist the supervisor and may even exercise functional control over the quality of the work of his department. This staff supervision and assistance do not relieve the supervisor of his responsibility for quality, but merely serve to assist him in meeting it. The supervisor alone cannot control or produce the quality desired from a department; only through the cooperation of his men can quality be met and standards maintained. The supervisor is responsible for cooperation, instruction, planning, leadership, and safety, which all play an integral part in producing, measuring, and maintaining quality standards. Workers seem to have a traditional pride in high quality. The pride that de-

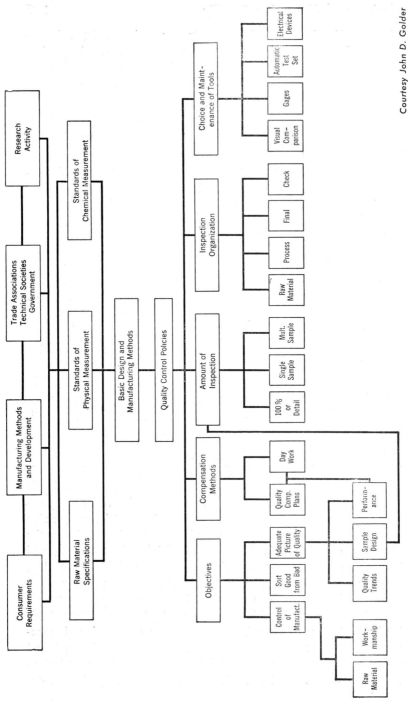

Courtesy John D. Golder

Figure 20.1. Chart showing the origin of quality control and factors considered in the effective use of quality control.

velops from men and their machines' meeting quality standards in terms of thousandths of an inch and holding these standards in producing large quantities can be as intense and as great a factor in building morale as any pride growing out of individual craftsmanship. The ability of men to control machines through the use of precision tools and measuring devices deserves the same praise as the ability of men to construct by hand an entire product. The supervisor can develop pride in this type of craftsmanship among his men if he handles them properly, and he can turn this sort of pride into a morale-building tool. This is not an easy assignment. It is more likely to be achieved through indirection than through a frontal attack. Pride in quality maintenance in mass-production industries usually accompanies pride in the company, a tradition of pride in the product (some companies are fortunate enough to have it), and pride in the membership in the department and loyalty to the dynamic leadership of the foreman. The production supervisor should be *quality-conscious*. He must be able to produce and measure quality in his department. This means he must make his men quality-conscious by instilling in them a pride in producing and maintaining quality.

Quality maintenance is a function of the materials used, the accuracy of the machines, and the performance of the worker. If equipment is defective it is the supervisor's responsibility to shut it down and to have the machinery repaired, or failing in this, to take the matter up with his superior for further instructions. This last step is important since the superior, in turn, is held responsible for the standards of quality by the persons above him. When equipment in the supervisor's department is inactive very long he is holding up a sequence of operations which precede and follow the work of his department. In mass-production industries machine troubles and delays in a single department can quickly cause production delays throughout the entire manufacturing process in the plant. If the material the supervisor receives is defective it is again his duty to report the facts immediately to his superior as well as to the inspection department. More labor or time may be required to achieve the quality standards when such materials must be utilized, but this does not excuse the supervisor from meeting and maintaining the established standards. He should report to his superior at once for instructions when labor costs are excessive. Such facts should also be reported to other departments concerned, including the department immediately preceding the supervisor's department, the inspection department, purchasing department, and other departments according to his company's procedure.

The organizational structure will determine whether or not the special function of quality measuring inspection is set up in a separate unit. Where quality standards are relatively easy to meet and of minor importance the inspection group may report to the supervisor. Where quality standards are relatively difficult to attain, a separate inspection department should measure quality. It is illogical to expect the same man to be responsible for producing quality under mass-production operating conditions and to be his own inspector of the attainment of that quality. The need increases for a separate inspection department, responsible to someone at a higher level of authority than the supervisor, in proportion to the difficulty of producing and measuring quality. In an organization where quality is vital, and this includes nearly all mass-production industries following the principles of specialization and interchangeable parts, the inspection department should report to the general superintendent or general manager. The supervisor or his representatives measure quality in most operations as part of their production responsibilities. The operator can be helpful in measuring the quality of work he does, but in the final analysis it is the supervisor who is held responsible for production's meeting standards. The supervisor must be certain the machine operators are trained to measure quality. In fact, save in the use of an automatic machine, the ability to measure quality is a requirement for producing an article of the desired standard.

Types of Inspection. With a full realization that there may be overlapping in any classification of inspection the following kinds of inspection may be found:

1. Remedial and preventive inspection
2. Centralized, floor, or a combination of centralized and floor inspection
3. Materials, work-in-process, finished product, or final inspection, and functional inspection
4. Visual, and nonvisual inspection, such as chemical composition, tensile strength, ductility

Remedial inspection lays its major emphasis upon catching defects that have already occurred, thus protecting the good name of the manufacturer as well as the consumer and eliminating further waste by adding more work to a defective part or product. Remedial inspection or corrective inspection strives to filter the good from the bad. Remedial inspection, of course, does not preclude the repair of a defective part or product.

Preventive inspection gives special attention to the accuracy of manufacturing processes in order to avoid defects and waste. Preventive or *constructive inspection* emphasizes the positive attitude rather than the negative. Constructive inspection strives to aid the manufacturing group to produce only those items that meet standard specifications. Corrective inspection catches parts that are defective, and the employee (who is on an incentive wage plan) is usually required to repair them, or he is not paid for them [2] if they must be scrapped, whereas preventive inspection often is used in connection with a special incentive for quality achievement. Neither preventive inspection nor remedial inspection has to be tied into any special wage scheme. The major difference between the two types of inspection is the emphasis of the one upon catching defects that have been produced and the other upon preventing their occurrence.

In *centralized inspection* the item is not inspected on the production floor but in a separate place set aside for inspection. Centralized inspection does not imply only one place for inspection. As a matter of fact, there might even be two or more places in one large department where parts are taken for inspection. Centralized inspection is often performed within an enclosure, especially adapted or equipped for the purpose. Centralized inspection carries the principle of specialization somewhat further than floor inspection. Advantages claimed for centralized inspection are:

1. There should be less interference with the workers in production and better shop housekeeping when the products are not held at the work place for inspection.

2. The inspector's output should be greater because of better working surroundings, less interference, and increased speed arising from specialization.

3. It is easier to supervise the inspectors; their tasks may be subdivided, and a less skilled type of worker may be used.

4. Production control is facilitated when parts pass through a central location, where a total count of approvals and rejections is made.

5. Records of approved and rejected parts, together with the source of each, are more readily kept under centralized inspection.

6. Centralized inspection facilitates the use of specialized and delicate equipment such as X-rays, radio amplification, special lights, and air conditioning.

---

[2] Of course, the earnings of the employee must meet the requirements of the national and state wages and hours laws.

7. Centralized inspection produces more impartial inspection; at least the inspector is not under the strain of rejecting the work of a man with whom he is in personal contact.

Centralized inspection tends to increase the amount of transporting material except where the inspection is performed in the stores department or stockroom. It is also apparent that centralized inspection is not feasible in progressive manufacturing, at least for the parts, although the final product may be centrally inspected. In some situations such as the manufacture of heavy parts or products, central inspection is highly impractical.

Floor inspection is the term applied to the inspecting of items on the floor at the point of production or adjacent to the place of production. The inspector may remain in one place or go from place to place to inspect as a "roving inspector." The character of the product, the type of processing, and the inspection itself control the movements of the inspector when inspection is performed on the production floor.

Material inspection usually refers to inspecting material on being received from a supplier or it may refer to the inspection of material before use. *Finished product inspection* refers to inspecting the product after it is finished or before shipping. *Work-in-process inspection* is carried on either as floor inspection or as centralized inspection.

In assembly industries inspection includes attention to accuracy of manufacture and to interchangeability. The American system of manufacture has been erected on the basis of interchangeable parts. From a production control standpoint, as well as from the standpoint of the assembly operations, this interchangeability of parts in assembled products is essential in order that specific parts, when started in manufacture, need not be designated as being for specific pieces of final product. Inspection of components during process affords the inspection department an especially good opportunity to practice preventive medicine in assembly industries.

Statistical quality control charts are valuable tools to aid the supervisor in detecting troubles before they get out of hand. These charts may be operated by the quality control group but the supervisor should make use of them as an aid in supervision.

Engineering inspection refers to the inspection of a product after it is finished to see if it meets specifications. Certain types of products, such as large machinery units, are completely fabricated on the assembly or erection floor and accurately tested by technical experts to determine their operating characteristics. Large motors, turbines, generators, etc., are tested in this manner by the Allis-Chalmers Corporation. In some instances representatives of the purchaser, particularly in governmental purchases, are present at these inspections. Airplanes and steamships are usually either flight-tested or given trial runs. *Functional inspection* is conducted by placing the part or assembly in a skeleton assembly as desired. *Visual inspection,* as the term implies, merely means inspection by vision for color, contour, roughness, or any other characteristic that can be checked by sight.

The Function of the Inspection Department. Many of the frictions arising between the operating supervisor, his men, and the inspection group would not arise if each member of the manufacturing team understood the functions of inspection. These may be summarized as follows:

1. To sort acceptable from defective raw materials or work in process (*remedial inspection*)
2. To aid in the location of the causes of defective work and cooperatively to assist in removing these causes (*preventive inspection*)
3. To control the quality standards of the manufacturing processes (*operative inspection*)
4. To provide management, through properly designed reports, with a picture of the quality of the product made, a statement of the quality of the raw materials received, and a measure of the efficiency of plant operations, which is often used as a basis of payment to the worker

Organization of the Inspection Department. When the organizational structure of the inspection department is clearly understood and accepted by the supervisor, the fixing of responsibility promotes mutual respect and harmonious working together. The inspection department should never be made directly subservient to the will of those who are engaged in increasing the quantity of production, unless quality of work is but a very small factor in the successful operation of the plant. This does not imply that the supervisor should not be interested in quality; quite the contrary, *the supervisor has as one of his major responsibilities the creation of a quality product.* Means should be provided to see that quantity production should not be credited to a supervisor unless quality is good. On the other hand the supervisor should not be charged with the final measurement of the quality he creates. The inspection department should have full control both over inspection of purchased materials and parts and over inspection during production. This enables it to maintain the material standards which have been set and makes possible the maintenance of product standards.

When quality standards are not of excessive importance in an industry, inspection forces may be maintained as a staff department under the superintendent. This places the supervisor in a position of receiving instructions from two sources regarding amount of product to be produced and the quality of that product. He must endeavor to correlate his instructions and if there is a conflict in instructions, the matter will naturally be referred to the superintendent for a decision. If quality is of maximum importance, as in the production of scientific instruments or in goods which are sold mainly on the basis of quality rather than on the basis of price, the inspection should probably become a major manufacturing function directly under the control of the works manager. The inspection function would thus hold a position analogous to that of the purchasing department or the engineering department. Though all errors cannot be corrected before their actual occurrence, if the inspection department will practice preventive medicine on the product, not only will it become a dividend-paying department of the organization, but it can more readily cooperate with the supervisors responsible for quality. The inspection department is an effective aid to the supervisor, the planning department, the training department, or the methods department, whichever of these may direct the methods of operation and instruction of the employee.

Factors Influencing Inspection. Where the number of supervisors is adequate to keep a close check on the quality of production, the amount of inspection necessary to measure quality is reduced. On the other hand, if the number of inspectors is increased the number of supervisors may be reduced. The ratio of inspectors to production employees depends upon several factors, namely, the nature of the production process, the relative quality group of the product, the type of equipment used, the organizational setup, etc. It is obvious that a continuous-process industry producing a single product would require less inspection than a jobbing type of industry producing many types of quality products. Institutions producing a high-quality precision type of product also require more inspectors than the same general type of industry producing a lower quality product. Again, the special-purpose machine used where volume justifies it requires less inspection of its product than where the same item is manufactured by general-purpose machines. It is true that the special-purpose machine itself may require more checking and maintenance than the general machine, but the maintenance group is not usually classified with the inspectors. Modern precision equipment and techniques have greatly reduced the number of inspectors required to maintain the desired quality.

In high-quality products, or products which are manufactured largely through the skill of the employee rather than the skill of the machine, much more of the product must be inspected than where the machine, once set up, is likely to turn out standard quality products without adjustment for a considerable time. The more automatic the machine, the less attention need be given to inspecting the product after the initial setup inspection. Where quality depends on the machine, inspection must be made frequently enough to ascertain that the equipment is operating satisfactorily and does not need adjustment other than the usual adjustment made by the men on the job. Where quality depends on human skill, frequently 100 per cent inspection will be necessary, that is, every unit of product must be inspected after every operation.

The Supervisor's Role in Maintaining Quality. When quality standards are not being met the supervisor's first step is to analyze the facts and take the necessary steps to get the desired quality. Scattered shotgun attempts at correcting quality deficiencies are not so effective as specific efforts to correct the exact cause. In his analysis of causes of low quality the supervisor may find: (1) lack of knowledge either of the standards or of methods of performing their work, (2) lack of ability (when the man lacks capacity for the work he should be transferred to work for which he is better suited), (3) not exercising proper care (every supervisor has met the careless employee who must either be cured, transferred, or discharged), and (4) defective equipment or materials (which are the supervisor's responsibilities once the man has informed the supervisor concerning them).

The producing of the desired quality is a positive requirement in leadership. When standards are not being met to maintain quality the supervisor must find out what is causing the defects and teach the men how to avoid them. The right man on the job is important and the supervisor must carry out his responsibilities for properly inducting, instructing, and, when necessary, transferring men to maintain quality in his department. Proper specifications as to the desired quality are necessary since no employee can be expected to work to tolerances unless he knows what they are. It is helpful when men know and understand the reasons for close tolerances. Showing them how their work ties into that of other departments and other men assists them in producing and measuring quality. Persistent follow-up by the supervisor is required and supervision must be especially close and instruction thorough where high-quality tolerances are required.

Quality maintenance is a team assignment by the supervisor. The supervisor should use his assistants, his group leaders, his setup men, and adjusters to attain quality. It is particularly important that these men be kept informed of quality requirements and standards. Successful supervisors develop their men's pride in quality achievement. In an age of specialization when a man frequently performs only a single operation on a product, developing pride in craftsmanship is difficult, but showing him where his part goes in the finished product will create interest on his part and assist in attaining quality production. The supervisor can use inspection, scrap, and rejection reports effectively in making his men quality conscious. He can develop competition between men and sections of his department as an aid in producing quality. The supervisor must create the conditions conducive to quality maintenance by paying especial attention to ma-

Courtesy Stewart-Warner Corporation

Figure 20.2. Quality control chart tells the worker whether or not his work comes within the prescribed standards

terials, machines, and working conditions. Finally, the supervisor should take immediate action when standards are not met, action to inform the men, to instruct the men, to repair machines, to provide satisfactory materials and tools, and to eliminate men who through carelessness or lack of ability lower his department's capacity to produce and measure quality.

The use of quality control [3] charts at the machine where the worker can see the results of his efforts provides a strong incentive for increased efforts at meeting standards (see Figure 20.2). The supervisor can promote quality control through the men themselves. He can let them know the standards and why these standards are necessary. He should provide instruction for both new and old men. He should use praise wherever possible since praise for good work is far more effective than censure for poor work. He should provide adequate supervision for the men through delegation of responsibilities to well-trained assistants. It is poor policy to pass work below standard one day and reject it the following day. The supervisor should see that his men have proper equipment, correct tools, satisfactory materials, and an even flow of work with as few changes as possible.

The tabulation that follows shows the analysis of a group of supervisors in a conference. They were striving to identify the cause of low quality and to suggest a remedy.

Causes	Remedy
1. Unskilled workmen	1. Instruct
2. Poor equipment	2. Proper supervision and maintenance
3. Carelessness of worker	3. Proper training and supervision
4. Lack of knowledge on the part of the worker	4. Teach quality requirements and reasons for same
5. Defective materials	5. Reject materials, report to proper authorities, and add extra work

6. Speed of production in
  6.1 Relation to machine capacity
  6.2 Relation to worker capacity
	6. To regulate:
	  6.1 Adjust or get new machines
	  6.2 Adjust, slow down, or teach new speed

7. Design of machine	7. Correct
8. Design of tool	8. Correct
9. Quality ideals of supervisors low	9. Instruct

[3] See Appendix A for a brief discussion of the use of statistical quality control in inspection.

The Supervisor's Responsibility for Promoting Cooperation with the Inspection Department. As stated earlier, a clear definition of the function of the inspection department and the acceptance of the responsibility for quality creation should promote a mutuality of interest between the producing and inspecting group. It is the supervisor's responsibility to create quality and to make use of the information provided him by the inspection department in meeting his responsibility. The supervisor should recognize that the function of inspection is to measure quality and should not feel that there is something personal in actions taken by inspectors. He should cooperate in and encourage preventive inspection and not merely acquiesce in remedial inspection. He should develop respect for the inspection department among his men and see that they cooperate with the inspectors. The supervisor may not always agree with the inspection department but he should never show this attitude before his men.

The supervisor must realize that quality maintenance is a cooperative program challenging the best efforts of the supervisor as an executive. Success in producing and measuring quality comes only to the supervisor who recognizes and applies the doctrine of individual differences in handling his men. To achieve quality maintenance requires careful organizing, deputizing responsibilities and authority to others since no supervisor can do it alone, and supervision that is inherent in leadership of the highest quality.

21 The Supervisor and Stores and Material Control

Definitions. *Raw material* is material, used in production, that has undergone little or no change since its receipt. *Material in process or worked material* is material that has work performed on it but is not yet ready for shipment to the customer, has not been placed in an assembly, or has not been delivered to the stock room. Finished parts in a stock room may or may not be classed as material in process. From an accounting standpoint finished parts in a stock room awaiting use in the department as a part of an assembly may be called finished parts. The same part on the production floor not yet delivered to the stock room might be called work in process. *Finished products* have been completed and are ready to be shipped to the consumer. Where there is a separate stock room or shipping department, the product is considered a finished product when it is turned over to this unit. *Supplies* are all the materials that are used as aids to production but are not part of the product itself. Such items as oil, sandpaper, and polishing compound come under this heading. Sometimes small tools, such as knives and hacksaw blades, may be classified under the general heading of supplies.

"Stores" is a term not always clearly differentiated in various plants. It is frequently used to refer to purchased raw material, supplies, or parts. Partly finished material awaiting use in the plant may also be classed as "stores." Finished parts awaiting shipment to the consumer may be called "stock," as may the finished product in which the part is used. This same part awaiting use in the plant might be called "stores" or worked material. The terms *storeroom* and *stock room* are used interchangeably in various plants.

249

The Relationship of the Supervisor to Materials and Store Control.
The proper care and handling of raw materials, work in process, and
the finished product is a major responsibility of the person in charge
of each department through which it passes. The waste arising from
improper use, misuse, or improper handling of materials is very great
indeed. While losses by theft may be substantial in the case of some
items, such losses are a small per cent of the other losses in the care
and handling of materials.

The attitude of the supervisor toward the proper use and care of
materials is more important than any particular technique or procedure.
Where the supervisor is conscious of the problem he usually is capable
of devising ways and means of reducing scrap and waste arising from
improper handling of materials. In a small company the department
supervisor may be solely responsible for the use and care of material.
In the medium-sized or large company many other persons are involved in the record keeping and issuance of materials. Even in the
large companies the actual care and use of materials in production
rest largely upon the supervisor. The production control representative may issue the *order* telling the stock room attendant to deliver
material or parts to the supervisor's department, the internal transportation department may deliver the material to the desired location,
but from that time on the use and handling of the material rest on
the production group.

The Supervisor's Aid in Determining Preferred Materials. While
the engineering department and the purchasing department are primarily responsible for material specifications the supervisor does have
an interest in these specifications. The purchasing department is constantly looking for new suppliers and new materials that may be used
for present materials. Materials from two different suppliers may
work differently in actual production even though both suppliers are
supposedly working to the same specifications. It is the responsibility
of the supervisor to report to the purchasing department or the other
responsible department these differences in workability of materials
supplied by different vendors. Frequently the purchasing department
makes a so-called "pilot purchase" from a new supplier just to see how
his product works out in production, or the purchasing department,
with the approval of the engineering department, may ask the supervisor to try out a substitute material. In all of these situations the
supervisor is a key person in approving or disapproving the sample
material. The inspector may do most of the observing, but the final

responsibility may rest on the shoulders of the supervisor. Nearly always he will personally inspect the new materials to make certain that they meet production requirements.

Frequently a new model may have parts that meet engineering specifications but are difficult to make or difficult to assemble. In such cases the supervisor often is in a position to suggest minor changes that will simplify the manufacture of the part or remove the difficulty encountered in its assembly. Not only does the supervisor often suggest modifications of design to reduce costs or simplify operations, but he should encourage his men to make suggestions for improvements. These suggestions may arise from a regularly organized suggestion program, or they may be encouraged by the supervisor as a part of his departmental leadership.

The Supervisor and the Purchasing Department. The functions of the purchasing department are:

1. To provide the necessary services, materials, equipment, facilities, and supplies according to established specifications
2. To provide these items according to a schedule or when needed
3. To purchase all materials, services, etc., at a price in keeping with the qualities required, not above the community price, and to take advantage of the fluctuations in the market
4. To be ever on the alert for new sources, equipment, or processes and new materials to be used in the place of current materials and equipment
5. To promote ethical standards in purchasing
6. In some cases to dispose of salvage
7. To perform all functions related to its basic purchasing assignment; this may include traffic, rendering aid to a supplier, participating in writing specifications, and similar acts
  7.1 In a few cases the purchasing function includes inventory control, materials control, and even occasionally material storage, handling, and issuing
  7.2 In a few other cases purchasing also has charge of production scheduling and control

Naturally the supervisor's relationship to purchasing will be determined in a large measure by the functions assigned to the purchasing department. As indicated earlier in this chapter, the supervisor frequently is called upon to report on the working of new material or the old material received from a new supplier. In ordering replacement parts for a machine, when this process is not handled by the maintenance department, the supervisor must give an exact description of the part and the machine number for which the part is needed.

The machine number enables the manufacturer to check his specifications and to send the part that will fit the particular machine. Not only in ordering parts but in all other requests made of the purchasing department the supervisor should give detailed instructions where these are needed. If detailed specifications are not required they may result in excessive costs when the standards are higher than needed. For instance, if a supervisor orders a brand-named supply it almost always costs more than the same thing ordered by its chemical name or chemical specification.

A supervisor is a better member of the production team when he understands the functions and operation of the other departments in his company. Figures 21.1 and 21.2 show the purchasing relationships and the route followed in issuing material to production.

Organization of the Materials and Stores Functions. As was indicated in discussion of purchasing, in a few cases the materials and supplies are purchased, stored, and delivered to the foreman by representatives of the purchasing department. This is not a common practice because material handling and storing is an activity quite unlike purchasing. Purchasing is essentially an office type of activity. Material handling and storage is a factory operating type of assignment.

Since production control issues the orders for actual production it frequently issues the orders to deliver to the foreman materials with which to do the work as well as issuing the order to the purchasing department to buy (see Figure 21.2). At times the people who handle the materials and store them report to the production control department. The same unlikeness of activities applies in this situation. Production control work is more nearly related to a clerical function than to a factory operation task. In many cases the material handling and stores functions are in a separate department reporting to the factory superintendent or to a superintendent of nonproductive workers. In such cases the orders to deliver materials to the foreman usually are issued by the production control department. Of course, in a smaller plant the materials may be under the control of a general foreman or even the foreman.

Accounting for Materials. The actual records of the receipt of materials and their issuance to production may be kept by the inventory clerk in the production control department, in the purchasing department, or in the materials department. Since it is a clerical operation it is more nearly related to production control or purchasing than to the work of handling and storing materials. When the order

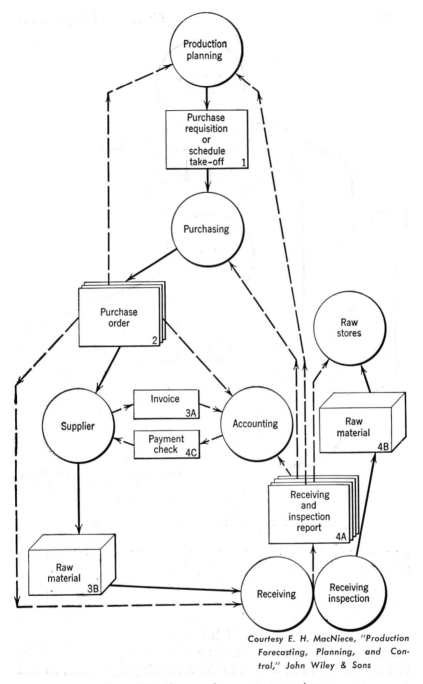

Courtesy E. H. MacNiece, "Production
Forecasting, Planning, and Control," John Wiley & Sons

Figure 21.1. The general procurement procedure.

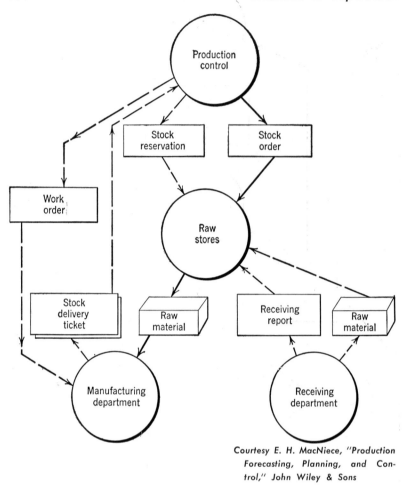

Figure 21.2. The general arrangement of stores control.

originates in a department other than the material storage department
it is usually issued in multiple copies. The order filler enters on the
order the amount sent to production, sends one copy back to the issuing clerk, and one copy to the accounting department; one copy may
go with the material and one copy may be kept by the materials department. If a part of the material is returned to the materials department the receiving clerk makes out a returned slip and sends copies
to the record clerk as well as to the accounting department, so that
appropriate credits are made.

Regardless of how carefully records are supposed to be kept, mechanical checks and other aids are often used to avoid running out of material. This is especially true of small parts. At times, bin cards are kept in the storage room. When the order clerk fills an order and subtracts the amount, he notifies production control if the amount remaining has reached a predetermined limit. In some cases this minimum quantity is placed in a bag or behind a partition in a bin. In such circumstances the order filler keeps right on filling orders until the free material in the bin is used up. He then notifies production control. The reserve is estimated so that it will last until the new supply can be ordered and arrive.

The foreman can be very helpful in keeping records correct by using materials according to specifications and on the appropriate orders for which they are assigned. He also should send excess materials back to storage at once rather than let them lie around in the department. Attention to the details in using materials characterizes the modern scientific minded supervisor.

Handling Materials. Naturally the nature and size of the material influences its method of handling. The quantity of the material used also is a controlling factor. For instance, if a cleaning liquid is used only occasionally it may be secured in small hand containers or buckets. If it is used in great quantities it may be piped in from the storage tank. If it is used in moderate quantities it may be brought in on electric trucks in drums. The drums may be placed on a special rack that would facilitate the use of the liquid.

If large quantities of the parts are used, such as in an automobile assembly line, the parts are usually brought to the assembly line in tote boxes on trucks. The material is ordinarily stored at the point of use on the assembly line in these tote boxes. Some items are easily scratched and must be handled on special racks. The racks can be taken by trucks to the point of use, if they are used in large quantities. In other instances, such as in airplane assembly, groups of parts may be placed in appropriate containers and delivered to the point of assembly. In other words, each situation has to be studied and the materials delivered according to specific needs. Sometimes parts are delivered to the assembly line on conveyors that are synchronized with the assembly line, and the parts are removed from the conveyor and placed directly into the assembly.

Storing Materials. Some materials such as liquids require special storage facilities. There is usually a compromise between storing materials close to the point of receipt and close to the point of use. If the material can be delivered to the point of use it reduces the cost of rehandling. However, it is usually impossible to provide sufficient storage space adjacent to the point of use for large quantities of bulky material. If the parts are small it creates a problem of controlling their use to store a two or three months' supply on the production floor. The resulting solution is often a separate storage place for relatively small items from which they are delivered to the point of assembly according to orders from the production control department.

The actual arrangement of the storage varies according to the size and nature of the material and the systems of identification. Here again there may have to be a compromise in the use of a particular system. In some cases the storage bins are numbered according to a logical system. This enables the stock clerk to go directly to a particular location when he learns the particular bin number from his card index. Items may be stored in keeping with their part numbers, provided these follow a logical pattern. Such a procedure might call for certain items being stored a considerable distance from the point of issuance. These same parts might be used daily. In this case it would be more logical to store the most frequently used items near the point of assembly of materials to be issued. In actual practice any system of storage may be modified to meet operating conditions, regardless of its doing violence to a neatly conceived pattern.

There is also the problem of issuing the oldest material first so as not to keep any particular item in storage too long. This problem is easily met when a dual storage bin system is followed. One bin is emptied before starting on the new bin. This system requires a larger total number of bins than the single bin system, which is in more common use. The single bin system would remove all of the older material from the bin when newer supplies are received. The new supply is placed in the bin and the older materials are then placed in the bin on top of the newer ones. Under this system the old parts are generally used before the new ones. Sometimes, movable partitions are used in the bins to separate the new supply from the older parts.

Securing Supplies on the Second or Third Shift. It is common practice to issue supplies and materials on the first shift in large enough quantities to take care of the needs of the second and third shifts. When this practice works as planned there is no problem. Unfortunately, the best laid plans sometimes are not properly carried out. In such instances the second or third shift foreman may have to make out his own requisition, get the keys to the stock room from the night superintendent or watchman, and get the supplies himself or have one of his men do it. This situation requires that the night foreman know a good deal about the systems of storage and issuance of materials. If proper records are not left so that the perpetual inventory entries are made by the regular inventory clerks the entire system breaks down. Proper materials control requires a high degree of cooperation by all parties. The supervisor is the key man in providing one side of this cooperation.

Salvage. Practically every company of any size has a salvage department where materials are assembled, sorted, returned to production, or sold. The supervisor's interest in this field is basically to keep all material in such shape that it will not have to go to salvage; and to send any material that *must* go to salvage promptly to this department. One item of basic importance is to make out adequate records of parts that are sent to salvage. Otherwise the proper count and costs cannot be kept. Sometimes material that otherwise would be sent to the salvage department may be saved by the supervisor by reworking. Reworking is costly but often less costly than selling the item for salvage.

22 | Waste Control

The Nature of Waste. In its broadest social and economic sense, waste is not the sole responsibility of any one segment of society. Overproduction, underproduction, excess costs of any phase of production, noneconomic buying or selling, or any activities that needlessly increase the cost of providing the goods or services to the customer are a waste. *Waste arises from the improper use of or the failure to use materials, manpower, equipment, or any measurable factor in production.*

Industrial waste in the broadest social and economic sense includes among other things: (1) unemployment during depressions, (2) speculation and overproduction during boom times, (3) excessive labor turnover, (4) labor conflicts, (5) failure in transportation of supplies, fuel, or power, (6) unbalanced seasonal production, (7) lack of standardization, (8) inefficient processing of materials, (9) uneconomic use of equipment, (10) inefficient use of manpower, (11) uneconomic use of supplies, (12) misuse of power, (13) deliberate restriction of production either by management or men, and (14) ill health and accidents. Many of these do not come within the control of the supervisor. Others are within his province and he can either take action himself to eliminate or control them or start action higher up by his suggestions and recommendations. The supervisor can control the use of power within his department, avoiding waste of it whenever possible. Recognizing the possibilities of restriction of output by his men, he can see that the conditions leading to such action are not present in his department. Each supervisor through safety instruction and supervision can take steps to reduce accidents. The supervisor may even recommend steps toward standardization within his own department and within the plant, as well as methods to eliminate unbalanced seasonal production.

Waste exists when either too much light or too little light is used. Waste develops when the wrong tool or a poorly designed machine is selected to do work that could be done more efficiently with other tools or better-designed equipment. Manpower is wasted any time a skilled man receiving a high wage rate is used on work that could be done equally well by a less skilled employee receiving a lower wage. Waste occurs if one department processes materials that could be handled more efficiently in another department. When work is done in any manner other than the one best-known way, waste occurs. Using material other than the material best suited for the particular job involved, or employing men who are not the best qualified to do the work, produces waste. Waste occurs just as easily in the engineering, purchasing, or personnel departments as in the production departments. Any supervisor can find wastes in his department. Many of them are of a kind that he can take immediate steps to eliminate or control. Other wastes may have to be referred to other departments, such as personnel, engineering, or purchasing, but at least the supervisor can recognize and raise the problem and wherever possible recommend action.

Waste Classified. There is no special value in a given classification unless it contributes to achieving a given objective. The control or elimination of waste is a prime objective of operating management. The various classifications of waste facilitate its recognition and that of its causes. Viewed from the standpoint of control, waste may be classified according to *time of occurrence, types,* and *what may be done about it.* Waste classified according to time of occurrence falls into: (1) *frequently recurring,* (2) *miscellaneous,* and (3) *epidemic.* Waste classified as to types includes: (1) *manpower,* (2) *equipment,* (3) *tools,* (4) *supplies,* (5) *materials,* and (6) *heat, light, and power.* Waste classified as to what can be done about it includes: (1) *avoidable,* (2) *semi-avoidable,* and (3) *unavoidable.* From the standpoint of the supervisor each of the above classifications has merit. Under "avoidable wastes" may be found those which are frequently recurring, such as manpower and equipment. The term "epidemic," as used here, refers to substantial waste, not recurring, such as a sudden burst of breaking tools or excess absenteeism arising at a given time. There is no single percentage allowance for waste that is characteristic of industry in general or for the same industry. If the waste can be reduced and the waste-reducing cost is not greater than the saving, it should be reduced.   Published records of successful waste-reducing efforts are relatively scarce.   The Westinghouse Electric and Manufacturing Company (East Springfield Works) found that, in general, their waste was distributed as follows: recurrent, 25 per cent; epidemic, 25 per cent; and miscellaneous, 50 per cent.[1]   Through winning employee cooperation this company was able in 1939 to reduce waste 31 per cent under 1938 and 47 per cent under 1937.

Responsibility for Waste and Its Control.   "Control is the function of constraining and regulating action in accordance with the requirements of a plan for the accomplishment of an objective.   It is achieved through the proper correlation and coordination of the activities of the business organization."[2]   Control may be either at the administrative or top management level, or at the operative level where the specific procedures take place.   Top management is interested in administrative controls because these are the ones for which it is directly responsible.   It is also interested in operational controls for if these are carried out as planned top management's controls will be made simple.   In fact, many of top management's controls are designed to effectuate operative controls, or at least to let top management know when the operative controls are not functioning as expected.

While top management is primarily responsible for many aspects of waste control, it must rely on its delegated representatives for the actual point-of-operation controls.   The supervisor is the key man in waste reduction.   Of course his efforts are confined to the over-all framework of established policy and available equipment and processes.

Waste arises from the buying habits of the consumer, from management's decisions and controls, and from the performance of workers. The public is both directly and indirectly responsible for many wastes that are very nearly unavoidable.   Buying habits, especially seasonal demands, are causes of waste that no management can cure.   Pressing into four weeks the buying for Christmas is an outstanding example that causes many manufacturers to compress their production into the few months just preceding this buying season.   Both management and the customer are responsible for certain wastes arising from style or model changes and the great variety of colors, styles, and sizes.   The customers, particularly women, seem to want style changes.   Management recognizes that sales may be increased by style changes and

[1] See T. O. Armstrong, *Employee Cooperation in Quality Control,* Bureau of Industrial Relations, University of Michigan, 1941.

[2] Ralph C. Davis, *The Fundamentals of Top Management,* Harper and Brothers, New York, 1951, p. 637.

hence encourages this desire of customers for the "latest" style or model.

Among the many examples that can be cited are women's clothing, radios, and refrigerators. To the demand of the consuming public for change must often be added that of the engineering departments and purchasing agents, whose demands for something different and for variations in dimensions or specifications are often amazing. It took World War I to start a movement toward simplification and stand-ardization that is yet a long way from completion. The responsibility for manufacturing waste may be traced to management and very often to the supervisors. It includes those wastes caused by poor planning or complete lack of planning, faulty organization, inadequate buildings or space, poor plant layout, expensive processes, inefficient methods, lack of controls, inadequate instruction and improper placement of employees, failure to give the men information that would make them waste- and standards-conscious, and the lack of standards or designs. The responsibility for waste can be charged against the men when they fail to acquire the necessary skill to perform their work, lack the will-ingness to cooperate, have the wrong attitude toward their work, their supervisor, and the company, when they deliberately restrict output, fail to learn and to follow the standards set for them, meet with acci-dents they could have avoided by taking proper precautions, and fail to pay the necessary attention to details. The first step in waste control is to get all the facts, then determine the causes and fix the responsi-bility, and finally to take the necessary action to control or eliminate the waste.

Records as a Basis for Waste Control. Any kind of record keeping is facilitated when the organizational structure has clearly defined lines of supervision and fixed responsibilities. Records which assist in waste controls can be kept only when functions and responsibilities are clearly defined and allocated from an organization standpoint, thus indicating defects for which the men are responsible or which are due to management inadequacies. To be useful, records must be specific and describe in workable detail the exact nature of the waste and to a considerable extent its cause. Records on waste should be compiled so that the waste can be allocated to a particular product, a specific item in that product, and so far as is practicable to a particular opera-tion and machine. Wherever possible they should fix responsibility on a shift and even on an operator. Waste records should be suffi-ciently comprehensive so that they can point to the cause, whether it be unsatisfactory raw materials, defective tools or equipment, poor workmanship, defective supplies, or auxiliary materials such as lubricants, improper design, routing, or inadequate handling or storing. Such records can be compiled only when specialized departments such as production control, cost, or inspection specifically collect them for preventive purposes and not merely as historical data.

Since a sizeable proportion of waste may be traceable to the failure of the men to meet standards of quality and performance, waste records must be in a form capable of being understood and used by the supervisor and his assistants. These records, especially when assembled by other departments, must be made available to the supervisor. Not only must the supervisor receive adequate records to enable him to locate needless waste, he must get this information currently. It is necessary for him to know, at the time, that the waste is being caused so that he may take the needed steps to correct it.

Many times it is advisable to give such records to the operator involved, but he must also be given an interpretation of causal relationships and have the standards re-explained to him. The Westinghouse Electric and Manufacturing Company screw machine department had a running feud with the fan department over the tolerances specified on a worm gear. When a committee of employees from the two departments came together to discuss the scrap situation it was discovered that the screw machine operators had never seen the inside of a fan before. When they had the opportunity to examine the parts of a fan and see for themselves the reasons for the close tolerances the trouble was ended.[3] Whenever men have the opportunity to see the reasons for the standards set for them, when they know the why of the job, the supervisor has taken a long step toward waste control.

The Supervisor's Role in Waste Control. The supervisor is not solely responsible for all of the waste that develops in his department. Defective raw material may be sent to him. Of course if it continues to be less than standard he may set up an inspection to detect it before his men spend time working on it. The following list of sources of waste in the department contains items entirely or in part within the control of the departmental supervisor:

    1. Scrap from the operation
    2. Wasted material arising from permitting it to lie around and become shop worn (in the case of small parts like nuts and bolts they may merely be mixed sizes)

[3] T. O. Armstrong, *op. cit.*

3. Idle machines
   3.1   Waiting for work
   3.2   Due to absenteeism of workers
4. Defective parts needing to be reworked
5. Inefficient workers (may produce defective work or merely substandard output)
6. Poor scheduling from the production control department or a failure of supervisor to follow the schedule
7. Accidents causing
   7.1   Personal injury
   7.2   Broken equipment
   7.3   Spoiled product
8. Poor housekeeping adds to accidents, increases janitor costs, and increases loss of materials or parts
9. Excess use of lights, compressed air or water, and electricity
10. Manpower (using a skilled man on an unskilled job)
11. Maintenance, not properly oiling or using equipment, or delaying minor repairs too long
12. Using a larger machine than is needed for the operation
13. Improper standards (they may be more rigid than is needed)

Space will not permit a detailed discussion of each of these items. Each of them has a common core with the others. The supervisor needs to know what is required to do the job efficiently, to train his men to do it properly, and to follow up to see that it is done according to standard.

Material Waste. When the supervisor has the majority of his men on piecework and begins to find too many men carrying day rates in his department, he should recognize it as a sign of the developing of waste. If he continues learners on day rate after they should go on incentive rates, waste is present. Indirect wastes of materials develop from specifications being incompletely checked. Too often the specifications are not drawn carefully enough to obtain the best possible finished product per unit of cost.

Accessory materials such as sandpaper and files, as well as many larger articles that are not supplies, are in universal use. There is usually a best size and type for each particular task. Sometimes excessive variety is the result of improper standardization. Indirect wastes of materials are often found in the methods of disbursement used. Disbursements should be made only on order and should be checked against production requirements. Unless proper storage methods are used to give materials protection against deterioration and to avoid pilfering, indirect wastes develop. Reclaiming materials is one way to control waste where such materials as oils, files, and tools are used. Many supervisors discard these materials when they could be salvaged at a cost lower than the cost of replacement. Other material wastes that are indirect, and go unnoticed until the supervisor studies his department, include oils, both cutting and lubricating, waste rags, waste paper, scrap metals, partially worn-out or greasy belting, soap, towels (where furnished), empty containers such as cartons, boxes, and barrels, broken castings, parts, and other materials. Many of these can be salvaged, reworked, or if properly handled sold to other companies instead of costing money to store or destroy.

The supervisor should be on the alert to see that materials are not wasted: (1) because they are improperly machined and do not meet specifications, (2) because they become mixed, for example, nuts, bolts, and washers, or (3) because regular processing leaves scrap such as that from stamping out parts, cutting out patterns, shavings, or defects arising from initial runs or setups. Frequently, materials, otherwise of no use to the company, can be salvaged or sold to firms specializing in scrapped materials. In many instances the costs of separating or baling are more than offset by the higher prices paid for the materials when they are sold according to grade and ready for processing.

Waste in the Use of Tools and Equipment. The supervisor may see that the wrong machines are being used, that heavy work is being done on light equipment, resulting in overloading and greater wear on machine parts, or that small operations are being performed on large and expensive equipment involving higher setup costs and operating expense. Wastes due to improper maintenance of machines and the lack of, or improper, repairing, oiling, or cleaning, may add materially to the cost of maintaining equipment.

The supervisor may find that available special attachments are not being used. Waste is present in every case where machines are not equipped with the best-designed cutting tools. The supervisor will uncover waste whenever his analysis of equipment discloses the fact that his machines are not producing up to capacity. The supervisor, as a result of studying his equipment and looking for waste, will frequently find that the operation sequence is improper and analysis of the operation will reveal a better procedure. When looking for waste, the supervisor will often uncover the use of dull tools, and frequently the causes of tool breakage will be discovered and reduced. Dull tools or tool breakage may result from improperly sharpened tools. Wastes occur in connection with equipment such as trays, racks, tote boxes, trucks, and containers that are used in machine operations. Contrary to popular opinion, great savings are often realized by motion-studying automatic or semi-automatic machinery. Not only should hand operations be motion-studied, but it is also essential to motion-study automatic equipment since it is possible to standardize the methods of setup and control of automatic equipment with consequent savings of machine time, material, operator time, and effort.

Waste in the Use of Manpower. A keen sense of motion analysis is a strong aid to any person who directs the efforts of a group of workers. An analysis of the manpower usage usually reveals waste in: (1) ineffective use of manpower, (2) inefficiency in the maintenance of manpower, (3) accidents and health, (4) unnecessary overtime, (5) excessive overtime, and (6) excessive nonproductive labor. Every supervisor who analyzes his department will usually find places where he is not utilizing his manpower to its maximum effectiveness. This may be due to wasted motions or to his men's not using the best possible method of performing the work. Usually this will be found true in departments where the jobs have not been motion-studied and the best possible procedure established. In other instances, supervisors will find that an employee is not on the job for which he is best fitted. Such waste is evident when a skilled man is being used on semiskilled or unskilled operations. When the supervisor knows his men, their interests, capacities, and opportunities, he will find that men are often on jobs that do not take full advantage of the individual's interests and capacities.

One of the major ways in which manpower is not used to its maximum effectiveness is in the failure to take advantage of the principles of specialization. Almost every supervisor will find in his department skilled men who spend part of their time on operations which could be performed by a helper or learner, freeing the experienced man for concentration on operations requiring his special skills and experience. Many supervisors will find men in their departments who wash up prior to quitting time or who are not at their workplaces at starting time. When this is a frequent occurrence, manpower losses are considerable. Ineffective use of manpower results when men deliberately restrict output or work rapidly until the standard is in sight and then loaf on the job. Some supervisors have found instances where one man operates a single machine when he could readily, with slight readjustments of equipment, operate two or more machines.[4] Poor departmental layout will result in ineffective use of manpower. When

---

[4] Of course such situations may be the result of union pressures over which the supervisor has little control.

men have to walk an excessive distance to get materials or tools, when their machines are not arranged in such fashion as to conserve both space and worker energy, and when the flow of materials from machine to machine is not properly laid out, manpower is being wasted. To have men waiting for materials is an ineffective use of manpower. A similar situation arises when men wait for job assignments or to punch time cards for new jobs. The supervisor may find that men walk long distances in order to get materials or work orders when orders and work should be brought to them.

Poorly selected men will cause high turnover, increased costs, and lowered morale in the department. Poorly placed men also communicate their discontent to other men in the department and lower departmental efficiency. The supervisor must constantly watch and control the selection and placement of the men assigned to his department and train or transfer men when the selections or placements are not satisfactory. Wastes of manpower are indicated when labor turnover increases. No department will utilize to their fullest extent the capacities of its men when there is a constant parade of men into and out of the department. Each employee will himself be wondering whether or not he will be the next one to go or if the turnover is due to men leaving for better jobs. The men who remain are also likely to be looking for other jobs and only staying on the job until a better opening appears. Excessive absences and tardinesses prevent the maintenance of manpower at the maximum point of efficiency. Poor discipline and low morale, which go hand in hand, increase the problems of the supervisor in effectively maintaining manpower.

When men are absent because of accidents, the production of the entire department is reduced. The man must be replaced, which results in delays and loss of time while the new man learns the work. There are the resultant losses to the company in compensation costs and decreased production. Unsatisfactory health conditions contribute to wastes in manpower. When bad lighting, ventilation, heating, or other unsatisfactory working conditions result in poor health, wastes develop. The money saved by decreasing light bills, reducing heat, by lack of guards, or the reduced medical costs when periodical medical examinations are not used may readily be lost many times over in the resultant wastes of manpower. Lack of heat may cause an epidemic of colds that will cost much in absenteeism and lowered production and morale. It costs money to surround hazardous occupations with the necessary safeguards and to provide regular medical checkups, but the savings more than offset the cost. The supervisor who takes the necessary steps to eliminate causes for accidents and illness will not only win the confidence of his men and build morale but will also increase his production and lower his departmental costs.

When poor planning results in the need for overtime, costs rise since the work will carry overtime rates and the production of men on overtime is lower than during their regular working hours. Overtime due to insufficient manpower leads to discontent and lowered morale. Desired production cannot be maintained long by men in an understaffed department, and the supervisor will do well to see that his department is not short on manpower. Frequently he will think when he loses a man by transfer or discharge that he can get along without a replacement by letting the rest of the men share the work. At times this may be desirable if the department is overstaffed. At other times the practice is fatal. The men easily see through such an action on the part of the supervisor and frequently this leads to the beginning of the restriction of output. If, however, the supervisor reorganizes the work of his department, finding more efficient methods of performing the work, and the men see that they are helped to do a better job, then the supervisor may not need the replacement.

Excessive day work allowances in departments on piecework or incentive plans indicate waste due to poor planning or lax supervision. When certain operations continue on day rate when they can be put on piecework or incentive, waste is occurring. Use of excessive nonproductive labor, such as clerks or inspectors, even though day rate may be the established method of wage payment, results in waste. The supervisor must be on the lookout constantly for unnecessary personnel in his department. It is easy to add men to a department when it is busy and production is rising, but the successful supervisor is the one who can control his labor costs in terms of his production within the possible limits imposed on him. When the supervisor has the majority of his men on piecework and begins to find too many men carrying day rates in his department, he should recognize it as a sign of the developing of waste. If he continues learners on day rate after they should go on incentive rates, waste is present and the cause should be sought.

Waste of Space, Heat, Power, and Light. Almost every supervisor will find power wastes in his department. Overloading of equipment in starting wastes power, as does starting all machines at once. Failure to take advantage of special rates on power constitutes a waste. Misuse of compressed air, such as the men's using the air hose to blow the dirt off their clothing, results in waste of power. Leaks in fittings and airlines waste power as does the use of compressed air for power when electricity is available. The use of excess horsepower in motors or constant overloading of motors are other wastes that the supervisor will do well to seek out and remedy. Waste of heat results whenever overheating takes place, or irregular control of heat is present, and whenever hot water is wasted by employees in the rest rooms or in the operation of equipment. The supervisor should seek to replace human controls with automatic controls of heat, power, and light whenever possible. The supervisor will find tremendous opportunities for controlling or eliminating wastes due to inefficient departmental layout, inefficient use, misuse, or nonuse of conveyors, and improper or lack of building maintenance.

The use of general lighting when point-of-operation lighting should be employed develops waste and at the same time is much less satisfactory to the operators. Misuse of light is a major waste in most departments and offers an excellent opportunity to the supervisor to show his ability to control or eliminate waste. Improper location of lighting fixtures and inadequate or excess lighting are frequently found in most departments. Lights that continue to burn when not needed constitute a common waste. Incorrect colors used in painting walls and ceilings result in increased light being required, with resultant waste. Windows, bowls, and bulbs that need to be cleaned, or bulbs that are too large, all contribute to power wastes which the supervisor can control or eliminate.

Eliminating Waste. As stated earlier, waste control requires knowing what to expect, training employees properly, and following up to see that standards are met. The supervisor, in controlling waste, must set up adequate controls as part of his method. These will include planning for and developing methods to care for his equipment. They go farther and involve the selection of the correct machine, the best tool, and the right accessories for the work. They require the proper use of equipment—avoid overloading machines or using one that takes too much time to set up when another machine is or can be made available. Carefully established controls, properly set up, will do something else for the supervisor: they will indicate when it is more profitable to replace equipment with more economical machines that are available, and not only will do more work at less cost, but will also absorb the cost of the discarded equipment with a margin of profit left over. Finally, the supervisor must see that his men use special-purpose equipment when the volume justifies it. The chart that follows illustrates some of the waste possibilities together with the re-

Waste in Industry

Waste Possibilities	Responsibility	Recommendation
1. Manpower		
1.1 Lost time on the job	Management	Better organization, closer supervision and planning
1.2 Labor turnover	Management	Better selection, training, placement, and closer supervision, planning, and cooperation
1.3 Accidents and illness	Management and men	Better selection, training, supervision, and follow-up of safe practices
1.4 Too few men	Management	Better planning, supervision, and managerial efficiency
1.5 Too many men to women	Management	Better planning, supervision, and managerial efficiency
1.6 Misfits	Management	Better selection, instruction supervision, transfer, and discharge
1.7 Lack of skill	Management	Better selection and training, transfer
1.8 Unnecessary overtime	Management and men	More careful planning and closer supervision
1.9 Tardiness and absenteeism	Management and men	Personal counsel, incentives, adjustment, transfer, discharge
1.10 Inefficiency	Management and men	Better instruction, planning, control, layout, discharge
1.11 Poor morale	Management	Strong carefully planned leadership
2. Material		
2.1 Metal, copper, zinc, brass, etc.	Management and men	Closer controls, supervision and cooperation
2.2 Solder, varnish, paint	Management and men	Closer controls, supervision and cooperation
2.3 Lead	Management and men	Closer controls, supervision and cooperation
2.4 Tools and equipment	Management and men	Better standards, closer controls, instruction, supervision and cooperation
2.5 Janitor supplies	Management and men	Better standards, proper controls, supervision and follow-up
2.6 Office supplies	Management and men	Better supervision, storage, issuance, standards and cooperation
2.7 Clothing that may be furnished	Management and men	Better selection, care, use, and maintenance

Waste in Industry (Continued)

Waste Possibilities	Responsibility	Recommendation
2.8 Cutting oils, lubricants	Management and men	Better specifications, closer supervision, issuance and cooperation
2.9 Cartons	Management and men	Closer supervision and cooperation
2.10 Lumber	Management and men	Better specifications, closer supervision, issuance and cooperation
2.11 Salvaging	Management and men	Organize to salvage and sell
3. Plant, building, heat, light, power, and equipment		
3.1 Unused space	Management	Better planning
3.2 Poor layout	Management	Better planning
3.3 Material storage and handling	Management and men	Better planning, closer supervision
3.4 Conveyors, aisles	Management and men	Better planning, supervision, follow-up, and cooperation
3.5 Heat	Management and men	Closer follow-up
3.6 Light	Management and men	Closer supervision and cooperation
3.7 Power	Management and men	Closer supervision, better planning and cooperation
3.8 Water	Management and men	Closer supervision and cooperation, and maintenance
3.9 Air	Management and men	Closer supervision, better maintenance and cooperation
3.10 Idle machines	Management and men	Better planning, closer supervision and cooperation
3.11 Improper machines	Management and men	Better planning
3.12 Unbalanced production	Management and men	Better planning
3.13 Handling equipment	Management and men	Training and supervision
3.14 Tool salvage	Management	Set up salvage procedure

sponsibility for these conditions and some recommendations for action which were developed in one large company.

Organization, Standards, and Procedures. Proper organization is essential in waste elimination. Definite lines of authority must be established and maintained. Responsibility must be fixed—everybody's job is nobody's job. The supervisor must see that authority accompanies responsibility. Standards that are clear-cut and readily understood must be established and they must be commercially feasible and no higher than needed. This determination of proper standards may often require redesigning of parts and materials. One method for the controlling of waste by the supervisor is the establishment of points of inspection to facilitate preventive inspection rather than reliance on remedial inspection. It is wise, where possible, to tie in remuneration with quality maintenance and scrap reduction or elimination. The supervisor should not become content with job performance up to established standards of scrap reduction but must re-evaluate the performance from time to time to see if newer or better methods may be devised. Research to develop better standards resulting in lowered waste is another step toward success in waste elimination. The supervisor through planning can control many situations that would otherwise develop waste. He should avoid emergencies and rush orders and, in so far as possible, special orders. Wherever possible he should try for runs of economical lot sizes. When the supervisor succeeds in developing versatility among his men he is well prepared to meet successfully any unexpected conditions and demands on his department without unnecessary waste taking place. The supervisor should plan for carefully scheduled repairs and maintenance of his machines and equipment and provide a steady flow of production to his men. These last two actions will contribute tremendously to any program of waste elimination and waste control the supervisor operates, and they are basic elements in his planning for his department.

23

The Supervisor and Cost Control

Introduction. The control of costs is a major concern of top management. Selling prices are not solely established by costs but costs do set a limit below which the product cannot be sold without a loss. Every operating and staff unit should be cost conscious. The foreman has within his province the control of many phases of costs. These phases include waste of any nature, materials, supplies, accidents, labor, heat, light, compressed air, and products that must be sold as seconds.

Management uses many devices for controlling costs. Among these are: (1) budgets, (2) standard specifications for the product and processes, (3) standards for each operation in terms of time, (4) standards for allowances for scrap (it is impossible to eliminate all scrap from processing), (5) standards for maintenance, (6) standard time allowances for changeovers from one operation to another, (7) labor turnover, (8) training, and (9) accident severity and frequency standards. The ideal for accidents would be *zero*. So long as people are subject to frailties there will be some accidents. Management's goal is to reduce these accidents to a minimum. Of course, top management has many other costs that it strives to minimize such as: (1) selling costs, (2) various phases of overhead costs, inventory of work-in-process, raw materials, and finished products, and (3) the costs of securing funds for expansion, interest charges, preferred stock dividend rates, and the cost of marketing securities. Most of these costs are of such a nature that the supervisor has little influence over them. Of course, the supervisor may exert some control over the inventory of work-in-process by not keeping up to schedule; however, the layout-by-process or -by-product may exert a tremendous influence on the inventory in process. Top management has more control over the type of layout used than the supervisor.

The Supervisor's Records as a Basis of Cost Control. Chapter 25 is devoted to records and reports. They will be considered here solely as they relate to cost control. It is entirely too easy for the enthusiast to blame all of the excess costs of a supervisor on his failure to keep or to use the records needed for decision making. Certainly it is difficult for a supervisor to make many of the decisions required of him in the absence of adequate records. On the other hand, balance is required in the allocating of the supervisor's time between record keeping and directing the operations from which the records are derived. Most operating supervisors are not record oriented. They are men of action not especially interested in nor qualified for record keeping. If a supervisor spends an hour a day making his records and analyzing them, during which time his men require training and supervising, he may readily lose more than he gains by his records. Two observations are in order in relation to the supervisor and the use of cost records, namely:

1. In so far as possible the supervisor should be relieved of the burden of record keeping. Most records can be kept more economically by one of the staff departments. The supervisor should be provided with adequate clerical assistance so that he can devote his time to those activities for which he is best qualified.

2. Records provided the supervisor should be in such form that they point out items for which he is responsible. The supervisor is not responsible for most overhead and it wastes his time to include such costs on his reports. He is responsible for economical use of the heat, light, and power in his department. He is also responsible for direct and indirect labor in his department. Records provided the supervisor by staff departments need to be current so that he can do something about deviations from attainable standards.

The Supervisor and His Budget. A budget is a predetermined standard of performance in terms of the controllable costs for any given volume of production covering a specific period of time. The budget may be a variable one covering a series of volumes of production. It should be clearly recognized that the budget does not control costs but is a standard established by carefully considering past experience, standards for materials and labor, and the expected performance in terms of these experiences and standards. The budget gives a target to shoot at and provides a measure against which to compare performance.

To construct a workable budget requires pre-planning of a high order. Records of past achievements serve as a basis for this effective planning. This pre-planning forces the supervisor to think through his entire operation. He must look at it as a whole. This looking at the entirety of the operation is sufficient justification for constructing the budget. In its construction the supervisor's superior should give counsel and advice. This promotes teamwork. If the projected budget calls for an increase or decrease in production it establishes a time schedule that guides the supervisor in hiring and training new men or in planning to cut back his work force. Of course, conditions may arise that upset the plan; where a cut-back was anticipated changed conditions may call for an increase. In spite of these unexpected changes orderly planning facilitates control and promotes increased efficiency. It is immeasurably to be preferred to operating off the cuff and to improvising with each change. The flexible budget is especially to be desired when unexpected changes are encountered. Such a budget may readily include a plan for an increase or decrease of 10 per cent over the budgeted production.

Some aspects of a budget may be more rigid than others. For instance, there may be a specific amount budgeted for maintenance. This amount may include painting. In such an event the supervisor may be restricted to a specific amount for this type of expenditure. On the other hand, emergency breakdowns have to be taken care of regardless of the budget. However, careful budgeting of maintenance expenditures tends to minimize or eliminate emergency breakdowns. The equipment will usually be so maintained that breakdowns will not occur.

Maximum benefits from a budget are derived when the record keeping is so designed as to give current reports to the supervisor regarding his performance. Several large companies have organized their reporting so that the supervisor gets pertinent information within a 24-hour period from the time of performance. For instance, one highly conveyorized company has carefully established standards of the ratio of indirect labor to direct labor. Actual performance reports for a given day are available to the supervisor by noon of the following day. Such budget reporting aids the supervisor in catching deviations. He can take the necessary steps to correct them before it is too late.

Cost Control over the Product and Process. Budget standards for a product are predicated on the use of standardized materials, machines, and methods. Labor costs may be too high because of a failure of employees to produce according to standard or because the material used required more labor than allowed for in the standard. Of course defective workmanship may call for excess reworking. If the reworking is done by the individuals who caused the defects there may be no additional direct labor cost provided the workers are on straight piecework or an equivalent incentive system. Even in such circumstances production will be lower and the overhead costs will be spread over a reduced number of units.

The supervisor's responsibility for controlling the costs of the product consists in his being able to influence his employees to produce the number of items of the quality desired with the allowed scrap, power usage, and due regard for proper care of equipment. In other words, the supervisor is responsible for the control of every item of cost that is chargeable to the product in his department. In the so-called chemical or semi-chemical industries defects may show up just before the product is ready for wrapping or packaging. The product may be satisfactory from a chemical standpoint but show slight defects as to appearance. For instance, the die through which soap is being extruded prior to being cut into bars may have marked the side of the soap. The soap has to be reprocessed to remove this blemish. The cost of reprocessing is an added cost to that of the accepted bars of soap. Failure at any stage of an operation to meet established standards adds to the cost of the product.

The Supervisor's Control of Scrap. It is well within the province of a supervisor to establish realizable norms for scrap and to get his men to achieve these standards. In the case of workers who are on an incentive wage plan it becomes, at times, a problem to get them to exercise the needed care to keep scrap to an acceptable minimum. In some instances an incentive system may include a factor for the minimizing of scrap. In most cases the keeping of scrap within established standards is achieved through close supervision and indoctrinating the workers in the necessity for working according to acceptable standards. Any system that shares the savings with the workers when scrap is lower than the established standard provides them with a strong incentive.

The problem of controlling scrap has plagued manufacturers from time immemorial. It never has been completely solved. Proper maintenance of equipment, care in handling of material, adequate instruction, careful control of issuance of material, and every technique of good management contribute to the control of scrap. Perhaps the strongest single item is the ability of the supervisor to develop in his men a scrap consciousness. Employee cooperation is more effective in reducing scrap than any special technique. Contests in which the individual workers strive to meet a given standard often get desired cooperation. The posting of daily scrap records may provide an effective method of calling the scrap item to the attention of the workers.

Close cooperation between the inspection department and the supervisor of the production department frequently aids in reducing unnecessary scrap. In other words, *preventive inspection* is a more productive approach than *remedial inspection*. Preventive inspection strives to eliminate the defect rather than to catch it once it has occurred. To the extent that the supervisor can develop in his men quality consciousness and the "will to produce" according to the established standards, the total amount of inspection may be reduced. As a matter of fact, inspection by an "outside inspector" or an inspector not a part of the actual productive process is an additional cost that need not be necessary when a well-trained quality conscious work group is properly led. One machine tool manufacturer had his workers do their own inspection. The only inspection given his product was that given by the supervisor. To be able to achieve this result requires a leadership and cooperation not found too often in modern industry. The fact still remains that a supervisor who really teaches and leads may cooperate with the inspection department to reduce the cost of scrap. It may also prevent adding additional labor costs to a piece that has already failed to meet specifications.

Reducing Overtime Costs. Overtime should not be required, save in unusual emergencies, when production control does its job as it should do it, when the personnel department has been able to fill the requests for needed employees, where the supervisor has properly trained his men and kept labor turnover within reasonable limits, and when equipment has been properly maintained so as to avoid breakdowns unless poor sales planning or budgeting is encountered. Of course, overtime in a few cases may be required when the available machines simply cannot handle the required production. Such a situation should only be temporary. In some instances it may be cheaper to use the available equipment five hours a week on an overtime basis than to have enough expensive equipment to get out the needed production in a forty-hour week. In such cases the problem is one of balancing production and facilities. The supervisor's role in keeping down overtime costs lies largely in: (1) knowing his production requirements and giving the employment department time to hire the needed men, (2) allowing time to train his men so that they can meet production requirements, (3) actually training the men to meet both quality and quantity standards, and (4) providing dynamic leadership so as to minimize absenteeism and tardiness. Of course, the planning ability of the supervisor frequently is his strongest ally in getting things done on time. Overtime is an unnecessary cost in most instances and should be studiously avoided save in emergencies. Good planning reduces emergencies to a minimum.

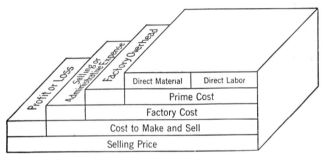

Figure 23.1. The cost steps.

The Supervisor's Knowledge of Cost Accounting. It is not expected that the average supervisor will be a technically trained cost accountant. However, there is practically nothing in cost accounting that cannot be readily understood by the average high school graduate who has had two years of mathematics. The supervisor is primarily concerned with those aspects of costs over which he has control and not the entire cost accounting system. The supervisor who is truly ambitious and looks forward to the time when he may be in charge of the entire operation should study cost accounting seriously. Figure 23.1 illustrates the various costs that go into the product. Naturally the selling price must include total costs of making and selling ± profit and loss.

Classification of Costs. *Factory expense* is composed of all those burden items that can be allocated to the factory, such as waste, depreciation, repairs, taxes, insurance, indirect labor, power, heat. light, and salaries of factory supervisors and clerical workers. *General expense* includes general administration and managerial costs, such as main-office salaries and expenses, legal costs, the portion of power, heat, light, and depreciation expenses that is chargeable to the central office group, accounting, and other items, such as communication expense, general office supplies, and sometimes institutional advertising, public relations expenses, and similar costs. *Selling expense* includes those items that are directly chargeable to selling. The exact breakdown of this expense, like all the others, may vary with the individual concern and the use made of the costs. Advertising, for instance, is frequently chargeable with little difficulty to sales; yet some institutions classify this item under general expense (see Figure 23.1).

From the standpoint of the operating factory executive the classification of costs as given below is helpful:

1. Prime costs = direct material cost + direct labor costs
2. Factory costs = prime cost + factory expense
3. Cost to make and sell = factory cost + selling expense
4. Total cost = cost to make and sell + general administrative expense
5. Selling price = total cost ± profit or loss

The Elements of Costs. Figure 23.1 shows direct materials and direct labor as being the two components of prime costs. Total costs are made up of the costs of material, labor, and expenses. *Direct materials* are those that go into the product and can be directly traced to it. *Indirect materials* are those that are necessary in the production process but are not directly used in the product itself, such as coal, oil, and sandpaper. Other materials that go into the products but are difficult to trace to a given product are often for practical reasons classed as indirect material, such as nails, glue, putty, and sometimes paint. The same material may be a direct material for one producer and an indirect material for another. Labor is also classified into two groups, direct, or productive, and indirect, or nonproductive labor.[1] *Direct labor* can be allocated to a specific product or products, whereas *indirect labor* cannot readily be thus assigned. The method of wage payment may influence the classification of labor as direct or indirect. A janitor is ordinarily paid on a day-rate basis, and his work is usually classified as indirect. In some departments the entire group, including

---

[1] "Productive" and "nonproductive" in a sense are inaccurate terms when applied to labor, although they are in common use. All labor should be productive or else abolished. The mere fact that labor may not be directly traceable to a given product does not mean it is nonproductive in the strict sense of the term.

the janitor, may be paid on a group piece-rate basis. In this case the janitor service is directly allocable to the product and therefore is classified as direct labor. Depreciation, interest, rent, taxes, heat, light, power, and similar items are just as much a matter of cost as materials and labor. These cost items are commonly called *overhead expense* or *burden*. *Fixed expenses* are those costs that tend to remain relatively constant regardless of the volume of production, such as the interest on bonds, taxes on land, buildings, and equipment, depreciation arising from the passage of time, and rent. *Variable expenses* are those items that tend to vary directly with the volume of production, such as depreciation arising from use, royalties paid on a volume basis, power, and salaries of minor clerks and some sub-foremen.

Distributing Expense. When the supervisor's department is charged for some minor construction job he becomes keenly aware that costs are not made up solely of materials and labor. Overhead is often greater than the labor costs.

Burden or expense can be allocated according to: (1) *the actual number of direct labor-hours worked* or (2) *the cost of the direct labor-hours worked*. These two methods give the same result when the men are paid at the same rate on a time basis. Such a condition seldom prevails; hence, the two systems are usually different. The distribution of expense on the basis of direct man-hours worked on a given product is predicated on the assumption that these expenses are proportional to the man-hours worked. When the rates paid the workers are relatively the same and the amount and the nature of the work vary only slightly, this system is accurate for most purposes. It has the advantage of emphasizing the time element in the distribution of indirect costs; however, it emphasizes only "worked" time and does not consider "elapsed" time, which is also an important item in costs. This system does not distinguish between the different kinds of equipment that may be used in processing work having different characteristics. It is self-evident that a carpenter working with hand tools is not in fact carrying so much burden as a man working on a large boring mill in the same department. The direct labor-cost basis of distributing expense is predicated on the assumption that burden is proportional to the direct labor cost. This system ignores the effect of elapsed time and does not emphasize the time worked quite so definitely as the direct labor-hour basis. The other advantages and disadvantages of the direct labor-cost basis are essentially the same as those of the direct labor-hour basis, but the direct labor-cost basis has an additional advantage in that the data are accumulated for other purposes and need not be specially segregated in the same sense that labor-hours have to be collected. Where the rates vary materially in the department, the results of the two systems will be different.

The distribution of expense on the basis of direct material is predicated on the theory that indirect costs vary in direct proportion to the direct material used. This system is logical for continuous-process manufacture of a standardized product. If more than one line is turning out products that are materially different or if the same line turns out different products this system tends to be less applicable. It is of doubtful value for burden distribution for an industry producing a variety of products. Burden distribution on the basis of prime costs is in reality a combination of the systems that have been described and possesses both the advantages and the disadvantages of each. The machine-rate basis of expense distribution in its more highly developed form strives to allocate to each machine its true expense when considering all costs, such as original cost of machine and expected life, power consumption, heat, light, floor space occupied, and maintenance. By carefully estimating the expected use of a machine and dividing all costs allocable to this machine for a given period by the total number of expected use-hours, the burden charge per hour can readily be obtained. By keeping a record of the time a machine is used in manufacturing a given product, the burden cost of each machine can be charged to the product. This method involves considerable record keeping, but it is theoretically preferable to many of the other systems.

Depreciation. *Depreciation is defined as the reduction in the value, or the elective economic life, of a product arising from the passage of time, use or abuse, wear and tear, influence of the elements, or the cessation of demand for use.*[2] Depreciation frequently is considered to include obsolescence and inadequacy or supercession. The mere passage of time creates physical decay or decrepitude in such things as buildings, boilers, rubber products, and other productive instruments. Wear and tear take place with use and are relatively proportional to use; however, the time element may influence the rapidity of wear. When a factor in production is being consumed in production, regardless of the cause, the value of that portion of the factor consumed is a cost of production. Fixed assets are constantly being

[2] See L. P. Alford, *Cost and Production Handbook*, Ronald Press Co., New York, 1937, pp. 1215–1221.

converted into expense that must in the long run be recovered in the selling price in order that the buildings and equipment may be repaired during their effective lives and replaced when they are no longer economically usable.[3] The expense arising from the conversion of fixed assets into the product sold may take several forms, such as wear and tear and physical decay resulting from the passage of time, obsolescence, and inadequacy.

Basis of Depreciation. The three common bases of depreciation are: (1) original cost, (2) replacement cost, and (3) present value or appraised cost. Depreciation on the basis of original cost, which includes transportation and installation costs, is simple and easily determined by referring to the equipment ledger. Depreciation on this basis will tend to retain the original investment intact. Some authorities argue that the objective should not be merely to preserve the original investment but to preserve the organization as a going concern, and that this purpose will not be accomplished by merely recovering original costs during a period of rising prices; hence they advocate depreciating the asset on the basis of its replacement cost. There is considerable merit to their argument, but its practical application involves a great deal of accounting and revision of depreciation charges as price levels fluctuate.

The *straight-line* method of depreciation assumes that the depreciation takes place in equal increments throughout the life of the equipment. The life expectancy of the machine is estimated, together with its scrap value. From the cost of the machines is subtracted the scrap value, and the remainder is distributed equally among the estimated years of life of the machine. For instance, a machine costing $2,000 and having an estimated life of 10 years and scrap value at the end of this period of $200 would have an annual depreciation of $180, computed as follows: ($2,000 − $200) ÷ 10 = $180. This method gives a constant depreciation rate for each year which in reality does not conform to actual depreciation, since a machine depreciates more during the first few years of its life than during the last years. Maintenance costs are greater during the later years of the life of a machine, and these, when added to the straight-line depreciation charge, will give an unequal charge against production. If it is desirable to have a relatively constant machine cost chargeable to production, the straight-line method is not satisfactory.

[3] Land is an exception to this statement.

The *sum-of-the-years-digits method* of computing depreciation was legalized by the Revenue Act of 1954. Simply stated, this system uses a declining depreciation cost per year based upon the sum of the number of years' life of the item as the denominator and the given number of years as the numerator. To illustrate, assume the life expectancy of the machine to be 5 years, the sum of the digits 5, 4, 3, 2, 1 = 15, the denominator. The depreciation for the first year would be $5/15$ or 33 and $\frac{1}{3}$ per cent; for the third year it would be $3/15$ or 20 per cent; and for the last or fifth year it would be $1/15$ or 6 and $\frac{2}{3}$ per cent. This system charges a heavy depreciation the first year with a declining cost for the later years when maintenance costs are likely to be higher.

It is frankly admitted that the supervisor will have little occasion to participate in the selecting of the system to be used in computing depreciation. On the other hand, as a key man in the operation of industry he should be informed on the cost aspects of business in addition to being able to get out production in his own department.

24   Maintaining Discipline

The Nature of Discipline. Before discussing the role of the supervisor in discipline it would be well to clarify the meaning of discipline. *Discipline may be thought of as that force which prompts an individual or group to observe rules, regulations, and procedures that are deemed necessary to the attainment of an objective; that force or fear of a force which restrains individuals or groups from doing things that are deemed destructive of group objectives; or the exercise of restraints or enforcement of penalties for the violation of group regulations.* Note that this definition includes three phases: positive discipline, or the force which *prompts* individuals, negative discipline, or the force which *restrains* individuals, and the actual imposing of penalties. Too often discipline is thought of only in terms of restraints and penalties. Effective discipline is educational and not punitive.

Discipline itself is a major factor in achieving smooth operation of the enterprise and the larger the organization the more essential discipline is to maintaining continued and successful operations. Discipline is not static but is always being developed in one form or another. In its highest form it is a process of growth; even in its lowest form, such as restraints and penalties, it must promote growth in broad areas of conformity if it is to be effective. The main objective of discipline is to facilitate coordination, the primary principle in organization, in order that the major objective of the group may be attained. Former President Alexander Ruthven of the University of Michigan has said, quoting Edmund Burke: "Society cannot exist unless a controlling power upon will and appetite be placed somewhere; and the less of it there is within, the more there must be without."

Positive Discipline. Positive discipline is a social force that marshals the collective sentiments of a group in support of the desired actions. Viewed from the standpoint of the individual, positive or constructive discipline proceeds from within and to a large extent is a habitual reaction to established values, customs, traditions, and regulations. Positive discipline does not restrict the individual but enables him to have a greater freedom because he enjoys a greater degree of self-expression in striving to achieve the group objective, which he identifies as his own. Habitual responses that conform to group activities do not enslave but set one free. Positive discipline enables the individual and group to divert destructive instincts into productive channels without a resultant feeling of frustration, and tends to promote emotional satisfactions rather than emotional conflicts. Positive discipline increases the strength of the individual and the group and does not dissipate its energies; it contributes to the community of interests, thus making possible a higher degree of attainment. Positive discipline promotes coordination and effective cooperation with a minimum of formal organization, but it can be achieved only when group objectives and procedures are well known and have become a part of the individual's reaction as the result of the process of indoctrination.

Negative Discipline. Negative discipline is the only phase of discipline that is recognized or understood by large numbers of supervisors and executives. Negative discipline, or discipline involving force or some outward influence in its extreme form, proceeds on the theory that compliance is secured by the use of punishment or by the fear of penalties. Negative discipline uses deterrent forces to secure the desired action. All forms of negative discipline are not extreme. In actual practice, discipline may vary from positive discipline as manifested by a well-trained group that takes great pride in its skill and ability to that of the sulky, rebellious worker who is on the job solely to earn enough to eat and whose *emotional set* is opposed to all authority. These various steps may proceed by imperceptible degrees from the highest to the lowest. Certain disciplinary actions may savor of both positive and negative discipline.

Nature's method of disciplinary action has one message for man, namely, its certainty. A failure to conform with natural laws brings with it deprivation, want, and at times great suffering or even death. The penalty for a failure to conform, or conformity only because of fear of the consequences of nonconformity, is negative discipline.

Conformity through fear of the results of nonconformity is not an extreme form of negative discipline unless the fear complex is a dominating one with the basic desires contrary to the action. To conform with natural laws results in satisfactions and positive rewards. When the individual identifies his own best interest with natural laws and strives to conform, he derives his greatest satisfactions and therefore this may be considered positive discipline. Such a reaction may be known as enlightened self-interest.

One of the basic criticisms leveled at scientific management by practical operating men is: "That is all right in theory but in practice things do not work out that way. Some people just do not respond to honest treatment." This statement contains a lot of truth. Some people for various and sundry reasons do challenge leadership regardless of the methods used. Negative discipline even to the point of discharge may be required at times. Negative discipline is required only when the action of the individual or group is contrary to the established mores, rules, or regulations. It has a place in industry only when the positive incentives or drives go wrong or fail to motivate the individual or the group to the desired action. Negative discipline of the fear type merely secures the minimum performance necessary to avoid the punishment. It usually secures physical compliance but emotional and mental rebellion. The person disciplined is likely to be "on side" physically but against the constituted authorities emotionally. The amount of resistance built up by negative discipline depends largely upon the degree of acceptance of the rule or regulation from which the discipline proceeds. When the rule or regulation, the violation of which requires discipline, is generally accepted by the group and at times by the offending person as reasonable and designed for the greater good, the response to the disciplinary action is usually not violent nor very unfavorable. At times it may even be welcomed and the individual may feel partly reinstated in his own mind when such discipline has been impartially meted out. When a given rule is fraught with great emotional bias and is supported by a slight majority of opinion or even a minority temporarily in control, disciplinary action intensifies resistance, builds up antagonism, and may provoke violence.

The Supervisor Must Lead. Inherent in the responsibility assumed by the supervisor when he accepts the position of leadership in his department is the necessity of making decisions. He is accountable for the use of the authority conferred upon him to enable him to discharge his responsibility. He cannot be accountable if the decisions are made by his subordinates. Naturally, enlightened leadership seeks the advice and counsel of the subordinates and strives to harmonize the wishes of the followers with the necessities of the situation. Nevertheless, the supervisor must assume the responsibility for the action taken to achieve the objective; he must make the decision. Most men have an actual need for positive leadership that is firm yet sympathetic. It provides them a high degree of certainty and the security of knowing what to expect. Dr. Douglas McGregor, President of Antioch College, in his farewell message to the alumni and friends of Antioch, summed up the responsibilities of the leader as follows:

It will require time to think back over the many events that have been crowded into these few years and to draw a proper meaning from them. However, two related convictions have developed slowly but steadily out of this experience.

The first is a conviction which has been derived from my personal struggle with the role of college president. Before coming to Antioch I had observed and worked with top executives as an adviser in a number of organizations. I thought I knew how they felt about their responsibilities and what led them to behave as they did. I even thought that I could create a role for myself which would enable me to avoid some of the difficulties they encountered.

I was wrong! It took the direct experience of becoming a line executive and meeting personally the problems involved to teach me what no amount of observation of other people could have taught.

I believed, for example, that a leader could operate successfully as a kind of adviser to his organization. I thought I could avoid being a "boss." Unconsciously, I suspect, I hoped to duck the unpleasant necessity of making difficult decisions, of taking the responsibility for one course of action among many uncertain alternatives, of making mistakes and taking the consequences. I thought that maybe I could operate so that everyone would like me—that "good human relations" would eliminate all discord and disagreement.

I couldn't have been more wrong. It took a couple of years, but I finally began to realize that a leader cannot avoid the exercise of authority any more than he can avoid responsibility for what happens to his organization. In fact, it is a major function of the top executive to take on his own shoulders the responsibility for resolving the uncertainties that are always involved in important decisions. Moreover, since no important decision ever pleases everyone in the organization, he must also absorb the displeasure, and sometimes severe hostility, of those who would have taken a different course.

A colleague recently summed up what my experience has taught me in these words: "A good leader must be tough enough to win a fight, but not tough enough to kick a man when he is down." This notion is not in the least inconsistent with humane, democratic leadership. Good human relations develop out of strength, not of weakness.

I'm still trying to understand and practice what is implied in my colleague's statement.

Discipline as a Tool of Supervision. Positive discipline is a standard in itself and thus acts in a reciprocal relationship to the work of employees who have been subjected to its influence. Positive discipline minimizes the amount of personal supervision required and aids in the maintenance of standards. The supervisor does not need to stand over an employee to see that he does his work properly. When a new employee has been properly introduced and carefully instructed, when he has come to know the supervisor and has confidence in that supervisor's ability to take care of him, when he willingly cooperates with the supervisor, that employee has been under positive discipline and can be put on his own to produce the quantity and quality desired. Negative discipline, the fear of dismissal, for example, to a limited extent may restrain certain individuals from an overt act or violation. It may serve to prevent the repetition of an act for which a specific penalty has been levied. Although this results in negative disciplinary action toward the offender and others, in mild cases it may be neutral or even instructional. Negative discipline may prompt individuals to perform according to the standard to avoid the penalty as, for example, docking for tardiness, time off for carelessly broken tools, lowered rating in companies where merit rating is used.

Causes of Disciplinary Problems. Surveys have shown that personality traits are primarily responsible for employee violations of established regulations.[1] Dr. John M. Brewer of Harvard University in studying 4,174 cases of discharge found that 62.4 per cent involved personal characteristics.[2] Mr. William C. Ackerey, Secretary of the New York Employment Managers Association, found the following causes for discharge.[3]

Carelessness	14%	Lateness	7%
Noncooperation	10%	Lack of effort	7%
Laziness	10%	Disloyalty	3%
Dishonesty	8%	Discourtesy	2%
Attention to outside interests	8%	Miscellaneous	24%
Lack of initiative	7%		

[1] See American Management Association, *Constructive Discipline in Industry,* Special Research Report No. 3, New York, 1943, p. 18.
[2] See American Management Association, *Personnel,* May 1940, p. 199.
[3] *Ibid.*

If the supervisor is to handle disciplinary problems intelligently he needs to get the facts in the given situation and strive to interpret these facts in terms of their basic causes. It is often easier to get the facts of the violation than to go behind these facts to the *real cause*. The basis for detection of violations is adequate records that fix responsibility. The supervisor should be certain that his inspection reports show the machine and the man responsible for the work. The job tickets must always indicate the man or men who worked on the job and the operations each performed. Detecting causes that demand negative discipline requires the supervisor to follow up to see that adequate instruction is given and that his instructions are being followed in the manner he prescribed. The supervisor's follow-up, however, is dependent on management's providing a sufficient number of supervisors so that each is not overloaded with work to the point where he does not have time to follow up his men. The supervisor, as an inspector, is neither a talebearer nor a spy. Inspection of the work of the men in his department is one of his routine duties and he should see to it that his men recognize it as such. Inspection is to be preferred to secret methods of securing information.

Every action of an employee in his work situation tends to be a reaction to previous experiences or a result of his inner adjustment to the many forces in life. These may include:

1. Frustrations arising from difficult personal problems which force themselves into the worker's reactions on the job. (It must ever be remembered that problem employees are not confined to the lowest level of work. They are found at every level of the executive hierarchy.) Family, social, financial, and even union pressures may provoke in a work situation an explosion that seemingly has no apparent cause.

2. Physical defects that were not present or not detected at the time of hiring. Vision may become impaired to the extent that excess spoilage or even breakage of equipment results. A negative thyroid may cause such a change in the reaction of the worker that he has excessive absences or tardiness or engages in daydreaming with the resultant work spoilage or accidents. The employee himself may not be aware of his defects but merely feel that things are "upside down."

3. Lack of training or inability to perform the job up to the required standards may be the cause of excess spoilage or other violations. If training is all that is needed the cause may readily be removed. On the other hand, if the worker is fundamentally short in native ability or capacity to meet the job requirements, this should be discovered and a transfer effected. This lack of ability may manifest itself not only in a failure to meet requirements but also in irritations and complaints at the work situation.

4. Emotional unbalance may make it impossible for the worker to conform to the requirements of the cooperative work situation. This

type of reaction may manifest itself in almost any form. The worker may have superior skill and productive capacity but be a constant griper and troublemaker. Obsessive thinking may cause substandard production in both quality and quantity. Excessive drinking may cause absences or tardiness. Alcoholism is often a manifestation of another cause and not the cause itself.

5. Insecurity may create an abnormal desire to please, at times leading to accidents or scrap merely because the worker followed instructions that were wrong. Of course, the person providing the instructions is primarily responsible in such cases, but the experienced worker who follows such instructions blindly is a potential menace to his associates and himself.[4]

Symptoms are tremendously important in detecting acts contrary to the desired standards. Any change in attitude is usually accompanied by a reaction similar to the attitude. Among the causes of offenses commonly listed are: ignorance, accident, failure to try hard enough, incapacity, challenge to existing authority, conflicts of duty and desire, jealousy, discontent, men not kept busy, fear of rate cut, dishonesty, carelessness, desire for money and managerial incompetence.[5] The causes of offenses requiring negative discipline, if permitted to continue, very often develop into acts that lead to a discharge. Negative discipline alone cannot cure these causes; positive discipline in one form or another must be used. Instruction is sometimes necessary, and explanations of policies or of the importance of the employee's work may be used. Incentives should be developed as needed to stimulate employees' interests. Positive and negative discipline supplement each other; neither stands alone but each must be used as the situation and the individual require.

Company Policies on Discipline. Company policies in relation to the foreman's role in discipline vary all the way from giving him practically full responsibility for all action within his department to the other extreme where he can only reprimand and recommend.[6] One company's policy in relation to discharge reads: "No dismissal of any employee of more than one year's service (except for reduction in force, dishonesty, or pronounced disloyalty or insubordination, or in cases where the employee's conduct is detrimental to the company's business) is to be made unless the employee has been previously

[4] See F. C. Smith, "Effective Use of Discipline," *Personnel Journal,* Vol. 27, No. 7, Dec. 1948, p. 259.

[5] For a fuller discussion of this point see Henry P. Dutton, *Principles of Organization,* McGraw-Hill Book Co., New York, 1931, pp. 273–290.

[6] See American Management Association, *Constructive Discipline in Industry,* p. 14.

informed in what respect his services were unsatisfactory and unless
he has been given reasonable opportunity to improve or to correct
objectionable traits. A dated record of such handling and warnings
given to the employee shall be kept in order that the facts on which
the decision to dismiss is based will be available as historical data."

Some companies spell out in minute detail the acts that call for
disciplinary action and the penalties for each on the first, second, and
third offenses. An illustration of this type of policy is as follows:

Offense	First	Second	Third
Drinking alcoholic beverages on the job or appearing on the job under the influence of intoxicating liquors	Warning notice, and suspension (2–8 days)	Warning notice, and suspension (7–12 days)	Dismissal
Smoking in prohibited area, marked "Explosive"	Dismissal		
Smoking in prohibited area—general	Warning notice	Warning notice, and suspension (1–3 days)	Dismissal
Violation of recognized safety rule	Warning notice	Warning notice, and suspension (1–4 days)	Dismissal
Fighting on premises	Warning notice to dismissal—depending on all the facts	Dismissal	
Stealing from fellow workers	Warning notice, suspension to dismissal	Dismissal	
Stealing from company	Warning notice, suspension to dismissal	Dismissal	

Companies using uniform penalties for disciplinary cases claim the
following advantages:

1. Subjective differences in handling similar offenses in the various departments of the same company are eliminated, in so far as possible.
(This is held to be especially significant where many new supervisors are
being appointed.)

2. Tendencies to extremes of harshness or leniency are overcome, since
the penalties are established in conference and represent the average of
the collective judgment with respect to particular violations.

3. The penalties are usually approved in advance by representatives of management, supervision, and the unions, thus minimizing the chances that discipline cases will reappear as grievances.

4. Penalties are graduated in proportion to the number of previous infractions, taking into account, of course, the length of the period over which the offenses are spread.

5. There is sufficient range allowed on each penalty for a given offense to permit ample consideration of qualifying factors.

6. The system is dependent on careful record-keeping and thus discourages the guesswork that is too often associated with matters of discipline.

7. The system is flexible in character, allowing for change in penalties when circumstances warrant such action.

Other companies state their company policies in very broad terms and make no attempt to spell out in any detail uniform penalties. These companies seem to be thoroughly satisfied with their practices. They strive to fit the punishment in each case to the gravity of the situation and the needs of the individual. A belligerent union may lead a liberal management to published statements of penalties for specific offenses. On the other hand, a legalistic management may insist on spelling out the details regardless of the union attitude. In all probability it is more important to have the representatives of management in substantial agreement with general penalties to be assessed and the procedures to be followed than to reduce them to writing. Discipline is a valuable subject for supervisory conferences. The use of actual cases in these conferences tends to build up a body of generally accepted practice in handling cases of discipline.

Union Participation in Disciplinary Action. Some unions participate in disciplinary matters only through the grievance procedure. Other unions have succeeded in working out agreements covering many aspects of the disciplinary process. For instance, where written reprimands are standard practice, a written reprimand becomes inactive after twelve months and cannot be presented in evidence against an employee who has a clean record for that long. On the other hand, if he has another reprimand during the twelve-month period the first reprimand may be used as supporting evidence of the unsatisfactory work of the employee. In some union contracts penalties for certain offenses are spelled out. In practically any union relationship a disciplinary action may be the subject of a grievance.

Promoting and Maintaining Discipline. Since most disciplinary situations arise in work situations it is the supervisor's responsibility to create a work atmosphere that promotes positive discipline. He can do this in practically all cases other than the ones involving the emotionally immature or the emotionally unstable person. High group morale and positive discipline go hand in hand. The conditions which will promote positive discipline have been discussed under group attitudes and group morale.[7] The factors which develop high group morale and also positive discipline in the group include: (1) good health, both physical and mental, (2) explicit purposes or objectives known to the group, (3) knowing the employees individually and collectively, (4) fair treatment of the individual in relation to the group, (5) a reasonable sense of security among the group, (6) a sense of "belonging" among the group, (7) a technically trained group, (8) recognition where recognition is due, (9) confidence by the supervisor in the ability of the group and the organization to meet all requirements, (10) prompt elimination of rumors, (11) issuance through proper channels of all information that is available, (12) strong effective leadership, (13) avoidance of errors, but willingness on the part of the supervisor to admit an error if it be made, (14) never making issues out of minor infractions, (15) never making personal issues out of matters that should be handled on an impersonal basis, (16) delegation of authority commensurate with responsibility, (17) use of authority sparingly and always without displaying it, (18) decisions made as far down in an organization as responsibility and competence exist, (19) knowledge that discipline cannot be completely routinized since individual differences control, (20) willingness of the men to come to their supervisor with their problems, and (21) supervisors who understand company policies and standards, who interpret them clearly, impartially, and understandingly, and who observe all regulations personally.

The Armstrong Cork Company, along with its many other modern personnel practices, has devised the following check list as an aid to handling disciplinary situations:

1. Have I secured the necessary facts?
   A. Did the employee have an opportunity to fully tell his side of the story?
   B. Did I investigate all other sources of information?
   C. Did I hold my interviews privately so as to avoid embarrassing the interested employee or employees?
   D. Did I exert every possible effort to verify the facts in the case?
   E. Did I check the employee's personnel folder to look at his past record?

[7] See Chapter 9

2. Have I considered all the facts in deciding upon the disciplinary measure?
    A. Have I found out what has been done in similar cases in my department?
    B. Have I found out what has been done in similar cases in other departments?
    C. Have I shown any discrimination toward an individual or group?
    D. Have I let personalities affect my decision?
    E. Does the measure fit the violation?
    F. Will the measure prevent a recurrence?
    G. Will the measure maintain morale?
    H. Will the measure encourage the employee's initiative?
    I. Will the measure create a desire on the part of the employee to do what is right?
    J. Have I checked this decision with my immediate supervisor?
3. Have I administered the corrective measure in the proper manner?
    A. Did I consider whether it should be done individually or collectively?
    B. Am I prepared to explain to the employee, or employees concerned, why the action is necessary?
        1. The effect of the violation on the Company, fellow-employees, and himself.
        2. To help him improve his efficiency and also that of the department.
    C. Am I prepared to discourage, effectively, a similar offense in the future?
    D. Am I prepared to deal with any resentment shown?
    E. Have I filled out a Personnel Folder Memo sufficiently covering the occurrence?
4. Have I made the necessary follow-up?
    A. Has the measure had the desired effect on the employee?
    B. Have I done everything possible to overcome any resentment?
    C. Is the employee convinced that the action was for his best interest?
    D. Have I endeavored to compliment him on his good work?
    E. Has the disciplinary action had the desired results on other employees in the department? [8]

W. S. Ferguson, writing in *Factory Management and Maintenance,* expressed in a very pertinent manner a check list to be kept in mind while handling personnel problems as follows:

Before Talking with the Employee
1. Get all of the background possible. Study this from the worker's viewpoint, putting yourself in his place.
2. Postpone talk until sure that you are in correct frame of mind. Talk privately. Allow sufficient time.
3. Review human characteristics below (to appeal to, or to guard against):

[8] Adapted from American Management Association, *Constructive Discipline in Industry,* 1943, p. 34.

a. We like to feel we're important.
b. We want recognition, credit, attention.
c. We have our own self-interest at heart.
d. We want to be better off tomorrow than today.
e. We want prompt action on our question.
f. We would rather talk than listen.
g. We would rather give advice than listen to it.
h. We generally resent too close supervision.
i. We resent change, generally.
j. We're all prone to be curious.

While Talking with the Employee

1. Know his name in advance; don't forget to use it.
2. Be friendly. Watch your tone of voice particularly. It may help to begin by discussing something else.
3. Find something about him to praise sincerely early in the talk.
4. Encourage him to talk; listen with sincere interest and respect.
5. Ask questions instead of giving orders.
6. Talk in terms of his interests; show sympathy with his desires.
7. Let him know that he fills a position of some importance, and that you value his services.
8. Try to call attention to mistakes and bad attitudes indirectly.
9. If necessary, state in a friendly manner management's side of the question, explaining to the employee in detail what bad effects are resulting from the situation that you are trying to correct.
10. Avoid arguing over points not absolutely vital. Do not challenge statements directly, but build up proof so he will see his own mistakes.
11. It sometimes helps to mention similar mistakes you yourself have made.
12. If you are wrong, admit it quickly.
13. Let him feel that the ideas are his.
14. Throw down a challenge.
15. Make the fault seem easy to correct, and try to make him feel happy about carrying out your suggestion.
16. If an ultimatum must be delivered, do it in a friendly way—but with firmness and without apology.
17. Try to leave the employee an "out" by which to save face.

After Talking with the Employee

1. Check for results.
2. Be sure to notice and praise each improvement as it appears.
3. If an ultimatum was delivered, follow it up, make it stick.
4. In later talks, repeat the above procedure.
5. If you finally have to discharge a man, don't rub it in. Don't forget: In such a case, *you* have failed too.[9]

Principles to Be Kept in Mind in the Use of Negative Discipline.
While the necessity for the use of negative discipline is to be deplored,

[9] This article by W. S. Ferguson appeared in *Factory Management and Maintenance,* Vol. 109, No. 6, June 1951, p. 109.

the cold facts of life reveal that it may have to be used at times. In the use of negative discipline it is the certainty of the punishment and not the severity that is the important factor. The punishment must never do violence to the group's sense of fair play and the supervisor must recognize the importance of the group's being in accord with the severity of the punishment he inflicts. Fines cannot be in proportion to the damage done to expensive equipment. Fines are usually of questionable merit unless they consist largely in withholding premiums or bonuses that would otherwise have been earned. Fines must be carefully handled or they will increase the breach between the men and the supervisor. Negative discipline has only a limited use so far as compliance is concerned. A parallel can be drawn between the supervisor's driving and leading his men, and his use of negative discipline will work just so long; then the effects are negligible so far as the desired results are concerned.

Negative discipline having been once administered should be forgotten, on the theory that the price has been paid. It should be made a matter of record, not to be mentioned again unless the same offense or other ones are repeated. However, careful records on the employee's qualification card should be kept for future guidance. Negative discipline should be kept on an impersonal basis and whenever possible should be meted out in private. In a mild form negative discipline may be helpful in attaining positive discipline from persons of average or less intelligence. The penalties inflicted as a part of this form of discipline should be relatively automatic, certain, and, in general, related to the offense. Anger should never enter into administering discipline. The disciplinary action should never destroy the individual's self-confidence but rather encourage him to build his confidence anew after the price has been paid. The penalty should not take away the incentive to remedy the error. On the other hand, special privileges should not be given to offenders over and above the conscientious employee who does his work.

In the event of discharge, causes should be carefully determined and recorded. The employee should be informed as to the reasons and the fact that the discharge is to be a matter of record. Along with the discharge record should go a statement as to whether or not the employee may be reemployed. Since a discharge almost invariably carries with it a loss of seniority the discharge is a more serious penalty than a suspension even though the elapsed time may be the same in case of rehiring. Cases where a rehiring may be indicated are illustrated by fighting. A supervisor's sentiments may be with an individual in certain situations but in his company fighting on the job may be one of the items calling for dismissal.   The penalty is assessed in this instance, but the employee may not be eliminated permanently.

An Analysis of Disciplinary Problems by a Group of Supervisors. In the author's experience in supervisory training, discipline has always been a live topic with foremen.   One group produced the following tabulation:

Violations	Causes	Cures
1. Criticism of working conditions	Jealousy, mismanagement, favors	Instructions, good example, if possible remove cause
2. Tardiness and absenteeism	See Chapter 19	
3. Dissatisfaction and spreading unrest	Work conditions, wages, equipment, leadership	Work conditions, transfer, square deal
4. Spread disloyalty to company	Discontent	Investigate, square deal, penalty
5. Willful disobedience	Lack of interest, spite, jealousy	Investigate, square deal, penalty
6. Fooling	Not enough work, clownishness	Keep busy, personal talk, morale of department
7. Misrepresenting management	Dissatisfaction, ignorance	Working conditions, square deal, transfer or discharge
8. Poor housekeeping	Carelessness, lack of interest	Personal talk, example, competition
9. Lack of appreciation and discontent	Lack of knowledge or interest	Create interest and instruction
10. Visiting	Not kept busy	Personal talk, square deal, firmness
11. Withholding efficiency	Fear of rate cut, short time	Honesty, square deal, personal talk
12. Washing up ahead of time	Rate too high, habit, washroom facilities, desire to get out	Correct rate, insist on quality of work, firmness
13. Reading	Break down, desire for news, out of material	Keep busy, insist on quality of work, permit reading in case of breakdown
14. Gossip	Jealousy, curiosity for news	Investigate, personal talk, square deal, remove cause, penalty
15. Slighting work	Desire for money, lack of knowledge, laziness	Personal talk, square deal, pride, close inspection, penalty
16. Dishonesty	Low wage, severity of discipline, natural crookedness	Investigation, pride, square deal, possible discharge
17. Removing safety devices	Greed, selfishness, indifference	Personal talk, square deal, danger to self, penalty
18. Minor waste	Lack of knowledge, desire for money, laziness	Personal talk, instruction, firmness, penalty

The Clinical Approach to Discipline. Throughout this chapter the clinical or analytical approach to discipline has been stressed. The emphasis is placed not on the violation but on the causes of the violation and the attitude of the person involved. Disciplinary actions are adjusted to suit the needs of each situation as determined by the causal relationships. This attitude toward discipline seeks to bring about a behavior change and is little concerned with the punishment aspect. Disciplinary action based on this approach presupposes an understanding of human nature. Too often the supervisor lacks this understanding and his handling of disciplinary cases reacts unfavorably both on the individual involved and on the supervisor.

Glen U. Cleeton developed the clinical approach in a challenging article in *Personnel*. The following tabulation itemizes the points at which he finds this understanding lacking and suggests methods of correction to be used.[10]

Points Often Overlooked	Methods of Correcting
1. The employee's "reasoning" is biased by feelings and emotions; hence, things that seem logical to management may not appear so to the employee.	1. Since reasoning is biased, repeated appeals to logic must be made. A lesson in the effect of repetition and dramatic presentations might be learned from advertisers.
2. Their daily experiences cultivate greater loyalty to their fellow workers than to the company.	2. Inter-employee loyalties are not in themselves destructive. Where antagonism to company policies has been reduced to a minimum, this sense of group loyalty may be an asset.
3. There is often a feeling of insecurity based on false beliefs concerning the attitude of foremen and supervisors.	3. The feeling of insecurity prevalent among many workers can be reduced by using discharge as a means of clearing out undesirables and incompetents rather than as a threat to secure compliance with regulations. It is no longer considered good personnel practice to permit foremen and supervisors to discharge workers on their own authority. This power should be centered in a higher official.

[10] Adapted from Glen U. Cleeton, "The New Approach to Employee Discipline," *Personnel*, May 1940, pp. 201–202.

4. Workers often feel that they deserve a better job than the one they now hold.

4. Pride in one's job can be encouraged. Some firms play up the importance of jobs in carefully written leaflets, house-organ stories, and special awards for competent performance.

5. Workers are subjected quite frequently (almost continuously of late years) to propaganda unfavorable to their employers.

5. Propaganda of an unfavorable character can be met better by counter-propaganda than by criticism and cursing the source of the unfavorable propaganda.

6. The immediate supervisor is the company to many workers (and he may be failing to carry out the policy of the company with respect to employee relations).

6. Since the immediate supervisor represents the company to the employees, the selection and training of foremen and supervisors is extremely important. Lack of skill and judgment on the part of a foreman often creates disciplinary problems. A foreman who knows human nature and likes men can secure employee cooperation and thereby reduce the necessity of having cases brought to the attention of higher-ranking officials.

7. Every worker wants individual recognition—to be known, praised, and given evidence of confidence in his work.

7. Foremen should know their men by name, show an interest in some of the personal elements in the lives of individual workers, and be ready to praise where credit is due.

8. The worker must have explicit and detailed instructions. *Human capacity for misunderstanding is almost limitless.*

8. Instructions should be patiently and clearly stated. Some instructions should be given both verbally and in written form. Repetition is often necessary. Every supervisor should be a good teacher.

9. He likes to express opinions and make suggestions, and if given an opportunity to do so is more likely to strive to do his job in the manner expected of him.

9. Encourage employees to offer suggestions. Give credit for good ones.

Summary. The problem of discipline is as old as leadership. The supervisor can never fully solve it. A wise leader enables his followers to widen their opportunities for self-realization and self-expression. Sound discipline is largely a teaching function with a minimum of deterrents. Constructive discipline tends to follow when a group is kept busy doing productive things, especially when the members of the group know *why*. A well-trained, efficient group is usually a well-disciplined group since the two relationships are reciprocal. Negative discipline is now supplemented largely by constructive discipline, but when negative discipline is used it should always be impersonal. Women tend to make a personal issue of most matters of discipline, thus raising complex problems in negative discipline. The leader who leads as a matter of right inherent in his ability, foresight, and temperament, and not in mere position, seldom encounters the need for negative discipline.

Discipline is that force which prompts an individual or group to observe rules, regulations, and procedures that are deemed necessary to the attainment of the objectives; that force or fear of a force which restrains individuals or groups from doing things that are deemed destructive of group objectives; or the exercise of restraints or enforcement of penalties for the violation of group regulations. The two types of discipline include negative discipline, which emphasizes the fear element or punishment factor, and positive discipline, which emphasizes the motivating factor or incentive. Positive discipline identifies the individual's and the group's objectives with those of the institution and is to be preferred to negative discipline. Almost the only phase of negative discipline that is permanently effective is certainty.

25 The Supervisor's Use of Records and Reports

Types of Reports. In general there are three main classifications of reports, namely, (1) the standardized periodic report, (2) the intermittent standardized report, and (3) special reports. The standardized periodic report is illustrated by such reports as those on daily or hourly production, inspection, spoilage, attendance, and absenteeism. The intermittent standardized reports include those on accidents, labor turnover, tool breakage, budget performance, and the like. Special reports may cover almost any subject at any time they are needed. They include such topics as a change in process, a change in personnel as from men to women, costs on manufacture of a new product, and a survey to decrease indirect costs such as waste or turnover. The supervisor may present to his superior special reports not required of him on facts he has observed, difficulties he has solved, or suggestions he may want to make.

Every report in part discharges the responsibility of a supervisor to his superior. Just as an order should communicate all information essential to appraisal of performance, every report should contain all the necessary facts to arrive at a sound decision. Too often reports will omit vital facts without which a decision is not possible or which may lead to decisions that will prove unsound.

Intermittent standardized reports are rendered when something unusual arises for which a report is required. A report of a specific accident is an example of the intermittent report. Such reports may be prepared by someone else in the department but must be reviewed carefully and usually investigated personally by the supervisor. Frequently these reports may indirectly form the basis of a criticism of the supervisor and his department and therefore he must be familiar with all the facts and must be prepared to defend or accept the responsibility for the act which gave rise to the report.

Special reports are required of the supervisor by his superior and by other departments, together with such reports as he may develop on his own initiative dealing with problems which he feels should be brought to the attention of others. There is a continuing demand for men with shop background who have the ability to analyze difficult situations and make recommendations for eliminating the difficulties. Management frequently has its attention called to a progressive supervisor by the clarity of his reports. This is especially true in the case of special reports. The ability to write a report is one of the most common specifications listed by management when seeking a person to bring along in the organization.

One type of special report met by many supervisors is the preliminary budget estimate wherein the supervisor must forecast his operations for the next period, which may be a month, three months, or even a year. This forecast together with those of other departments may properly form the basis for the company's budget, an estimate of all expenditures for the period. The right way for the supervisor to approach any special report is to put himself in the other fellow's position; in the case of the budget the other fellow is management. Management must know in advance the needs of the various departments, their requirements in terms of manpower, machines, materials, and all the other factors that go into the operation of the department. This is information even the supervisor should have if he is to assist management in controlling the operation of the enterprise as a whole and his department as a part of it. He will analyze the past experience in his department, consulting the records which are available to him. He will analyze the current conditions in his department, the condition of his equipment, the turnover of his personnel. In the course of such an analysis he will uncover facts that should enable him to operate his department more efficiently in the future than in the past.

The Need for Reports. The application of mass-production techniques to manufacturing makes controls a necessity. If the company is to produce its products in the quantity required, at the time specified for delivery, and at the estimated cost, each operation on the product must be performed at the specified time, in the required amount, and at or near the estimated cost. This is facilitated only through controls derived from reports and records. The supervisor needs to become control-minded also. He must learn to operate his department in the same way management plans the operation of the entire enterprise, and to base his decisions and actions on the reports he receives from his men, the reports he prepares for his supervisors, and the records that are available to him or that he develops for his own use.

Reports and records are the lifeblood of the business. They give the facts concerning the operation of the enterprise and point out the progress of the work and its cost. Their preparation and use make possible the elimination of guesswork by management. Only through records can the supervisor keep informed about his men and their work, the materials he uses, his equipment, and the inspection of the work produced by his department. Most important among records are cost records, because every business financed by private funds must control its costs or fail to survive. Yet it is only through the reports made by the supervisor and his men that management can compile the records that will give them control over operations and keep them informed of current progress and that will bring to light the trouble spots.

A report is a statement of facts concerning a particular situation and may be either verbal or written. Written reports become the basis for records which tabulate and summarize reports. In the final analysis both reports and records are only a substitute for memory. In the early days of industrial history when the owner-manager had his own shop and did all his own work, records were comparatively unnecessary to him. When the individual enterpriser's shop grew and he hired a helper, reports and records became a necessity for continued growth and expansion.

Reports are essential to the successful operation of any enterprise. They are the basis for decisions and serve to check the judgment in past decisions. A report of today's operations is a check on yesterday's judgment. The steps in formulating sound judgment include securing all the facts and analyzing those facts. The average person must record facts as he collects them in order to have them available for analysis. Careful analysis of facts requires that they be arranged and then rearranged in written form for study if sound judgment is to be exercised and well-considered decisions reached. The larger the enterprise the greater the need for reports and records since many decisions must be made far removed from the place of operations and can be based only on reports and records. The more departmentalized the organization is, the more highly it is functionalized, the greater the need of each department for reports from those other departments with which its work must be coordinated. Every enterprise depends on coordination for successful operation, but coordination is impossible unless facts are available and facts are only available in a large enterprise in written form as reports. Mass production is based on standardization of parts and standardization of manufacturing procedure. Standardization can be made effective only when reports are available to determine deviations from standards.

The supervisor must keep the other departments with which he must coordinate his operations informed of the operations in his department, and he likewise requires reports of the conditions in the other departments in order to cooperate with them. He requires reports from his own department since he should not depend on verbal opinions from his own men who rely on their memories for the facts he needs. Reports and records replace "hunches" and are the facts the supervisor must have today if he is to operate his department successfully.

Balance in the Use of Records and Reports Is Needed. A perfectly good management procedure may do more harm than good when used excessively or in a manner to be out of balance with other activities. Aside from their historical value, records and reports have no value other than their use for purposes of pricing, planning, and control. Too many reports are costly to prepare and file. Too few reports may even be more costly than too many, when action is taken that should be based on facts and the facts are not available. Although system is essential to a successful organization and is largely dependent on reports and records, if carried too far it can defeat its own purpose. Whenever the cost of reporting and records is greater than the savings they account for, such reports and records should immediately be discarded. Ideally, the right number and kind of reports and records compiled from them tell the management the exact status of the business as a whole and in detail. The supervisor may often need certain records and reports for his own use that are not required by management. He must also be careful not to require too many or too few records of his own men. He must be certain that the reports he receives give him the information he needs to be well informed, and at the same time that they do not include unnecessary data. The test of any good report is whether or not it provides the information needed at the time and on the subject under consideration. The supervisor should strive to make the reports and records in his department meet the ideal of providing an accurate picture of his department as a whole and at the same time show the details necessary for efficient operation.

Another aspect of records and reports that should be mentioned is the filing of them in such a manner as to be able to find them when needed. The supervisor seldom has enough clerical help to justify an elaborate cross-indexed filing system. Most supervisors and clerical employees would not know how to set up an elaborate filing system if they had the time. The important reports that the foreman receives from his superiors should be kept in separate folders or on separate clip boards. These folders should be marked with the main topic. It is better to have an extra folder than to have to leaf through an entire file to locate something that is needed. In case certain basic material is kept up to date by the central office, such as standing orders or specifications, it is frequently advisable to preserve it in a three-ring loose-leaf binder. In this event the old page should be removed as soon as a new one is received. A little care in initial filing saves an enormous amount of time when it is necessary to locate the record.

The Supervisor's Responsibility for Reports. It will be recalled that the four operating fundamentals are closely related to records and reports. These fundamentals stated briefly are: (1) the development of adequate system, (2) the establishment of adequate records, (3) the laying down of proper operating rules and regulations, and (4) the exercise of effective leadership. System is predicated on adequate records. Operating rules require proper reports and records. The exercise of effective leadership also requires supporting information that can only be provided by proper records. Adequate records can be maintained only if the necessary reports are available, even in a simple form, from which to compile the records. Reports range all the way from the inspector's report to the comprehensive survey.

Frequently supervisors complain about the excess clerical detail for which they are responsible. They often give their clerical work as an excuse for not being out on the floor actually directing the operation of their department. Some supervisors have insisted that they were responsible only for production, not for record keeping and reports, and that the accounting, statistical, and production control departments which required reports of them were nonproductive departments. These complaints from supervisors usually are not factual. It may take longer for some men to keep adequate records than it should, merely because they are not systematic in this work and do it very inefficiently. If, in fact, it does require too much of a foreman's time to keep the needed records he should be provided with clerical assistance. Even when the foreman has clerical help to do the actual clerical work, he needs to spend some time to make certain that the proper records are being kept. He also needs to use these records for his own guidance. There are some records that only the supervisor should initiate. These items pertain largely to positive or negative aspects of merit rating. The clerk may enter the foreman's notation on the employee's record but the supervisor alone should determine what is to be entered. Management today, however, is placing increased emphasis on reports, and the success of mass-production methods, the split-second timing of assembly lines, are in a large measure made possible by reports and records. Each supervisor must assume the responsibility for reports and the successful supervisor recognizes *the place and the importance of reports in the effective operation of the enterprise, his responsibility for reporting, the need for records in his own department, and the ways in which he may use them to operate his department more efficiently.*

The supervisor who has become record-conscious and handles reports and records effectively has a promotional asset, for management today is on the lookout for such men. A department and its supervisor stand out when the reports of that department come in on time, clearly written, and the operation of that department indicates that the supervisor is basing his actions and decisions on the analysis of the facts contained in these reports. Every supervisor in his contacts with his superior must constantly answer questions concerning his department, its production, down time of the machines, costs, and waste. He cannot have the facts available to answer such questions unless they are assembled in advance and are available in the form of reports and records.

The supervisor should accustom himself to making good written reports because it is one of the ways by which he is judged. Initiative, knowledge of his job, ability to handle men and get out production are qualities which are always sought in a supervisor, but these may not be sufficient when he is being considered for promotion. If in addition he can make a clear concise report which deals directly with the subject at hand and contains all the essential facts without unnecessary detail, he proves to management that he is the master of his job. Such a report indicates a clear understanding of the work of his department and gives evidence of his ability to confront a situation, analyze its elements, and solve it intelligently.

Compiling Records and Reports. As a general operating procedure the supervisor should review every periodic and intermittent standardized report that goes out of his department. *He should see that it is properly made out, that all the items are accounted for, and that it is neat, legible, and accurately compiled.* Occasionally a supervisor, when some difficulty arises, has had his superior check back to the original report that gave the facts and has been ashamed of the appearance, inaccuracy, and inadequacy of the report when they looked it over together. Frequently the supervisor is not able to see all the reports that leave his department, but he should delegate the responsibility for those reports to someone whom he has carefully instructed and indoctrinated with the need for neat, legible, and accurate reports.

Reports that are late are often compiled in a hurry and are likely not only to be inaccurate but also to delay the making of decisions. One late minor report from one supervisor may delay the preparation of an entire major report for management, perhaps resulting in a faulty decision. The supervisor whose reports are always on time, legible, and accurate is meeting one of the major responsibilities of his position.

Planning the Approach. Facts that can be treated statistically should be reduced to this basis, for figures will illustrate the comparative situation far better than page after page of written material. Wherever possible graphs and charts should be used to visualize facts. Management will grasp facts more readily if they are presented simply and clearly through the use of tables of figures and charts. The report should also state the method used to arrive at the conclusions. The supervisor may test his report by examining it to see if it gives the facts in such a form that a busy executive can grasp the objective, method, and conclusions immediately and then, if he desires, find clearly stated within the report the answers to any questions he may have about the conclusions or methods used. In preparing his report the supervisor will find that planning is essential. He should prepare an outline in advance and develop his report from this outline, revising his writing until it says simply and clearly what he wants to say.

The little "black book" that some foremen carry in their pockets provides the source of much of the information that goes into the supervisor's reports, particularly about his men. His memory, unless it is unusual, will never hold all this information. A notebook with a page devoted to each man and recording each unusual contact will enable the supervisor to have a complete record of his men should it be required. Such a notebook can also be used to record facts about problems in his department concerning material, inspection, storage, waste, and other items as they arise. This notebook can provide material for a report by the supervisor on his men and his department whenever required. The time required to maintain this record is relatively slight compared to its value in making decisions. The supervisor who has learned the lesson of "putting it down" instead of depending on his memory has laid the foundation for meeting his responsibility for reports. Reports are no problem to the man who has the facts readily available.

Using Records and Reports. The material in the supervisor's notebook should form the basis of merit rating, especially on those factors pertaining to cooperation and the other intangible items. In merit rating on productivity, the employee's actual production record should be consulted. He must have reports from his subordinates and records of his own to substantiate discharges when they are necessary. Promotions and transfers should be based on records so that the supervisor can defend and justify his action should it be questioned by his men or superiors. No supervisor ought to depend solely on his memory for important data.

Reports and records are his way of eliminating the need for remembering a mass of facts, whether they are about his men, the production of his department, or other pertinent items. The supervisor will find reports and records invaluable to him in operating his department. Reports made to him by his men and records compiled from past reports are the foundations of his planning. The proper handling of the standardized reports required of his department will indicate to other departments his willingness to cooperate and will tend to win their cooperation for him. When the supervisor gives assistance to the inspection department in solving a difficulty by including extra data on the regular reports or setting up additional controls and reporting on them, he earns their confidence and in return gains their cooperation. It is difficult to see how any progressive supervisor could possibly discharge his responsibilities without the aid of reports that he initiates as well as the ones he receives from others. Proper use of records and reports gives the supervisor a confidence in the rightness of his actions. When he acts in terms of the facts of the situation, he can dismiss one act and look forward to his next problem without being disturbed about his previous decision.

While the supervisor has a responsibility for properly making reports and using reports sent to him, top management also has a basic responsibility for the reports it requests and for the persons to whom reports are sent. Literally thousands of dollars can often be saved in large organizations by checking from time to time on the need for reports.   One such annual check of reports reduced report costs by $30,000.   This survey discovered (as frequently is the case) that many persons get reports that they do not need, that reports were still being sent to the offices of persons who had resigned, and in one case that reports were being sent to the office of a man who had died. Seldom does a person ask that his name be removed from the list for a given report.   It is management's responsibility to check the use of reports just as it checks inventories and other important matters.

The Supervisor
and Labor Relations

Labor Relations or Industrial Relations. Terminology has not been clearly defined in the area of personnel management. The terms personnel management, industrial relations, and personnel administration are often used interchangeably. In many parts of the Midwest the term industrial relations includes all of the personnel functions together with many subsidiary functions including "labor relations," which refers to union-management relationships. In other areas the major function is referred to as personnel management, personnel administration, or occasionally as personnel administration and management. In this group terminology the department under the personnel division that handles the union relationships is usually called the industrial relations department. In this chapter we are using the term labor relations to refer to union-management relationships.

A group of personnel men has said: "The objective of Personnel Management, Personnel Administration, or Industrial Relations in an organization is to attain maximum individual development, desirable working relationships between employers and employees, and employees to employees, and effective molding of human resources as contrasted with physical resources." [1] It can be seen that this statement can readily be interpreted to include "labor relations" as a part of the bigger personnel function.

What Is Collective Bargaining? The Norris-La Guardia Act of 1932, the National Industrial Recovery Act of 1933, and the National

[1] See *Personnel,* July 1947, p. 6; also, Walter D. Scott, Robert C. Clothier, and William R. Spriegel, *Personnel Management,* McGraw-Hill Book Co., New York, 1954, pp. 22–23.

Labor Relations Act of 1935 were the forerunners of the National Labor-Management Relations Act of 1947 and more recent modifications. Collective bargaining, as defined by Title 1, Section 101, Subsection 6 (d) of the 1947 National Labor-Management Relations Act, is:

the performance of the mutual obligation of the employer and the representative of the employees to meet at reasonable times and confer in good faith with respect to wages, hours, and other terms and conditions of employment, or the negotiation of an agreement, or any question arising thereunder, and the execution of a written contract incorporating any agreement reached if requested by either party, but such obligation does not compel either party to agree to a proposal or require the making of a concession. . . .

It will be observed that this statutory definition contains the following requirements:

1. To meet at reasonable times to confer in good faith with respect to wages, hours, and other terms and conditions of employment, or
2. The negotiation of
    2.1   An agreement, or
    2.2   Any questions arising thereunder, and
    2.3   The execution of a written contract embodying the agreement reached if requested by either party

It should be noted that, by definition, neither party is required to agree to a proposal nor to make concessions. The definition includes the adjusting of grievances as a part of collective bargaining. It can thus be seen that the supervisor has an important role in collective bargaining since he often is the key person in handling the first step in the grievance procedure.

The Supervisor and the Labor Management Relations Act. The National Labor Management Relations Act guarantees the exercise by workers of full freedom of association, self-organization, and designation of representatives of their own choosing, for the purpose of negotiating the terms and conditions of their employment or other mutual aid or protection. However, Section 101, Subsections 2 and 11, define a supervisor and exclude him from being an employee as covered by the act, as follows:

Section 2: (3) The term "employees" shall include any employee, and shall not be limited to the employees of a particular employer, unless the Act explicitly states otherwise, and shall include any individual whose work has ceased as a consequence of, or in connection with, any current labor dispute or because of any unfair labor practice, and who has not obtained any other regular and substantially equivalent employment, but shall not include any individual employed as an agricultural laborer, or in the domestic service of any family or person at his home, or any individual employed by his parent or spouse, or any individual having the status of an independent contractor, or any individual employed as a supervisor, or any individual employed by an employer subject to the Railway Labor Act, as amended from time to time, or by any other person who is not an employer as herein defined.

Section 2: (11) The term "supervisor" means any individual having authority, in the interest of the employer, to hire, transfer, suspend, lay off, recall, promote, discharge, assign, reward, or discipline other employees, or responsibility to direct them, or to adjust their grievances, or effectively to recommend such action, if in connection with the foregoing the exercise of such authority is not of a merely routine or clerical nature, but requires the use of independent judgment.

The Act specifically rules out the supervisor as being an employee entitled to protection of collective bargaining. The Act of 1935 was silent on this matter and the Board had ordered management to bargain with some foremen's unions. There is considerable logic in not having management's representatives as members of a union (or at least of the same union as the workers to whom the supervisor represents management). This statement is in keeping with the philosophy as expressed in Section 101, Subsection 9, which says:

Provided, that the Board shall not decide that any unit is appropriate for such purposes if it includes, together with other employees, any individual employed as a guard to enforce against employees and other persons rules to protect property of the employer or to protect the safety of persons on the employer's premises; but no labor organization shall be certified as the representative of employees in a bargaining unit of guards if such organization admits to membership, or is affiliated directly or indirectly with an organization which admits to membership, employees other than guards.

In other words, a guard is not eligible for membership in a union that admits workers who are under the surveillance of the guard.

While the supervisor is not eligible for the protection of the National Labor-Management Relations Act from the standpoint of a personal interest in collective representation, he is subject to the provisions of the Act as a representative of management in dealing with "employees" who are covered by the Act. In fact, the supervisor is the key person in many of the "unfair labor practice" charges brought against management.

The Supervisor and Unfair Labor Practices. The original National Labor Relations Act of 1935 listed a series of unfair labor practices of which management could be found guilty in case of certain activities. The 1935 Act did not list "unfair labor practices" that might be committed by labor organizations, but the revision of 1947 listed unfair labor practices that might be charged against labor unions in case of certain acts and retained the original list of unfair labor practices that might be charged against management. The unfair labor practices that are chargeable to an employer [Section 101, Subsection 8 (a)] may be summarized as follows:

1. Employers must not interfere with their employees in the exercise of their right to self-organization, to form or to join labor organizations, and to bargain collectively through representatives of their own choosing.

2. Employers must not dominate or interfere with the formation or administration of any labor organization or contribute financial aid to the support of such labor organization.

3. Employers must not encourage or discourage membership in any labor organization by discriminating in hiring, discharge, or in any other condition of employment. This does not forbid a union shop when the union-shop agreement is entered into through an agreement between the duly authorized representatives of the employer and the employees. (Prior to the amendment of 1951 the union shop could not be granted unless in an election supervised by the National Labor Relations Board a majority of all the eligible employees had voted in favor of it. The amendment removed the requirement of the election.)

4. Employers must not in any way discriminate against employees who file charges against the company under the act or who give testimony before the Board under the act.

5. Employers must not refuse to bargain collectively with duly accredited representatives of their employees.

6. An employer may not terminate an existing contract with a labor organization without first serving on the labor organization a 60 days' notice prior to its termination date, offering to meet and confer with the labor organization for the purpose of negotiating a new contract containing the proposed modifications, and notifying the Federal Mediation Service within 30 days of the existence of a dispute. In case the dispute is in a state or territory having a mediation or conciliation service, notice also has to be served on the state or territorial service at the same time that the notice is served on the Federal Mediation Service.

Items 1–5 are ones that the foreman as a representative of management must be constantly on guard against violating in fact, or even giving the appearance of violating. Item 6 is almost always in the hands of top management. In order that the foreman may know when the union is violating the "unfair labor" provisions of the act [Section 101, Subsection 8 (c)], these are listed below:

1. A labor organization shall not restrain or coerce employees in the exercise of their rights to organize and belong to a union of their choice or to refrain from belonging to a union except to the extent that the right not to belong to a union may be modified by a contract with an employer for a union shop as described above under item 3 for unfair labor practices for an employer.

1.1 The labor organization is not restricted in its right to prescribe its own rules with respect to the acquisition or retention of membership in the union. On the other hand, in the case of a duly authorized union shop, "no employer shall justify any discrimination against an employee for nonmembership in a labor organization (A) if he has reasonable grounds for believing that such membership was not available to the employee on the same terms and conditions generally applicable to other members, or (B) if he has reasonable grounds for believing that membership was denied or terminated for reasons other than the failure of the employee to tender the periodic dues and the initiation fees uniformly required as a condition of acquiring or retaining membership" [Section 101, Subsection 8 (a) (3)].

1.2 The labor organization not only may not restrain or coerce employees in relation to the selection of their representatives, neither can it restrain or coerce "an employer in the selection of his representatives, for the purpose of collective bargaining or adjustment of grievances."

2. A labor organization may not "cause or attempt to cause an employer to discriminate" against an applicant for employment or an employee because of membership or nonmembership in a union, subject, of course, to the terms of a union-shop agreement duly entered into according to the act. (See item 3 above, under Unfair Labor Practices, and 1.1 above, regarding unfair labor practices of labor organizations.) A labor organization may refuse to accept a member who does not meet its standards or dismiss one for cause, but the employer may not discriminate against such an employee if he has paid or offered to pay all regular dues and initiation fees. An employer may dismiss an employee for cause, but the cause cannot be the loss of union membership for any reason other than a failure to pay dues or initiation fees. The union may deny membership to a Communist. An employer in his own right may discharge the same man for being a Communist but not because the union has denied him membership for being a Communist. The reverse is also true. An employer may discharge a Communist to whom a union gives membership. In this case, as in the other, the sole basis for discharge would be Communist affiliation, not union membership.

3. A union that is the duly designated or selected agent for employees may not refuse to bargain collectively with the employer for the employees represented. By definition in Section 101, Subsection 8 (d), collective bargaining includes "the execution of a written contract incorporating any agreement reached if requested by either party." Therefore, a refusal to sign a contract covering an agreement reached through collective bargaining is an unfair labor practice for either an employer or a labor organization refusing to sign.

4. A labor organization may not engage in a jurisdictional strike, boycott another employer's goods, or force an employer to cease doing business with another employer.

4.1 This does not require employees to enter the premises of any employer (other than his own employer) whose employees are striking at the request of an appropriately designated union. For instance, truck drivers are not required to cross picket lines in such instances to deliver or to get goods. On the other hand, they cannot refuse to handle these goods in their own plant.

5. A labor union may not charge fees, "as a condition precedent to becoming a member of such organization . . . in an amount which the Board finds excessive or discriminatory under all circumstances."

6. A labor organization may not "cause or attempt to cause an employer to pay or deliver or agree to pay or deliver any money or other thing of value, in the nature of an exaction, for services which are not performed or not to be performed."

The actual interpretation of each of these "unfair labor practices" is at times highly technical. Many companies send to their supervisors legal interpretations that provide them with current practices. Several magazines that foremen read carry digests of Board decisions as well as court decisions. A careful reading of these reports will keep a progressive supervisor aware of the trend in labor legislation interpretation.

Are the Foreman's Hands Tied by Union-Management Relations?
The answer to this question tends to be "yes" if viewed from the freedom of action enjoyed before the union entered the picture in a given situation. The answer is "no" in all situations other than the freedom to try to influence workers in their choice of representatives to speak for them in collective bargaining. The right of collective bargaining has been recognized by the basic laws of our country. With this as a background, management has conditioned its attitude to recognize the rights of its employees to be represented by persons of their own choosing.

The management-union relationship places certain responsibilities upon the supervisor in dealing with his men and sets up procedures that hold him accountable for following the generally accepted rules inherent in collective bargaining. Within this framework of operating procedures the *supervisor is free to exercise his supervisory responsibilities.* He can insist upon the maintenance of quality standards, regularity and promptness in attendance, the observance of safety rules and regulations, the meeting of production standards as to quantity, and the observance of all reasonable regulations that are applicable to all persons in the same situation. In other words, the supervisor is clothed with all of the needed authority to run his department within the framework of the union contract. He cannot penalize a worker for filing an "unfair labor practice" complaint. To permit a foreman to do this would nullify the protection established for the worker. The foreman may discharge a man for anything that he could have discharged him for prior to unionization other than his union membership and his legitimate actions in relation to this affiliation. Of course, a grievance may be filed challenging the foreman's action. If the foreman has applied the same regulations to others he will be sustained in his action. On the other hand, if it can be shown that he has discriminated against the complaining worker he will probably be reversed. The foreman still can manage his department, but he is more accountable for his actions than formerly.

The Supervisor and the Union Agreement. Since the foreman is most frequently the person who is closest to the enforcement of the terms of the union agreement he frequently knows more about the causes of friction than anyone else. Some managements consult their foremen before opening negotiations for a new contract to learn of the difficulties encountered in administering the old one.[2] Armed with these facts, management is in a better position to bargain for a more workable contract. It is rare indeed that the foremen sit in on the actual contract negotiations.

Day to day operations under the union agreement are primarily the foreman's responsibilities. Particularly in the early days of operating under a new contract the foreman may have to seek advice from his superiors for their interpretation of new clauses or provisions. Management usually conducts conferences with its foremen to acquaint them with the terms of a new contract and the proper interpretation of the contract. When in doubt a supervisor should always seek advice in applying a contract to a specific situation. It is immeasurably better to seek guidance before taking action than to be reversed later. When the workers know that their supervisor sincerely strives to live within both the letter and the spirit of their union agreement he will have established a sound basis for his actions. He may occasionally be wrong but he will be given the benefit of sincerity of purpose. This reputation will cause fewer grievances to be filed. In so far as he can the foreman should strive to give his men reasons for his actions.[3]

[2] See Guy B. Arthur, Jr., "Supervisors Participate in Contract Administration," *Personnel,* Vol. 24, No. 2, Sept. 1947, pp. 107–112.

[3] See *The Foreman's Guide to Labor Relations,* Bulletin No. 66, United States Department of Labor, Division of Standards, Washington, D. C., 1944, p. 13.

The Foreman and Union Status. The security status of the bargaining agent is a matter of contractual agreement on which the foreman has little influence. However, the manner in which the foreman explains the exact status has a lot to do with its general acceptance by his workers. For instance, the foreman's own sentiments may be in favor of an open shop, yet his company may have accepted a union shop. In this case the foreman should explain the responsibilities of operating under the agreement signed by his company.

The union contract usually sets forth: (1) a statement of the limits of the bargaining unit, (2) the union's representation rights, and (3) the status of union security. The contract may cover one plant only or a number of plants. It may designate the union as the bargaining agent for all of the employees in the unit or only a part of them, such as the factory employees or even so small a unit as the teamsters or truck drivers. The union status as to security might be: (1) a *closed shop* (not legal under the Labor-Management Act of 1947), (2) *the union shop,* (3) *the open shop,* and (4) *the dues shop.* Section 101, Subsection 8 (b) (3) states:

no employer shall justify any discrimination against an employee for non-membership in a labor organization (A) if he has reasonable grounds for believing that such membership was not available to the employee on the same terms and conditions generally applicable to other members, or (B) if he has reasonable grounds for believing that membership was denied or terminated for reasons other than the failure of the employee to tender the periodic dues and the initiation fees uniformly required as a condition of acquiring or retaining membership.

The *open shop* permits management to hire any employee it wants to hire. He may or may not join the union. His employment is not contingent on union membership. The "dues shop" differs from the union shop in that all the employee has to do is to agree to pay the regular initiation fee and regular dues. The employer does not have to discharge him if the union decides he is in bad standing for anything but a failure to pay his dues. The restriction quoted above as a limitation of the union shop [Section 101, Subsection 8 (b) (3)] in effect produces a dues shop. The only responsibility of a foreman in relation to union status in a *union shop* or a *dues shop* is to explain to each employee the exact status and to discharge him if he fails to pay his dues or at least try to, even though the union may not accept the dues. In the case of the open shop the supervisor is obliged to explain the status when questioned about it or as the occasion may arise. In a few cases of *dues shops* the employee is not required to offer to join the union but merely to pay the union dues required of all members. This protects the man who does not want to become a union member.

The Supervisor and the Shop Steward. The union steward occupies the same position in relation to the union as the supervisor occupies in relation to the company.[4] He may be a good fellow or he may suffer from an emotional block in relation to all representatives of management. He *is the representative of the union* and the supervisor should strive to understand his method of handling things and learn to get along with him as well as possible. In most cases this is not a difficult assignment. In no case should the supervisor deviate from sound practice merely to strive to gain the cooperation of an emotionally immature individual. In the main the supervisor gets the kind of cooperation with the steward that he gives.

One of the best methods of dealing with the steward is to try to look at his problems from the steward's viewpoint. The supervisor should ask himself "what kind of information would I like to have if I were steward" and then give it. Again—the supervisor should avoid trying to embarrass the steward in the eyes of his union associates. When the supervisor can help the steward "save face" he should do so. This type of recognition usually pays off in a mutual respect for each other's problems.

A good illustration of enlightened cooperation with a union steward arises when departmental layout changes are being considered. The supervisor usually is not required to discuss these with the steward, but he is building up a reservoir of good will when he does. The supervisor should not be offended when the steward presses strenuously for a given item requested by his men. The steward has a responsibility to represent the will of his associates.

The Supervisor and Grievances. This subject was treated in detail in Chapter 8. It is sufficient here to point out the essential responsibilities in handling the grievances. Of course, the most ideal situation would be one in which grievances did not arise. This is a goal worth working toward but it is never fully realized. The supervisor should accept the grievance with an open mind and a sincere desire to get the facts and resolve the complaint in terms of these facts. The supervisor should handle grievances as if they were emergencies. They

---

[4] The word "steward" is used to indicate the union representative. Some companies do not have stewards but call their representatives committeemen, chairman, or any other appropriate designation.

demand immediate attention but not so speedy that a decision is rendered without getting the facts. The decision should be given in terms of company policy and not mere opportunism. Grievances settled "on the cuff" are likely to rebound with two grievances instead of the one that was thought to have been settled. The supervisor must recognize that he cannot settle all grievances at his level. He must not get stage fright at the thought of an appeal. All he has to do is to prepare his decision with all the care that would be used were he going to appeal the case himself. With thorough preparation and policy orientation in handling grievances the supervisor can approach each grievance as an opportunity for leadership rather than as something to be dreaded.

An occasional supervisor is puzzled over whether it is the union's responsibility to process a grievance for a member of the bargaining unit who is not a union member. The answer to this query is "Yes." The union is supposed to represent all workers in the bargaining unit; however, a lukewarm steward may not press the non-union member's grievance with vigor. There is little that the supervisor can do about this type of poor representation.

27 Managerial Coordination and the Supervisor

The Need for Coordination. Organization is the *structural relationship* of the various factors in the enterprise. Organization is not an end in itself but an aid in attaining the objective of the enterprise. Organization is designed to create in the enterprise an atmosphere that will facilitate harmonious operating in terms of the objective; it releases the energies of the people for productive purposes and minimizes the frictions that so often arise when persons work in groups. "Organization, therefore, refers to more than the frame of the edifice. It refers to the completed body, with all its correlated functions. It refers to these functions, as they appear in action, the very pulse and heartbeats, the circulation, the respiration, the vital movement, so to speak, of the organized unit." [1]

Oliver Sheldon views organization as "the process of so combining the work which individuals or groups have to perform with the faculties necessary for its execution that the duties, so formed, provide the best channels for the efficient, systematic, positive, and coordinated application of the available effort." [2]

Organization is designed to help achieve and support the objective or purpose of the enterprise. Organizing is also one of the primary responsibilities of an executive. The other two basic functions of the executive are *planning* and *operating*. The all pervasive function in organization, the one that permeates all other functions, is *coordina-*

[1] James D. Mooney and Alan C. Reiley, *The Principles of Organization,* Harper and Brothers, New York, 1939, p. 3.

[2] Oliver Sheldon, *The Philosophy of Management,* Sir Isaac Pitman & Sons, London, 1923, p. 32.

tion. In other words, coordination may be considered the support for the planning and operating activities. Coordination is the process of so arranging activities in relation to time, place, and effort that each item will be taken care of according to the needs of the situation.[3] Coordination is as essential to the perpetuation of an effective organization as leadership is to a dynamic enterprise. With the devolution of function, as the enterprise grows, comes "empire building" on the part of the specialists in the various functions. It seems to be impossible to keep all parties in the organization so imbued with the company's objective or purpose that they will place the greater good ahead of personal aggrandizement through "empire building." It is the function of executives at the top to see to it that all of the functions of the enterprise are in balance and are coordinated. This coordination of effort keeps the business on the track, moving steadily toward its *purpose.* Even in the absence of any selfish motive to build one division out of all proportion to its needs, and assuming that good will permeates the entire executive personnel, coordination is still necessary. To be effective, men of competence and good intentions must know *when, where,* and *how* to exert their efforts. The function of coordination is to provide the plans, the schedule as to when, the specific place (where), and the "how" (Fig. 27.1).

The Supervisor's Interest in Coordination. The supervisor is a part of management. If he is to perform his duties effectively he must operate in a climate that encourages his assumption of full responsibility. This cannot be done in the absence of careful, purposeful coordination. Not only must the supervisor's role be coordinated with the roles of his counterparts in the other functional units, he, himself, must coordinate the activities directly under his control. He must also have an interest in striving to maintain a coordinated pace with other departments on a level horizontal with his. Likewise he must keep pace with the departments occupying a vertical relationship to his. If he holds up the department that uses his product, coordination is not in balance. On the other hand, if he cannot take the material from the department preceding him in the manufacturing cycle the scheduling is also out of balance. Coordinating the manufacturing process in a large enterprise is not the sole function of a central production planning and control department. It is entirely too big an assignment for any such agency. It requires willing cooperation all

[3] See William K. Spriegel and Ernest C. Davies, *Principles of Business Organization and Operation,* Prentice-Hall, New York, 1952, pp. 36, 43, 544–555, 564.

along the line to make the centrally conceived plan work. *Coordination is a dynamic function, not merely a clerical and dispatching activity.*

Coordination and the Line Executive. The foreman is a line officer and as such is directly responsible to his superior for coordinating his production with that of others and with the established schedule. It would be possible (though not truly efficient) to achieve coordination in an organization with a minimum of staff assistance from the production planning and control department, a staff department. For instance, the factory manager could give each division superintendent a copy of demands for finished products by days, weeks, and months, and each superintendent could establish for his unit the daily requirements of all of the parts and assemblies for which his unit was responsible. The division superintendents would do likewise with their foremen and each foreman would make up his own schedule to meet the bigger requirements. On this basis each executive would be devoting an excess amount of his time to planning and scheduling, leaving less time than is needed to supervise the carrying out of the established schedule. The principle of specialization so effectively recognized by Frederick W. Taylor would not sanction such an inefficient method of securing the needed coordination of production requirements. Taylor pointed out that the old-line foreman in charge of a machine shop needed to have the following qualifications.

First. He must be a good machinist—and this alone calls for years of special training, and limits the choice to a comparatively small class of men.

Second. He must be able to read drawings readily, and have sufficient imagination to see the work in its finished state clearly before him. This calls for at least a certain amount of brains and education.

Third. He must plan ahead and see that the right jigs, clamps, and appliances, as well as proper cutting tools, are on hand, and are used to set the work correctly in the machine and cut the metal at the right speed and feed. This calls for the ability to concentrate the mind upon a multitude of small details, and take pains with little, uninteresting things.

Fourth. He must see that each man keeps his machine clean and in good order. This calls for the example of a man who is naturally neat and orderly himself.

Fifth. He must see that each man turns out work of the proper quality. This calls for the conservative judgment and the honesty which are the qualities of a good inspector.

Sixth. He must see that the men under him work steadily and fast. To accomplish this he should himself be a hustler, a man of energy, ready to pitch in and infuse life into his men by working faster than they do, and this quality is rarely combined with the painstaking care, the neatness and the conservative judgment demanded as the third, fourth, and fifth requirements of a gang boss.

Seventh. He must constantly look ahead over the whole field of work and see that the parts go to the machines in their proper sequence, and that the right job gets to each machine.

Eighth. He must, at least in a general way, supervise the timekeeping and fix piecework rates. Both the seventh and eighth duties call for a certain amount of clerical work and ability, and this class of work is almost always repugnant to the man suited to active executive work, and difficult for him to do; and the rate-fixing alone requires the whole time and careful study of a man especially suited to its minute detail.

Ninth. He must discipline the men under him, and readjust their wages; and these duties call for judgment, tact, and judicial fairness.[4]

Item three in Taylor's list of qualifications is the planning function that he delegated to one of his eight functional foremen, *the order-of-work and route clerk.*[5] Today this function is largely carried on in the production planning and control department. In spite of the fact that the bulk of the clerical and planning work is performed in this department the supervisor has a basic interest in contributing to the smooth functioning of the production control department's schedules. He cannot divorce himself entirely from the coordinating process.

The Supervisor and Committee Action as a Phase of Coordination. The committee as an organic entity is often used as a substitute for sound organization. This is a tragic misuse of an organizational unit that has a real function, provided the organizational structure is what it should be in the first instance. When committees are properly constituted, have their objective clearly defined, and are used for purposes for which they are suited they serve a useful purpose. Under proper circumstances the committee may be used successfully as an agency for: (1) decision making and policy making, (2) coordination, (3) judicial determination, (4) giving advice, and (5) for educational purposes. The committee may be a rather expensive method of securing some of the foregoing values. As a coordinating agency, the committee may include among its functions advice, education, and at times, decision making.

An executive at any level may establish a coordinating committee of his key subordinate line as well as staff associates. The supervisor's immediate superior may establish such a committee and call it an

[4] See Frederick Winslow Taylor, *Shop Management,* Harper and Brothers, New York, 1911, pp. 96–98.

[5] Frederick Winslow Taylor, *op. cit.,* p. 102.

operating committee or a *coordinating committee*. When such a committee discusses a common operating problem each supervisor learns what is required of him and his department. If the demands on his department come within his present forces' and equipment's capacities, the only problem remaining is timing. The foreman is provided the needed information as to time and the detailed requirements by a common discussion with his superior and his associates. All that is necessary for men of good will, who are thoroughly trained and indoctrinated in company objectives, is to give them the facts, and they will live up to expectations. The committee discussion of the total requirements gives each member an opportunity to learn all the facts and to harmonize any differences of opinion. Actually, it is not the committee that secures the coordination but the general manager's discussion of requirements with the group. Coordination, then, is a by-product of the instruction and advice by the general manager and the advice given the members of the group by each interested party. Coordination is effected through the authority of ideas and instruction —not through the authority of the committee as an entity. As a matter of fact, coordination can usually be achieved immeasurably better by a specialist or functional department than by a committee acting as an entity trying to achieve it. This statement is in no manner intended to play down the value of the group discussion of common problems as a means of disseminating information and harmonizing differences of opinion. It simply indicates that in many cases committees are used as a method of coordination because of lack of experience with other methods. While recognizing that the committee may not be the most effective method of securing coordination it is realized that there are other by-products of properly led committees. Mutuality of understanding and cooperative appreciation of the common purpose arise from committee work provided the meetings are not held so often as to keep the supervisors away from their real jobs. If the committee work causes the men to develop a feeling of futility because of neglect of their own work the desirable by-products listed above are usually not realized.

Committee coordination at the level of top management frequently is more productive than much of it at the foremen's or supervisors' level. There are two reasons for this: (1) the expected results at the top levels are usually passed on down the line to the supervisors, and (2) top management men are not required to give the detailed personal supervision to their subordinates that the first line supervisors have to give; hence, they can afford to give more time to committee work without neglecting their jobs. When there is friction, bickering, and "buck passing" at the top division level this same attitude tends to prevail all down the line. On the other hand when the divisional heads have a common appreciation of each other's problems this same mutuality of understanding is reflected down to the work level. Coordination through the operating committee at the top echelons of management is more effective than at the supervisory level.

Coordination in Personnel Matters and the Supervisor. The broad personnel policies of any organization emanate from top management. This is inevitably true and is as it should be, for top management alone can make the basic decisions and pay the price to put them into effect. Nevertheless, personnel policies and procedures are likely to be no more effective than the first line supervisor's interpretation and actual following of the personnel policies established by top management. Personnel management is closely associated with actual production. The real personnel management takes place at the point of operations at the departmental level. Training is a function handled in part by the personnel department and in part by the supervisor. The supervisor really is in a better position than the personnel department to know how long it takes to train a new employee to the point where he keeps up his load in production. In case of an increase in production calling for additional men a close coordination between hiring, training, and the production required is called for. Often it falls on the supervisor to requisition the men. He may do this in consultation with the production control department and the personnel department. It is expensive to have men in training before they are needed and possibly even more expensive to need the men and not have them.

There is also real need for close cooperation and coordination of the training carried on in vestibule schools with the actual needs of the operating department. Some supervisors sit back and criticize the training division without doing anything to help them. They often engage in a substantial amount of retraining, taking the attitude that it is inevitable. This attitude is almost never justified. The training instructors are nearly always eager to keep up with all technological changes and operational changes in the departments and welcome information regarding these changes and suggestions as to how they can prepare the trainees for their jobs. The supervisor can well afford an occasional visit to the vestibule school to assist the instructors in their tasks. Close cooperation between the supervisor and the training department may result in the shortening of the training off the job and some additional on-the-job training.

There is also need for close coordination in interpreting new personnel policies. This is especially true when policies have been changed as a result of collective bargaining. The major responsibility for initiating the action in such cases rests on top management. The supervisor cannot interpret or carry out a changed policy until he is told what it is. Sometimes the communications between the union and the employees is faster than between top management, including its supervisors, and its employees. This puts the supervisor at a disadvantage.

Some companies conduct extensive training for employees on the "economics of enterprise." These courses are often conducted by representatives of the personnel department. The supervisor has a basic interest in this program. He can give it his support and cause it to be immeasurably more effective if he shows an interest in it and participates in informal discussions with his men on the subjects taught in these courses. To do this, of course, the supervisor must understand the subjects discussed. As a matter of fact, it would be an ideal situation if the supervisor could conduct the courses himself. He seldom has the time to do this because of his many other pressing departmental duties. Nevertheless, the success or failure of such a program often rests on the attitude and informal approval of the supervisor.

Coordination Is a Universal Requirement. In every phase of departmental operation that is influenced by a staff agency outside the department, there is need for coordination between this agency and the efforts of the supervisor. The activities of the *director of safety,* the director of the *suggestion systems,* and the *maintenance superintendent* are excellent illustrations of the need for coordinated efforts.

The real *safety* of any department rests in the hands of the operating supervisor in the department. This statement is predicated on the assumption that top management has provided the normal safety devices that are available. In most large companies there is a director of safety who, as a staff officer, devotes all of his time to studying the safety needs of his company, analyzing the accident records, promoting safety education, and doing anything within his power to get his associates to work safely. The supervisor should plan his own safety work to dovetail with that of the safety director. Coordination both in timing and objective among all persons interested in safety really gets results.

An entire chapter (Chapter 15) has been devoted to the supervisor's relationship to the suggestion system. Suffice it to say here that the focusing of the energies of the supervisor and the director of the suggestion system at the same time and in the same direction gives a real impetus to the interest of employees in suggesting improvements. Unfortunately, a few supervisors take a negative attitude toward their workers' turning in suggestions regarding their work. This attitude arises from a false notion that the supervisor should have thought of the improvement himself. A lukewarm attitude toward suggestions by a supervisor places the program at a distinct disadvantage. On the other hand, coordinating the efforts of all parties to the suggestion program produces better results than the same effort expended individually without regard to the timing of the other. Not only should the efforts of all be synchronized as to timing but they should harmonize as to purpose and interpretation of policy.

In some organizations there is constant friction between the maintenance department and the departmental supervisor, particularly when the maintenance department is responsible for the janitor service. This arises in part from the tempo that generally prevails in the work force

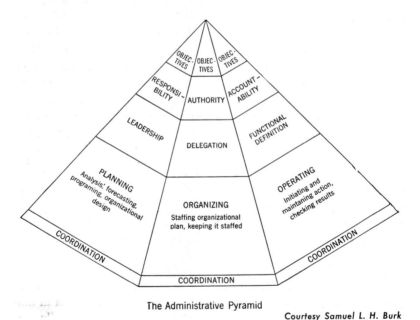

The Administrative Pyramid

Courtesy Samuel L. H. Burk

Figure 27.1.

in the maintenance department in contrast with the tempo among the production workers. It also arises in part because the production personnel frequently do not give the equipment the careful attention it requires. Both of these situations arise from a lack of full appreciation of the problems of each department. Maintenance workers seldom are paid on incentive; hence, the motive is lacking to produce up to the production man's idea of what should be done. Because of the nature of their jobs, the maintenance workers cannot be so closely supervised as most production workers. This is a place where the departmental supervisor can assist the maintenance supervisor. He can report soldiering on the job. He can also help the maintenance man by reporting the actual trouble in so far as he can, rather than merely phoning in the information "My overhead fan does not start." Again, some supervisors keep the equipment running just as long as it will run even though they may observe that things are not as they should be.

When both the supervisor and the maintenance man realize that they are working for the same objective their efforts will be directed in the same manner rather than one's complaining at the inefficiency of the other. When asking for a minor addition to the department or a modification of layout the supervisor will check in detail all of the changes required rather than to keep adding to his request as the work progresses. It is not at all unusual for four or five additional requests to be added to an original maintenance order. This adds to the costs. If all the changes had been included in the original request the work could have been planned more efficiently at a lower cost. One of the most pressing needs for coordination between the maintenance department and the departmental supervisor arises when the entire department or a part of it is moved from one location to another. In such cases planning and coordination of a high order are called for.

Summary. The entire concept of the need for coordination and its relationship to the other functions in operating a business may be illustrated by Figures 2.1 and 27.1. It is difficult to portray a pyramid on a printed page, but the supervisor may visualize the organizational relationships as a pyramid resting on the foundation of coordination. All of the efforts and various stages come to a focus at the top of the pyramid as the objective. In the original establishment of the enterprise the organization structure evolves from the objective. *Responsibility* is related to the objective. *Authority* [6] is derived from *responsibility* and accountability is required from those persons entrusted with

[6] See Chapter 2, pp. 12–13, for definitions of these terms.

authority. Responsibility supported by authority is discharged through *leadership*. Leadership is multiplied by *delegation* and clarified through *functional definition*. The executive process requires *planning, organizing,* and *operating*. Effective planning, organizing, and operating require *coordinating*.

Viewed from the standpoint of a going concern, the executive process is permeated at all times by coordination. Every step in operations should be coordinated to focus on the discharge of the responsibility for achieving the objective. When the entire personnel is thoroughly indoctrinated with the objective and aware of its responsibility, coordination will enable it to move slowly but resolutely toward the company goal. Personal satisfactions in such a balanced situation will arise from a high degree of integration of company and individual interests.

appendix

A   Statistical Quality Control[1]

The Supervisor's Interest in Statistical Quality Control. Since the primary responsibility for the quality of the product rests squarely on the shoulders of the supervisor, he should be interested in any procedure or device that will help him meet the established standards. Statistical techniques provide a technical mathematical picture of how closely the product meets requirements. Relatively few supervisors are sufficiently trained in mathematics to derive the formulas used in statistical quality control. However, any eighth grade student can read the charts made from the use of the technical statistical procedures. A substantial number of supervisors could readily master the procedures used in statistical quality control even though many of them might be unable to establish the system in the first place.

The supervisor's interest in statistical quality control is basically one of its use. The charts easily tell the foreman how his quality is coming. They also may indicate that trouble is ahead or that performance is well within the requirements. When the supervisor becomes thoroughly accustomed to the use of these aids in quality control he will fight to keep them.

Statistical Quality Control in Practice.[2] For purposes of explanation, the technique of statistical quality control can be divided into two major parts:

1. *Control charts,* which are based upon sampling at the process.

2. *Acceptance sampling,* which may be applied at any stage of the manufacturing operation. It is often used by purchasers to check the quality of products received from vendors.

The functions of *control charts* in a manufacturing process are similar

---

[1] A substantial part of the material in Appendix A was provided by Dr. Richard Henshaw of the Bureau of Business Research of the College of Business Administration of The University of Texas.

[2] See William R. Spriegel and Richard H. Lansburgh, *Industrial Management,* John Wiley & Sons, fifth edition, New York, 1955, Chapter 10, which has been quoted freely in this section.

to the job of a detective in attempting to establish the possible guilt of a person suspected of a crime. In both cases, associations in time are essential facts needed for solving the problems. Control-chart applications are based upon the principle that some quality variations are inherent to any production process. The setting of tolerances and the manufacturing of a product are recognized as inseparable problems. Control-chart analysis of pilot runs and data relating to similar manufacturing methods are used as indicators of the probable capabilities of various processes. Information about the process is summarized in regard to its ability to hold a given average and as to variation (degree of uniformity) about that average. Beyond a certain point it has been found to be impractical to eliminate chance variations. From statistical measures of such chance variations the so-called *natural process dispersion* is estimated. The natural process dispersion tells the design engineer what specifications the process can meet while under control. The use of control charts in the subsequent manufacturing operation shows whether or not the product is being produced within the desired tolerance limits. Shifts of process average and variations in excess of the natural process dispersion are indicated by *out-of-control points* on the charts. It is important that the sample be inspected promptly after the items are produced and the results immediately plotted on the charts. Thus the exact time that assignable causes of variation occur will be indicated by out-of-control points, and such information is invaluable for identifying and eliminating manufacturing troubles. Equally important, the control chart tells when to leave the process alone.

The control-chart approach operates on the theory that it is better to make the product right in the first place. Control charts are primarily a diagnostic device, and although their use often makes possible a substantial curtailment of inspection, this is distinctly a secondary objective.

Many successful applications of control charts are based upon 100-per-cent inspection, with the contribution in such cases accruing from the detection and elimination of sources of trouble. However, in most cases it is possible to reduce the amount of inspection needed through continued use of the control charts.

Measurements on continuous scales are said to be expressed by variables, while classifications on the basis of conformity or nonconformity of articles to any specified requirements are said to be expressed by attributes.

Problems of controlling variables (i.e., dimensions, weights, tensile strength, etc.) are attacked by use of control charts for $\overline{X}$ and R, or $\overline{X}$ and σ.[3]

Control of quality where the articles inspected are simply classified as either acceptable or defective utilizes the control chart for fraction defective p.

A third type of control chart is useful for regulating the number of defects per article or per unit sample. This is called the c chart and may be applied to such things as number of seeds (small air pockets) in glass

---

[3] $\overline{X}$ refers to the average of a sample, and R (range) and σ (standard deviation) are measures of dispersion.

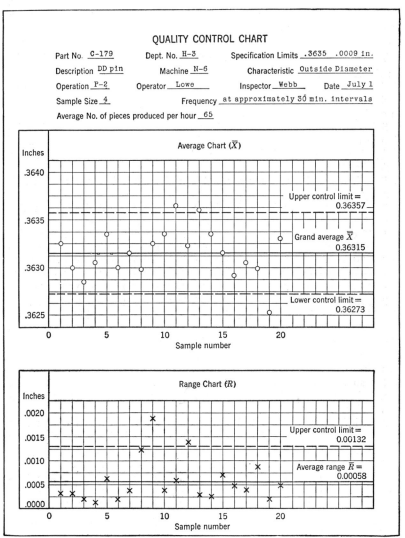

Courtesy, Richard Henshaw, Bureau
of Business Research, University
of Texas

Figure A.1.   Quality control charts.

bottles, blemishes on painted surfaces, defects in complex assemblies, etc.

Control charts for averages $\overline{X}$ and ranges R are generally used together. The $\overline{X}$ chart is useful for indicating shifts in process average while the R chart shows changes in process dispersion. Figure A-1 portrays the measurements taken of the outside diameter of a machined part.

Three points (samples 11, 13, and 19) are outside the control limits on the $\overline{X}$ chart. Two points (samples 9 and 12) are outside the control limits on the R chart. This indicates the presence of assignable causes of variation in the machining process, i.e., factors contributing to the variation in quality which it should be possible to identify and eliminate.

Subsequent use of the charts helped find the assignable causes of variation in the process centering, primarily related to machine setting, and the assignable cause of variation in the process dispersion, mostly related to lack of skill of the operator.

Retraining of the operator resulted in a significant improvement in uniformity of the product.

Some other extremely useful facts which can be derived from this control-chart analysis are as follows:

1. If control (in the statistical sense) can be maintained, the natural tolerances of this process seem to be about ± 0.0007 inches. Therefore, by maintaining statistical control and by close attention to adjustments in process average at a level of about 0.3635 inches, it should be possible to make parts all within the specification limits of 0.3635 ± 0.0009 inches.

2. Process average at present is a little too low at 0.36315 inches. It should be shifted up to 0.3635 inches so that no parts will be produced below the lower specification limit, which would require expensive scrapping. Furthermore, since it is possible to rework any parts for which the outside diameter is occasionally too large to satisfy the upper specification limit, the operator should be instructed to keep process centering adjusted so that it does not fall below 0.3635. This should prevent the production of any parts with outside diameters below the lower specification limit which have to be scrapped.

3. If it is found that control of the process can be maintained for long periods with all points falling inside the control limits, consideration should be given to the possibility of eliminating 100-per-cent inspection and using the control-chart results instead. In this case, measurements of the outside diameter of four parts at hourly intervals might replace 100-per-cent inspection with the go and no-go gauges, except when the control chart showed lack of control. The quality assurance afforded by an acceptance procedure of this kind might actually be superior to that offered in the case of 100-per-cent inspection before the control charts were used. The reason for this is that inspection fatigue makes it impossible for even 100-per-cent inspection to eliminate defectives from lots of small, mass-produced items.

It should be clear to the reader by now that control charts are mainly used for process control. On the other hand, acceptance sampling is primarily a post-mortem operation which seeks to determine the quality of product that has already been produced. In many actual situations, a clearcut division between the purposes of control charts and acceptance sampling does not exist. That is, a product is often accepted on the basis of control-chart records, and likewise the results of acceptance sampling are often useful in process control.

Just as there are different types of control charts, there are also acceptance sampling plans based upon inspection by attributes, by variables, and by number of defects per unit. Most sampling plans by attributes can, in addition, be applied to number of defects per unit problems. For all three of the above types of inspection (attributes, variables, and number of defects per unit) sampling plans utilizing single, double, multiple, and sequential sampling procedures are available.

Sampling is based upon the principle that a random sample will be representative of the lot from which it is drawn. The amount of sampling error to be expected in a random sample has been mathematically proved *to be inversely proportional to the square root of the number of items in the sample.* By making use of this and other facts from the theory of mathematical probability, it is possible to determine scientifically how large a sample needs to be inspected in order to attain a desired quality assurance in regard to any given production lot.

The adoption of a sampling inspection plan is based on the premise that a *certain percentage of the output will not conform to the standard specifications.* An allowable percentage of defective product in any lot inspected may be specified in determining between a satisfactory lot and a rejected lot. According to the laws of chance, a sample will occasionally give a *favorable indication for a bad lot,* resulting in the passing of this lot for use in further production or for delivery to the consumer.[4] This is often called the "consumer's risk." In addition to the consumer's risk there is another measure, namely, a value for the *upper limit of defective product that will be accepted from any supplier over a long period of time.* This ceiling value is known as the "average outgoing quality limit" or "AOQL."

A third factor needed in the choice of a good sampling plan is a knowledge of the average percentage of defective parts existing in the product submitted for inspection. This factor, known as the "incoming process average," is obtained from inspection records of previously inspected lots and is an estimate of the expected quality under normal conditions.

The *Sampling Inspection Tables* by Dodge and Romig [5] probably enjoy the widest use in industry. These sampling plans are of the acceptance/rectification type, that is, the remaining portion of any lot rejected by the sample can be expected to minimize the total amount of inspection necessary to achieve any desired degree of quality assurance. The user is given the choice of either single or double sampling plans. A much wider range of sampling plans can be found in *Sampling Inspection,* prepared by the Statistical Research Group (SRG) of Columbia University.[6]

[4] H. F. Dodge and H. G. Romig, "A Method of Sampling Inspection," *The Bell System Technical Journal,* October 1929, p. 628.

[5] Harold F. Dodge and Harry G. Romig, *Sampling Inspection Tables—Single and Double Sampling,* New York, John Wiley & Sons, 1944.

[6] H. A. Freeman, Milton Friedman, Frederick Mosteller, and W. A. Wallis, editors, *Sampling Inspection,* New York, McGraw-Hill Book Co., 1948.

The most recent of the sampling acceptance schemes being used by the armed forces of the United States, Military Standard 105A,[7] is an excellent example of an acceptance/rejection sampling procedure. Because of the cost or due to lack of inspection personnel and facilities, screening of rejected lots by the consumer may be impractical. Essentially, these sampling plans are designed to accept or reject the producer's process, that is, they accept nearly all of the submitted lots if the quality level of his process is at or better than the acceptable quality level, and they reject a substantial fraction of his lots if the quality is lower than the acceptable level.

The three types of sampling schemes which have been discussed apply to inspection by attributes. With slight modification they can also be used for number of defects per unit. Since by far the greatest amount of acceptance sampling is done by attributes, no further discussion of sampling schemes by number of defects per unit or by variables will be given here.[8]

It should be acknowledged here that in actual practice much of the inspection by sampling is not based upon scientific use of statistical methods but rather upon empirical judgment. This accounts in part for some of the turmoil in which inspection departments and producing units frequently find themselves.

Statistical quality control has increased in popularity during the past decade. Through its use many companies have increased their control over quality, and some have phenomenally reduced inspection costs at the same time. It is highly important that a statistical quality-control system be installed by a specialist. Having been properly installed by competent specialists, it may be operated by a person of normal technical and clerical ability. However, it is far better not to try to use this technique than to have it installed by a person not qualified both in statistical theory and practice. Of course, it must be remembered that statistical quality control does not produce a quality product. It merely informs management when things are not going as they should go. Management must then take the needed technical action to remove the causes of failure.

[7] *MIL-STD-105A, Sampling Procedures and Tables for Inspection by Attributes,* Superintendent of Documents, Government Printing Office, Washington, D. C., 1950.

[8] A complete discussion of sampling acceptance schemes can be found in E. L. Grant, *Statistical Quality Control,* New York, McGraw-Hill, 1952, pp. 311–437.

Bibliography

Alford, L. P., *Cost and Production Handbook,* Ronald Press Co., New York, 1937.

————, and J. R. Bangs, *Production Handbook,* Ronald Press Co., New York, 1944.

American Management Association, *Organization and Function of the Safety Department,* Research Report No. 18, New York, 1951.

————, *Management Education for Itself and Its Employees,* Part I: "Management Education in American Business: General Summary," by Lyndall F. Urwick; Part II: "A Survey of Management Development: The Qualitative Aspects," by Joseph M. Trickett; Part III: "Case Studies in Management Development: Theory and Practice in Ten Selected Companies," by Robert G. Simpson with the assistance of Allison V. MacCullough and company personnel; Part IV: "The Education of Employees: A Status Report with a Proposal for Further Research," by Douglas Williams and Stanley Peterfreund, Douglas Williams Associates with the assistance of Roscoe Edlund and Ott Lerbinger, New York, 1954.

Apple, James M., *Plant Layout and Materials Handling,* Ronald Press Co., New York, 1950.

Barnard, Chester I., *The Functions of the Executive,* Harvard University Press, Cambridge, Mass., 1938.

————, *Organization and Management: Selected Papers,* Harvard University Press, Cambridge, Mass., 1948.

Barnes, Ralph M., *Motion and Time Study,* John Wiley & Sons, New York, third edition, 1949.

Begeman, Myron L., *Manufacturing Processes,* John Wiley & Sons, third edition, New York, 1952.

Beishline, John R., *Military Management for National Defense,* Prentice-Hall, New York, 1950.

Belcher, David W., *Wage and Salary Administration,* Prentice-Hall, New York, 1955.

335

Berrien, F. K., *Comments and Cases on Human Relations,* Harper and Brothers, New York, 1951.

Bethel, Lawrence L., Franklin S. Atwater, George H. E. Smith, and Harvey A. Stackman, *Industrial Organization and Management,* McGraw-Hill Book Co., New York, third edition, 1956.

Blum, Fred H., *Toward a Democratic Work Process,* Harper and Brothers, New York, 1953.

Bowen, Howard R., *Social Responsibilities of the Businessman,* Harper and Brothers, New York, 1953.

Bower, Marvin, *The Development of Executive Leadership,* Harvard University Press, Cambridge, Mass., 1949.

Bowker, Albert H., and H. P. Goode, *Sampling Inspection by Variables,* McGraw-Hill Book Co., New York, 1952.

Bunting, J. Whitney, *Ethics for Modern Business Practice,* Prentice-Hall, New York, 1953.

Bursk, Edward C., *Getting Things Done in Business,* Harvard University Press, Cambridge, Mass., 1953.

———, *How to Increase Executive Effectiveness,* Harvard University Press, Cambridge, Mass., 1954.

———, *The Management Team,* Harvard University Press, Cambridge, Mass., 1954.

Busch, Henry M., *Conference Methods in Industry,* Harper and Brothers, New York, 1949.

Cabot, Hugh, and Joseph A. Kahl, *Human Relations,* Vols. I and II, Harvard University Press, Cambridge, Mass., 1953.

Calhoon, Richard P., *Problems in Personnel Administration,* Harper and Brothers, New York, 1949.

Childs, Marquis W., and Douglass Cater, *Ethics in a Business Society,* Harper and Brothers, New York, 1954.

Copeland, Melvin T., *The Executive at Work,* Harvard University Press, Cambridge, Mass., 1951.

Copley, F. B., *Frederick W. Taylor,* Harper and Brothers, New York, 1923.

Cushman, Frank, *Foremanship and Supervision,* John Wiley & Sons, second edition, New York, 1938.

———, *Training Procedure,* John Wiley & Sons, New York, 1940.

Dale, Ernest, *Planning and Developing the Company Organization Structure,* American Management Association, Research Report No. 20, New York, 1952.

Davis, Ralph C., *Fundamentals of Top Management,* Harper and Brothers, New York, 1951.

Dennison, Henry, *Organization Engineering,* McGraw-Hill Book Co., New York, 1931.

Dooher, M. Joseph, and Vivienne Marquis, *The Supervisor's Management Guide,* American Management Association, New York, 1949.

———, *The Development of Executive Talent,* American Management Association, New York, 1952.

———, *Effective Communication on the Job,* American Management Association, New York, 1956.

Fayol, Henri, *General and Industrial Management,* Sir Isaac Pitman & Sons, London, 1949.

Filipetti, George, *Industrial Management in Transition,* Richard D. Irwin, Homewood, Ill., 1953.

Finlay, William W., A. Q. Sartain, and Willis M. Tate, *Human Behavior in Industry,* McGraw-Hill Book Co., New York, 1954.

Folts, Franklin E., *Introduction to Industrial Management,* McGraw-Hill Book Co., fourth edition, New York, 1954.

Freeman, G. L., and E. K. Taylor, *How to Pick Leaders,* Funk & Wagnalls Co., New York, 1950.

Glover, John D., and Ralph M. Hower, *The Administrator,* Richard D. Irwin, Homewood, Ill., 1954.

Gomberg, William, and David Dubinsky, *A Trade Union Analysis of Time Study,* Prentice-Hall, New York, 1955.

Guetzkow, Harold, *Groups, Leaders, and Men,* Carnegie Press, Pittsburgh, Pa., 1951.

Halsey, George D., *How to Be a Leader,* Harper and Brothers, New York, 1938.

Hersey, Rexford, *Better Foremanship—Key to Profitable Management,* Chilton Co., Philadelphia, 1955.

————, *Zest for Work,* Harper and Brothers, New York, 1955.

Heyel, Carl, *The Foreman's Handbook,* McGraw-Hill Book Co., New York, 1949.

Holden, Paul E., Lounsbury S. Fish, and Hubert L. Smith, *Top Management Organization and Control,* McGraw-Hill Book Co., New York, 1951.

Hoslett, Schuyler, *Human Factors in Management,* Harper and Brothers, New York, 1951.

Immer, John R., *Layout Planning Techniques,* McGraw-Hill Book Co., New York, 1950.

————, *Materials Handling,* McGraw-Hill Book Co., New York, 1953.

Ireson, William G., and Eugene L. Grant, *Handbook of Industrial Engineering and Management,* Prentice-Hall, Englewood Cliffs, N.J., 1955.

Jamison, Charles L., *Business Policy,* Prentice-Hall, New York, 1953.

Juran, J. M., *Management of Inspection and Quality Control,* Harper and Brothers, New York, 1945.

Katz, Daniel, Nathan Maccoby, Gerald Gurin, and Lucretia G. Floor, *Productivity, Supervision and Morale Among Railroad Workers,* Institute for Social Research, University of Michigan, Ann Arbor, Mich., 1951.

Kienzle, George J., and Edward H. Dare, *Climbing the Executive Ladder,* McGraw-Hill Book Co., New York, 1950.

Kimball, Dexter S., Sr., and Dexter S. Kimball, Jr., *Principles of Industrial Organization,* McGraw-Hill Book Co., New York, 1947.

Knowles, William H., *Personnel Management: A Human Relations Approach,* American Book Co., New York, 1955.

Koepke, Charles A., *Plant Production Control,* John Wiley & Sons, second edition, New York, 1949.

Landy, Thomas M., *Production Planning and Control,* McGraw-Hill Book Co., New York, 1950.

Lanham, E., *Job Evaluation,* McGraw-Hill Book Co., New York, 1955.

Learned, Edmund P., David N. Ulrich, and Donald R. Booz, *Executive Action,* Harvard Business School, Division of Research, Boston, Mass., 1950.

Lesperance, J. P., *Economics and Techniques of Motion and Time Study,* Wm. C. Brown Company, Dubuque, Iowa, 1953.

Lytle, Charles Walter, *Wage Incentive Methods,* Ronald Press Co., New York, 1942.

————, *Job Evaluation Methods,* Ronald Press Co., New York, 1954.

McCormick, Charles Perry, *Multiple Management,* Harper and Brothers, New York, 1939.

McLarney, William J., *Management Training,* Richard D. Irwin, Homewood, Ill., 1955.

McNaughton, Wayne L., *Employer-Employee Relations,* Golden State Publishers, Westwood Village, Los Angeles, Calif., 1946.

Maier, Norman R. F., *Principles of Human Relations,* John Wiley & Sons, New York, 1952.

Mallick, Randolph W., and Armand T. Gaudreau, *Plant Layout: Planning and Practice,* John Wiley & Sons, New York, 1951.

March, C. A., *Building Operation and Maintenance,* McGraw-Hill Book Co., New York, 1950.

Maynard, Harold B., *Effective Foremanship,* McGraw-Hill Book Co., New York, 1941.

————, G. J. Stegemerten, and John L. Schwab, *Methods-Time Measurement,* McGraw-Hill Book Co., New York, 1948.

Mayo, Elton, *The Social Problems of an Industrial Civilization,* Graduate School of Business Administration, Division of Research, Harvard University, Boston, Mass., 1945.

————, *The Human Problems of an Industrial Civilization,* Graduate School of Business Administration, Division of Research, Harvard University, Boston, Mass., 1946.

Mee, John F., *Personnel Handbook,* Ronald Press Co., New York, 1951.

Merrill, Harwood F., *The Responsibilities of Business Leadership,* Harvard University Press, Cambridge, Mass., 1948.

Mooney, James D., *The Principles of Organization,* Harper and Brothers, New York, 1947.

Moore, Franklin G., *Manufacturing Management,* Richard D. Irwin, Homewood, Ill., 1953.

Mundel, Marvin E., *Motion and Time Study: Principles and Practices,* Prentice-Hall, New York, 1955.

Newman, William H., *Administrative Action,* Prentice-Hall, New York, 1951.

Niles, Mary Cushing H., *Middle Management,* Harper and Brothers, New York, 1949.

Noland, E. William, and E. Wright Bakke, *Workers Wanted,* Harper and Brothers, New York, 1949.

Nunn, Henry L., *The Whole Man Goes to Work,* Harper and Brothers, New York, 1953.

Otis, Jay L., and Richard H. Leukart, *Job Evaluation,* Prentice-Hall, New York, 1954.

Parker, Willard E., and Robert W. Kleemeier, *Human Relations in Supervision,* McGraw-Hill Book Co., New York, 1951.

Peterson, Elmore, and E. Grosvenor Plowman, *Business Organization and Management,* Richard D. Irwin, Homewood, Ill., 1953.

Pigors, Paul, and Faith Pigors, *Human Aspects of Multiple Shift Operations,* Massachusetts Institute of Technology, Cambridge, Mass., 1944.

——, and Charles A. Myers, *Personnel Administration,* McGraw-Hill Book Co., New York, 1956.

——, *Readings in Personnel Administration,* McGraw-Hill Book Co., New York, 1952.

Planty, Earl G., and J. Thomas Freeston, *Developing Management Ability,* Ronald Press Co., New York, 1954.

Riegel, John W., *Executive Development,* University of Michigan Press, Ann Arbor, Mich., 1952.

Ritchie, William E., *Production and Inventory Control,* Ronald Press Co., New York, 1951.

Roethlisberger, F. J., *Management and Morale,* Harvard University Press, Cambridge, Mass., 1939.

——, and William J. Dickson, *Management and the Worker,* Harvard University Press, Cambridge, Mass., 1939.

Ronken, Harrier O., and Paul R. Lawrence, *Administering Changes,* Graduate School of Business Administration, Division of Research, Harvard University, Boston, Mass., 1952.

Schell, Erwin H., *Administrative Proficiency in Business,* McGraw-Hill Book Co., New York, 1936.

——, *New Strength for New Leadership,* Harper and Brothers, New York, 1942.

——, *The Technique of Executive Control,* McGraw-Hill Book Co., New York, 1950.

——, *Techniques of Administration,* McGraw-Hill Book Co., New York, 1951.

Scott, Walter D., Robert C. Clothier, and William R. Spriegel, *Personnel Management,* McGraw-Hill Book Co., fifth edition, New York, 1954.

Sheldon, Oliver, *The Philosophy of Management,* Sir Isaac Pitman & Sons, London, 1923.

Slichter, Sumner H., *The Challenge of Industrial Relations,* Cornell University Press, Ithaca, N.Y., 1947.

Smith, George A., and C. Roland Christensen, *Policy Formulation and Administration,* Richard D. Irwin, Homewood, Ill., 1955.

Smith, Howard, *Developing Your Executive Ability,* McGraw-Hill Book Co., New York, 1946.

Snider, Joseph L., *The Guarantee of Work and Wages,* Graduate School of Business Administration, Division of Research, Harvard University, Boston, Mass., 1947.

Spriegel, William R., and Ernest C. Davies, *Principles of Business Organization and Operation,* Prentice-Hall, New York, 1952.

——, and Richard H. Lansburgh, *Industrial Management,* John Wiley & Sons, fifth edition, New York, 1955.

Spriegel, William R., and Clark E. Myers, editors, *The Writings of the Gilbreths,* Richard D. Irwin, Homewood, Ill., 1953.

Strong, Jay V., *Employee Benefit Plans in Operation,* Bureau of National Affairs, Washington, D.C., 1951.

Taylor, Frederick Winslow, *Shop Management,* Harper and Brothers, New York, 1911.

———, *Scientific Management,* Harper and Brothers, New York, 1947.

Tead, Ordway, *The Art of Leadership,* McGraw-Hill Book Co., New York, 1935.

Terry, George R., *Principles of Management,* Richard D. Irwin, Homewood, Ill., 1953.

Thomason, Calvin C., *Human Relations in Action,* Prentice-Hall, New York, 1947.

Thompson, Claude E., *Personnel Management for Supervisors,* Prentice-Hall, New York, 1948.

Tibbits, Clark, *Living Through the Older Years,* University of Michigan Press, Ann Arbor, Mich., 1951.

Urwick, L., *The Elements of Administration,* Harper and Brothers, New York, 1943.

———, *The Golden Book of Management,* Newman Neame, London, 1956.

Viteles, Morris S., *Motivation and Morale in Industry,* W. W. Norton & Co., New York, 1953.

Walker, Charles R., *Steeltown,* Harper and Brothers, New York, 1950.

———, and Robert H. Guest, *The Man on the Assembly Line,* Harvard University Press, Cambridge, Mass., 1952.

Whitehill, Arthur M., *Personnel Relations,* McGraw-Hill Book Co., New York, 1955.

Yoder, Dale, *Personnel Management and Industrial Relations,* McGraw-Hill Book Co., New York, 1955.

———, *Personnel Principles and Policies,* Prentice-Hall, New York, 1952.

Zaleznik, A., *Foreman Training in a Growing Enterprise,* Graduate School of Business Administration, Division of Research, Harvard University, Boston, Mass., 1951.

Index